An *Odyssey* Reader

An *Odyssey* Reader

Selections from Homer's *Odyssey*, Books 1-12

with notes and vocabulary by
P. A. Draper

THE UNIVERSITY OF MICHIGAN PRESS
Ann Arbor

Published in the United States of America by
The University of Michigan Press
Printed and bound by CPI Group (UK) Ltd, Croydon, CR0 4YY

2016 2015 2014 2013 4 3 2 1

A CIP catalog record for this book is available from the British Library.

ISBN 978-0-472-07192-0 (cloth : alk. paper)
ISBN 978-0-472-05192-2 (pbk. : alk. paper)

Contents

List of Illustrations

Preface

This is a reader for students who have learned the basics of Greek grammar but have not had much experience reading long passages of unabridged ancient texts. Homer is a great place to begin, though the differences between Attic and Homeric Greek will require some adjustment. Vocabulary, grammar, and other explanatory notes are included liberally, but in the interests of increasing vocabulary and reading speed, I urge readers to try to read the Greek text without looking at the notes first, then to use them as needed. Words marked with a tilde (~) will be seen again more than once and should be learned, though if the next appearance is several books away, a repeat definition may appear.

In the preparation of this reader, I owe an enormous debt to the many commentaries (especially the Oxford commentary of Heubeck, West, Hainsworth, and Hoekstra), annotated readers, books, and articles that I consulted. Credit for ideas, explanations, and interpretations taken from them is given in the Source Notes appendix (p. 189) rather than in the notes themselves so as not to lessen the focus of the notes – providing immediate help with reading and understanding. The Readings appendix lists several of these sources, as well as others that readers may want to peruse for more information. The Greek text is based mainly on the 1993 Teubner edition edited by P. Von Der Muehll, but alternate readings from other editions were used when commentators or other editors offered persuasive arguments for changes.

I am extremely grateful to all the people who helped me with this project: the anonymous reviewers, whose suggestions led to significant improvements; the Interlibrary Loan Office of the Clemson University Libraries, especially Victoria Hamilton; Jeffrey B. Wilcox of the Museum of Art and Archaeology at the University of Missouri, for his help in locating and reproducing the illustrations; and Ellen Bauerle, Chris Hebert, Alexa Ducsay, Mary Sexton, and Andrea Olson at the University of Michigan Press.

Special thanks to several fellow Clemson University faculty members: Elizabeth Carney and Margaret Thompson, who agreed to read the text in our weekly Greek reading sessions and provided many useful ideas as well as catching many a typo; Stephen Satris, for meticulously combing the manuscript for inconsistencies and making many helpful suggestions; and Peg Tyler, for letting me take advantage of her editorial skill when she didn't really have time to lend it.

My deep gratitude to my husband, Richard Cowan, who was always supportive and encouraging and who never complained about the hours I spent on this project.

Finally, there aren't words to sufficiently thank the two people who have given so much of their time and expertise (reading every word of several versions of the manuscript, writing out pages of notes and suggestions, helping locate illustrations) and without whose support, encouragement, and advice this book would never have made it to publication, Cathy Callaway and Robert Seelinger.

Introduction

Odysseus, the king of Ithaca and the Greek hero in the Trojan War who devised the Trojan horse (the trick that led to Greek victory over Troy), has been trying to get home for a long time. When the ten-year war ended, he set sail from Troy, eager to return to his family.

The first three years of the journey back to Ithaca brought death to all of Odysseus' men and the destruction of his ships. For the next seven years, the nymph Calypso held Odysseus prisoner on the island of Ogygia. She wants to marry him and make him immortal; he is desperate to reach home.

On the island of Ithaca, no one knows where he is. His wife, Penelope, has been using tricks of her own to fend off dozens of local nobles who want to marry her, but they have invaded the palace, constantly demanding food and entertainment. They are now becoming increasing insistent that she choose one of them as her new husband. Odysseus' son, Telemachus, a baby when his father left home and now an inexperienced young man, cannot defend his mother alone.

So things stand at the beginning of the *Odyssey*. Odysseus must use all his wiles, as well as help from, among others, a goddess, a princess, a sea nymph, and a sorceress, to finally make it safely back to Ithaca, where he will face ruthless foes who would kill him on sight.

This book consists of readings from Books 1-12 of the *Odyssey*, the great epic poem written by Homer. Or was it? Was there really a Homer? Did he write the *Odyssey* or compose it orally? When did he live? Could he have been a she? Are the places he describes real? These are just a few of the questions that have been asked about the author whom the ancient Greeks considered the greatest of poets. To say there has been much research, theorizing, and speculation about the man called Homer and his works would be a considerable understatement. Take a look at the Readings appendix (p. 215) for sources of more information about these and other questions.

A few things before you begin:

Homer — We have no idea who Homer was, or even if he was a real person. The ancient Greeks believed he was a blind itinerant poet who lived sometime after the Trojan War and was the author of two great epics, the *Iliad* and the *Odyssey*. Several cities claimed to be his birthplace. Linguistic evidence places him in the eighth century B.C.E., probably from somewhere in Ionia (the central area of the west coast of modern Turkey). His poetry is in the style of traveling oral poets in the generations before the eighth century, who had no written texts and composed while they performed, using formulaic phrases, lines, and scenes as well as their own invention to tell stories. But was Homer himself a traveling oral poet? Are the works we have entirely the work of one man or were they originally composed by one person, then transmitted by other oral poets, who themselves added to the works? Or did he write down or dictate his compositions, merely using the oral style? Or is he someone who never existed at all and what we ascribe to "Homer" is just a collection of the works of several poets? It's even been suggested that he was a woman. These questions have been debated for centuries but we have no definitive answers.

Language There are differences between Homeric Greek and Attic Greek. Take a look at the Forms and Grammar appendix (p. 197) to get a preview of what you will encounter.

Meter The *Odyssey* is a poem written in dactylic hexameter. To learn the patterns of this meter and how to scan the lines, look at the Meter and Scansion appendix (p. 209).

Timeline In following the story of the *Odyssey*, it's important to remember that the poem begins very near the end of the story. When Athena asks Zeus to let Odysseus leave Calypso's island, it has been ten years since the end of the Trojan War. The adventures Odysseus relates to the Phaeacians in Books 9-12 are flashbacks; they occurred in the first three years after the war ended. Calypso kept him on her island for the next seven. The events Homer describes in Ithaca, Ogygia, and Phaeacia happen shortly before Odysseus finally returns home.

Geography There has been endless speculation on the identity of the places described in Odysseus' voyage from Troy to Ithaca, even argument about the identity of Ithaca itself. From ancient times until the present, people have debated whether the places described were completely fictional or reflected actual places (*e.g.*, locating Scylla and Charybdis in the Straits of Messina or making Sicily the home of Nausicaa). For those who thought the places were real, theories ranged from placing Odysseus' travels mostly in the eastern

Mediterranean to having him sail as far away as to North America and Scotland. For a good overview of the many ideas, both ancient and modern, of Odysseus' itinerary, see Chapter 9 (Geography) in Mark's *Homeric Seafaring*.[1]

Epithets

You'll see these frequently in Homer's poetry. Epithets are words or phrases describing or characterizing a person or a thing. For example, Zeus the cloud gatherer (**νεφεληγερέτα Ζεύς**, 1.63; earth-holding Poseidon (**Ποσειδάων γαιήοχος**, 1.68; the swift ship (**θοὴ νηῦς**, 10.244); rosy-fingered Dawn (**ῥοδοδάκτυλος Ἠώς**, 5.121). Just as the language used in the poetry was developed by itinerant oral bards over several hundred years (see Grammar appendix, p. 197), so also were standard descriptive epithets (as well as longer formulaic phrases, lines, and indeed, entire scenes) that oral poets used as building blocks for the poetry that they composed as they performed.

Whether Homer himself performed his works, they were meant for performance before a live audience. For these occasions, epithets may have had a very practical purpose. If the poet who was performing marked a change in speakers only with the name of the new speaker ("and Zeus said" or "then Athena answered"), a listener might miss the name of the speaker. (Since performances were probably done during or after a meal in aristocratic homes, at festivals, or at games, it seems likely that someone's attention could be momentarily distracted.) But if an epithet accompanied the name ("and Zeus the cloud-gatherer said"), even if you missed Zeus, "cloud-gatherer" would still let you know who was talking.[2]

Notes

There are many notes accompanying the text to help you with unfamiliar vocabulary and grammar. There is also a section containing the Greek text without notes and vocabulary (p. 221). After you read a passage using the notes, read it again in this section, trying not to look back at the notes. The more practice you have reading, the easier it will be to remember vocabulary and grammar.

---

[1] Marks, Samuel. *Homeric Seafaring* (College Station, TX: Texas A&M University Press, 2005): 161-178.

[2] Michalopoulos, André. *Homer* (New York: Twayne, 1966): 69-70.

The Gaps As you read the selections in this book, you will be missing the parts of the story that happen in between them. It would be a good idea to fill in the gaps by reading these parts of the poem in translation. This will give the narrative more continuity and provide more food for thought about major themes, motifs, and issues. For example:

- Hospitality, its proper forms and its abuse, is a major theme in the *Odyssey*. In how many episodes can you find references to it?
- Why is the story of Agamemnon mentioned so often? Does it provide parallels, contrasts, or warnings for Odysseus?
- Was Odysseus in any way responsible for the death of his companions?
- What does Odysseus learn as he makes his way home and how does he apply this knowledge?

The *Odyssey* has adventure, romance, horrible monsters, a clever hero (and heroine), hardships and suffering to be overcome, triumph, disaster, and ultimately a happy ending, at least for the family at the center of the story. Whoever wrote it and however he (or she or they) did it, the poem is a remarkable creation, containing characters and situations that have continually fascinated us for nearly three thousand years.

carmina sola carent fato mortemque repellent.
carminibus vives semper, Homere, tuis.[3]

[3] Baehrens, Emil, ed. *Poetae Latini Minores*, Vol. 4. New York and London: Garland Publishing, 1979: 68 (*Anthologia Latina* 27: "Memoriam per litteras manere," lines 9-10; attributed to Seneca); this is a reprint of the 1882 edition published by B. G. Teubner, Leipzig.

Odyssey Book 1.1-95

The Odyssey begins...

Book 1.1-95

The poet calls on a Muse to tell him about an ***ἀνήρ****. When the Trojan War ended, this* ***ἀνήρ*** *suffered many hardships (****ἄλγεα****) while trying to bring about a homecoming (****νόστος****) for himself and his comrades (****ἑταῖροι****).*

Ἄνδρα μοι ἔννεπε, Μοῦσα, πολύτροπον, ὃς μάλα πολλὰ
πλάγχθη, ἐπεὶ Τροίης ἱερὸν πτολίεθρον ἔπερσε·
πολλῶν δ' ἀνθρώπων ἴδεν ἄστεα καὶ νόον ἔγνω,
πολλὰ δ' ὅ γ' ἐν πόντῳ πάθεν ἄλγεα ὃν κατὰ θυμόν,
ἀρνύμενος ἥν τε ψυχὴν καὶ νόστον ἑταίρων.

---

1 **ἄνδρα**—the first word of the *Odyssey* announces its subject – a man. Although the **ἀνήρ** is not named until 1.21, the details in the introductory lines would have told the audience that the story was going to be about Odysseus. Or perhaps Homer intentionally concealed the name for twenty-one lines, foreshadowing Odysseus' frequent concealment of his own identity.

ἐννέπω—tell of, tell about, tell the tale of.

Μοῦσα—the Muse who inspires the poet. The Muses are goddesses of song, music, and poetry. In Homer's time, they did not have individual names and areas of responsibility, as they did later. In addition to acknowledging her as his source of inspiration, calling upon the Muse may be the poet's signal for the audience to be quiet since the performance is beginning.

πολύτροπος,-ον—ingenious, much-wandering (Even in antiquity there was dispute over which definition of **πολύτροπος** was intended in this line. Translating it "of many moves" would be one way to convey both ideas.)

πολλά—greatly, much (neuter adjective used as adverb).

2 **πλάζω**—drive from one's course; *middle and passive*, be tossed about, be forced to wander; **πλάγχθη = ἐπλάγχθη** – aorist passive, 3rd pers. sing. (In Homeric Greek, augments are often absent.)

πτολίεθρον,-ου, τό—city (There are several theories as to why Troy is called a sacred city – **ἱερὸν πτολίεθρον**. It may refer to the story that two gods, Poseidon and Apollo, built its original walls. It may be because of its many temples. Or the adjective may simply mean "impressive" or "awe-inspiring," without any religious connotation.)

πέρθω, (aor.) **ἔπερσα**—sack, destroy.

3 **ἴδεν**—aorist of **ὁράω**.

ἄστυ,-εος, τό—city, town.

~ **νόος,-ου, ὁ**—mind, nature, attitude, outlook, way of thinking.

ἔγνω—aorist active, 3rd pers. sing. of **γιγνώσκω** – "he learned," "he gained knowledge of."

4 **ὁ**—"he" (In Homeric Greek it is common for the article to be used as a personal, demonstrative, or relative pronoun.)

~ **πόντος,-ου, ὁ**—sea, open sea.

~ **πάθεν = ἔπαθεν**—aorist of **πάσχω.**

~ **ἄλγος,-εος, τό**—pain, suffering; *plural*, hardships, misfortunes.

~ **ὅς, ἥ, ὅν**—his own, her own, its own; **ὃν κατὰ θυμόν** – "within his heart."

How many forms of **πολλός** do you find in the first four lines? What facts does this repetition emphasize?

5 **ἄρνυμαι**—achieve, gain; **ἀρνύμενος** – "trying to achieve," "trying to gain" (a CONATIVE present, *i.e.*, a present form expressing an attempt or intention).

τε...καί—both...and.

ἥν...ψυχήν—"his own life."

~ **νόστος,-ου, ὁ**—return, homecoming.

~ **ἑταῖρος,-ου, ὁ**—companion, comrade (refers to the men who accompanied Odysseus to Troy and fought under his command).

Scanning Notes

1 **μοι** is scanned as a short syllable. This is an example of CORREPTION, scanning as short a long vowel or diphthong at the end of a word when the next word begins with a vowel.

2 The final syllable of **πλάγχθη** is scanned short, another example of CORREPTION.

4 The **υ** in **θυμόν** is long.

5 The last syllable of **ἀρνύμενος** is scanned long because **ἥν** was originally spelled **σϝήν**, putting two consonants after the short o. The digamma, **ϝ**, pronounced like the English *w*, was a consonant used in early Greek but no longer in use in Homer's time. Sometimes, as here, the digamma still affects the determination of long and short syllables.

τε is scanned long because **ψ** is considered a double consonant.

The **υ** in **ψυχήν** is long.

ἀλλ’ οὐδ’ ὧς ἑτάρους ἐρρύσατο, ἱέμενός περ·
αὐτῶν γὰρ σφετέρῃσιν ἀτασθαλίῃσιν ὄλοντο,
νήπιοι, οἳ κατὰ βοῦς Ὑπερίονος Ἠελίοιο
ἤσθιον· αὐτὰρ ὁ τοῖσιν ἀφείλετο νόστιμον ἦμαρ.
τῶν ἁμόθεν γε, θεά, θύγατερ Διός, εἰπὲ καὶ ἡμῖν.

*All the others who escaped utter destruction (**αἰπὺς ὄλεθρος**) are now home. Odysseus alone (**οἶος**) is not because the nymph Calypso, who wants him to be her husband (**πόσις**), is holding him prisoner in a hollow cave (**ἐν σπέεσι γλαφυροῖσι**).*

ἔνθ’ ἄλλοι μὲν πάντες, ὅσοι φύγον αἰπὺν ὄλεθρον,

6 ~ **ὧς**—so, thus.

~ **ἕταρος,-ου, ὁ** = **ἑταῖρος**.

ῥύομαι, (aor.) **ἐρρυσάμην**—rescue, save, protect.

~ **ἱέμενος**—present middle participle of **ἵημι** – "desiring."

~ **περ**—although, even though.

7 **σφέτερος,-η,-ον**—their; **αὐτῶν...σφετέρῃσιν** – "their very own."

ἀτασθαλίαι,-ῶν, αἱ—recklessness, criminal folly, wickedness; **σφετέρῃσιν ἀτασθαλίῃσιν** = **σφετέραις ἀτασθαλίαις** – DATIVE OF CAUSE.

ὄλοντο—unaugmented aorist middle of **ὄλλυμι**.

Line 7 has been called the moral of the *Odyssey* – human beings bring suffering and destruction upon themselves when they engage in **ἀτασθαλίαι**, *i.e.*, wicked behavior for which they deserve to suffer. Here Homer refers to the death of Odysseus' men for killing and eating Helios' cattle, something they had been repeatedly warned about and they had sworn not to do. The idea that humans must take responsibility for their actions will occur again in 1.34ff., when Zeus talks about Aegisthus, as well as several times later in the *Odyssey* with reference to the behavior of Penelope's suitors.

8 **νήπιος,-η,-ον**—foolish, thoughtless; **νήπιοι** – "the fools."

~ **βοῦς, βοός, ὁ, ἡ**—bull, cow; *plural*, cattle; **βοῦς** – acc. plur.

Ὑπερίων,-ονος, ὁ—Hyperion (a name or title for Helios, the sun god).

Ἠέλιος,-ου, ὁ—Helios, the sun god (= Attic **Ἥλιος**); **Ἠελίοιο** – gen. sing. (Note: **-οιο** is frequently used as the second declension genitive singular ending).

9 **κατεσθίω**—eat, devour; **κατά** (line 8)...**ἤσθιον** is treated like a compound verb (**κατήσθιον**) whose parts are separated. In Homeric poetry, a preposition could be used with a verb to convey an idea that in later Greek would be expressed by a compound verb formed from their union. The relationship between these prepositions and verbs has traditionally been referred to as TMESIS (from **τέμνω**

– cut). This is actually an incorrect application of the term, since in Homeric Greek the preposition has not been "cut" from the verb. Rather, the two have not yet evolved into a compound verb. (It is correctly applied to instances in Attic Greek where true tmesis occurs and words are actually cut apart, usually for emphasis or parody.)

~ **αὐτάρ**—but, however.

ὁ—refers to Helios.

τοῖσιν—"from them" (dat. plur. article used as a personal pronoun).

ἀφαιρέομαι, (aor) **ἀφειλόμην**—take away (what is taken is in the accusative and the person from whom it is taken is in the dative).

νόστιμος,-ον—belonging or pertaining to a return (**νόστος**) or homecoming.

~ **ἦμαρ,-ατος, τό**—day.

The story of Helios' revenge for the death of his cattle is told in Book 12.

10 **τῶν**—"of these things," "in this story" (article used as demonstrative pronoun).

ἁμόθεν—from any point, from somewhere; **τῶν ἁμόθεν** – "from some point in this story."

θεά—refers to the **Μοῦσα** of 1.1.

θύγατερ—vocative.

Ζεύς, Διός, ὁ—Zeus, king of the gods.

~ **εἶπον** (aor.)—say, tell; **εἰπὲ καὶ ἡμῖν** – The meaning of this phrase is not completely clear. It may mean "tell us *also,*" *i.e.,* share what you know with us (the poet and the audience). Or possibly "also tell *us* [as you have told others before]."

11 **ἔνθ' = ἔνθα**—"then" is the tenth year after the fall of Troy, the twentieth since Odysseus left home.

ἄλλοι...πάντες—*i.e.*, all the others who had gone to fight at Troy.

ὅσ(σ)ος,-η,-ον—as many as.

φύγον = ἔφυγον.

~ **αἰπύς,-εῖα,-ύ**—utter, merciless (**αἰπύς** literally means "steep" or "precipitous." It's theorized it may have originally been used in descriptions of warriors falling to their deaths off city walls, then later taken on the meaning seen here.)

~ **ὄλεθρος,-ου, ὁ**—destruction, death.

Scanning Notes

6 The **υ** in **ἐρρύσατο** is long.

The **ι** in **ἱέμενος** is long.

8 The **ι** in **Ὑπερίονος** is long.

10 The **α** in **θεά** is long.

οἴκοι ἔσαν, πόλεμόν τε πεφευγότες ἠδὲ θάλασσαν·
τὸν δ' οἶον, νόστου κεχρημένον ἠδὲ γυναικός,
νύμφη πότνι' ἔρυκε Καλυψώ, δῖα θεάων,
ἐν σπέεσι γλαφυροῖσι, λιλαιομένη πόσιν εἶναι.
ἀλλ' ὅτε δὴ ἔτος ἦλθε περιπλομένων ἐνιαυτῶν,
τῷ οἱ ἐπεκλώσαντο θεοὶ οἶκόνδε νέεσθαι
εἰς Ἰθάκην, οὐδ' ἔνθα πεφυγμένος ἦεν ἀέθλων
καὶ μετὰ οἷσι φίλοισι· θεοὶ δ' ἐλέαιρον ἅπαντες
νόσφι Ποσειδάωνος· ὁ δ' ἀσπερχὲς μενέαινεν

---

12 **οἴκοι**—at home.
ἔσαν = **ἦσαν**—imperfect of **εἰμί**.
πεφευγότες—perfect active participle, nom. plur. masc. of **φεύγω**.
~ **ἠδέ**—and; **τε...ἠδέ**—both...and.
~ **θάλασσα,-ης, ἡ**—the sea.

13 **τόν**—"this man," *i.e.*, Odysseus (article used as a demonstrative pronoun).
~ **οἶος,-η,-ον**—alone.
χράομαι, χρήσομαι, ἐχρησάμην, κέχρημαι—yearn for, desire, long for (+ gen.); **κεχρημένον** – "desiring," "longing for" (perfect middle participle modifying **τόν**).
~ **γυνή,-αικός**—woman, wife.

14 ~ **νύμφη,-ης, ἡ**—nymph (Nymphs are minor female divinities, of lesser rank than major goddesses, and usually associated with an aspect of nature (trees, mountains, springs, rivers, the sea) or places (caves, islands).)
πότνια (fem. adj.)—honored, revered (a title of honor given to goddesses and women); **πότνι'...Καλυψώ** – "the Lady Calypso," "queenly Calypso."
ἐρύκω, ἐρύξω, ἤρυξα—detain, restrain; **ἔρυκε** – unaugmented imperfect.
Καλυψώ,-όος or **-οῦς, ἡ**—Calypso, a nymph, daughter of Atlas (Calypso lived on the island of Ogygia, where she detained Odysseus for seven years. Because there are no stories about Calypso in any other context than that of the *Odyssey*, her character may have been invented by Homer to keep Odysseus away from home long enough for his son Telemachus to grow up. Telemachus was a baby when Odysseus left to fight in the Trojan War. The war lasted ten years; his travels before he reached Ogygia took three more. Seven years spent with Calypso meant Telemachus would be a young man when Odysseus reached Ithaca.)
~ **δῖος,-α,-ον**—divine, glorious, bright, famous, noble; **δῖα θεάων** – "glorious among goddesses."

15 ~ **σπέος** or **σπεῖος, σπείους, τό**—cave, cavern; **σπέεσι** – dat. plur. used for sing.

~ **γλαφυρός,-ή,-όν**—hollow; **γλαφυροῖσι = γλαφυροῖς.**

λιλαίομαι—desire.

πόσις,-ιος, ὁ—husband; **λιλαιομένη πόσιν εἶναι** – "desiring [Odysseus] to be [her] husband."

16 ~ **ἔτος,-εος, τό**—year.

περιπέλομαι—go around, revolve; **περιπλομένων** – aorist participle.

ἐνιαυτός,-οῦ, ὁ—year, a cycle of seasons; **περιπλομένων ἐνιαυτῶν** – "as the seasons revolved" (GENITIVE ABSOLUTE).

17 **τῷ**—"in which" (article used as relative pronoun; refers to **ἔτος** in the previous line).

~ **οἱ**— "to him" (dat. sing. of **εἶο**).

ἐπικλώθω, (aor.) **ἐπέκλωσα**—*active and middle,* assign as one's destiny, grant.

οἶκόνδε—to one's home, homewards (The suffix **-δε** indicates motion towards. **–δε** is an enclitic. When an enclitic is attached to a word, the word is accented as though the enclitic were a separate word. Since **οἶκον** has a circumflex accent on the penult (next-to-the-last syllable), it gets an additional acute accent on the ultima (last syllable) and the enclitic has no accent. Hence, **οἶκόνδε** has two accents.)

~ **νέομαι**—go or come back, return; **νέεσθαι = νεῖσθαι** – present infinitive.

18 **'Ιθάκη,-ης, ἡ**—Ithaca, an island off the west coast of Greece; Odysseus' home.

πεφυγμένος—perfect middle participle of **φεύγω.**

ἦεν = ἦν—imperfect, 3rd pers. sing. of **εἰμί.**

ἄεθλος,-ου, ὁ—contest; *plural*, troubles, struggles.

οὐδ' ἔνθα πεφυγμένος ἦεν ἀέθλων—"not even then was he free from his troubles."

19 **οἷσι = οἷς**—from **ὅς, ἥ, ὅν** (his own, her own, its own).

φίλοισι = φίλοις.

ἐλεαίρω—pity, feel pity for; **ἐλέαιρον** – unaugmented imperfect.

ἅπας, ἅπασα, ἅπαν = πᾶς, πᾶσα, πᾶν.

20 **νόσφι(ν)**—except (+ gen.).

ἀσπερχές—vehemently.

μενεαίνω—rage, be enraged, be angry at; **μενέαινεν** – unaugmented imperfect.

Scanning Notes

14 The **υ** in **ἔρυκε** is long.

The **α** in **θεάων** is long.

20 The **α** in **Ποσειδάωνος** is long.

ἀντιθέῳ Ὀδυσῆϊ πάρος ἣν γαῖαν ἱκέσθαι.

*Poseidon is away from Mt. Olympus visiting the Ethiopians. While he was enjoying himself (**τέρπετο**) receiving sacrifices and banqueting with them, the other **θεοί** gather in the palace (**ἐνὶ μεγάροισιν**) of Zeus, who is pondering the fate of Aegisthus.*

ἀλλ' ὁ μὲν Αἰθίοπας μετεκίαθε τηλόθ' ἐόντας,
Αἰθίοπας, τοὶ διχθὰ δεδαίαται, ἔσχατοι ἀνδρῶν,
οἱ μὲν δυσομένου Ὑπερίονος, οἱ δ' ἀνιόντος,
ἀντιόων ταύρων τε καὶ ἀρνειῶν ἑκατόμβης.
ἔνθ' ὅ γε τέρπετο δαιτὶ παρήμενος· οἱ δὲ δὴ ἄλλοι

---

21 ~ **ἀντίθεος,-η,-ον**—godlike, *i.e.*, strong, good-looking; *does not imply moral superiority.*

Ὀδυσ(σ)ευς,-ῆος, ὁ—Odysseus.

ἀντιθέῳ Ὀδυσῆϊ—"against godlike Odysseus" (first mention of Odysseus' name).

πάρος—before; *with an aorist infinitive*, "before ___ing. "

ἥν—from **ὅς, ἥ, ὅν**.

~ **γαῖα,-ης, ἡ**—earth, land, country, native land.

~ **ἱκνέομαι, ἵξομαι, ἱκόμην**—arrive at, reach, come to.

πάρος ἣν γαῖαν ἱκέσθαι—"until [he] reached his native land" (*literally*, before reaching his native land).

Poseidon is angry because Odysseus blinded the Cyclops Polyphemus, Poseidon's son (the story is told in Book 9 of the *Odyssey*).

22 **ὁ**—"he" (= Poseidon).

Αἰθίοπες,-ων, οἱ—Ethiopians, a mythical race noted for piety and righteousness, loved and often visited by the gods. (There is no clear evidence that Homer and his audience were aware of the real Ethiopians living south of Egypt. The first definite indication of Greek knowledge of these people is in the work of the sixth century B.C. historian Hecataeus. Whether the Greeks of Homer's time were acquainted with any black Africans is uncertain, though some argue the description of a character in Book 19.246-248 of the *Odyssey* suggests that they were.)

μετακιάθω—visit.

τηλόθι—far away.

ἐόντας = **ὄντας**—present participle, acc. plur. masc. of **εἰμί**; **τηλόθ' ἐόντας** – "who were far away" (literal translation?).

23 **τοί** = **οἱ**—nom. plur. masc. of **ὁ**, used here as a relative pronoun.

διχθά—in two.

δαίω—divide; **δεδαίαται** = **δέδαινται** – perfect passive, 3rd pers. plur.

ἔσχατος,-ον—most remote.

24 **δύω, δύσω, ἔδυν** or **ἔδυσα**—*active or middle,* go, enter, make one's way, plunge; *with reference to the sun or a constellation,* go into the Ocean, set; **δυσομένου** – aorist middle participle, gen. sing. masc.; translate as present. (This is a MIXED AORIST, that is, an aorist with the **σ** of the "first" aorist and the thematic vowel (**ο** or **ε**) of a "second" aorist.)

ἄνειμι—go up; *with reference to the sun,* rise; **ἀνιόντος** – present active participle, gen. sing. masc.

οἱ μὲν δυσομένου Ὑπερίονος, οἱ δ' ἀνιόντος—"some where Hyperion sets, some where he rises." The Ethiopians were usually thought to live far to the east (**Ὑπερίονος...ἀνιόντος**), but Homer also places them in the far west (**δυσομένου Ὑπερίονος**).

25 **ἀντιόω, ἀντιόω**—receive, accept (+ gen.); **ἀντιόων** – FUTURE PARTICIPLE OF PURPOSE (refers to Poseidon).

ἀρνειός,-οῦ, ὁ—ram.

ἑκατόμβη,-ης, ἡ—hecatomb, sacrificial offering of a large number of animals; **ἑκατόμβης** – object of **ἀντιόων** (Literally, the word means a sacrifice of one hundred (**ἑκατόν**) oxen (**βοῦς**), but it was used for sacrifices of fewer than one hundred animals and not necessarily oxen.)

26 **ἔνθ'** = **ἔνθα**—there.

τέρπω, τέρψω, ἔτερψα—delight, cheer; *middle and passive,* enjoy oneself; **τέρπετο** = **ἐτέρπετο.**

δαίς, δαιτός, ἡ—feast, banquet; **δαιτί** – dat. with **παρήμενος**; refers to the feast following the sacrifice. After the animals were killed, bits of raw meat and the thigh bones wrapped in fat were burned for the gods, who enjoyed the smell of burnt meat. The rest of the meat was roasted and eaten by those making the sacrifice.

πάρημαι—sit at, sit in enjoyment of (+ dat.).

ἄλλοι [θεοί].

Scanning Notes

21 The last syllable of **πάρος** is scanned long because **ἥν** was originally spelled **σϝήν**, putting two consonants after the short **ο**.

22 The **ι** in **μετεκίαθε** is long.

24 The first **υ** in **δυσομένου** is long.

The **ι** in **Ὑπερίονος** is long.

Ζηνὸς ἐνὶ μεγάροισιν Ὀλυμπίου ἁθρόοι ἦσαν. 27
τοῖσι δὲ μύθων ἦρχε πατὴρ ἀνδρῶν τε θεῶν τε· 28
μνήσατο γὰρ κατὰ θυμὸν ἀμύμονος Αἰγίσθοιο, 29
τόν ῥ᾽ Ἀγαμεμνονίδης τηλεκλυτὸς ἔκταν᾽ Ὀρέστης· 30
τοῦ ὅ γ᾽ ἐπιμνησθεὶς ἔπε᾽ ἀθανάτοισι μετηύδα· 31

---

27 **Ζηνός** = **Διός**—gen. sing. of **Ζεύς**.

~ **ἐνί** = **ἐν**.

~ **μέγαρον,-ου, τό**—great hall, main room, dining hall, house, palace; *plural often used for singular*; **μεγάροισιν** = **μεγάροις**.

Ὀλύμπιος,-ον—Olympian.

ἁθρόοι,-αι,-α—all together.

28 **τοῖσι** = **τοῖς**—"to them."

~ **μῦθος,-ου, ὁ**—word, speech; *plural*, a speech.

ἄρχω, ἄρξω, ἦρξα—begin; **μύθων ἦρχε** – "began to speak."

πατὴρ ἀνδρῶν τε θεῶν τε—*i.e.*, Zeus.

29 **μιμνήσκομαι, μνήσομαι, ἐμνησάμην**—remember, call to mind; *can take a genitive object*; **μνήσατο** = **ἐμνήσατο**.

ἀμύμων,-ον—The meaning of this adjective is much disputed. Often translated "blameless" (from **ἀ-** (negative prefix) + **μῶμος** – blame, fault), it seems an inappropriate adjective to describe Aegisthus. Several theories have been put forth to explain its use here: 1) He was blameless with respect to his birth, *i.e.*, he was of noble birth, an aristocrat. 2) It was a careless use of an epithet by the poet who needed a word to fill out the syllable in the line and simply used this one. 3) It is an honorary epithet, like "good" in "my good sir," and doesn't necessary imply the person described has the quality indicated by the adjective. 4) It means "handsome," *i.e.* "blameless" with respect to physical features. 5) It means "cunning" or "crafty," *i.e.*, "blameless" or "excellent" with respect to one's skill, Aegisthus' skill being his cunning. 6) Because Aegisthus, in killing Agamemnon, was avenging the atrocities committed against Aegisthus' father Thyestes by Agamemnon's father Atreus (Atreus murdered Thyestes' children and served them to their father for dinner), Aegisthus was only doing what human and divine law demanded, hence he actually was "blameless."

Αἴγισθος,-ου, ὁ—Aegisthus, the cousin of Agamemnon (the king of Mycenae and leader of the Greek forces in the Trojan War). Aegisthus became the lover of Agamemnon's wife Clytemnestra while Agamemnon was fighting at Troy, then murdered him upon his return. (In contrast to the version of the story in Aeschylus' *Agamemnon*, in which Clytemnestra is the murderer of Agamemnon, Homer stresses Aegisthus' role as the killer. He serves as a parallel to the suitors in the *Odyssey* and their plans for Telemachus and Penelope.)

30 **τόν**—"whom" (article used as relative pronoun).

ῥ' = **ἄρα**.

Ἀγαμεμνονίδης,-ου, ὁ—son of Agamemnon (Orestes) (The suffix **-δης** adds the meaning "son of" to the name to which it is attached. Such names are called patronymics, literally, "names from the father.")

τηλεκλυτός,-όν—far-famed, famous, well-known.

~ **κτείνω, κτενέω, ἔκτεινα** or **ἔκτανον** or **ἔκταν**—kill; **ἔκταν'** = **ἔκτανε**.

Ὀρέστης,-αο, ὁ—Orestes.

31 **τοῦ**—"him" (Aegisthus); genitive with **ἐπιμνησθείς**.

ὁ—"he" (Zeus).

ἐπιμιμνήσκομαι, (aor.) **ἐπεμνήσθην**—remember, think of (+ gen.); **ἐπιμνησθείς** – aorist participle: "remembering," "thinking of."

~ **ἔπος,-εος, τό**—word; **ἔπε'** = **ἔπεα**.

~ **ἀθάνατος,-η,-ον**—immortal; *plural as a noun,* the immortals, the gods.

μεταυδάω—speak, utter; **μετηύδα** – imperfect active, 3rd pers. sing.; **ἔπε' ἀθανάτοισι μετηύδα** – "he addressed the gods" (literal translation?).

Fig. 1. Triobol depicting head of Zeus. Greek, Hellenistic period, ca. 195-182 BCE. Minted for the Arcadian League at Megalopolis, Greece. Silver. 67.191. Museum of Art and Archaeology, University of Missouri.

Scanning Notes

27 The last syllable of **ἐνί** is scanned long. A short final syllable ending in a vowel and followed by a word beginning with **μ** can be scanned long.

Find two examples of CORREPTION in this line.

28 The **υ** in **μύθων** is long.

29 The **υ** in **θυμόν** is long.

The **υ** in **ἀμύμονος** is long.

31 The first **α** in **ἀθανάτοισι** is long.

*Zeus says that mortals (**βροτοί**) blame the **ἀθάνατοι** for evil (**κακόν**), but it is by their own folly (**ἀτασθαλίαι**) that they bring suffering upon themselves. We sent Hermes to warn Aegisthus not to kill (**κτείνειν**) Agamemnon and marry his wife (**ἄλοχος**). But he was not able to change Aegisthus' mind (**φρήν**).*

“ ὢ πόποι, οἷον δή νυ θεοὺς βροτοὶ αἰτιόωνται.
ἐξ ἡμέων γάρ φασι κάκ’ ἔμμεναι· οἱ δὲ καὶ αὐτοὶ
σφῇσιν ἀτασθαλίῃσιν ὑπὲρ μόρον ἄλγε’ ἔχουσιν,
ὡς καὶ νῦν Αἴγισθος ὑπὲρ μόρον Ἀτρεΐδαο
γῆμ’ ἄλοχον μνηστήν, τὸν δ’ ἔκτανε νοστήσαντα,
εἰδὼς αἰπὺν ὄλεθρον, ἐπεὶ πρό οἱ εἴπομεν ἡμεῖς,
Ἑρμείαν πέμψαντες, ἐΰσκοπον Ἀργεϊφόντην,
μήτ’ αὐτὸν κτείνειν μήτε μνάασθαι ἄκοιτιν·

---

32 **ὢ πόποι**—expresses Zeus' vexation or displeasure; possible translations: “look at this!” or “good grief” or “it's amazing!” or “how perverse!”

οἷον—“to think how!”

~ **νυ**—indeed; *may be used to add emphasis.*

~ **βροτός,-οῦ, ὁ** or **ἡ**—mortal, mortal man, man.

αἰτιάομαι—blame; **αἰτιόωνται** – present, 3rd pers. plur.

33 **ἡμέων** = **ἡμῶν**—gen. of **ἡμεῖς.**

~ **φημί, φήσω, ἔφησα**—say, declare, assert; **φασι** – present, 3rd. pers. plur.

~ **κακόν,-οῦ, τό**—evil, misfortune; **κάκ’** = **κακά.**

ἔμμεναι = **εἶναι**—present infinitive of **εἰμί.**

δὲ καί—“but indeed.”

34 **σφός, σφή, σφόν**—their own; **σφῇσιν ἀτασθαλίῃσιν** – DATIVE OF CAUSE.

μόρος,-ου, ὁ—fate, destiny; **ὑπὲρ μόρον** – “beyond what is fated,” “beyond what destiny allots.” In other words, the choices people make can cause them to experience a larger share of **ἄλγεα** than fate originally allotted for them.

ἄλγε’ = **ἄλγεα**—acc. plur. of **ἄλγος.**

What group did Homer mention in the opening lines of the *Odyssey* who perished because of their **ἀτασθαλίαι**?

35 **ὡς καὶ νῦν**—“just as in this case.”

Ἀτρεΐδης,-αο or **-εω, ὁ**—son of Atreus (another patronymic which refers to Agamemnon in this line; it can also refer to his brother, Menelaus).

36 **γαμέω, γαμέω, ἔγημα**—marry; **γῆμ’** = **ἔγημε.**

~ **ἄλοχος,-ου, ἡ**—wife.

μνηστός,-ή,-όν—lawfully married, wedded.

τόν—"whom" (refers to **Ἀτρεΐδαο** in the preceding line).

~ **νοστέω, νοστήσω, νόστησα**—return; **νοστήσαντα** – aorist active participle, acc. sing. masc.; **τόν...νοστήσαντα** – "whom, having returned" or "whom, when he returned."

37 ~ **οἶδα** (perfect, translate as present)—know; **εἰδώς** – perfect active participle, nom. sing. masc.: "knowing."

πρό—beforehand, in advance.

38 **Ἑρμείας, Ἑρμείω, ὁ**—Hermes, the messenger of the gods.

ἐΰσκοπος,-ον—sharp-sighted.

~ **Ἀργεϊφόντης,-ου, ὁ**—Argeiphontes, an epithet of Hermes, most likely understood by Homer and his audience to mean "slayer of Argus," referring to the story of Zeus and Io, a mortal woman with whom Zeus was having an affair. About to be discovered with her by his wife, the goddess Hera, Zeus turned Io into a cow. Hera, knowing full well what was going on, asked for the cow as a gift, a request Zeus could not refuse without confessing the truth. Hera set the hundred-eyed creature Argus to guard the cow. Zeus turned for help to Hermes, who lulled Argus to sleep, then killed him. The original meaning of **Ἀργεϊφόντης** is not known. Among suggestions by modern scholars: "dog-killer;" "shining in splendor;" "killer at Argos;" "shining at Argos."

39 **μήτε...μήτε**—neither…nor.

αὐτόν—"him" (= Agamemnon).

μνάομαι—woo, court; **μνάασθαι = μνᾶσθαι** – present infinitive.

ἄκοιτις,-ιος, ἡ = ἄλοχος.

Scanning Notes

33 **-εων** in **ἡμέων** is scanned as one long syllable. This is an example of SYNIZESIS (two vowels run together and pronounced as one long syllable).

The **α** in **φασι** is long.

35 The second **α** in **Ἀτρεΐδαο** is long.

39 The first **α** in **μνάασθαι** is long.

ἐκ γὰρ Ὀρέσταο τίσις ἔσσεται Ἀτρεΐδαο,
ὁππότ' ἂν ἡβήσῃ τε καὶ ἧς ἱμείρεται αἴης.
ὣς ἔφαθ' Ἑρμείας, ἀλλ' οὐ φρένας Αἰγίσθοιο
πεῖθ' ἀγαθὰ φρονέων· νῦν δ' ἁθρόα πάντ' ἀπέτεισε."

*Athena answers (**ἀμείβεται**) that Aegisthus deserved his fate. Long-suffering Odysseus, however, is being held on an island (**ἐν νήσῳ**) by Atlas' **θυγάτηρ**. Is Zeus' heart (**ἦτορ**) not moved by the sacrifices Odysseus made beside the ships (**παρὰ νηυσί**) at Troy?*

τὸν δ' ἠμείβετ' ἔπειτα θεὰ γλαυκῶπις Ἀθήνη·

---

40 **Ὀρέσταο**—gen. of **Ὀρέστης**.

τίσις,-εως, ἡ—revenge, vengeance, retribution; **τίσις...Ἀτρεΐδαο** – "revenge for the son of Atreus (*i.e.*, Agamemnon)."

ἔσσεται = ἔσται—future tense of **εἰμί**.

41 **ὁππότ' = ὁππότε**—when, whenever; *with* **ἄν** *and a subjunctive verb, it indicates something that will happen in the future.*

ἡβάω, ἡβήσω, ἥβησα—be in the prime of youth, be young; *aorist*, come to manhood; **ἡβήσῃ** – aorist subjunctive, 3rd pers. sing.

ἧς—from **ὅς, ἥ, ὅν**; agrees with **αἴης**.

ἱμείρομαι, (aor.) **ἱμειράμην**—long for, long, wish, desire (+ gen.); **ἱμείρεται = ἱμείρηται** (**ἱμείρεται** is a SHORT VOWEL SUBJUNCTIVE. In Homer, long thematic vowels, the **η** or **ω** before the verb endings of the subjunctive, may be shortened to **ε** or **ο**.)

~ **αἶα,-ης, ἡ**—country, land, homeland, native land (Orestes was a child when Aegisthus killed his father. He was either away from Mycene when the murder took place or was taken away to safety shortly after. When he grew up, he returned and killed Aegisthus to avenge his father's death.)

The story of Agamemnon, Clytemnestra, and Orestes is mentioned frequently in the *Odyssey* and serves as an important parallel/contrast to the action of the poem. It is a warning to Odysseus of what he may face when he gets home. For Telemachus, it provides an example of a young man who took revenge on someone who destroyed his family. It is a vindication of Penelope, who was faithful to her husband, unlike Clytemnestra. Zeus introduces the story and uses it here to illustrate his point that humans bring their own misfortune on themselves, even when they are warned that certain actions will bring dire consequences.

Homer's audience will have been familiar with both the story of Agamemnon and of Odysseus. They will likely have seen Aegisthus representing Penelope's suitors (**μνηστῆρες**). Homer's choice of the word **μνάασθαι** ("to woo") for what Aegisthus is told not to do will bring **μνηστῆρες** to mind, even though the suitors have not been formally introduced into the story yet.

Another possible effect the frequent mention of Agamemnon's story could have is the creation of suspense. It may cause the audience to worry about the ultimate happy ending they expect for the story of Odysseus. Is this version of the story going to end as it always does or will Odysseus suffer the same fate as Agamemnon? Repeated references to Agamemnon's fate suggest they should pay close attention and perhaps be a bit concerned.

42 **ἔφαθ'** = **ἔφατο**—imperfect middle with active meaning of **φημί**.

~ **φρήν, φρενός, ἡ**—mind, heart; midriff, diaphragm; *plural often used for singular* (The Greeks thought of the midriff or chest area as the seat of thought and emotion.)

43 **πεῖθ'** = **ἔπειθε**.

φρονέω—intend, desire; **φρονέων** = **φρονῶν; ἀγαθὰ φρονέων** – "despite his good intentions" (*literally*, intending good things); **φρονέων** agrees with **Ἑρμείας** in the preceding line.

πάντ' = **πάντα**—acc. plur. neut.; **ἀθρόα πάντ'** – "everything all at once" (referring both to taking Agamemnon's wife and killing Agamemnon).

ἀποτίνω, ἀποτείσω, ἀπέτεισα—pay for, pay the penalty for.

44 **τόν**—"him."

~ **ἀμείβω, ἀμείψω, ἤμειψα**—exchange; *middle,* answer, reply; **ἠμείβετ'** = **ἠμείβετο**.

γλαυκῶπις,-ιδος (fem. adj.)—epithet of Athena, usually translated "gleaming-eyed," "bright-eyed," "flashing-eyed" (**γλαυκός** – gleaming + **ὦπα** – eye).

Ἀθήνη,-ης, ἡ—Athena, goddess of the arts, intelligence, and war.

Scanning Notes

40 The **α** in **Ὀρέσταο** is long.

The final syllable (**-ο**) in **Ὀρέσταο** is scanned long, even though its vowel is short. Occasionally, a final syllable ending in a short vowel is arbitrarily scanned long simply because it occupies a position in the line that requires a long syllable.

The second **α** in **Ἀτρεΐδαο** is long.

41 The first **ι** in **ἱμείρεται** is long.

42 The **α** in **Ἑρμείας** is long.

44 The **α** in **θεά** is long.

“ ὦ πάτερ ἡμέτερε Κρονίδη, ὕπατε κρειόντων,
καὶ λίην κεῖνός γε ἐοικότι κεῖται ὀλέθρῳ,
ὡς ἀπόλοιτο καὶ ἄλλος ὅτις τοιαῦτά γε ῥέζοι.
ἀλλά μοι ἀμφ’ Ὀδυσῆϊ δαΐφρονι δαίεται ἦτορ,
δυσμόρῳ, ὃς δὴ δηθὰ φίλων ἄπο πήματα πάσχει
νήσῳ ἐν ἀμφιρύτῃ, ὅθι τ’ ὀμφαλός ἐστι θαλάσσης,
νῆσος δενδρήεσσα, θεὰ δ’ ἐν δώματα ναίει,
Ἄτλαντος θυγάτηρ ὀλοόφρονος, ὅς τε θαλάσσης
πάσης βένθεα οἶδεν, ἔχει δέ τε κίονας αὐτὸς
μακράς, αἳ γαῖάν τε καὶ οὐρανὸν ἀμφὶς ἔχουσι.

---

45 **πάτερ ἡμέτερε**—vocative (Zeus is the actual father of many of the gods and goddesses – Athena, Apollo, Artemis, Hermes, Hephaestus, Ares, Dionysus, and, in Homer, Aphrodite.)

Κρονίδης,-ου, ὁ—son of Cronus (another patronymic); **Κρονίδη** – voc.

ὕπατος,-η,-ον—highest, supreme.

κρείων,-οντος, ὁ—ruler, king, lord.

46 **λίην**—very much; **καὶ λίην** – truly, surely.

~ **κεῖνος,-η,-ο** = **ἐκεῖνος,-η,-ο**—that, that one; **κεῖνος** refers to Aegisthus.

ἔοικα (perfect, translate as present)—be fitting, be suitable; **ἐοικότι** – perfect active participle, dat. sing. masc.: “fitting,” “suitable.”

~ **κεῖμαι**—lie, lie dead.

ἐοικότι...ὀλέθρῳ—“in a fitting death.”

47 ~ **ἀπόλλυμι, ἀπολέσσω, ἀπώλεσα, ἀπόλωλα**—destroy, kill, lose; *middle, passive, and perfect active,* perish, die; **ἀπόλοιτο** – present middle optative; OPTATIVE OF WISH.

ὅτις = **ὅς τις**—whoever, anyone who, whosoever.

τοιοῦτος, τοιαύτη, τοιοῦτον—such, of such a kind.

ῥέζω, ῥέξω, ἔρεξα—do; **ῥέζοι** – present active optative, 3rd pers. sing. (When there is an optative of wish in the main clause, a verb in a subordinate clause may be optative by assimilation.)

Athena’s wish for the destruction of anyone else who would do such things (court a man’s wife and murder him when he came home) foreshadows what will happen at the end of the *Odyssey* to Penelope’s **μνηστῆρες**.

48 **μοι**—DATIVE OF INTEREST expressing possession; refers to **ἦτορ**.

ἀμφ’ = **ἀμφί**—about, concerning (+ dat.).

δαΐφρων,-ονος—wise, skillful.

δαίεται—"is troubled," "is distressed," "is torn" (from **δαίω** – divide).

~ **ἦτορ, τό** (only in nom. and acc. sing. forms)—heart, spirit.

49 **δύσμορος,-ον**—ill-fated, unlucky.

δηθά—for a long time, long.

φίλων ἄπο = **ἀπὸ φίλων**—the accent on the first syllable of **ἀπό** indicates it goes with the preceding word.

~ **πῆμα,-ατος, τό**—suffering, woe, misery.

50 ~ **νῆσος,-ου, ἡ**—island.

ἀμφίρυτος,-η,-ον—encircled by the sea, sea-girt.

ὅθι—where, at the place where; **ὅθι τ'** – "just where."

ὀμφαλός,-οῦ, ὁ—the navel, the center.

ὅθι τ' ὀμφαλός ἐστι θαλάσσης—locating Calypso's island at the center of the sea is not very specific (which sea?). There are many theories, both ancient and modern, as to where Homer envisioned it.

51 **δενδρήεις,-εσσα,-εν**—woody, wooded, full of trees.

ἐν—there, on it, *i.e.*, on the **νῆσος** (adverbial use of **ἐν**).

~ **δῶμα,-ατος, τό**—house; **δώματα** – plural used for singular.

ναίω—live, dwell.

52 **Ἄτλας, Ἄτλαντος, ὁ**—Atlas; **Ἄτλαντος θυγάτηρ** is Calypso.

ὀλοόφρων,-ονος—malicious, destructive, malevolent (Why Atlas is described so negatively is unknown.)

53 **βένθος,-εος, τό**—depth (of the sea); *plural,* the depths, the deep recesses (of the sea).

ἔχει—"holds."

κίων,-ονος, ὁ or **ἡ**—pillar, column.

54 **ἀμφίς**—apart.

This picture of Atlas is different from Hesiod's description of him standing on land holding up the sky with his hands (*Theogony* 517-19). Here he is in the sea, holding pillars that keep the earth and sky apart. Homer seems to have combined Near Eastern stories of pillars supporting the sky and a sea-dwelling giant who has the earth and heaven built upon him with the story of the Titan Atlas condemned by Zeus to support the sky.

Scanning Notes

46 The **ι** in **λίην** is long.

51 The **α** in **θεά** is long.

53 The **ι** in **κίονας** is long.

54 The second **α** in **μακράς** is long.

τοῦ θυγάτηρ δύστηνον ὀδυρόμενον κατερύκει,
αἰεὶ δὲ μαλακοῖσι καὶ αἱμυλίοισι λόγοισι
θέλγει, ὅπως Ἰθάκης ἐπιλήσεται· αὐτὰρ Ὀδυσσεύς,
ἱέμενος καὶ καπνὸν ἀποθρῴσκοντα νοῆσαι
ἧς γαίης, θανέειν ἱμείρεται. οὐδέ νυ σοί περ
ἐντρέπεται φίλον ἦτορ, Ὀλύμπιε; οὔ νύ τ' Ὀδυσσεὺς
Ἀργείων παρὰ νηυσὶ χαρίζετο ἱερὰ ῥέζων
Τροίῃ ἐν εὐρείῃ; τί νύ οἱ τόσον ὠδύσαο, Ζεῦ; "

*Zeus replies that it is Poseidon the earth-shaker (**ἐνοσίχθων**) who is keeping Odysseus from his native land (**ἀπὸ πατρίδος αἴης**). He is angry because Odysseus blinded his son. But it is time for Poseidon to give up his anger (**χόλος**). He will not be able (**δυνήσεται**) to stand alone (**οἶος**) against all the other **θεοί**.*

τὴν δ' ἀπαμειβόμενος προσέφη νεφεληγερέτα Ζεύς·

---

55 **τοῦ**—"his," *i.e.*, Atlas'.
δύστηνος,-ον—miserable, unhappy.
ὀδύρομαι—weep, grieve; **δύστηνον ὀδυρόμενον** is Odysseus.
κατερύκω—detain, keep from leaving.

56 ~ **αἰεί = ἀεί**.
μαλακός,-ή,-όν—soft, gentle.
αἱμύλιος,-ον—wheedling, flattering; **μαλακοῖσι καὶ αἱμυλίοισι λόγοισι** – DATIVE OF MEANS.

57 **θέλγω, θέλξω, ἔθελξα**—bewitch, beguile.
~ **ὅπ(π)ως**—so that, in order that.
ἐπιλανθάνομαι, ἐπιλήσομαι—forget (+ gen.).
ὅπως Ἰθάκης ἐπιλήσεται—PURPOSE CLAUSE (In poetry, a future indicative verb was often used in a purpose clause rather than a subjunctive when the clause was introduced by **ὅπως**.)

58 **καπνός,-οῦ, ὁ**—smoke; **καὶ καπνόν** – "even the smoke."
ἀποθρῴσκω—rise up from (+ gen.).
νοέω, νοήσω, ἐνόησα—see, observe, perceive.

59 **ἧς**—from **ὅς, ἥ, ὅν**.
θνήσκω, (aor.) **ἔθανον**—die; **θανέειν = θανεῖν** – aorist infinitive.

ἱμείρομαι, (aor.) **ἱμειράμην**—long for, long, wish, desire (+ gen.).

σοι—DATIVE OF INTEREST showing possession; with **ἦτορ** in the next line.

περ—at all.

60 **ἐντρέπομαι**—care, be moved.

φίλον—"own;" **σοί...φίλον ἦτορ** – "your own heart."

Ὀλύμπιε—vocative; "Olympian" is used here as a noun referring to Zeus.

τ' = τοι = σοι.

61 **Ἀργεῖοι,-ων, οἱ**—Argives (one of the names Homer uses for Greeks).

~ **νηῦς, νηός, ἡ**—ship; **νηυσί** – dat. plur. (**Ἀργείων παρὰ νηυσί** refers to the Greek ships beached on the shore during the Trojan War. When the Greeks arrived at Troy, they drew their ships out of the water onto the shore and built their camp beside them.)

χαρίζομαι—honor, seek favor (+ dat.).

ἱερα,-ῶν, τά—sacrifices, offerings; **ἱερὰ ῥέζων** – "making sacrifices."

62 **Τροίῃ**—"the Troad" (the area in the northwest corner of Asia Minor of which Troy (the city) was the capital).

~ **εὐρύς,-εῖα,-ύ**—broad, wide.

τί—why?

τόσον—so much, so greatly.

ὀδύσσομαι, (aor.) **ὠδυσάμην**—be angry with, hate (+ dat.); **ὠδύσαο** – aorist, 2nd pers. sing. (**ὠδύσαο** is a pun on Odysseus' name. In the previous lines Athena used other words which also echo his name and stress his unhappiness and misfortune: **δυσμόρῳ** (1.49) – unlucky; **δύστηνον** (1.55) – miserable; **ὀδυρόμενον** (1.55) – weep.)

63 ~ **ἀπαμείβομαι**—answer.

~ **πρόσφημι**—speak to, address; **προσέφη** – imperfect.

νεφεληγερέτα,-αο, ὁ—the cloud-gatherer (**νεφέλη** – cloud + **ἀγείρω** – gather) (an epithet of Zeus).

Scanning Notes

55 The **υ** in **ὀδυρόμενον** is long.

The **υ** in **κατερύκει** is long.

56 **δέ** is scanned as a long syllable. A short final syllable that ends in a vowel and is followed by a word beginning with **μ** can be scanned long.

59 The first **ι** in **ἱμείρεται** is long.

61 The **ι** in **ἱερά** is long.

“ τέκνον ἐμόν, ποῖόν σε ἔπος φύγεν ἕρκος ὀδόντων.
πῶς ἂν ἔπειτ’ Ὀδυσῆος ἐγὼ θείοιο λαθοίμην,
ὃς περὶ μὲν νόον ἐστὶ βροτῶν, περὶ δ’ ἱρὰ θεοῖσιν
ἀθανάτοισιν ἔδωκε, τοὶ οὐρανὸν εὐρὺν ἔχουσιν;
ἀλλὰ Ποσειδάων γαιήοχος ἀσκελὲς αἰὲν
Κύκλωπος κεχόλωται, ὃν ὀφθαλμοῦ ἀλάωσεν,
ἀντίθεον Πολύφημον, ὅου κράτος ἐστὶ μέγιστον
πᾶσιν Κυκλώπεσσι· Θόωσα δέ μιν τέκε νύμφη,
Φόρκυνος θυγάτηρ, ἁλὸς ἀτρυγέτοιο μέδοντος,
ἐν σπέεσι γλαφυροῖσι Ποσειδάωνι μιγεῖσα.

---

64 **τέκνον,-ου, τό**—child.

ποῖος,-η,-ον—what kind!, what sort!

φύγεν = ἔφυγεν.

ἕρκος,-εος, τό—barrier, fence.

ὀδούς, ὀδόντος, ὁ—tooth; **ἕρκος ὀδόντων** – “lips” or “mouth” (*literally*, the barrier of teeth) (Grammatically, **σε** and **ἕρκος ὀδόντων** are in apposition, **ἕρκος ὀδόντων** specifying the part of **σε** affected. Translate **σε** as though it were a possessive: “what sort of word escaped your mouth!” or “what are you saying!”)

65 **θεῖος,-η,-ον**—godlike, excellent; **θείοιο** – gen. sing. masc.

~ **λανθάνω, λήσω, ἔλαθον**—escape the notice of; *middle,* forget (+ gen.); **λαθοίμην** – aorist optative; **πῶς...λαθοίμην** – POTENTIAL OPTATIVE: “how could I forget.”

66 **περίειμι**—be superior, surpass (+ gen.); **περὶ...ἐστί = περίεστι** – TMESIS.

νόον—“in intelligence” (ACCUSATIVE OF RESPECT).

πέρι (after the comma)—exceedingly, beyond measure.

ἱρά = ἱερά.

67 **τοί = οἱ**—nom. plur. masc. of **ὁ**, used here as a relative pronoun.

68 **γαιήοχος,-ον**—earth-holding (an epithet of Poseidon, possibly referring to the ocean surrounding or supporting the earth).

ἀσκελές—unrelentingly.

~ **αἰέν = ἀεί.**

69 **Κύκλωψ,-ωπος, ὁ**—Cyclops. (The Cyclopes were a race of barbarous one-eyed giants.); **Κύκλωπος** – genitive of cause. With verbs of emotion, a genitive can indicate the cause of the emotion.

χολόω, χολώσω, ἐχόλωσα, (perf. mid.) **κεχόλωμαι**—enrage, make angry; *middle and passive*, be angry

ἀλαόω, ἀλαώσω, ἀλάωσα—blind, make [acc.] blind in [gen.].

70 **Πολύφημος,-ου, ὁ**—Polyphemus, a Cyclops who is Poseidon's son.

ὅου = οὗ—relative pronoun, gen. sing. masc.: "whose."

κράτος,-εος, τό—strength, power.

71 **πᾶσιν Κυκλώπεσσι**—"among all the Cyclopes;" DATIVE OF PLACE.

Θόωσα,-ης, ἡ—Thoosa.

~ **μιν**—"him," *i.e.*, Polyphemus; acc. sing. of **εἷο**.

τίκτω, τέξω, ἔτεκον—give birth to, bear; **τέκε = ἔτεκε**.

72 **Φόρκυς,-υνος, ὁ**—Phorcys, a sea god.

~ **ἅλς, ἁλός, ἡ**—sea.

ἀτρύγετος,-ον—There is uncertainty about the meaning of this word. It is usually translated "barren," "unfruitful," or "unharvested" (contrasting the sea to the earth). Other suggested meanings are "tireless," "restless," "noisy," "enduring," or "never runs dry" (in contrast to pools or rivers, which can dry up).

μέδων,-οντος, ὁ—ruler, lord.

73 **μίσγω, μίξω, ἔμιξα,** (aor. pass.) **ἐμίγην**—mix, mingle; *middle and passive,* mingle with, join (+ dat.); have sex with (+ dat.); **μιγεῖσα** – aorist passive participle, nom. sing. fem., modifies **Θόωσα** (1.71).

Scanning Notes

66 The final syllable of **ἐστι** is not scanned long even though it is followed by two consonants. If the first consonant is a mute or stop (**π, β, φ, κ, γ, χ, τ, δ,** or **θ**) and the second is either **λ** or **ρ**, the preceding syllable can be scanned short.

The **ι** in **ἱρά** is long.

68 The **α** in **Ποσειδάων** is long.

72 The **υ** in **Φόρκυνος** is long.

73 The **α** in **Ποσειδάωνι** is long.

ἐκ τοῦ δὴ Ὀδυσῆα Ποσειδάων ἐνοσίχθων
οὔ τι κατακτείνει, πλάζει δ' ἀπὸ πατρίδος αἴης.
ἀλλ' ἄγεθ' ἡμεῖς οἵδε περιφραζώμεθα πάντες
νόστον, ὅπως ἔλθῃσι· Ποσειδάων δὲ μεθήσει
ὃν χόλον· οὐ μὲν γάρ τι δυνήσεται ἀντία πάντων
ἀθανάτων ἀέκητι θεῶν ἐριδαινέμεν οἶος."

Athena urges that Hermes be sent to Ogygia, the ***νῆσος*** *where Calypso lives, to inform her of the gods' decision that stout-hearted (****ταλασίφρων****) Odysseus must be allowed to go home. She herself will go to Ithaca to encourage Odysseus'* ***υἱός*** *Telemachus to speak out against the suitors (****μνηστῆρες****). She will send him to Sparta and Pylos to seek news of his* ***πατήρ****.*

τὸν δ' ἠμείβετ' ἔπειτα θεὰ γλαυκῶπις Ἀθήνη·
"ὦ πάτερ ἡμέτερε Κρονίδη, ὕπατε κρειόντων,
εἰ μὲν δὴ νῦν τοῦτο φίλον μακάρεσσι θεοῖσι,
νοστῆσαι Ὀδυσῆα πολύφρονα ὅνδε δόμονδε,

---

74 **ἐκ τοῦ δή**—from that time on, since then, ever since.

~ **ἐνοσίχθων,-ονος, ὁ**—earth-shaker (an epithet of Poseidon, who was believed to cause earthquakes).

75 ~ **τι**—in any way, at all.

κατακτείνω—kill; **οὔ τι κατακτείνει** – "although he does not kill" or possibly a CONATIVE present, "he is not in any way trying to kill."

πλάζω—drive, drive away from.

~ **πατρίς,-ίδος** (fem. adj.)—of one's fathers; *with* ***αἶα****,* one's fatherland, home, native land.

76 ~ **ἄγεθ' = ἄγετε**—come! (imperative of **ἄγω** used as an interjection).

περιφράζομαι—consider, think about; **περιφραζώμεθα** – "let us consider" (HORTATORY SUBJUNCTIVE).

ἡμεῖς οἵδε...πάντες—"all of us here," *i.e.*, all the gods except Poseidon.

77 ~ **ὅπ(π)ως**—how, in what way.

ἔλθῃσι—aorist subjunctive, 3rd pers. sing. of **ἔρχομαι** (**νόστον** and the clause **ὅπως ἔλθῃσι** ("how he will come [home]") are both direct objects of **περιφραζώμεθα**. After a verb meaning "consider," in a clause introduced by **ὅπθς** or **ὡς** that expressed what was to be considered, Homer used a subjunctive or optative verb. In Attic, a clause like this would have a future indicative verb.)

μεθίημι, μεθήσω, μεθῆκα—let go, give up.

78 **χόλος,-ου, ὁ**—anger, wrath.

~ **δύναμαι, δυνήσομαι, ἐδυνησάμην** or **ἐδυνάσθην**—be able.

ἀντία—against (+ gen.).

79 **ἀέκητι**—against the will of (+ gen.); **ἀντία...ἀέκητι** – "in opposition against the will of" (the use of both words which are synonymous reinforces the idea that Poseidon will be standing alone against all the other gods).

ἐριδαίνω, (aor.) **ἐρίδηνα**—contend; **ἐριδαινέμεν = ἐριδαίνειν** – present active infinitive.

81 Compare 1.44-45 with 1.80-81.

82 **φίλον**—"pleasing;" **εἰ μὲν δὴ νῦν τοῦτο φίλον** [**ἐστί**].

~ **μάκαρ,-αρος** (masc. and fem. adj.)—happy, blessed; **μακάρεσσι** – dat. plur. masc.

83 **πολύφρων,-ονος** (masc. and fem. adj.)—much-thinking, intelligent.

~ **δόμος,-ου, ὁ**—house, home; **ὅνδε δόμονδε = ὃν δόμον** plus the suffix **-δε** (indicating motion toward) added to both words: "to his own home."

Fig. 2. Tetradrachm depicting head of Athena. Greek, Hellenistic period, ca. 91-90 BCE. Minted at Athens, Greece. Silver. 61.41. Museum of Art and Archaeology, University of Missouri.

Scanning Notes

74 The **α** in **Ποσειδάων** is long.

77 The **α** in **Ποσειδάων** is long.

78 Find an example of CORREPTION in this line.

80 The **α** in **θεά** is long.

Ἑρμείαν μὲν ἔπειτα, διάκτορον Ἀργεϊφόντην,
νῆσον ἐς Ὠγυγίην ὀτρύνομεν, ὄφρα τάχιστα
νύμφῃ ἐϋπλοκάμῳ εἴπῃ νημερτέα βουλήν,
νόστον Ὀδυσσῆος ταλασίφρονος, ὥς κε νέηται.
αὐτὰρ ἐγὼν Ἰθάκηνδε ἐλεύσομαι, ὄφρα οἱ υἱὸν
μᾶλλον ἐποτρύνω καί οἱ μένος ἐν φρεσὶ θείω,
εἰς ἀγορὴν καλέσαντα κάρη κομόωντας Ἀχαιοὺς
πᾶσι μνηστήρεσσιν ἀπειπέμεν, οἵ τέ οἱ αἰεὶ
μῆλ' ἀδινὰ σφάζουσι καὶ εἰλίποδας ἕλικας βοῦς.

---

84 **διάκτορος,-ου, ὁ**—guide (epithet of Hermes; refers to the fact that he serves as a guide for travelers and for the dead as they go to the Underworld).

85 ~ **ἐς = εἰς**.

Ὠγυγίη,-ης, ἡ—Ogygia, the island on which Calypso lived.

ὀτρύνω, ὀτρυνέω, ὤτρυνα—send; **ὀτρύνομεν** – "let us send" (HORTATORY SUBJUNCTIVE); **ὀτρύνομεν = ὀτρύνωμεν** – SHORT VOWEL SUBJUNCTIVE.

~ **ὄφρα**—so that, in order that (introduces a PURPOSE CLAUSE here).

τάχιστα—most quickly, at once.

86 ~ **ἐϋπλόκαμος,-ον**—with beautiful braids, having well-braided hair.

εἴπῃ—subjunctive, 3rd pers. sing. of **εἶπον**; **ὄφρα...εἴπῃ** – PURPOSE CLAUSE.

νημερτής,-ές—certain, true; **νημερτέα** – acc. sing. fem.; **νημερτέα βουλήν** – "[our] sure decree," *i.e.*, a decree that will be enforced.

87 **ταλασίφρων,-ονος** (masc. and fem. adj.)—steadfast, stout-hearted.

~ **κε(ν)**—may add an idea of indefiniteness or indicate a condition; where Attic used **ἄν**, Homer much more often used **κε(ν)**; here it is part of a PURPOSE CLAUSE.

νέηται—present subjunctive, 3rd pers. sing. of **νέομαι**.

νόστον—in apposition to **βουλήν**; further amplified by **ὥς κε νέηται** – "that he may go home."

88 ~ **ἐγών = ἐγώ.**

Ἰθάκηνδε = Ἰθάκην + -δε.

οἱ—"his," *i.e.*, Odysseus'; DATIVE OF INTEREST used as possessive; **οἱ υἱόν** is Telemachus.

89 ~ **μᾶλλον**—more, much, the more.

ἐποτρύνω—urge on, rouse to action; **ἐποτρύνω** – present subjunctive.

οἱ—"his," *i.e.*, the son's.

μένος,-εος, τό—courage, spirit, determination.

φρεσί—dat. plur. of **φρήν**.

θείω—aorist subjunctive of **τίθημι**; **ἐποτρύνω** and **θείω** are verbs in the PURPOSE CLAUSE introduced by **ὄφρα**.

90 **καλέσαντα**—aorist active participle, acc. sing. masc. of **καλέω**. It refers to **οἱ** in the previous line, but has become accusative in an accusative/infinitive construction.

κάρη, κρατός, τό—head; **κάρη** – ACCUSATIVE OF RESPECT.

κομάω—have long or abundant hair, wear long hair; **κομόωντας** – present active participle, acc. plur. masc.; **κάρη κομόωντας** – "long haired" (*literally*, having long hair with respect to the head). In Homer, heroes and gods have long hair.

~ **Ἀχαιοί,-ῶν, οἱ**—Achaeans (the name Homer most commonly uses for Greeks. In the *Odyssey*, it is often used to refer to the people of Ithaca and the surrounding islands.)

91 ~ **μνηστήρ,-ῆρος, ὁ**—suitor; **μνηστήρεσσιν** – dat. plur. (The suitors are mentioned here for the first time in the *Odyssey* with no explanation of who they are (young men from the best families in Ithaca) or what they are doing (besieging the household rather than offering gifts to woo Penelope). This suggests that the story of Penelope's suitors was a very familiar one to the audience.)

ἀπεῖπον (aor.)—speak one's mind freely; **ἀπειπέμεν** – infinitive with **καλέσαντα** (1.90): "that he, having summoned…speaks his mind to…"

οἵ—relative pronoun.

οἱ—"his."

92 ~ **μῆλον,-ου, τό**—sheep; *plural,* flocks of sheep; **μῆλ' = μῆλα**.

ἁδινός,-ή,-όν—thick-thronging.

σφάζω—slaughter.

εἰλίπους,-πουν (gen. **-ποδος**)—with rolling gait, lumbering.

ἕλιξ,-ικος (masc. and fem. adj.)—with twisted horns.

Scanning Notes

85 The **υ** in **ὀτρύνομεν** is long.

89 The **υ** in **ἐποτρύνω** is long.

92 The last syllable of **εἰλίποδας** is scanned long because **ἕλικας** was originally spelled **ϝέλικας**, putting two consonants after the short **α**.

πέμψω δ' ἐς Σπάρτην τε καὶ ἐς Πύλον ἠμαθόεντα
νόστον πευσόμενον πατρὸς φίλου, ἤν που ἀκούσῃ,
ἠδ' ἵνα μιν κλέος ἐσθλὸν ἐν ἀνθρώποισιν ἔχῃσιν."

---

93 **πέμψω**—understand "him" as the object.

Σπάρτη,-ης, ἡ—Sparta, the chief city of Laconia, home of King Menelaus and his wife Helen.

Πύλος,-ου, ἡ—Pylos, a kingdom on the southwestern coast of the Peloponnese; ruled by Nestor, who fought in the Trojan War with Odysseus.

ἠμαθόεις,-εσσα,-εν—sandy (an epithet of Pylos, probably because it was close to the sea).

94 **πεύθομαι, πεύσομαι**—learn of, find out about; **πευσόμενον** – FUTURE PARTICIPLE OF PURPOSE, accusative to agree with the understood object of **πέμψω**.

ἤν = εἰ ἄν—if by chance, in the hope that (+ subjunctive).

~ **που**—somewhere, perhaps.

ἀκούσῃ—aorist subjunctive of **ἀκούω**; it has an understood object: "something" or "some news."

95 **κλέος, τό** (only found in nom. and acc. forms)—fame, glory, report, reputation, honor; **κλέος** in this line is nom.

~ **ἐσθλός,-ή,-όν**—good, excellent.

ἔχῃσιν—present active subjunctive, 3rd pers. sing. of **ἔχω**; **ἵνα...ἔχῃσιν** – PURPOSE CLAUSE (In English, a person possesses a good reputation. In Greek, the **κλέος ἐσθλόν** possesses **μιν**. Athena's assumption is that Telemachus will win praise for his efforts to find his **πατήρ**.)

Odyssey Book 2.85-110

Telemachus summoned the people of Ithaca to an assembly where he protested the outrageous behavior of his mother's suitors. The suitors protested in return.

Book 2.85-110

Antinous, one of the ***μνηστῆρες****, replies that they are not to blame. Penelope raised their hopes and made promises to each man (****ἀνὴρ ἕκαστος****) while actually devising a* ***δόλος****. She told them her wedding must wait until she finished weaving a burial robe for Laertes, Odysseus'* ***πατήρ****. But during the nights (****νύκτας****) she unraveled what she wove during the day.*

" Τηλέμαχ' ὑψαγόρη, μένος ἄσχετε, ποῖον ἔειπες
ἡμέας αἰσχύνων, ἐθέλοις δέ κε μῶμον ἀνάψαι.
σοὶ δ' οὔ τι μνηστῆρες Ἀχαιῶν αἴτιοί εἰσιν,
ἀλλὰ φίλη μήτηρ, ἥ τοι περὶ κέρδεα οἶδεν.
ἤδη γὰρ τρίτον ἐστὶν ἔτος, τάχα δ' εἶσι τέταρτον,
ἐξ οὗ ἀτέμβει θυμὸν ἐνὶ στήθεσσιν Ἀχαιῶν.
πάντας μὲν ῥ' ἔλπει, καὶ ὑπίσχεται ἀνδρὶ ἑκάστῳ,
ἀγγελίας προϊεῖσα· νόος δέ οἱ ἄλλα μενοινᾷ.
ἡ δὲ δόλον τόνδ' ἄλλον ἐνὶ φρεσὶ μερμήριξε·

---

85 **Τηλέμαχ'= Τηλέμαχε**—vocative.
ὑψαγόρης,-ου, ὁ—bold talker, boaster; **ὑψαγόρη** – vocative.
μένος,-εος, τό—spirit, anger, passion; **μένος** – ACCUSATIVE OF RESPECT.
ἄσχετος,-ον—unrestrained, ungovernable; **ἄσχετε** – vocative.
ἔειπες—aorist, 2nd pers. sing. of **εἶπον**; **ποῖον ἔειπες** – "what a speech!" (an exclamation of surprise or anger; *literally*, what sort of thing you said).

86 **ἡμέας = ἡμᾶς**.
αἰσχύνω—blame, put to shame.
ἐθέλοις...κε—"you may wish" (POTENTIAL OPTATIVE).
μῶμος,-ου, ὁ—fault, disapproval (normally refers to a trivial fault, slight criticism or disapproval).
ἀνάπτω, (aor.) **ἀνῆψα**—attach, fasten upon; **ἐθέλοις δέ κε μῶμον ἀνάψαι** – "and I suppose you want to put the blame on us for this minor matter" (*literally*, and you may wish to fasten this trivial fault [on us]).

By refusing to take Telemachus seriously (calling him **ὑψαγόρης** and referring to the suitors' behavior as a **μῶμος**), Antinous tries to undermine Telemachus' attempt to assert his authority and minimize the seriousness of what the suitors are doing.

87 **σοί**—"for what has happened to you."

~ **οὔ τι**—not at all.

αἴτιος,-η,-ον—at fault, to blame.

88 ~ **τοι**—in truth, certainly, indeed.

περί—beyond all others, to an extraordinary degree.

κέρδος,-εος, τό—profit, device, plan; *plural,* cunning arts, craft, guile; **περὶ κέρδεα οἶδεν** – "is exceedingly crafty" (*literally*, knows the cunning arts beyond all others).

89 ~ **ἤδη**—now, already.

τρίτος,-η,-ον—the third.

τάχα—soon, quickly.

εἶσι—present, 3rd pers. sing. of **εἶμι**.

τέταρτος,-η,-ον—fourth; **εἶσι τέταρτον** – "the fourth [year] is passing."

90 **ἐξ οὗ**—since.

ἀτέμβω—mistreat, toy with; **ἐξ οὗ ἀτέμβει** – "since she began mistreating," "since she has been toying with."

~ **στῆθος,-εος, τό**—*always plural, translate as singular,* breast, chest; **στήθεσσιν** – dat. plur.

91 **ἔλπω**—cause to hope, give hope to, make hopeful.

ὑπίσχομαι—give a promise, make promises.

~ **ἕκαστος,-η,-ον**—each.

92 **ἀγγελίη,-ης, ἡ**—message.

προΐημι—send; **προϊεῖσα** – present active participle, nom. sing. fem.

οἱ—"her" (DATIVE OF INTEREST).

μενοινάω—plan, turn over [in one's mind]; **μενοινᾷ** – present active, 3rd pers. sing.

93 ~ **δόλος,-ου, ὁ**—trickery, guile, trick.

τόνδ᾽ = τόνδε.

ἄλλον—"besides," "in addition."

φρεσί—dat. plur. of **φρήν**.

μερμηρίζω, (aor.) **ἐμερμήριξα**—devise, contrive; **μερμήριξε = ἐμερμήριξε**.

Scanning Notes

86 The **υ** in **αἰσχύνων** is long.

90 The **υ** in **θυμόν** is long.

91 **αι** in **καί** is a diphthong, yet the word is scanned short. Why?

93 The **ι** in **μερμήριξε** is short, but the penultimate (next to the last) syllable is scanned long. Why?

στησαμένη μέγαν ἱστὸν ἐνὶ μεγάροισιν ὕφαινε,
λεπτὸν καὶ περίμετρον· ἄφαρ δ' ἡμῖν μετέειπε·
κοῦροι, ἐμοὶ μνηστῆρες, ἐπεὶ θάνε δῖος Ὀδυσσεύς,
μίμνετ' ἐπειγόμενοι τὸν ἐμὸν γάμον, εἰς ὅ κε φᾶρος
ἐκτελέσω, μή μοι μεταμώνια νήματ' ὄληται,
Λαέρτῃ ἥρωϊ ταφήϊον, εἰς ὅτε κέν μιν
μοῖρ' ὀλοὴ καθέλῃσι τανηλεγέος θανάτοιο,
μή τίς μοι κατὰ δῆμον Ἀχαιϊάδων νεμεσήσῃ,
αἴ κεν ἄτερ σπείρου κεῖται πολλὰ κτεατίσσας.

---

94 **στησαμένη**—"having set up" (aorist middle participle of **ἵστημι**).

ἱστός,-οῦ, ὁ—warp (the vertical threads on a loom). **ἱστός** can also mean the loom itself or the cloth being woven, but here it refers to the warp that Penelope put on the loom. The loom was an upright framework, two perpendicular beams about six feet high and three or four feet apart connected by a cross-piece at the top. The warp hung from the top piece of the frame and the weaver stood in front of the loom, moving back and forth as she wove.

ἐνὶ μεγάροισιν—"in the palace."

ὑφαίνω, (aor.) **ὕφηνα**—weave; **ὕφαινε** – "she began to weave."

95 **λεπτός,-ή,-όν**—of fine threads (The finer the thread, the longer it would take to finish.)

περίμετρος,-ον—very large, very long, "consisting of long threads." (**λεπτόν** and **περίμετρον** modify **μέγαν ἱστόν** in the preceding line.)

ἄφαρ—immediately, without delay, at once.

μετέειπον (aor.)—address, speak to (+ dat.).

96 **κοῦρος,-ου, ὁ**—young man.

ἐμοί—nom. plur. masc. of **ἐμός,-ή,-όν**.

θάνε = **ἔθανε**—aorist of **θνῄσκω**; **ἐπεὶ θάνε δῖος Ὀδυσσεύς** – To win their confidence, Penelope pretends to accept the suitors' assumption that Odysseus is dead.

97 **μίμνω**—wait; **μίμνετ'** = **μίμνετε**.

ἐπείγω—be eager for; **ἐπειγόμενοι** – "even though eager for."

γάμος,-ου, ὁ—marriage, wedding; **τὸν ἐμὸν γάμον** is the object of **ἐπειγόμενοι**.

εἰς ὅ κε—until (+ subjunctive).

φᾶρος,-εος, τό—robe; **φᾶρος** – "this robe," referring to one she has already begun.

98 **ἐκτελέω,** (aor.) **ἐξετέλεσσα**—finish, complete; **ἐκτελέσω** – aorist subjunctive.

μοι—"my" (DATIVE OF INTEREST).

μεταμώνιος,-ον—coming to nothing, vain, useless.

νῆμα,-ατος, τό—yarn, thread; *plural,* weaving, woven work; **νήματ'** = **νήματα.**

ὄληται—aorist middle subjunctive, 3rd pers. sing. of **ὄλλυμι.**

μή μοι μεταμώνια νήματ' ὄληται—"so that my weaving might not be done in vain" (*literally,* so that my weaving might not come to nothing, be useless [as it would if she married and never finished it]) (PURPOSE CLAUSE).

99 **Λαέρτης,-ου, ὁ**—Laertes, Odysseus' father (Laertes appears to have been the king of Ithaca before Odysseus, but he had resigned or stepped down even before Odysseus left for the Trojan War. Now an old man, he lives on a small farm in the country. Why he retired and why he did not come out of retirement while Odysseus was away is a mystery.)

ἥρως, ἥρωος, ὁ—warrior, hero.

ταφήϊος,-η,-ον—of or for burial; **ταφήϊον** – shroud, burial robe; in apposition to **φᾶρος**, 1.97.

εἰς ὅτε κέν—for the time when (+ subjunctive).

100 **μοῖρα,-ης, ἡ**—fate, destiny, doom; **μοῖρ'** = **μοῖρα.**

ὀλοός,-ή,-όν—destructive, deadly.

καθαιρέω, (aor.) **καθεῖλον**—seize, take; **καθέλησι** – aorist subjunctive, 3rd pers. sing.

τανηλεγής,-ές—pitiless, remorseless.

101 **δῆμος,-ου, ὁ**—community, land, country.

Ἀχαιϊάς,-άδος, ἡ—Achaean woman.

νεμεσάω, (aor.) **ἐνεμέσησα**—reproach, blame (+ dat.); **νεμεσήσῃ** – aorist subjunctive, 3rd pers. sing.

μή τίς μοι κατὰ δῆμον Ἀχαιϊάδων νεμεσήσῃ—PURPOSE CLAUSE.

102 **αἴ**—if.

ἄτερ—without (+ gen.).

σπεῖρον,-ου, τό—shroud.

κεῖται—present subjunctive.

κτεατίζω, (aor.) **κτεάτισσα**—gain, acquire, win; **κτεατίσσας** – "although having acquired," "who had won" (describing Laertes, the subject of **κεῖται**).

αἴ κεν ἄτερ σπείρου κεῖται πολλὰ κτεατίσσας—protasis of a future more vivid condition: "if he, who had won many things, lies without a shroud."

Scanning Notes

94 The last syllable of **ἐνί** is scanned long. A short final syllable ending in a vowel and followed by a word beginning with **μ** can be scanned long.

ὣς ἔφαθ', ἡμῖν δ' αὖτ' ἐπεπείθετο θυμὸς ἀγήνωρ. 103
ἔνθα καὶ ἠματίη μὲν ὑφαίνεσκεν μέγαν ἱστόν, 104
νύκτας δ' ἀλλύεσκεν, ἐπεὶ δαΐδας παραθεῖτο. 105
ὣς τρίετες μὲν ἔληθε δόλῳ καὶ ἔπειθεν Ἀχαιούς· 106
ἀλλ' ὅτε τέτρατον ἦλθεν ἔτος καὶ ἐπήλυθον ὧραι, 107
καὶ τότε δή τις ἔειπε γυναικῶν, ἣ σάφα ᾔδη, 108
καὶ τήν γ' ἀλλύουσαν ἐφεύρομεν ἀγλαὸν ἱστόν. 109
ὣς τὸ μὲν ἐξετέλεσσε καὶ οὐκ ἐθέλουσ', ὑπ' ἀνάγκης· 110

---

103 **ἔφαθ'** = **ἔφατο**—imperfect middle with active meaning of **φημί**; Penelope is the subject.

ἡμῖν—"our."

~ **αὖτ'** = **αὖτε**—furthermore, in turn; *may simply mark a transition.*

ἐπιπείθομαι—be persuaded; **ἐπεπείθετο** – imperfect.

ἀγήνωρ,-ορος (masc. and fem. adj.)—manly, bold, proud.

104 **ἠμάτιος,-η,-ον**—by day, during the daytime; **ἠματίη** agrees with "she," the subject of **ὑφαίνεσκεν**. Homer uses a predicate adjective (an adjective agreeing with the subject) where English would use an adverb or an adverbial phrase.

ὑφαίνεσκεν—"she kept weaving;" ITERATIVE imperfect, 3rd pers. sing. of **ὑφαίνω** (Iterative imperfects and aorists are formed by adding **-σκ-** and personal endings to the stem. Usually unaugmented, they indicate repeated past action.)

ἱστόν—"the piece of cloth."

105 **νύκτας**—"during the nights."

ἀλλύω—undo, unravel; **ἀλλύεσκεν** – ITERATIVE imperfect.

δαΐς,-ΐδος, ἡ—torch.

παρατίθημι, (aor.) **παρέθηκα**—set or place beside; **παραθεῖτο** – aorist middle optative (an optative is used in a temporal (time) clause (**ἐπεὶ δαΐδας παραθεῖτο**) when the verb in the main clause (**ἀλλύεσκεν**) is an imperfect denoting past repeated action); **ἐπεὶ δαΐδας παραθεῖτο** – "when she had set torches at her side."

106 **τρίετες**—for three years.

λήθω—escape the notice of.

δόλῳ—DATIVE OF MEANS.

ἔπειθεν Ἀχαιούς [that she was really making a shroud for Laertes].

107 **τέτρατος,-η,-ον**—fourth.

ἐπέρχομαι, (aor.) **ἐπῆλθον** or **ἐπήλυθον**—come round, return.
ὥρη,-ης, ἡ—season.
108 **τις...γυναικῶν**—"one of the female servants."
ἔειπε—"told [us]."
σάφα—clearly, well, exactly.
ᾔδη—pluperfect, 3rd pers. sing. of **οἶδα**; translate as imperfect; **σάφα ᾔδη** – "knew exactly [what Penelope was doing]."
109 **τήν**—"her."
ἀλλύουσαν—present active participle, acc. sing. fem. of **ἀλλύω**.
ἐφευρίσκω, (aor.) **ἐφεῦρον**—discover, find, surprise.
ἀγλαός,-ή,-όν—splendid; **ἀγλαὸν ἱστόν** – object of **ἀλλύουσαν**.
110 **τό**— "it," *i.e.*, the shroud.
ἐθέλουσ' = ἐθέλουσα—present active participle, nom. sing. fem.
ἀνάγκη,-ης, ἡ—compulsion.

In Homer, weaving often signifies the subordinate position of women. In *Odyssey* 1.356-7, Telemachus tells his mother to retire to her room and look after her own work, the loom and the distaff (a staff used to spin wool or flax into thread for weaving). He uses the same words when he tells her to withdraw in *Odyssey* 21.350-1, as does Hector in *Iliad* 6.490-1, when he tells Andromache to leave war to men. It is ironic that Penelope gains the upper hand over men using her loom.

The verb used to designate Penelope's weaving – **ὑφαίνω** – is also used metaphorically to mean scheming and plotting in several Homeric passages. Very appropriate, then, that she is weaving literally and metaphorically.

Scanning Notes

103 The **υ** in **θυμός** is long.
105 The **υ** in **ἀλλύεσκεν** is long.
109 The first **υ** in **ἀλλύουσαν** is long

Odyssey Book 5.116-191

Hermes went to Calypso's island and delivered Zeus' command that she allow Odysseus to return home.

Book 5.116-191

Addressing Hermes, Calypso complains that the ***θεοί*** *are jealous of* ***θεαί*** *who take mortal men as lovers. When Eos loved Orion, Artemis killed him. When Demeter took Iasion as a lover, Zeus killed him with a thunderbolt (****κεραυνός****).*

ὣς φάτο, ῥίγησεν δὲ Καλυψώ, δῖα θεάων,
καί μιν φωνήσασ' ἔπεα πτερόεντα προσηύδα·
" σχέτλιοί ἐστε, θεοί, ζηλήμονες ἔξοχον ἄλλων,
οἵ τε θεαῖς ἀγάασθε παρ' ἀνδράσιν εὐνάζεσθαι
ἀμφαδίην, ἥν τίς τε φίλον ποιήσετ' ἀκοίτην.
ὣς μὲν ὅτ' Ὠρίων' ἕλετο ῥοδοδάκτυλος Ἠώς,
τόφρα οἱ ἠγάασθε θεοὶ ῥεῖα ζώοντες,

---

116 **φάτο = ἔφατο**—imperfect middle with active meaning of **φημί**; Hermes is the subject.

ῥιγέω, ῥιγήσω, ἐρρίγησα—shudder; **ῥίγησεν = ἐρρίγησεν**.

117 ~ **φωνέω, φωνήσω, ἐφώνησα**—speak; **φωνήσασ' = φωνήσασα** – "speaking;" aorist active participle, nom. sing. fem.

ἔπεα—acc. plur. of **ἔπος**.

~ **πτερόεις,-εσσα,-εν**—winged; **ἔπεα πτερόεντα** – "winged words," a poetic phrase conveying the idea of words flying through the air from speaker to listener.

~ **προσαυδάω**—speak to, address; **προσηύδα** – imperfect, 3rd pers. sing. (This verb can take two accusatives: she spoke **ἔπεα πτερόεντα** to **μιν**.)

118 **σχέτλιος,-η,-ον**—cruel, hard-hearted.

ἐστε—present, 2nd pers. plur. of **εἰμί**.

ζηλήμων,-ον (gen. **–ονος**)—jealous, envious.

ἔξοχον—beyond (+ gen.).

119 **οἵ**—"(you) who."

ἄγαμαι—grudge, begrudge, be jealous of (+ dat.); **ἀγάασθε** – present, 2nd pers. plur.

ἀνδράσιν—dat. plur. of **ἀνήρ**; object of **παρ'...εὐνάζεσθαι**.

παρευνάζομαι—lie beside, go to bed with, sleep with (implies a sexual relationship) (+ dat.); **παρ'...εὐνάζεσθαι** – TMESIS.

120 **ἀμφαδίην**—openly, publicly.

ἤν = **εἰ ἄν**—if (+ subjunctive).

ποιήσετ' = **ποιήσεται**—aorist middle subjunctive (a SHORT VOWEL SUBJUNCTIVE).

ἀκοίτης,-ου, ὁ—husband.

ἤν τίς τε φίλον ποιήσετ' ἀκοίτην—protasis of a present general condition: "if one [of us goddesses] makes [him] a beloved husband."

121 **ὅτ'** = **ὅτε**; **ὣς μὲν ὅτ'** – "so [it was] when."

'Ωρίων,-ωνος, ὁ—Orion, a great hunter; **'Ωρίων'** = **'Ωρίωνα**.

ἕλετο—"chose for herself," "took as her own;" aorist middle of **αἱρέω**.

ῥοδοδάκτυλος,-ον—rosy-fingered (from **ῥόδον** – rose and **δάκτυλος** – finger); refers to the rays of rosy light that appear in the sky before sunrise.

'Ηώς, 'Ηοῦς, ἡ—Eos, goddess of dawn.

122 **τόφρα**—"for so long," "then constantly."

οἱ—"her" (dative of **εἷο**); object of **ἠγάασθε**.

ἠγάασθε—imperfect, 2nd pers. plur. of **ἄγαμαι**.

ῥεῖα—easily, with ease.

ζώω—live; **ῥεῖα ζώοντες** – "who live at ease" (*literally,* living at ease); an epithet of the gods.

Scanning Notes

116 The **ι** in **ῥίγησεν** is long

The **α** in **θεάων** is long.

117 The **α** in **φωνήσασ'** is long.

You would expect the final syllable of **πτερόεντα** to be scanned long because it is followed by two consonants. However, if the first consonant is a mute or stop (**π, β, φ, κ, γ, χ, τ, δ,** or **θ**) and the second is either **λ** or **ρ**, the preceding syllable can be scanned short.

119 The first **α** in **εὐνάζεσθαι** is short, but the second syllable of the word is scanned long. Why?

121 The **ι** in **'Ωρίων'** is long.

The last syllable of **ἕλετο** is scanned long. A short final vowel followed by a word beginning with **ρ** can be scanned long.

122 The first **α** in **ἠγάασθε** is long.

Why is the final syllable of **ῥεῖα** scanned long?

ἕως μιν ἐν Ὀρτυγίῃ χρυσόθρονος Ἄρτεμις ἁγνὴ 123
οἷσ' ἀγανοῖσι βέλεσσιν ἐποιχομένη κατέπεφνεν. 124
ὣς δ' ὁπότ' Ἰασίωνι ἐϋπλόκαμος Δημήτηρ, 125
ᾧ θυμῷ εἴξασα, μίγη φιλότητι καὶ εὐνῇ 126
νειῷ ἔνι τριπόλῳ· οὐδὲ δὴν ἦεν ἄπυστος 127
Ζεύς, ὅς μιν κατέπεφνε βαλὼν ἀργῆτι κεραυνῷ. 128

*In the same way, she is not allowed to have this **βροτὸς ἀνήρ** with her, even though she saved him when Zeus destroyed his swift ship (**νηῦς θοή**) with a **κεραυνός**, leaving him alone on the wine-dark (**οἶνοψ**) sea. The wind (**ἄνεμος**) brought him to this place (**δεῦρο**), where she cared for him.*

ὣς δ' αὖ νῦν μοι ἄγασθε, θεοί, βροτὸν ἄνδρα παρεῖναι. 129

---

123 **ἕως**—until.

Ὀρτυγίη,-ης, ἡ—Ortygia (The name means Quail Island, from **ὄρτυξ,-υγος** – quail. May refer to the island of Delos, the birthplace of Apollo and Artemis, or to a nearby island.)

χρυσόθρονος,-ον—with a golden throne, golden-throned.

Ἄρτεμις,-ιδος, ἡ—Artemis, goddess of the hunt, sister of Apollo, daughter of Zeus and Leto.

ἁγνός,-ή,-όν—holy, pure.

124 **ἀγανός,-ή,-όν**—gentle; here, describing the arrows Artemis shot, the implication is "painless" or "bringing a quick painless death."

βέλος,-εος, τό—arrow; **οἷσ' ἀγανοῖσι βέλεσσιν** – DATIVE OF MEANS.

ἐποίχομαι—attack.

καταφένω, (aor.) **κατέπεφνον**—kill, slay.

125 **ὀπότ'** = **ὀπότε**.

Ἰασίων,-ωνος, ὁ—Iasion, a mortal from Crete; he and Demeter were the parents of Plutus, the god of wealth.

ἐϋπλόκαμος,-ον—with beautiful braids, having well-braided hair.

Δημήτηρ,-τερος or **–τρος, ἡ**—Demeter, sister of Zeus, goddess of grain, the harvest, and agriculture.

126 **εἴκω**, (aor.) **εἶξα**—yield to (+ dat.); **εἴξασα** – aorist active participle, nom. sing. fem.; **ᾧ θυμῷ εἴξασα** – "yielding to her desire."

μίγη = ἐμίγη—"mingled with," "joined with;" aorist passive, 3rd pers. sing. of **μίσγω**; **'Ιασίωνι** in the preceding line is the object.

φιλότης, φιλότητος, ἡ—love.

~ **εὐνή,-ῆς, ἡ**—bed; **φιλότητι καὶ εὐνῇ** – "in a bed of love" (*literally*, in love and in bed); **μίγη φιλότητι καὶ εὐνῇ** – "had sex with."

127 **νειός,-οῦ, ἡ**—a fallow field, *i.e.*, a field that has been plowed but left unplanted.

τρίπολος,-ον—triple-furrowed (Though often translated "thrice-plowed," it probably refers to a ritual in which three furrows were plowed, rather than to plowing the entire field three times); **νειῷ ἔνι τριπόλῳ = ἐν νειῷ τριπόλῳ**.

δήν—for a long time, for long.

ἦεν—imperfect, 3rd pers. sing. of **εἰμί**.

ἄπυστος,-ον—unaware, without knowledge.

128 **μιν**—refers to Iasion.

βαλών—"striking;" aorist active participle, nom. sing. masc.

ἀργής,-ῆτος (masc. and fem. adj.)—bright, flashing.

κεραυνός,-οῦ, ὁ—thunderbolt; **ἀργῆτι κεραυνῷ** – DATIVE OF MEANS.

129 **αὖ**—again.

θεοί—voc.

πάρειμι— be here with (+ dat.).

μοι ἄγασθε, θεοί, βροτὸν ἄνδρα παρεῖναι—"you, gods, are jealous that a mortal man is here with me."

Scanning Notes

123 **ἕως** is scanned as one long syllable. This is an example of SYNIZESIS (two vowels run together and pronounced as one long syllable).

The **υ** in **χρυσόθρονος** is long.

125 The first **ι** in **'Ιασίωνι** is long.

126 The **υ** in **θυμῷ** is long.

The first **α** in **εἴξασα** is long.

127 The last syllable of **οὐδέ** is scanned long because **δήν** was originally spelled **δϝήν**.

τὸν μὲν ἐγὼν ἐσάωσα περὶ τρόπιος βεβαῶτα 130
οἶον, ἐπεί οἱ νῆα θοὴν ἀργῆτι κεραυνῷ 131
Ζεὺς ἐλάσας ἐκέασσε μέσῳ ἐνὶ οἴνοπι πόντῳ. 132
ἔνθ' ἄλλοι μὲν πάντες ἀπέφθιθεν ἐσθλοὶ ἑταῖροι, 133
τὸν δ' ἄρα δεῦρ' ἄνεμός τε φέρων καὶ κῦμα πέλασσε. 134
τὸν μὲν ἐγὼ φίλεόν τε καὶ ἔτρεφον ἠδὲ ἔφασκον 135
θήσειν ἀθάνατον καὶ ἀγήραον ἤματα πάντα. 136

---

130 **σαόω, σαώσω, ἐσάωσα**—save.

περιβαίνω, περιβήσομαι, περιέβην, περιβέβηκα—be astride, straddle, have a leg on each side of (+ gen.); **περὶ...βεβαῶτα** – TMESIS; perfect active participle, acc. sing. masc., modifying **τόν**.

τρόπις, τρόπιος, ἡ—a ship's keel (the beam of wood running down the center of the bottom of a ship); **περὶ τρόπιος βεβαῶτα** – "when he was straddling a keel" (when Odysseus' ship was destroyed and his crew killed in a storm sent by Zeus [described in 12.403-425], he lashed the mast and keel together and rode them until he reached Calypso's island). It has also been suggested that **τρόπις**, while usually translated "keel," in this passage actually refers to the mast step. The mast step is the platform resting on the keel that supports the lower end of the mast.

131 **οἶον**—modifies **τόν** in the preceding line.

οἱ—"his."

~ **θοός,-ή,-όν**—swift.

132 **ἐλαύνω,** (aor.) **ἤλασα**—drive, strike; **ἐλάσας** – aorist active participle: "striking."

κεάζω, (aor.) **ἐκέασσα**—split, shatter, break in pieces.

μέσος,-η,-ον—the middle of.

~ **οἶνοψ,-οπος** (masc. adj.)—dark like wine, wine-dark, purple.

133 **ἀποφθίνω,** (aor. pass.) **ἀπεφθίθην**—destroy; *middle and passive*, die, perish; **ἀπέφθιθεν** – aorist passive, 3rd pers. plur.

134 ~ **δεῦρ' = δεῦρο**—to this place, hither.

~ **ἄνεμος,-ου, ὁ**—wind; **φέρων** describes **ἄνεμος** – "the carrying wind," "the wind [that was] carrying."

~ **κῦμα,-ατος, τό**—wave, waves (of the sea).

πελάζω, πελάσω, ἐπέλασ(σ)α—bring, carry; **πέλασσε = ἐπέλασσε**.

135 **φίλεον = ἐφίλεον**—"I welcomed."

τρέφω—tend, look after.

φάσκω—say, promise.

136 **θήσειν**—"to make;" future infinitive of **τίθημι**. **με** is the understood accusative subject in the indirect statement after the verb **ἔφασκον**. **τόν** is the object of **θήσειν**, as well as of **φίλεον** and **ἔτρεφον**.

ἀγήραος,-ον—ageless, not subject to old age.

ἤματα πάντα—"all his days;" accusative of extent of time.

The story of Eos and Tithonus illustrates the importance of Calypso offering not just immortality but also eternal youth. Eos asked for immortality for Tithonus, her mortal lover, but forgot to request eternal youth. Tithonus kept getting older and older until he was completely helpless. In some versions of the story, Eos locks him away in a room forever. In others, she takes pity on him and turns him into a grasshopper.

Scanning Notes

132 The second **α** in **ἐλάσας** is long.

133 Why is the last syllable of **ἐσθλοί** scanned short even though it contains a diphthong?

136 The first **α** in **ἀθάνατον** is long.

*She agrees, however, to do as Zeus has commanded, for it is not possible in any way (**πως**) to evade Zeus' will. She cannot provide Odysseus with **νῆες** or **ἑταῖροι**, but will give him advice **ὥς κε ἣν πατρίδα γαῖαν ἵκηται**.*

ἀλλ' ἐπεὶ οὔ πως ἔστι Διὸς νόον αἰγιόχοιο
οὔτε παρεξελθεῖν ἄλλον θεὸν οὔθ' ἁλιῶσαι,
ἐρρέτω, εἴ μιν κεῖνος ἐποτρύνει καὶ ἀνώγει,
πόντον ἐπ' ἀτρύγετον. πέμψω δέ μιν οὔ πῃ ἐγώ γε·
οὐ γάρ μοι πάρα νῆες ἐπήρετμοι καὶ ἑταῖροι,
οἵ κέν μιν πέμποιεν ἐπ' εὐρέα νῶτα θαλάσσης.
αὐτάρ οἱ πρόφρων ὑποθήσομαι οὐδ' ἐπικεύσω,
ὥς κε μάλ' ἀσκηθὴς ἣν πατρίδα γαῖαν ἵκηται."

---

137 ~ **πως**—in any way; **οὔ πως** – in no way, not at all.

ἔστι—"it is possible."

νόον—"intent," "will;" object of the two infinitives in the next line.

αἰγίοχος,-η,-ον—aegis-holding, aegis-bearing (The aegis is Zeus' shield, which he often allowed Athena to carry. With the head of the Gorgon Medusa mounted on it, the aegis created terror among men. Medusa was one of three Gorgons, monstrous women with snakes for hair; just looking at their faces turned men to stone. She was killed by Perseus, who looked at her in the reflection of his shield while he cut off her head.)

138 **παρεξέρχομαι**, (aor.) **παρεξῆλθον**—slip past, get past, defeat.

ἄλλον θεόν—"another god."

οὔθ' = οὔτε.

ἀλιόω, (aor.) **ἠλίωσα**—frustrate.

οὔτε παρεξελθεῖν ἄλλον θεὸν οὔθ' ἀλιῶσαι—an accusative/infinitive construction that is the subject of **οὔ πως ἔστι**.

οὔ in 5.137 and **οὔτε... οὔθ'** form a double negative which emphasizes the impossibility of thwarting Zeus' will. (This is very difficult to translate literally and include all the negative words. To keep the intensity conveyed by the three negative words, we might say "but since it is completely impossible" or "but since in absolutely no way is it possible for another god to defeat or frustrate the will of aegis-bearing Zeus.")

139 **ἔρρω**—go (with an implication of pain, difficulty, or misfortune); **ἐρρέτω** – present imperative, 3rd pers. sing.: "let him be off [to his destruction]," "let him go and destroy himself."

μιν—*i.e.*, Odysseus.

κεῖνος—*i.e.*, Zeus.

ἐποτρύνω—urge.

~ **ἀνώγω**, (perf.) **ἄνωγα**—order, command.

140 **ἀτρύγετος,-ον**—There is uncertainty about the meaning of this word. It is usually translated "barren," "unfruitful," or "unharvested" (contrasting the sea to the earth). Other suggested meanings are "tireless," "restless," "noisy," "enduring," or "never runs dry" (in contrast to pools or rivers, which can dry up).

πέμψω—used in the sense of "convey" or "provide the means to go."

πῃ—anywhere.

ἐγώ γε—note how the use of **γε** adds emphasis to **ἐγώ**.

141 **πάρα = πάρεισι**—"are available to."

ἐπήρετμος,-ον—fitted with oars.

142 **πέμποιεν**—present optative, 3rd pers. plur.; POTENTIAL OPTATIVE.

~ **νῶτον,-ου, τό**—back; **νῶτα** – plural used for singular; **νῶτα θαλάσσης**: "the surface of the sea."

143 **πρόφρων,-ονος** (masc. and fem. adj. often used as an adverb)—cheerful(ly), gracious(ly), kind(ly), willing(ly).

ὑποτίθημι, ὑποθήσω—place under; *middle*, give advice.

ἐπικεύθω, ἐπικεύσω—conceal, hide; understand "anything" as the object of **ἐπικεύσω**.

144 **ἀσκηθής,-ές**—unhurt, unharmed.

ἵκηται—aorist subjunctive of **ἱκνέομαι**.

ὥς κε μάλ' ἀσκηθὴς ἣν πατρίδα γαῖαν ἵκηται—PURPOSE CLAUSE.

χαλεπαίνω, (aor.) **ἐχαλέπηνα**—do violence to, be hard upon (+ dat.); **χαλεπήνῃ** – aorist active subjunctive, 3rd pers. sing.

Scanning Notes

139 The **υ** in **ἐποτρύνει** is long.

143 **οἱ** was originally spelled **ϝοι**.

τὴν δ' αὖτε προσέειπε διάκτορος Ἀργεϊφόντης· 145
"οὕτω νῦν ἀπόπεμπε, Διὸς δ' ἐποπίζεο μῆνιν, 146
μή πώς τοι μετόπισθε κοτεσσάμενος χαλεπήνῃ." 147

*After Hermes leaves, Calypso finds great-hearted **(μεγαλήτωρ)** Odysseus sitting on the shore. His eyes **(ὄσσε)** were never without tears **(δάκρυα)** as he longed for his **νόστος**. At night, unwilling, he slept beside Calypso **ἐν σπέεσι γλαφυροῖσι**; each day, he sat weeping and looking out at the **πόντος**.*

ὣς ἄρα φωνήσας ἀπέβη κρατὺς Ἀργεϊφόντης· 148
ἡ δ' ἐπ' Ὀδυσσῆα μεγαλήτορα πότνια νύμφη 149
ἤϊ', ἐπεὶ δὴ Ζηνὸς ἐπέκλυεν ἀγγελιάων. 150
τὸν δ' ἄρ' ἐπ' ἀκτῆς εὗρε καθήμενον· οὐδέ ποτ' ὄσσε 151
δακρυόφιν τέρσοντο, κατείβετο δὲ γλυκὺς αἰὼν 152
νόστον ὀδυρομένῳ, ἐπεὶ οὐκέτι ἥνδανε νύμφη. 153

---

145 ~ **προσέειπον** (aorist)—speak to, address.

διάκτορος,-ου, ὁ—messenger, runner, guide (an epithet of Hermes, the messenger of the gods and the one who guided the dead to the Underworld).

146 ~ **οὕτω**—in this way, thus, so.

ἀποπέμπω—send on one's way, arrange for one's departure; **μιν** or **Ὀδυσσῆα** is the understood object of **ἀπόπεμπε**.

ἐποπίζομαι—respect, have regard for; **ἐποπίζεο** – imperative.

μῆνις,-ιος, ἡ—anger, wrath.

147 **μή**—"lest;" introduces a clause indicating what Calypso should fear if she does not send Odysseus away.

τοι—dat. sing. of **σύ**.

μετόπισθε—in the future.

κοτέομαι, κοτέσσομαι—be angry with (+ dat.); *aorist*, grow angry with; **κοτεσσάμενος** – aorist participle, nom. sing. masc.; describes he (Zeus), the subject of **χαλεπήνῃ**.

χαλεπαίνω, (aor.) **ἐχαλέπηνα**—do violence to, be hard upon (+ dat.); **χαλεπήνῃ** – aorist active subjunctive, 3rd pers. sing.

148 **φωνήσας**—aorist active participle.

ἀποβαίνω, ἀποβήσομαι, ἀπέβην—depart, go away.

κρατύς (masc. adj.)—strong, mighty.

149 ~ **μεγαλήτωρ,-ορος** (masc. and fem. adj.)—great-hearted, great, daring, heroic.

πότνια (fem. adj.)—honored, revered; a title of honor given to goddesses and women.

150 **ἤϊ' = ἤϊε**—imperfect 3rd pers. sing. of **εἶμι**.

Ζηνός = Διός—gen. sing. of **Ζεύς**.

ἐπέκλυον (aor.)—hear, listen to (+ gen.); **ἐπεὶ...ἐπέκλυεν**: "when she had heard."

ἀγγελιάων—"the message."

151 **ἀκτή,-ῆς, ἡ**—beach, shore.

~ **εὑρίσκω,** (aor.) **εὗρον**—find, come upon.

κάθημαι—sit; **καθήμενον** describes **τόν**.

~ **ὄσσε** (only in nom./acc. dual neut. forms)—eyes.

In Books 1-4 of the *Odyssey*, the audience heard about Odysseus from his son, his wife, his wife's suitors, his friends, the goddess Athena, etc., but this is the first time they actually meet him.

152 ~ **δάκρυον,-ου, τό**—tear; **δακρυόφιν**—gen. plur.

τέρσομαι—be dry, become dry; **τέρσοντο = ἐτέρσοντο**.

κατείβω—let flow, shed; *middle*, flow, pass away, ebb away; **κατείβετο** – imperfect.

γλυκύς,-εῖα,-ύ—sweet.

~ **αἰών,-ῶνος, ὁ**—life.

153 **ὀδύρομαι**—weep for, long for; **ὀδυρομένῳ** – present participle, dat. sing. masc.; DATIVE OF INTEREST showing possession; **νόστον ὀδυρομένῳ** – "of the man longing for his return."

~ **οὐκέτι**—no longer, no more.

ἁνδάνω, ἁδήσω, ἕαδον—be pleasing, please, delight.

Scanning Notes

148 The **α** in **φωνήσας** is long.

149 The **α** in **'Οδυσσῆα** is short but is scanned long. A short final syllable ending in a vowel and followed by a word beginning with **μ** can be scanned long.

150 The second **α** in **ἀγγελιάων** is long.

153 The **υ** in **ὀδυρομένῳ** is long.

ἀλλ' ἦ τοι νύκτας μὲν ἰαύεσκεν καὶ ἀνάγκῃ
ἐν σπέεσι γλαφυροῖσι παρ' οὐκ ἐθέλων ἐθελούσῃ·
ἤματα δ' ἂμ πέτρῃσι καὶ ἠϊόνεσσι καθίζων
δάκρυσι καὶ στοναχῇσι καὶ ἄλγεσι θυμὸν ἐρέχθων
πόντον ἐπ' ἀτρύγετον δερκέσκετο δάκρυα λείβων.
ἀγχοῦ δ' ἱσταμένη προσεφώνεε δῖα θεάων·

*Calypso tells Odysseus to build a seagoing vessel (**σχεδίη**) for she is sending him away. She will put food (**σῖτος**) and water (**ὕδωρ**) and wine (**οἶνος**) in his **σχεδίη** and send a fair wind (**οὖρος**) behind him.*

" κάμμορε, μή μοι ἔτ' ἐνθάδ' ὀδύρεο, μηδέ τοι αἰὼν
φθινέτω· ἤδη γάρ σε μάλα πρόφρασσ' ἀποπέμψω.
ἀλλ' ἄγε δούρατα μακρὰ ταμὼν ἁρμόζεο χαλκῷ

---

154 ~ **ἦ**—in truth, truly, indeed; **ἦ τοι** is an emphatic form of **ἦ**.

νύκτας—acc. plur. of **νύξ**; cognate accusative, *i.e.*, an accusative containing the same idea as the verb.

ἰαύω—sleep, pass the night; **ἰαύεσκεν** – ITERATIVE imperfect.

ἀνάγκῃ—under compulsion, of necessity.

155 **σπέεσι**—dat. plur. used for sing. of **σπέος**.

παρ' = **παρά**.

ἐθέλων and **ἐθελούσῃ** are present active participles of **ἐθέλω**. **οὐκ ἐθέλων** describes Odysseus, the subject of **ἰαύεσκεν**. **ἐθελούσῃ** is the object of **παρ'** and refers to Calypso. By inserting **οὐκ ἐθέλων** between **παρ'** and **ἐθελούσῃ** and putting the contrasting **οὐκ ἐθέλων** next to **ἐθελούσῃ**, Homer stresses the difference in the feelings of the two.

156 **ἤματα δ'**—"during the days" (in contrast to **νύκτας μέν** in 5.154).

ἄμ = **ἀνά**—on, upon (+ dat.)

~ **πέτρη,-ης, ἡ**—rock, cliff; **πέτρῃσι** – dat. plur.

ἠϊών,-όνος, ἡ—beach, shore; **ἠϊόνεσσι** – dat. plur.

καθίζω—sit.

157 **δάκρυσι**—dat. plur. of **δάκρυ** = **δάκρυον**.

στοναχή,-ῆς, ἡ—groan, sigh.

ἄλγεσι—"expressions of distress or pain," "misery," "pain."

ἐρέχθω—break, rend.

158 **πόντον ἐπ' ἀτρύγετον = ἐπ' ἀτρύγετον πόντον.**

δέρκομαι, (aor.) **ἔδρακον**—look; **δερκέσκετο** – ITERATIVE imperfect.

λείβω—shed, pour out.

159 **ἀγχοῦ**—near, close by.

ἱσταμένη—"coming to stand;" present middle participle, nom. sing. fem. of **ἵστημι.**

προσφωνέω, προσφωνήσω—speak.

160 **κάμμορος,-ον**—ill-fated, wretched.

μή...ἔτ' = μή...ἔτι—no longer.

ἐνθάδ' = ἐνθάδε—here.

ὀδύρεο—"weep," "lament;" present imperative of **ὀδύρομαι; μοι...ὀδύρεο** – "lament to me."

161 **φθίνω**—waste away; **φθινέτω** – present imperative, 3rd pers. sing.; **αἰών** in the preceding line is its subject: "nor let your life waste away."

πρόφρασσα—"willingly;" an alternate nom. sing. fem. form of **πρόφρων.**

162 ~ **ἄγε**—come! (imperative of **ἄγω** used as an interjection).

δόρυ, δούρατος, τό—tree.

τάμνω, (aor.) **ἔταμον**—cut; **ταμών** – aorist active participle.

ἁρμόζω—put together, construct; **ἁρμόζεο** – "construct for yourself;" present middle imperative, 2nd pers. sing.

χαλκός,-οῦ, ὁ—ax.

Scanning Notes

157 The **υ** in **θυμόν** is long.

159 The **α** in **θεάων** is long.

160 The **υ** in **ὀδύρεο** is long.

161 The **ι** in **φθινέτω** is long.

εὐρεῖαν σχεδίην· ἀτὰρ ἴκρια πῆξαι ἐπ' αὐτῆς 163
ὑψοῦ, ὥς σε φέρῃσιν ἐπ' ἠεροειδέα πόντον. 164
αὐτὰρ ἐγὼ σῖτον καὶ ὕδωρ καὶ οἶνον ἐρυθρὸν 165
ἐνθήσω μενοεικέ', ἅ κέν τοι λιμὸν ἐρύκοι, 166
εἵματά τ' ἀμφιέσω· πέμψω δέ τοι οὖρον ὄπισθεν, 167
ὥς κε μάλ' ἀσκηθὴς σὴν πατρίδα γαῖαν ἵκηαι, 168
αἴ κε θεοί γ' ἐθέλωσι, τοὶ οὐρανὸν εὐρὺν ἔχουσιν, 169
οἵ μευ φέρτεροί εἰσι νοῆσαί τε κρῆναί τε." 170

*Odysseus is suspicious and refuses to do as Calypso says until she swears a great oath (**μέγας ὅρκος**) that she is not planning any other **πῆμα κακόν** for him.*

ὣς φάτο, ῥίγησεν δὲ πολύτλας δῖος Ὀδυσσεύς, 171
καί μιν φωνήσας ἔπεα πτερόεντα προσηύδα· 172

---

163 **σχεδίη,-ης, ἡ**—although traditionally translated as "raft," this word probably meant "vessel" or "craft." Based on the description of how Odysseus built the **σχεδίη** (5.234-57), it appears what he constructed was a small ship rather than a raft.

ἀτάρ = αὐτάρ—"and then."

ἴκρια,-ων, τά—deck, planks of the deck.

πήγνυμι, πήξω, ἔπηξα—construct, build; **πῆξαι** – aorist middle imperative, 2nd pers. sing.

αὐτῆς—"it," *i.e.*, the vessel.

164 **ὑψοῦ**—aloft, high.

φέρῃσιν—present active subjunctive, 3rd pers. sing. of **φέρω**; its subject is "it," *i.e.*, the vessel.

ἠεροειδής,-ές—misty.

What kind of clause is **ὥς σε φέρῃσιν**?

165 ~ **σῖτος,-ου, ὁ**—bread, food.

~ **ὕδωρ,-ατος, τό**—water.

~ **οἶνος,-ου, ὁ**—wine.

ἐρυθρός,-ά,-όν—red.

166 **ἐντίθημι, ἐνθήσω**—put upon, put on board.

μενοεικής,-ές—abundant, plentiful; **μενοεικέ' = μενοεικέα** – neut. plur. acc. describing **σῖτον, ὕδωρ**, and **οἶνον** in the previous line.

ἅ—"which;" nom. plur. neut. referring to the provisions.

τοι—"from you."

λιμός,-οῦ, ὁ—hunger.

ἐρύκω, ἐρύξω, ἤρυξα or **ἠρύκακον**—ward off, keep [something] from; **ἐρύκοι** – present optative, 3rd pers. sing.; POTENTIAL OPTATIVE.

167 ~ **εἷμα,-ατος, τό**—garment; *plural* – clothes, clothing.

ἀμφιέννυμι, ἀμφιέσω—put [clothing] on.

οὖρος,-ου, ὁ—fair wind.

ὄπισθεν—behind.

168 **ἀσκηθής,-ές**—unhurt, unharmed.

~ **σός, σή, σόν**—your, yours.

ἵκηαι—aorist subjunctive, 2nd pers. sing. of **ἱκνέομαι**.

What kind of clause is **ὥς κε μάλ' ἀσκηθὴς σὴν πατρίδα γαῖαν ἵκηαι**?

Compare this line with 5.144. In what two ways are they different? To whom is Calypso speaking in 5.144?

169 **αἴ κε** + subjunctive—provided that.

τοί = οἱ.

170 **μευ**—gen. sing. of **ἐγώ**; GENITIVE OF COMPARISON.

φέρτερος,-η,-ον—stronger, more powerful.

νοῆσαι—aorist active infinitive of **νοέω**.

κραίνω, (aor.) **ἔκρηνα**—accomplish, bring to pass, carry out; **νοῆσαι** and **κρῆναι** – "at perceiving and carrying out [future events];" the infinitives are used as ACCUSATIVES OF RESPECT.

171 **ῥιγέω, ῥιγήσω, ἐρρίγησα**—shudder; **ῥίγησεν = ἐρρίγησεν**.

πολύτλας (masc. adj.)—much-enduring.

172 Compare 5.116-117 with 5.171-172. What are the differences?

Scanning Note

166 The **ι** in **λιμόν** is long.

The **υ** in **ἐρύκοι** is long.

171 The **ι** in **ῥίγησεν** is long.

172 The **α** in **φωνήσας** is long.

You would expect the final syllable of **πτερόεντα** to be scanned long because it is followed by two consonants. However, if the first consonant is a mute or stop (**π, β, φ, κ, γ, χ, τ, δ,** or **θ**) and the second is either **λ** or **ρ**, the preceding syllable can be scanned short.

“ ἄλλο τι δὴ σύ, θεά, τόδε μήδεαι οὐδέ τι πομπήν,
ἥ με κέλεαι σχεδίῃ περάαν μέγα λαῖτμα θαλάσσης,
δεινόν τ’ ἀργαλέον τε· τὸ δ’ οὐδ’ ἐπὶ νῆες ἐῖσαι
ὠκύποροι περόωσιν, ἀγαλλόμεναι Διὸς οὔρῳ.
οὐδ’ ἂν ἐγώ γ’ ἀέκητι σέθεν σχεδίης ἐπιβαίην,
εἰ μή μοι τλαίης γε, θεά, μέγαν ὅρκον ὀμόσσαι
μή τί μοι αὐτῷ πῆμα κακὸν βουλευσέμεν ἄλλο. ”

*Calypso swears, calling the **γαῖα** and the **οὐρανός** and the **ὕδωρ** of the River Styx as witnesses, the **τε μέγιστος ὅρκος δεινότατός τε** there is for the **θέοι**, that she is not planning any other **πῆμα κακόν** for him.*

ὣς φάτο, μείδησεν δὲ Καλυψώ, δῖα θεάων,
χειρί τέ μιν κατέρεξεν ἔπος τ’ ἔφατ’ ἔκ τ’ ὀνόμαζεν·

---

173 **ἄλλο τι**—“some other thing.”

τόδε—“in this,” “with respect to this,” referring to what she just said.

μήδομαι, μήσομαι—plan, plot, devise; **μήδεαι** – present, 2nd pers. sing.

πομπή,-ῆς, ἡ—a sending away, a sending home.

174 **ἥ**—refers to **σύ**: “you who.”

~ **κέλομαι, κελήσομαι**—order, command, urge; **κέλεαι** – present, 2nd pers. sing.

περάω—cross, traverse, make one’s way across; **περάαν** – present active infinitive.

λαῖτμα,-ατος, τό—gulf, abyss.

175 **ἀργαλέος,-η,-ον**—difficult [to traverse]; **δεινόν** and **ἀργαλέον** modify **λαῖτμα**.

τό—refers to the **μέγα λαῖτμα θαλάσσης, / δεινόν τ’ ἀργαλέον τε**; object of **ἐπί**.

οὐδ’—“not even.”

νῆες – full-sized ships, as opposed to the **σχεδίη** she has told him to build.

ἐΐσος,-η,-ον—well-balanced (and therefore able to turn quickly).

176 **ὠκύπορος,-ον**—swift-sailing.

περόωσιν—present active, 3rd pers. plur. of **περάω**.

ἀγάλλομαι—exult in, delight in (+ dat.); **ἀγαλλόμεναι** – present participle; modifies **νῆες ἐῖσαι / ὠκύποροι**.

177 **ἀέκητι**—without the good will of, against the will of (+ gen.).

σέθεν—gen. sing. of **σύ**.

~ **ἐπιβαίνω**, (aor.) **ἐπέβην**—set foot upon, board [a ship] (+ gen.); **ἐπιβαίην** – aorist active optative, 1st pers. sing.

178 **εἰ μή**—"unless."

~ **τλάω, τλήσομαι, ἔτλην**—bear, endure, bring oneself (to do something); **τλαίης** – aorist optative.

~ **ὅρκος,-ου, ὁ**—oath.

~ **ὄμνυμι, ὀμοῦμαι, ὤμοσα**—swear.

οὐδ'...ἐγώ...ἐπιβαίην, / εἰ μή...τλαίης...ὀμόσσαι—"I would not set foot on…unless you should bring yourself to swear" (future less vivid condition).

179 **μοι αὐτῷ**—"for me," "against me."

βουλευσέμεν—future active infinitive; **μή...βουλευσέμεν** spells out the oath Odysseus wants her to swear: "not to be going to devise…"

τί, κακὸν, and **ἄλλο** modify **πῆμα**.

This is the first time in the *Odyssey* the audience hears Odysseus speak. We receive an impression of a man who does not trust Calypso, realizes the difficulties of the voyage she suggests, does not accept her orders without question, and insists on an oath to protect himself. Alertness, quick understanding, aggressive self-preservation, suspicion – these are all characteristics Odysseus will demonstrate throughout the *Odyssey*.

180 **μειδάω**, (aor.) **μείδησα**—smile.

181 ~ **χείρ, χειρός, ἡ**—hand.

καταρρέζω, (aor.) **κατέρεξα**—stroke, caress, pat.

ἔφατ' = ἔφατο.

~ **ὀνομάζω, ὀνομάσω, ὠνόμασα**—call by name (**ὄνομα**), speak to, address; **ὀνόμαζεν = ὠνόμαζεν**; **ἔπος τ' ἔφατ' ἔκ τ' ὀνόμαζεν** – "she addressed."

Scanning Notes

173 The **α** in **θεά** is long.

174 **-λεαι** in **κέλεαι** is scanned as one long syllable. This is an example of SYNIZESIS (two vowels or a vowel and a diphthong run together and pronounced as one long syllable).

178 The **α** in **θεά** is long.

180 The **α** in **θεάων** in long.

“ ἦ δὴ ἀλιτρός γ’ ἐσσὶ καὶ οὐκ ἀποφώλια εἰδώς,
οἷον δὴ τὸν μῦθον ἐπεφράσθης ἀγορεῦσαι.
ἴστω νῦν τόδε γαῖα καὶ οὐρανὸς εὐρὺς ὕπερθε
καὶ τὸ κατειβόμενον Στυγὸς ὕδωρ, ὅς τε μέγιστος
ὅρκος δεινότατός τε πέλει μακάρεσσι θεοῖσι,
μή τί τοι αὐτῷ πῆμα κακὸν βουλευσέμεν ἄλλο.
ἀλλὰ τὰ μὲν νοέω καὶ φράσσομαι, ἅσσ’ ἂν ἐμοί περ
αὐτῇ μηδοίμην, ὅτε με χρειὼ τόσον ἵκοι·
καὶ γὰρ ἐμοὶ νόος ἐστὶν ἐναίσιμος, οὐδέ μοι αὐτῇ
θυμὸς ἐνὶ στήθεσσι σιδήρεος, ἀλλ’ ἐλεήμων. ”

---

182 **ἀλιτρός,-οῦ, ὁ**—rogue, rascal.

ἐσσί = **εἶ**—present, 2nd pers. sing. of **εἰμί**.

ἀποφώλιος,-ον—empty, useless.

εἰδώς—perfect active participle, nom. sing. masc. of **οἶδα** – “knowing;” **οὐκ ἀποφώλια εἰδώς**—“no fool,” “shrewd,” “sagacious” (*literally*, knowing not-useless things).

183 **οἷον**—“because,” “seeing that.”

ἐπιφράζω, (aor. pass.) **ἐπεφράσθην**—*middle and passive*, think of (+ infinitive to express what one is thinking of doing).

~ **ἀγορεύω, ἀγορεύσω, ἠγόρευσα**—speak, say, utter.

184 **ἴστω**—“let it witness,” “be witness” (*literally*, let it know); imperative, 3rd pers. sing. of **οἶδα**.

τόδε—“this;” object of **ἴστω**.

ὕπερθε—above.

γαῖα and **οὐρανός** and **Στυγὸς ὕδωρ** in the next line are the subjects of **ἴστω**, although it is a singular verb.

185 **κατειβόμενον**—“down flowing.”

Στύξ, Στυγός, ἡ—the Styx, the underworld river by which the gods swore their most solemn oaths. According to Hesiod, *Theogony* 793-806, violating an oath sworn in this way led to lying prostrate without breathing, speaking, or eating for a year, then nine years banishment from association with the other gods.

ὅς—“which.”

186 ~ **πέλω** or **πέλομαι**—be.

187 **τοι αὐτῷ**—"against you," "for you."

Compare this line with 5.179. How is it different?

188 **νοέω**—"I am planning."

φράζω, φράσω, ἔφρασα—point out, show; *middle*, consider, plan, devise; **φράσσομαι = φράσομαι** – "I will devise."

ὅς τις, ἥ τις, ὅ τι—whoever, whatever; **ἅσσα = ἅ τινα** – neut. acc. plur.

περ—very, even, indeed.

189 **μήδομαι, μήσομαι**—plan, contrive, plot, devise, intend.

ὅτε—"whenever" (+ optative).

χρείω,-οῦς, ἡ—need.

τόσον—(adverb) so much, so greatly, to so great an extent.

ἵκω, ἱξῶ, ἷξον—come to, come upon.

ἅσσ' ἂν ἐμοί περ / αὐτῇ μηδοίμην, ὅτε με χρειὼ τόσον ἵκοι—"whatever things I would devise for myself, whenever need might come upon me so greatly."

190 **καὶ γάρ**—"for indeed."

ἐμοί—DATIVE OF POSSESSION; **ἐμοὶ νόος ἐστίν = ἔχω νόον.**

νόος—"intentions."

ἐναίσιμος,-ον—intent on what is right.

191 **σιδήρεος,-η,-ον**—made of iron, hard as iron.

ἐλεήμων,-ον—compassionate, merciful.

οὐδέ μοι αὐτῇ [ἐστι] / θυμὸς ἐνὶ στήθεσσι σιδήρεος, ἀλλ' ἐλεήμων

Scanning Notes

185 The **υ** in **ὕδωρ**, which is sometimes treated as a long vowel and sometimes as a short one, is long in this line.

189 The first **ι** in **ἵκοι** is long.

191 The **υ** in **θυμός** is long.

Odyssey Book 5.203-227

After returning to the cave, Odysseus and Calypso dined, then she spoke to him again.

Book 5.203-227

Calypso knows Odysseus wants to go ***ἐς πατρίδα γαῖαν*** *at once (****αὐτίκα****). If he knew the troubles (****κήδεα****) in store for him before he gets there, she says, he would stay with her, even though he longs to see his* ***ἄλοχος****, who as a mortal woman (****θνητή****) surely cannot be as attractive as she.*

" διογενὲς Λαερτιάδη, πολυμήχαν' Ὀδυσσεῦ, 203
οὕτω δὴ οἶκόνδε φίλην ἐς πατρίδα γαῖαν 204
αὐτίκα νῦν ἐθέλεις ἰέναι; σὺ δὲ χαῖρε καὶ ἔμπης. 205
εἴ γε μὲν εἰδείης σῇσι φρεσίν, ὅσσα τοι αἶσα 206
κήδε' ἀναπλῆσαι, πρὶν πατρίδα γαῖαν ἱκέσθαι, 207
ἐνθάδε κ' αὖθι μένων σὺν ἐμοὶ τόδε δῶμα φυλάσσοις 208
ἀθάνατός τ' εἴης, ἱμειρόμενός περ ἰδέσθαι 209
σὴν ἄλοχον, τῆς τ' αἰὲν ἐέλδεαι ἤματα πάντα. 210
οὐ μέν θην κείνης γε χερείων εὔχομαι εἶναι, 211
οὐ δέμας οὐδὲ φυήν, ἐπεὶ οὔ πως οὐδὲ ἔοικε 212
θνητὰς ἀθανάτῃσι δέμας καὶ εἶδος ἐρίζειν. " 213

---

203 **διογενής,-ές**—descended from Zeus (epithet of heroes); **διογενές** – voc.

Λαερτιάδης,-εω, ὁ—son of Laertes (Odysseus); **Λαερτιάδη** – voc.

πολυμήχανος,-ον—resourceful, ever-ready; **πολυμήχαν'** = **πολυμήχανε** – voc.

Ὀδυσσεῦ—voc.

205 ~ **αὐτίκα**—at once.

ἰέναι—infinitive of **εἶμι**.

χαῖρε—farewell, good luck to you.

ἔμπης—all the same, nevertheless; **καὶ ἔμπης** conveys the idea "even though your eagerness to leave is hardly flattering to me."

206 **εἰδείης**—perfect optative, 2nd pers. sing. of **οἶδα**; **εἴ...εἰδείης** – "if you should know," "if you knew," "if you only knew."

ὅσσα—"how many;" describes **κήδε'** in the next line.

αἶσα,-ης, ἡ—fate, destiny; understand **ἐστι** with **αἶσα** – "it is your fate."

207 **κῆδος,-εος, τό**—trouble, pain; *plural* – sorrows, troubles, sufferings; **κήδε'** = **κήδεα.**

ἀναπίμπλημι, (aor.) **ἀνέπλησα**—endure.

πρίν + aorist infinitive—before ____ing.

208 **κ' = κε.**

αὖθι—here; **ἐνθάδε...αὖθι** – "right here."

~ **μένω, μενέω, ἔμεινα**—remain, stay.

φυλάσσω, φυλάξω—guard, watch over, look after.

209 **εἴης**—present optative, 2nd pers. sing. of **εἰμί.**

εἴ...εἰδείης...κ'...φυλάσσοις...τ' εἴης (5.206-209)—future less vivid condition – "if you knew [should know]...you would look after...and be..."

ἱμείρομαι, (aor.) **ἱμειράμην**—wish, desire, long for; **ἱμειρόμενός περ** – "even though you wish" (*literally*, even though wishing).

ἰδέσθαι—aorist middle infinitive of **ὁράω**; translate as active.

210 **τῆς**—"whom."

ἐέλδομαι—long for (+ gen.); **ἐέλδεαι** – present, 2nd pers. sing.

ἤματα πάντα—"every day."

211 **θην**—in truth, surely.

κείνης—GENITIVE OF COMPARISON.

χερείων,-ον—inferior, less worthy.

εὔχομαι, εὔξομαι, ηὐξάμην—claim, declare; **εὔχομαι εἶναι = εἰμί.**

212 **δέμας, τό** (only in nom. and acc.)—body, figure; **δέμας** – ACCUSATIVE OF RESPECT.

φυή,-ῆς, ἡ—stature; **φυήν** – ACCUSATIVE OF RESPECT. (Goddesses were thought to be taller than mortal women.)

ἐπεὶ οὔ πως οὐδὲ ἔοικε—"since in no way is it likely," "since it is not at all likely" (the double negative stresses the complete unlikelihood).

213 ~ **θνητός,-ή,-όν**—mortal; **θνητάς** – mortal women.

ἀθανάτῃσι—immortal women (*i.e.*, goddesses); dat. plur.

εἶδος,-εος, τό—appearance, form, looks.

δέμας, εἶδος—ACCUSATIVES OF RESPECT.

ἐρίζω—compete with, rival (+ dat.); **θνητὰς...ἐρίζειν** – accusative/infinitive after **ἔοικε**: "that mortal women [could] compete with..."

Scanning Notes

203 The **ι** in **διογενές** is long.

The first **α** in **Λαερτιάδη** is long.

209 The first **α** in **ἀθάνατος** is long.

The first **ι** in **ἱμειρόμενος** is long.

213 The **α** in **θνητάς** is long.

The first **α** in **ἀθανάτῃσι** is long.

Odysseus admits that Penelope cannot compare to Calypso, but he longs ***ἤματα πάντα*** *to go home (****οἴκαδε****) and* ***νόστιμον ἦμαρ ἰδέσθαι****. Even if it means more suffering* ***ἐνὶ οἴνοπι πόντῳ****, he will endure it. When the sun (****ἠέλιος****) set, they went to the innermost part of the* ***σπεῖος γλαφυρόν*** *and made love.*

τὴν δ' ἀπαμειβόμενος προσέφη πολύμητις Ὀδυσσεύς· 214
" πότνα θεά, μή μοι τόδε χώεο· οἶδα καὶ αὐτὸς 215
πάντα μάλ', οὕνεκα σεῖο περίφρων Πηνελόπεια 216
εἶδος ἀκιδνοτέρη μέγεθός τ' εἰσάντα ἰδέσθαι· 217
ἡ μὲν γὰρ βροτός ἐστι, σὺ δ' ἀθάνατος καὶ ἀγήρως. 218
ἀλλὰ καὶ ὧς ἐθέλω καὶ ἐέλδομαι ἤματα πάντα 219
οἴκαδέ τ' ἐλθέμεναι καὶ νόστιμον ἦμαρ ἰδέσθαι. 220
εἰ δ' αὖ τις ῥαίῃσι θεῶν ἐνὶ οἴνοπι πόντῳ, 221
τλήσομαι ἐν στήθεσσιν ἔχων ταλαπενθέα θυμόν· 222
ἤδη γὰρ μάλα πολλὰ πάθον καὶ πολλὰ μόγησα 223
κύμασι καὶ πολέμῳ· μετὰ καὶ τόδε τοῖσι γενέσθω. " 224

---

214 **πολύμητις, -ιος** (masc. and fem. adj.)—crafty, shrewd, of many devices. Compare this line with 1.63. To whom does **τήν** refer in each line?

215 **πότνα** (fem. adj.)—revered, honored.

χώομαι—be angry; **χώεο** – present imperative.

καί—"also."

αὐτός—modifies "I," the subject of **οἶδα**.

216 **οὕνεκα**—that.

σεῖο—GENITIVE OF COMPARISON.

περίφρων (masc. and fem. adj.)—prudent, wise, sensible.

217 **εἶδος**—ACCUSATIVE OF RESPECT.

ἀκιδνότερος,-η,-ον—less admirable; **Πηνελόπειά [ἐστι] ἀκιδνοτέρη**.

μέγεθος,-εος, τό—height, stature; **μέγεθος** – ACCUSATIVE OF RESPECT. (Height was considered a requirement for Greek beauty.)

εἰσάντα—in the face, face to face; **εἰσάντα ἰδέσθαι** – to look in the face, to look at face to face.

218 **σὺ δ' [ἐσσί] ἀθάνατος.**

ἀγήρως = ἀγήραος—ageless, not subject to old age.

219 **καὶ ὥς**—"even so."

ἐέλδομαι—wish, desire (+ infinitive).

220 **οἴκαδε**—home, to one's home, homewards.

ἐλθέμεναι—aorist active infinitive of **ἔρχομαι.**

221 **αὖ**—again (Odysseus is on Calypso's island because Zeus destroyed his ship after his **ἑταῖροι** ate Helios' cattle.)

ῥαίω, ῥαίσω, ἔρραισα—shatter, wreck; **ῥαίῃσι** – present subjunctive, 3rd pers. sing.; understand "my ship" as its object.

θεῶν—with **τις**: "one of the gods," "some god."

222 **ἔχων**—present participle, nom. sing. masc.; modifies the subject of **τλήσομαι** – "I, having…"

ταλαπενθής,-ές—patient in suffering, bearing up against trouble.

εἰ δ' αὖ τις ῥαίῃσι θεῶν ἐνὶ οἴνοπι πόντῳ, τλήσομαι—future more vivid condition: "If some god again shatters [my ship]…, I will endure."

223 **πάθον = ἔπαθον**—aorist of **πάσχω.**

~ **μογέω,** (aor.) **ἐμόγησα**—suffer; **μόγησα = ἐμόγησα.**

224 **κύμασι**—dat. plur. of **κῦμα**; DATIVE OF PLACE – "in the waves," "on the sea."

πολέμῳ—DATIVE OF PLACE.

τοῖσι—object of **μετά**: "among these [other hardships]."

γενέσθω—aorist imperative, 3rd pers. sing.; **τόδε…γενέσθω** – "let this [*i.e.*, another shipwreck] be [one more]."

Scanning Notes

215 The **α** in **θεά** is long.

218 The first **α** in **ἀθάνατος** is long.

222 The **υ** in **θυμόν** is long.

224 The **υ** in **κύμασι** is long.

ὣς ἔφατ', ἠέλιος δ' ἄρ' ἔδυ καὶ ἐπὶ κνέφας ἦλθεν·
ἐλθόντες δ' ἄρα τώ γε μυχῷ σπείους γλαφυροῖο
τερπέσθην φιλότητι, παρ' ἀλλήλοισι μένοντες.

---

225 **ἠέλιος** = Attic **ἥλιος**.

δύω, δύσω, ἔδυν—go, enter; *with reference to the sun or a constellation* – go into [the Ocean], set.

κνέφας,-αος, τό—darkness, night.

ἐπὶ...ἦλθεν—TMESIS; **ἐπὶ κνέφας ἦλθεν** – "darkness came upon them," *i.e.*, night fell.

226 **ἐλθόντες**—plural participle modifying a dual subject (**τώ**).

τώ—nom. dual masc.: "the two of them"; when referring to a group of mixed gender, in this case, one female and one male, the masculine form is used.

μυχός,-οῦ, ὁ—the innermost part; **μυχῷ** – DATIVE OF PLACE.

σπείους—gen. sing. of **σπεῖος**.

227 **τερπέσθην**—imperfect middle, 3rd pers. dual of **τέρπω** – *middle*, enjoy oneself, take pleasure, give oneself up to pleasure or enjoyment.

φιλότητι—"sex," "making love" (DATIVE OF MEANS).

~ **ἀλλήλων** (gen. plur.)—one another, each other; **ἀλλήλοισι** – dat. plur.

Odysseus' sexual relationship with Calypso (and that with Circe, which we will hear about in Book 10) does not negate his loyalty to his wife nor stigmatize him as a unfaithful husband. By the double standards of ancient Greece, only wives were expected to be faithful to their spouses. Monogamy did not mean monogamous sexuality for the male.

Scanning Notes

225 The **υ** in **ἔδυ** is long.

Odyssey Book 5.333-353

Sailing home in his small craft, Odysseus was caught in a terrible storm sent by Poseidon. Leucothea came to his rescue.

Book 5.333-353

The sea nymph Leucothea sees and pities Odysseus. Rising from the sea and seating herself ***ἐπὶ σχεδίης****, she tells him to take off his* ***εἵματα****, leave the* ***σχεδίη****, and swim to land, since it is his fate (****μοῖρα****) to escape (****ἀλύξαι****). She gives him her veil to protect him, then plunges back (****ἄψ****)* ***ἐς πόντον****.*

τὸν δὲ ἴδεν Κάδμου θυγάτηρ, καλλίσφυρος Ἰνώ,
Λευκοθέη, ἣ πρὶν μὲν ἔην βροτὸς αὐδήεσσα,
νῦν δ' ἁλὸς ἐν πελάγεσσι θεῶν ἐξέμμορε τιμῆς.
ἥ ῥ' Ὀδυσῆ' ἐλέησεν ἀλώμενον, ἄλγε' ἔχοντα·
αἰθυίῃ δ' εἰκυῖα ποτῇ ἀνεδύσετο λίμνης,
ἷζε δ' ἐπὶ σχεδίης καί μιν πρὸς μῦθον ἔειπε·
"κάμμορε, τίπτε τοι ὧδε Ποσειδάων ἐνοσίχθων
ὠδύσατ' ἐκπάγλως, ὅτι τοι κακὰ πολλὰ φυτεύει;

---

333 **τόν**—"him" (Odysseus).

ἴδεν—aorist of **ὁράω**.

Κάδμος,-ου, ὁ—Cadmus, founder of Thebes, the leading city in Boeotia.

καλλίσφυρος,-ον—with beautiful ankles.

Ἰνώ,-όος, ἡ—Ino, daughter of Cadmus and wife of Athamas, the king of Orchomenus. When she jumped into the sea to save herself from her insane husband, the gods transformed her into the sea goddess Leucothea.

334 **Λευκοθέη,-ης, ἡ**—Leucothea.

πρίν—formerly, once, before.

ἔην—imperfect, 3rd pers. sing. of **εἰμί**.

αὐδήεις,-εσσα—speaking with human voice (as opposed to the way the gods speak).

335 **ἁλός**—gen. sing. of **ἅλς**.

πέλαγος,-εος, τό—the deep sea; **ἁλὸς ἐν πελάγεσσι** – "in the depths of the sea."

θεῶν—"from the gods."

ἐκμείρομαι—have, have one's share of (+ gen.); **ἐξέμμορε** – perfect, 3rd pers. sing.

τιμή,-ῆς,-ἡ—honor, respect.

336 **ἥ**—"she."

'Οδυσῆ' = **'Οδυσῆα**.

ἐλεέω, (aor.) **ἠλέησα**—pity; **ἐλέησεν** = **ἠλέησεν**.

ἀλάομαι—wander, rove; **ἀλώμενον** – present participle, acc. sing. masc., describing **'Οδυσῆ'**.

ἄλγε' = **ἄλγεα**.

ἔχοντα—present active participle describing **'Οδυσῆ'**.

337 **αἴθυια,-ης, ἡ**—some type of diving sea bird, possibly a cormorant.

εἰκυῖα—like, resembling (+ dat.); perfect active participle, nom. sing. fem. of **ἔοικα**.

ποτή,-ῆς, ἡ—flight; **ποτῇ** – "in flight."

ἀναδύομαι, ἀναδύσομαι, ἀνεδυσάμην—rise up from out of, emerge from (+ gen.); **ἀνεδύσετο** = **ἀνεδύσατο** (MIXED AORIST).

λίμνη,-ης, ἡ—the sea.

338 **ἵζω**—sit down, seat oneself.

μιν—object of **πρός**.

339 **κάμμορος,-ον**—ill-fated, wretched.

τίπτε—why?

~ **ὧδε**—thus, in this way.

340 **ὀδύσσομαι**, (aor.) **ὠδυσάμην**—be angry with, hate (+ dat.); **ὠδύσατ'** = **ὠδύσατο** – aorist, translate as present; **ὠδύσατ'** may be a pun on Odysseus' name.

ἐκπάγλως—vehemently, strongly, exceedingly.

ὅτι—in that, seeing that, "since I see that."

φυτεύω—cause, bring about.

Scanning Notes

333 The **ι** in **'Ινώ** is long.

335 The **ι** in **τιμῆς** is long.

337 The **υ** in **ἀνεδύσετο** is long.

339 The **α** in **Ποσειδάων** is long.

οὐ μὲν δή σε καταφθίσει, μάλα περ μενεαίνων.
ἀλλὰ μάλ' ὧδ' ἔρξαι, δοκέεις δέ μοι οὐκ ἀπινύσσειν·
εἵματα ταῦτ' ἀποδὺς σχεδίην ἀνέμοισι φέρεσθαι
κάλλιπ', ἀτὰρ χείρεσσι νέων ἐπιμαίεο νόστου
γαίης Φαιήκων, ὅθι τοι μοῖρ' ἐστὶν ἀλύξαι.
τῆ δέ, τόδε κρήδεμνον ὑπὸ στέρνοιο τανύσσαι
ἄμβροτον· οὐδέ τί τοι παθέειν δέος οὐδ' ἀπολέσθαι.
αὐτὰρ ἐπὴν χείρεσσιν ἐφάψεαι ἠπείροιο,
ἂψ ἀπολυσάμενος βαλέειν εἰς οἴνοπα πόντον
πολλὸν ἀπ' ἠπείρου, αὐτὸς δ' ἀπονόσφι τραπέσθαι."

---

341 **καταφθίω, καταφθίσω, κατέφθισα**—destroy.

μάλα περ—even though.

μενεαίνω—rage, be enraged, be angry at; **μενεαίνων** describes "he," the subject of **καταφθίσει**.

342 **ὧδ'** = **ὧδε**; **μάλ' ὧδ'** – "just like this."

ἔρδω, ἔρξω, ἔρξα—do, perform, accomplish; **ἔρξαι** – aorist infinitive used as an imperative.

δοκέω—seem, appear; **δοκέεις** = **δοκεῖς**.

ἀπινύσσω—lack sense; **οὐκ ἀπινύσσειν** – *i.e.*, to have good sense [enough to take my advice].

343 **ταῦτ'** = **ταῦτα**.

ἀποδύω, ἀποδύσω, ἀπέδυν—take off; **ἀποδύς** – aorist active participle, nom. sing. masc.; modifies the understood "you," the subject of **κάλλιπε** in the next line.

φέρεσθαι—present passive infinitive.

344 **καταλείπω, καλλείψω, κάλλιπον**—leave behind, abandon; **κάλλιπ'** = **κάλλιπε** – aorist imperative, 2nd pers. sing.

χείρεσσι—DATIVE OF MEANS.

νέω—swim.

ἐπιμαίομαι—struggle for, strive for (+ gen.); **ἐπιμαίεο** – present imperative, 2nd pers. sing.

νόστου—in this line, rather than "return" or "homecoming," **νόστου** means "arrival at" or "reaching a specific place."

345 **Φαίηκες,-ων, οἱ**—the Phaeacians, a people noted for their seafaring skill who lived on the island of Scheria (probably an imaginary place); **γαίης Φαιήκων**—"in the land of the Phaeacians."

ὅθι—where.

τοι—DATIVE OF POSSESSION.

μοῖρ' = μοῖρα—fate, destiny.

~ **ἀλύσκω, ἀλύξω, ἤλυξα**—escape.

346 **τῆ**—here! come! (followed by an imperative).

κρήδεμνον,-ου, τό—veil, woman's head-covering.

στέρνον,-ου, τό—chest.

τανύω, τανύω, ἐτάνυσσα—stretch, put, place; **τανύσσαι** – aorist middle imperative, 2nd pers. sing.

347 **ἄμβροτος,-ον**—immortal, divine; **ἄμβροτον** describes the **κρήδεμνον** in the previous line.

παθέειν—aorist infinitive of **πάσχω**.

~ **δέος, δέους, τό**—fear, reason for fear; **τί...δέος** – "any reason for fear."

ἀπολέσθαι – aorist middle infinitive of **ἀπόλλυμι**.

οὐδέ [ἐστί] τι τοι παθέειν δέος οὐδ' ἀπολέσθαι—"There is not any reason for you to fear suffering or perishing."

348 **ἐπήν = ἐπεὶ ἄν**—when, after, as soon as (+ subjunctive).

ἐφάπτομαι—touch (+ gen.); **ἐφάψεαι = ἐφάψηαι = ἐφάψῃ** – aorist middle subjunctive, 2nd pers. sing. (a SHORT-VOWEL SUBJUNCTIVE (**ε** for **η**) and an uncontracted 2nd pers. sing. ending).

ἤπειρος,-ου, ἡ—the land (as opposed to the sea).

349 ~ **ἄψ**—back.

ἀπολύω, ἀπολύσω, ἀπέλυσα—loosen; *middle*, undo, loosen from.

βαλέειν—aorist active infinitive of **βάλλω** used as an imperative; **κρήδεμνον** is the understood object.

350 **πολλόν**—far.

ἀπ' = ἀπό.

αὐτός—"you yourself."

ἀπονόσφι—away.

τρέπω, τρέψω, ἔτρεψα or **ἔτραπον**—turn; **τραπέσθαι** – aorist middle infinitve used as an imperative.

Scanning Notes

341 The first **ι** in **καταφθίσει** is long.

349 The **υ** in **ἀπολυσάμενος** is long.

ὣς ἄρα φωνήσασα θεὰ κρήδεμνον ἔδωκεν, 351
αὐτὴ δ' ἂψ ἐς πόντον ἐδύσετο κυμαίνοντα 352
αἰθυίῃ εἰκυῖα· μέλαν δέ ἑ κῦμ' ἐκάλυψεν. 353

---

352 **αὐτή**—"she herself."

ἐδύσετο = ἐδύσατο—"plunged" (**ἐδύσετο** is a MIXED AORIST.)

κυμαίνω—surge; **κυμαίνοντα** – present active participle, acc. sing. masc.; modifies **πόντον**.

353 **αἰθυιῃ εἰκυῖα**—In what other line was Leucothea described with this phrase? How are her actions in 5.352-353 different from what she was doing in the earlier line?

ἑ—"her" (acc. sing. of **εἷο**).

κῦμ' = κῦμα.

καλύπτω, καλύψω, ἐκάλυψα—cover, hide.

Scanning Notes

351 The first **α** in **φωνήσασα** is long.

352 The **υ** in **ἐδύσετο** is long.

The **υ** in **κυμαίνοντα** is long.

Odyssey Book 6.115-161

Having spent two days and two nights in the ocean after the destruction of his vessel, Odysseus was at last able to swim to shore in the land of the Phaeacians. Exhausted, he fell asleep beneath some bushes.

The next morning, Princess Nausicaa, inspired by Athena in a dream, brought her maids to the same place to do the family's laundry. As the clothes were drying, the young women sang and tossed a ball to one another.

Fig. 3. Marc Chagall (Belorussian, 1887-1985). *The Odyssey: The Waves Swallow Up Ulysses*, 1974. Color lithograph. 92.80. Museum of Art and Archaeology, University of Missouri. Gilbreath-McLorn Museum Fund.

Book 6.115-161

*Awakened by the sound of the young women playing with the ball (**σφαῖρα**), Odysseus, sitting up (**ἑζόμενος**), wonders where he is.*

σφαῖραν ἔπειτ' ἔρριψε μετ' ἀμφίπολον βασίλεια·
ἀμφιπόλου μὲν ἅμαρτε, βαθείῃ δ' ἔμβαλε δίνῃ.
αἱ δ' ἐπὶ μακρὸν ἄϋσαν· ὁ δ' ἔγρετο δῖος Ὀδυσσεύς,
ἑζόμενος δ' ὥρμαινε κατὰ φρένα καὶ κατὰ θυμόν·
"ὤ μοι ἐγώ, τέων αὖτε βροτῶν ἐς γαῖαν ἱκάνω;
ἤ ῥ' οἵ γ' ὑβρισταί τε καὶ ἄγριοι οὐδὲ δίκαιοι,
ἦε φιλόξεινοι καί σφιν νόος ἐστὶ θεουδής;
ὥς τέ με κουράων ἀμφήλυθε θῆλυς ἀϋτή,
Νυμφάων, αἳ ἔχουσ' ὀρέων αἰπεινὰ κάρηνα
καὶ πηγὰς ποταμῶν καὶ πίσεα ποιήεντα·

---

115 **σφαῖρα,-ης, ἡ**—ball.

~ **ῥίπτω, ῥίψω, ἔρριψα**—throw.

ἀμφίπολος,-ου, ἡ—female servant, maid.

βασίλεια,-ης, ἡ—princess (refers to Nausicaa).

116 **ἁμαρτάνω, ἁμαρτήσομαι, ἥμαρτον**—miss, fail to hit (+ gen.); **ἅμαρτε** = **ἥμαρτε**; Nausicaa is the subject.

βαθύς,-εῖα,-ύ—deep.

ἐμβάλλω, (aor.) **ἐνέβαλον**—throw [something (acc.)] into [something (dat.)]; **ἔμβαλε** = **ἐνέβαλε**; Nausicaa is the subject, **σφαῖραν** the understood object.

δίνη,-ης, ἡ—whirlpool, eddy [in a river].

117 **αἱ**—"they," *i.e.*, the girls.

ἐπί—"thereupon," "at this."

μακρόν—loudly.

αὔω, ἀΰσω, ἤϋσα—shout, cry out; **ἄϋσαν** = **ἤϋσαν**.

ἐγείρω, ἐγερῶ, ἤγειρα—awaken [someone], wake [someone] up; *middle*, wake up; **ἔγρετο** – aorist middle.

118 ~ **ἕζομαι**, (aor.) **εἶσα**—sit, sit up.

ὁρμαίνω, (aor.) **ὥρμηνα**—ponder, consider; **ὅρμαινε** = **ὥρμαινε**.

119 ὤ μοι ἐγώ—"alas for me."

τέων = τίνων (gen. plur. masc. of τίς); interrogative pronoun used as an adjective modifying βροτῶν.

αὖτε—*indicates impatience*, "now!" "this time." (Although the audience has not yet heard the tales of the many lands Odysseus has come to on his long trip home, for him this is yet another strange land. αὖτε expresses his weary exasperation at yet another one.)

~ ἱκάνω—come to; ἱκάνω—"I have come to;" present with perfect sense.

120 ὑβριστής,-οῦ, ὁ—violent person.

ἄγριος,-η,-ον—fierce, savage, barbarous, uncivilized.

δίκαιος,-α,-ον—civilized.

εἰσί is the understood verb for this question: "are they?"

121 ἦε—or.

φιλόξεινος,-ον—hospitable, friendly to strangers.

~ σφιν—them (dat. plur. of εἷο); DATIVE OF POSSESSION.

θεουδής,-ές—god-fearing.

122 ~ κούρη,-ης, ἡ—young woman, girl; ὥς...κουράων—"as of young women."

ἀμφέρχομαι, (aor.) ἀμφήλυθον—surround.

θῆλυς,-υ—feminine, female.

ἀϋτή,-ῆς, ἡ—shout, cry.

123 ἔχουσ' = ἔχουσι—"inhabit."

ὄρος,-εος, τό—mountain.

αἰπεινός,-ή,-όν—steep, towering.

κάρηνον,-ου, τό—top, summit.

124 πηγή,-ῆς, ἡ—spring, source [of a river].

πῖσος,-εος, τό—meadow.

ποιήεις,-εσσα,-εν—grassy.

Note the alliteration in this line.

Scanning Notes

116 The ι in δίνῃ is long.

117 The υ in ἄϋσαν is long.

118 The υ in θυμόν is long.

119 τέων is scanned as one long syllable (SYNIZESIS).

The α in ἱκάνω is long.

122 The α in κουράων is long.

The υ in ἀϋτή is long.

123 The α in Νυμφάων is long.

124 The ι in πίσεα is long.

ἦ νύ που ἀνθρώπων εἰμὶ σχεδὸν αὐδηέντων.
ἀλλ' ἄγ', ἐγὼν αὐτὸς πειρήσομαι ἠδὲ ἴδωμαι."

*Odysseus, naked (**γυμνός**), emerges from the bushes, covering his genitals with a leafy branch. Frightened, all the girls except the **θυγάτηρ** of Alcinous flee. Odysseus considers whether to clasp her knees (**γοῦνα**) and beseech the **κούρη** or to stand at a distance and beg with pleasing words (**ἐπέεσσιν μειλιχίοισι**), in the hope that she would show him the way to a **πόλις** and give him **εἵματα**.*

ὣς εἰπὼν θάμνων ὑπεδύσετο δῖος Ὀδυσσεύς,
ἐκ πυκινῆς δ' ὕλης πτόρθον κλάσε χειρὶ παχείῃ
φύλλων, ὡς ῥύσαιτο περὶ χροῒ μήδεα φωτός.
βῆ δ' ἴμεν ὥς τε λέων ὀρεσίτροφος, ἀλκὶ πεποιθώς,
ὅς τ' εἶσ' ὑόμενος καὶ ἀήμενος, ἐν δέ οἱ ὄσσε
δαίεται· αὐτὰρ ὁ βουσὶ μετέρχεται ἢ ὀΐεσσιν

125 **ἦ νύ που**—"is it possible?" "can it be perhaps?"

σχεδόν—near, close to (+ gen. or dat.).

αὐδήεις,-εσσα—speaking with human voice (as opposed to speaking the speech of immortals, as would the Nymphs he has just mentioned).

126 **πειράομαι, πειρήσομαι, ἐπειρησάμην**—try, try to find out, try to discover; **πειρήσομαι** – aorist subjunctive; HORTATORY SUBJUNCTIVE – "let me try to find out." **πειρήσομαι** (SHORT-VOWEL SUBJUNCTIVE) = **πειρήσωμαι**.

ἴδωμαι—HORTATORY SUBJUNCTIVE.

127 **θάμνος,-ου, ὁ**—bush, shrub; *plural*, a thicket.

ὑποδύομαι, ὑποδύσομαι, ὑπεδυσάμην—emerge from under, come out from under (+ gen.); **ὑπεδύσετο** – a MIXED AORIST form.

128 **πυκινός,-ή,-όν**—thick, dense.

ὕλη,-ης, ἡ—forest, woods.

πτόρθος,-ου, ὁ—branch [of a tree].

κλάω, κλάσω, ἔκλασα—break, break off; **κλάσε** = **ἔκλασε**.

παχύς,-εῖα,-ύ—strong; **χειρὶ παχείῃ** – DATIVE OF MEANS.

129 **φύλλον,-ου, τό**–leaf; **πτόρθον...φύλλων** – "a leafy branch."

ῥύομαι, (aor.) **ἐρρυσάμην**—cover; **ῥύσαιτο** – aorist optative; its subject is an understood **πτόρθος**; **ὡς ῥύσαιτο** – PURPOSE CLAUSE.

χρώς, χρωτός, ὁ—body; χροΐ – dat. sing.; περὶ χροΐ – "[when held] round his body."

μήδεα,-ων, τά—genitals.

~ φώς, φωτός, ὁ—person, man.

130 βῆ = ἔβη.

ἴμεν = ἰέναι—present infinitive of εἶμι; βῆ...ἴμεν – "he went."

ὥς begins a simile comparing Odysseus to a lion.

~ λέων,-οντος, ὁ—lion (Often mentioned by Homer, lions are not found in Greece today. Lions in Europe date back to Palaeolithic times but by Homer's time they probably only remained in the wildest regions. The historian Herodotus reported lions still living in the remote regions of northern Greece at the time of the Persian invasion. Homer himself may never have actually seen a lion, but knew of them from stories and depictions in art.)

ὀρεσίτροφος,-ον—mountain-bred.

ἀλκή,-ῆς, ἡ—strength, might; ἀλκί = ἀλκῇ.

πεποιθώς—perfect active participle, nom. sing. masc. of πείθω: "trusting in," "relying on" (+ dat.).

131 εἶσ' = εἶσι—present tense, 3rd pers. sing. of εἶμι.

ὕω—rain; *passive*, be rained on; ὑόμενος – "rained on," "drenched by rain."

ἄημι—blow; ἀήμενος – "blown [by the wind]," "beaten [by the wind]."

ἐν δέ—and nevertheless, moreover.

132 δαίω—set on fire; *passive*, blaze, burn; the subject is the dual ὄσσε – eyes. Homer sometimes uses a singular verb with a dual subject.

βουσί—dat. plur. of βοῦς.

μετέρχομαι, μετελεύσομαι, μετῆλθον—go among (+ dat.); go after, pursue (+ acc.).

ὄϊς, οἰός, ὁ or ἡ—sheep; ὀΐεσσιν – dat. plur.

Scanning Notes

127 The second υ in ὑπεδύσετο is long.

128 The υ in ὕλης is long.

129 The υ in ῥύσαιτο is long.

131 The υ in ὑόμενος is long.

ἠὲ μετ' ἀγροτέρας ἐλάφους· κέλεται δέ ἑ γαστὴρ
μήλων πειρήσοντα καὶ ἐς πυκινὸν δόμον ἐλθεῖν·
ὣς Ὀδυσεὺς κούρῃσιν ἐϋπλοκάμοισιν ἔμελλε
μείξεσθαι, γυμνός περ ἐών· χρειὼ γὰρ ἵκανε.
σμερδαλέος δ' αὐτῇσι φάνη κεκακωμένος ἅλμῃ,
τρέσσαν δ' ἄλλυδις ἄλλη ἐπ' ἠϊόνας προὐχούσας.
οἴη δ' Ἀλκινόου θυγάτηρ μένε· τῇ γὰρ Ἀθήνη
θάρσος ἐνὶ φρεσὶ θῆκε καὶ ἐκ δέος εἵλετο γυίων.

---

133 **μετ' = μετά**—"after;" refers back to **μετέρχεται** – "he goes after…"

ἀγρότερος,-η,-ον—wild.

ἔλαφος,-ου, ἡ—deer.

ἑ—"him" (acc. sing. of **εἷο**).

γαστήρ,-έρος, ἡ—belly.

134 **πειρήσοντα**—FUTURE PARTICIPLE OF PURPOSE: "to make an attempt on," "to attack" (+gen.).

καί—"even."

δόμον—"an enclosure for sheep," "a sheep-fold." **πυκινὸν δόμον** – perhaps a "strongly-built" or a "tightly-thronged" sheep-fold.

135 **ὥς**—"in this way," "in this manner."

κούρῃσιν—dat. plur.

μέλλω—be going, be about (+ infinitive).

136 **μείξεσθαι**—aorist middle infinitive from **μίσγω** – "to put himself among" (+ dat.).

γυμνός,-ή,-όν—naked.

περ—even though.

ἐών = ὤν—present participle, nom. sing. masc. of **εἰμί**.

χρείω,-οῦς, ἡ—need, necessity; **χρειὼ γὰρ ἵκανε**—"for necessity had compelled [him]" (*literally*, for necessity had come upon [him]); **ἵκανε** – imperfect used in pluperfect sense.

137 **σμερδαλέος,-η,-ον**—terrible.

~ **φαίνω, φανέω, ἔφηνα**, (aor. pass.) **ἐφάνην**—show, reveal; *middle and passive*, appear; **φάνη = ἐφάνη**—aorist passive, 3rd pers. sing.

κακόω—befoul, make dirty; **κεκακωμένος** – perfect passive participle.

ἅλμη,-ης, ἡ—seawater, brine, dried sea spray.

While Odysseus was not really charging the girls like a hungry lion seeking prey, the unexpected appearance of a filthy naked stranger frightened them as the attack of a wild animal would have. The simile underscores his desperate situation, his weather-beaten appearance, and the fear he inspired in the girls.

138 **τρέω**, (aor.) **ἔτρεσα**—flee, run away frightened; **τρέσσαν = ἔτρεσαν**.

ἄλλυδις—in another direction, to another place; **ἄλλυδις ἄλλη** – some in one direction, some in another.

ἠϊών,-όνος, ἡ—beach.

προέχω or **προὔχω**—jut out, project; **προὐχουσας** – present active participle, acc. plur. fem.; **ἠϊόνος προὐχούσας** – probably refers to spits (narrow points of land projecting into the water) that jut into the sea at the mouth of the river.

139 **Ἀλκίνοος,-ου, ὁ**—Alcinous, king of the Phaeacians and Nausicaa's father.

μένε = ἔμενε.

τῇ—"her" (DATIVE OF INTEREST showing possession with **φρεσί** in the next line).

140 **θάρσος,-εος, τό**—courage, boldness.

θῆκε = ἔθηκε.

ἐξαιρέω, (aor.) **ἐξεῖλον**—take out; *middle*, take [something – acc.] away from [someone or something – gen.]; **ἐκ...εἵλετο** – TMESIS.

γυῖα,-ων, τά—limbs.

Scanning Notes

133 The second **α** in **ἀγροτέρας** is long.

136 The **α** in **ἵκανε** is long.

στῆ δ' ἄντα σχομένη· ὁ δὲ μερμήριξεν Ὀδυσσεύς,
ἢ γούνων λίσσοιτο λαβὼν εὐώπιδα κούρην,
ἦ αὔτως ἐπέεσσιν ἀποσταδὰ μειλιχίοισι
λίσσοιτ', εἰ δείξειε πόλιν καὶ εἵματα δοίη.
ὣς ἄρα οἱ φρονέοντι δοάσσατο κέρδιον εἶναι,
λίσσεσθαι ἐπέεσσιν ἀποσταδὰ μειλιχίοισι,
μή οἱ γοῦνα λαβόντι χολώσαιτο φρένα κούρη.
αὐτίκα μειλίχιον καὶ κερδαλέον φάτο μῦθον·

Odysseus addresses her, asking if she is a ***θεός*** *or a* ***βροτός****. If a* ***θεός****, she seems most like Artemis. If she is one of those who dwell upon the earth (****ἐπὶ χθονὶ ναιετάουσι****), her* ***πατήρ*** *and her* ***μήτηρ*** *and her brothers (****κασίγνητοι****) are* ***μάκαρες****.* ***Μακάρτατος*** *is* ***κεῖνος*** *who will marry her.*

" γουνοῦμαί σε, ἄνασσα· θεός νύ τις ἦ βροτός ἐσσι;
εἰ μέν τις θεός ἐσσι, τοὶ οὐρανὸν εὐρὺν ἔχουσιν,
Ἀρτέμιδί σε ἐγώ γε, Διὸς κούρῃ μεγάλοιο,
εἶδός τε μέγεθός τε φυήν τ' ἄγχιστα ἐΐσκω·

141 **στῆ** = **ἔστη**.

ἄντα—facing [him], in front of [him].

σχομένη—aorist middle participle, nom. sing. fem of **ἔχω**: "holding [her position], "holding [herself].

μερμηρίζω, (aor.) **ἐμερμήριξα**—ponder, consider; **μερμήριξεν** = **ἐμερμήριξεν**.

142 ~ **γόνυ, γουνός** or **γούνατος, τό**—knee; **γούνων** – object of **λαβών**.

λίσσομαι—beg, entreat, supplicate; **λίσσοιτο** – present optative; **ἢ...λίσσοιτο** – indirect question. (A person begging or approaching someone as a suppliant would crouch or kneel and grasp the knees of the person they are entreating, unless physical contact is considered unwise – the issue Odysseus is pondering here.)

λαβών—aorist active participle, nom. sing. masc. of **λαμβάνω**.

εὐῶπις,-ιδος (fem. adj.)—attractive, fair-faced.

143 **αὔτως**—merely, only.

ἀποσταδά—standing at a distance.

~ **μειλίχιος,-η,-ον**—pleasing, winning, gentle, mild; **ἐπέεσσιν...μειλιχίοισι** – DATIVE OF MEANS.

144 **λίσσοιτ' = λίσσοιτο.**

εἰ—in the hope that, if by chance (+ optative).

~ **δείκνυμι, δείξω, ἔκειξα**—show, point out; **δείξειε** – aorist optative, 3rd pers. sing.; **εἰ δείξειε πόλιν** – "in the hope that she might show [him the way to] the city."

δοίη—aorist optative, 3rd pers. sing. of **δίδωμι.**

145 **φρονέω**—consider, debate, ponder; **φρονέοντι** – present active participle, dat. sing. masc.; describes **οἱ**.

δοάσσατο (impersonal aorist)—it seemed (= Attic **ἔδοξε**).

κερδίων,-ον—better, best.

147 **γοῦνα**—acc. plur. of **γόνυ.**

χολόω, χολώσω, ἐχόλωσα—make angry; *middle and passive*, be angry at (+ dat.); **χολώσαιτο** – aorist middle optative; **μή...χολώσαιτο** – PURPOSE CLAUSE.

φρένα—ACCUSATIVE OF RESPECT: "in her heart."

148 **κερδαλέος,-η,-ον**—cunning, shrewd, wily.

149 **γουνοῦμαι**—entreat, beseech, humbly beg (originally, the word meant to clasp the knees as an act of entreaty, but later came to mean to beg or entreat without the accompanying action. Why does he not actually touch her knees?)

ἄνασσα,-ης, ἡ—queen, lady (a word normally used only for goddesses, so a very flattering way to address her).

ἐσσι = εἶ.

150 **τοί = οἱ**—article used as relative pronoun: "[one of those] who."

151 **μεγάλοιο**—gen. sing. masc. of **μέγας.**

152 **εἶδος,-εος, τό**—appearance, form, looks.

φυή,-ῆς, ἡ—stature.

ἄγχιστα—most closely, very closely.

εἶδος, μέγεθος, φυήν—ACCUSATIVES OF RESPECT.

ἐΐσκω—consider (someone/thing – acc.) like (someone/thing – dat.).

Scanning Notes

151 The second **ι** in **Ἀρτέμιδι** is long.

152 Why is the first **τε** scanned as a long syllable?

εἰ δέ τίς ἐσσι βροτῶν, οἳ ἐπὶ χθονὶ ναιετάουσι, 153
τρὶς μάκαρες μὲν σοί γε πατὴρ καὶ πότνια μήτηρ, 154
τρὶς μάκαρες δὲ κασίγνητοι· μάλα πού σφισι θυμὸς 155
αἰὲν ἐϋφροσύνῃσιν ἰαίνεται εἵνεκα σεῖο, 156
λευσσόντων τοιόνδε θάλος χορὸν εἰσοιχνεῦσαν. 157
κεῖνος δ' αὖ περὶ κῆρι μακάρτατος ἔξοχον ἄλλων, 158
ὅς κέ σ' ἐέδνοισι βρίσας οἶκόνδ' ἀγάγηται. 159
οὐ γάρ πω τοιοῦτον ἴδον βροτὸν ὀφθαλμοῖσιν, 160
οὔτ' ἄνδρ' οὔτε γυναῖκα· σέβας μ' ἔχει εἰσορόωντα. 161

---

153 **χθών, χθονός, ἡ**—the earth.

ναιετάω—live, dwell, have one's home; **ναιετάουσι** – uncontracted present tense.

154 **τρίς**—three times, thrice.

Understand **εἰσί** as the verb.

155 **κασίγνητος,-ου, ὁ**—brother.

που—no doubt.

σφισι—dat. plur. of **εἶο**.

156 **ἐϋφροσύνη,-ης, ἡ**—gladness, happiness, joy; *plural can be used for singular.*

ἰαίνω, (aor.) **ἴηνα**—warm, gladden, cheer; **ἐϋφροσύνῃσιν ἰαίνεται** – "is warmed with joy."

εἵνεκα—because of, on account of (+ gen.).

σεῖο—gen. sing. of **σύ.**

157 **λεύσσω**—see; **λευσσόντων** – "when they see," "as they see" (*literally*, seeing); gen. in agreement with the possessive idea of **σφισι.**

τοιόσδε,-ήδε,-όνδε—such, of such nature.

θάλος,-εος, τό—young person (*literally*, a young shoot or branch).

χορός,-οῦ, ὁ—dancing, the dance.

εἰσοιχνέω—enter; **εἰσοιχνεῦσαν** – present active participle, acc. sing. fem.; describes **θάλος** but is feminine because Nausicaa is female. (This is an example of *constructio ad sensum* (construction according to sense), in which an adjective or participle agrees with the real gender rather than the grammatical gender.)

158 **δ' αὖ**—on the other hand.

περί—exceedingly.

~ **κῆρ, κῆρος, τό**—heart, soul, *i.e.*, the seat of emotion and feeling; **κῆρι** – DATIVE OF PLACE: “in his heart.”

μακάρτατος—superlative of **μάκαρ**; **κεῖνος...μακάρτατός** [ἐστι].

ἔξοχον—beyond (+ gen.).

159 **σ’** = **σε** (object of **ἀγάγηται**).

ἔεδνα,-ων, τά—bridal gifts given to the bride’s father for the hand of the bride; **ἐέδνοισι** – DATIVE OF MEANS.

βρίθω, βρίσω, ἔβρισα—prevail.

οἶκόνδ’ = **οἶκόνδε**.

ἀγάγηται—aorist subjunctive used for future; **οἶκόνδ’ ἀγάγηται** – marry, take as a wife.

160 ~ **πω**—ever, yet; **οὐ πω** – never, never yet.

τοιοῦτος, τοιαύτη, τοιοῦτον—such, of such a kind.

161 **ἄνδρ’** = **ἄνδρα**.

σέβας, τό (only in nom., acc., and voc. forms)—wonder, a feeling of awe.

εἰσοράω—look at, see; **εἰσορόωντα** – present active participle, acc. sing. masc.; agrees with **μ’** – “looking at [you],” “as I look at [you].”

Scanning Notes

155 The **υ** in **θυμός** is long.

Odyssey Book 6.186-197

Odysseus told the princess he had been shipwrecked and asked for clothing and directions to a city.

Book 6.186-197

Replying to Odysseus, Nausicaa agrees to help him and tells him the Phaeacians ***τήνδε πόλιν καὶ γαῖαν ἔχουσιν****. She is the* ***θυγάτηρ*** *of their king,* ***μεγαλήτωρ*** *Alcinous.*

τὸν δ᾽ αὖ Ναυσικάα λευκώλενος ἀντίον ηὔδα·
"ξεῖν᾽, ἐπεὶ οὔτε κακῷ οὔτ᾽ ἄφρονι φωτὶ ἔοικας,
Ζεὺς δ᾽ αὐτὸς νέμει ὄλβον Ὀλύμπιος ἀνθρώποισιν,
ἐσθλοῖσ᾽ ἠδὲ κακοῖσιν, ὅπως ἐθέλῃσιν, ἑκάστῳ·
καί που σοὶ τά γ᾽ ἔδωκε, σὲ δὲ χρὴ τετλάμεν ἔμπης.
νῦν δ᾽, ἐπεὶ ἡμετέρην τε πόλιν καὶ γαῖαν ἱκάνεις,
οὔτ᾽ οὖν ἐσθῆτος δευήσεαι οὔτε τευ ἄλλου,
ὧν ἐπέοιχ᾽ ἱκέτην ταλαπείριον ἀντιάσαντα.
ἄστυ δέ τοι δείξω, ἐρέω δέ τοι οὔνομα λαῶν·
Φαίηκες μὲν τήνδε πόλιν καὶ γαῖαν ἔχουσιν,
εἰμὶ δ᾽ ἐγὼ θυγάτηρ μεγαλήτορος Ἀλκινόοιο,
τοῦ δ᾽ ἐκ Φαιήκων ἔχεται κάρτος τε βίη τε."

186 **αὖ**—in reply, now.

λευκώλενος,-ον—white-armed (Fair arms may have been considered a sign of feminine beauty, or a woman may have been called white-armed because basic female attire, the **πέπλος**, was sleeveless, hence her arms appeared pale in contrast to the colored garment. Another possibility is that white arms were a sign of upper-class status, indicating a woman who did not have to work outdoors.)

αὐδάω, αὐδήσω, ηὔδησα—say, speak; *with* **ἀντίον** – address.

187 ~ **ξεῖνος,-ου, ὁ**—stranger; **ξεῖν᾽ = ξεῖνε** – voc.

ἄφρων,-ον—foolish.

ἔοικας—"you seem to be" (+ dat.); perfect (translate as present), 2nd pers. sing. of **ἔοικα**.

She does not complete the thought begun in this line until 6.191, as she now digresses for a few lines on how even good people can experience suffering.

188 **νέμω**—allot, assign, distribute.

ὄλβος,-ου, ὁ—good fortune, prosperity, happiness.

189 **ἐθέλῃσιν**—present subjunctive, 3rd pers. sing. of **ἐθέλω**; subjunctive with **ὅπως** – "as he wishes."

190 **που**—no doubt, I suppose.

τά—*i.e.*, these misfortunes.

χρή (impersonal)—there is need, it is necessary.

τετλάμεν—perfect infinitive of **τλάω**, translate as present; **σὲ...τετλάμεν** – accusative/infinitive with **χρή**.

ἔμπης—in any case, "as best you can."

192 **οὖν**—now, therefore.

ἐσθής,-ῆτος, ἡ—clothing.

δεύομαι, δευήσομαι—lack, be without (+ gen.); **δευήσεαι** – future, 2nd pers. sing.

τευ—gen. sing. of **τίς**; **τευ ἄλλου** – "any other thing."

193 **ὧν**—which (gen. after an understood **μὴ δεύεσθαι**).

ἐπέοιχ' = **ἐπέοικε** (impersonal)—it is fitting (+ acc. and infinitive).

ἱκέτης,-ου, ὁ—suppliant.

ταλαπείριος,-ον—much-suffering.

ἀντιάω, (aor.) **ἠντίασα**—meet, encounter; **ἀντιάσαντα** – aorist active participle, acc. sing. masc.

"which it is fitting that a much-suffering suppliant, having met [someone who can help him not lack]."

194 **ἄστυ,-εος, τό**—city, town.

~ **εἴρω, ἐρέω**—tell.

οὔνομα,-ατος, τό = **ὄνομα.**

~ **λαός,-οῦ, ὁ**—*singular and plural,* people.

197 **τοῦ...ἐκ** = **ἐκ τοῦ**—"on him."

ἔχεται—"depend."

κάρτος,-εος, τό—strength.

βίη,-ης, ἡ—power, might.

Scanning Notes

186 The final **α** in **Ναυσικάα** is long.

191 The **α** in **ἱκάνεις** is long.

194 The **α** in **λαῶν** is long.

Odyssey Book 9.252-306

[Odysseus is telling the Phaeacians about his adventures on the way home from the Trojan War. At this point in the story, Odysseus' twelve ships have reached the land of the Cyclopes, a race of lawless giants.]

Leaving eleven of the ships at an island in the harbor, Odysseus took his own ship to the mainland to find out who lived there. From the beach, they saw a cave surrounded by a courtyard and pens for flocks. Odysseus ordered most of the crew to remain with the ship while he and twelve men went to the cave. When they arrived, no one was there. They entered the cave, helped themselves to the food and drink they found, and awaited the return of the cave's inhabitant.

Polyphemus, a huge Cyclops, and his flocks returned to the cave for the night. After blocking the entrance with an enormous rock, he saw Odysseus and his men.

Book 9.252-306

*The Cyclops asks who they are. Though frightened by the monster (**πέλωρον**), Odysseus tells him they are **Ἀχαιοί** going **οἴκαδε** from the Trojan War who seek his hospitality in the hope that he will give them a guest gift (**ξεινήϊον**). He urges the Cyclops to respect the **θεοί**. They are suppliants (**ἱκέται**) and Zeus is the protector of **ἱκέται** and **ξεῖνοι**.*

“ ὦ ξεῖνοι, τίνες ἐστέ; πόθεν πλεῖθ’ ὑγρὰ κέλευθα;
ἤ τι κατὰ πρῆξιν ἦ μαψιδίως ἀλάλησθε
οἷά τε ληϊστῆρες ὑπεὶρ ἅλα, τοί τ’ ἀλόωνται
ψυχὰς παρθέμενοι, κακὸν ἀλλοδαποῖσι φέροντες; ”
ὣς ἔφαθ’, ἡμῖν δ’ αὖτε κατεκλάσθη φίλον ἦτορ,
δεισάντων φθόγγον τε βαρὺν αὐτόν τε πέλωρον.
ἀλλὰ καὶ ὥς μιν ἔπεσσιν ἀμειβόμενος προσέειπον·
“ ἡμεῖς τοι Τροίηθεν ἀποπλαγχθέντες Ἀχαιοὶ
παντοίοισ’ ἀνέμοισιν ὑπὲρ μέγα λαῖτμα θαλάσσης,
οἴκαδε ἱέμενοι, ἄλλην ὁδὸν ἄλλα κέλευθα
ἤλθομεν· οὕτω που Ζεὺς ἤθελε μητίσασθαι.

---

252 **πόθεν**—from what place.
πλέω—sail, sail over; **πλεῖθ’** = **πλεῖτε** – present active, 2nd pers. plur.
ὑγρός,-ή,-όν—liquid, watery.
κέλευθα,-ων, τά—ways, paths; **ὑγρὰ κέλευθα** – watery ways, *i.e.*, the sea.

253 **τι**—“in any way.”
πρῆξις,-ιος, ἡ—business; **κατὰ πρῆξιν** – “on business,” “on a trading voyage;” **ἤ τι κατὰ πρῆχιν** – “[are you] on some trading voyage?”
μαψιδίως—at random, without a determined course.
ἀλάομαι—wander, rove; **ἀλάλησθε** – perfect, 2nd pers. plur.; translate as present.

254 **οἷα**—just like, just as.
ληϊστήρ,-ῆρος, ὁ—pirate.
ὑπείρ = **ὑπέρ**.
τοί = **οἱ**—who.
ἀλόωνται—present, 3rd pers. plur. of **ἀλάομαι**.

255 **παρθέμενοι**—aorist middle participle, nom. plur. masc. of **παρατίθημι**; **ψυχὰς παρθέμενοι** – “risking their lives.”

ἀλλοδαπός,-ή,-όν—foreign, belonging to another land; **ἀλλοδαποῖσι** – "to people of other lands."

The Cyclops' questions, to a modern reader, seem quite natural. Asking your guests if they are pirates may sound insulting, but in the world of the *Odyssey*, being a pirate was, if not always completely respectable, not as disgraceful and disreputable as we would judge it today. However, the Cyclops asked the questions before his guests had been welcomed and fed. By the standards of Homer's world, he displayed extremely bad manners and betrayed his ignorance of the laws of hospitality. (Odysseus had not adhered strictly to the laws of hospitality himself, since he and his men entered the Cyclops' cave without invitation and took food, something for which he makes no apology in his reply. Even so, the Cyclops' subsequent actions seem extreme.)

256 **ἔφαθ' = ἔφατο**—imperfect middle with active meaning of **φημί**.

ἡμῖν—DATIVE OF INTEREST expressing possession.

κατακλάω, (aor.) **κατέκλασα**, (aor. pass.) **κατεκλάσθην**—break.

φίλον—"own."

257 ~ **δείδω, δείσομαι, ἔδεισα**—fear, be afraid; **δεισάντων** – aorist active participle, gen. plur. masc. Understand **ἡμῶν**, the genitive implied by **ἡμῖν** in the preceding line, to form a genitive absolute.

φθόγγος,-ου, ὁ—voice.

βαρύς,-εῖα,-ύ—heavy, grievous; *referring to a voice*, deep.

πέλωρον, τό (only nom. and acc. forms)—monster.

258 **καὶ ὧς**—even so, nevertheless, for all that.

ἔπεσσιν—dat. plur. of **ἔπος**.

259 **Τροίηθεν**—from Troy (the suffix **-θεν** adds the meaning "from").

ἀπεπλάγχθην (aor. pass.)—be driven off course; **ἀποπλαγχθέντες** – aorist passive participle.

260 **παντοῖος,-η,-ον**—of all sorts, of every kind; *with reference to winds*, all, blowing from all directions. What kind of dative is **παντοίοισ' ἀνέμοισιν**?

λαῖτμα,-ατος, τό—gulf, abyss.

261 **ἱέμενοι**—"being eager [to go]", "hastening."

ἄλλην ὁδόν, ἄλλα κέλευθα—"another way, other paths," *i.e.*, other ways or paths than those leading home.

262 **που**—"I suppose."

μητίομαι, μητίσομαι, ἐμητισάμην—devise, plan, bring about.

Scanning Notes

253 The last syllable of **πρῆξιν** is scanned long. A final syllable containing a short vowel can be scanned long if it ends with **ν, ρ,** or **ς**.

255 The **υ** in **ψυχάς** is long.

257 The last syllable of **βαρύν** is scanned long. A final syllable containing a short vowel can be scanned long if it ends with **ν, ρ,** or **ς**.

261 The first **ι** in **ἱέμενοι** is long.

262 The first **ι** in **μητίσασθαι** is long.

λαοὶ δ' Ἀτρεΐδεω Ἀγαμέμνονος εὐχόμεθ' εἶναι,
τοῦ δὴ νῦν γε μέγιστον ὑπουράνιον κλέος ἐστί·
τόσσην γὰρ διέπερσε πόλιν καὶ ἀπώλεσε λαοὺς
πολλούς· ἡμεῖς δ' αὖτε κιχανόμενοι τὰ σὰ γοῦνα
ἱκόμεθ', εἴ τι πόροις ξεινήϊον ἠὲ καὶ ἄλλως
δοίης δωτίνην, ἥ τε ξείνων θέμις ἐστίν.
ἀλλ' αἰδεῖο, φέριστε, θεούς· ἱκέται δέ τοί εἰμεν.
Ζεὺς δ' ἐπιτιμήτωρ ἱκετάων τε ξείνων τε,
ξείνιος, ὃς ξείνοισιν ἅμ' αἰδοίοισιν ὀπηδεῖ."

*The Cyclops with his pitiless heart (**νηλεὴς θυμός**) calls Odysseus a fool (**νήπιος**) and informs him that Cyclopes care nothing for Zeus or the **θεοὶ μάκαρες**. He then asks him where his well-made (**εὐεργής**) **νηῦς** is moored.*

ὣς ἐφάμην, ὁ δέ μ' αὐτίκ' ἀμείβετο νηλέϊ θυμῷ·
"νήπιός εἰς, ὦ ξεῖν', ἢ τηλόθεν εἰλήλουθας,
ὅς με θεοὺς κέλεαι ἢ δειδίμεν ἢ ἀλέασθαι.

---

263 **εὐχόμεθ' εἶναι**—"we declare ourselves to be."

264 **τοῦ**—"whose."
ὑπουράνιος,-ον—under heaven (**ὑπό** + **οὐρανός**), "far and wide," "on earth."
κλέος, τό (only found in nom. and acc. forms)—fame, glory.

265 **τόσσος,-η,-ον**—so great, of such magnitude.
διαπέρθω, (aor.) **διέπερσα**—sack, lay waste, destroy utterly.
ἀπώλεσε—aorist of **ἀπόλλυμι** – destroy, kill.

266 **κιχάνομαι**—arrive at, come to, find oneself at; **κιχανόμενοι** – "finding ourselves [here]."

267 **ἱκόμεθ' = ἱκόμεθα**—aorist of **ἱκνέομαι**.
εἰ—[to see] if, in the hope that (+ optative).
~ **πόρω**, (aor.) **ἔπορον**—give; **πόροις** – aorist active optative, 2nd pers. sing.
ξεινήϊον,-ου, τό—guest gift, *i.e.*, a gift given by a host to a guest. (In Homeric society, the proper reception of a guest includes offering him gifts, as well as feeding and entertaining him, all *before* asking his identity.)
ἄλλως—"in another way."

268 **δοίης**—aorist active optative, 2nd pers. sing. of **δίδωμι**.
δωτίνη,-ης, ἡ—gift, present.

ἥ—"which" (refers to both **ξεινήϊον** and **δωτίνην**, but is feminine because it has been attracted into the gender of **θέμις**).

θέμις,-ιστος, ἡ—customary right, what is due according to custom.

ἥ τε ξείνων θέμις ἐστίν—"which it is customary [to give to] strangers [as a gesture of friendship]" (*literally*, which is the right of strangers).

269 **αἰδέομαι**—honor, respect; **αἰδεῖο** – present imperative, 2nd pers. sing.

φέριστος,-η,-ον—best, noblest; *used in the vocative as a form of address:* "noblest sir."

ἱκέτης,-ου, ὁ—suppliant.

δέ—"for."

270 **Ζεὺς δ' [ἔστιν]**.

ἐπιτιμήτωρ,-ορος, ὁ—protector, avenger.

271 **ξείνιος,-α,-ον**—protective of guests and strangers; **Ζεὺς ξείνιος** is Zeus, protector of guests and strangers.

ὅς—"the one who."

αἰδοῖος,-η,-ον—worthy of respect.

ὀπηδέω—follow, accompany, act as a protector (+ dat.); **ἅμ'...ὀπηδεῖ** – is with as a protector.

272 **ἐφάμην**—imperfect middle with active meaning, 1st pers. sing. of **φημί**.

ἀμείβετο = ἠμείβετο.

~ **νηλεής,-ές**—pitiless.

273 **νήπιος,-η,-ον**—foolish; **νήπιος** – "a fool."

εἶς—present, 2nd pers. sing. of **εἰμί**.

ξεῖν' = ξεῖνε.

τηλόθεν—from far away.

εἰλήλουθας—perfect active, 2nd pers. sing. of **ἔρχομαι**.

274 **ὅς**—"[you] who," "since you."

κέλεαι—present, 2nd pers. sing. of **κέλομαι**.

δειδίμεν—perfect active infinitive of **δείδω**.

ἀλέομαι, (aor.) **ἠλευάμην**—avoid; **ἀλέασθαι = ἀλεύασθαι**.

Scanning Notes

263 The **α** in **λαοί** is long.

-δεω in **Ἀτρεΐδεω** is scanned as one long syllable. This is an example of synizesis (two vowels run together and pronounced as one long syllable).

265 The **α** in **λαούς** is long.

266 The **α** in **κιχανόμενοι** is long.

267 The **ι** in **ἱκόμεθ'** is long.

268 The **ι** in **δωτίνην** is long.

270 The second **ι** in **ἐπιτιμήτωρ** is long.

The **α** in **ἱκετάων** is long.

272 The **υ** in **θυμῷ** is long.

οὐ γὰρ Κύκλωπες Διὸς αἰγιόχου ἀλέγουσιν 275
οὐδὲ θεῶν μακάρων, ἐπεὶ ἦ πολὺ φέρτεροί εἰμεν· 276
οὐδ' ἂν ἐγὼ Διὸς ἔχθος ἀλευάμενος πεφιδοίμην 277
οὔτε σεῦ οὔθ' ἑτάρων, εἰ μὴ θυμός με κελεύοι. 278
ἀλλά μοι εἴφ', ὅπῃ ἔσχες ἰὼν εὐεργέα νῆα, 279
ἤ που ἐπ' ἐσχατιῆς ἦ καὶ σχεδόν, ὄφρα δαείω." 280

*Odysseus tells the Cyclops that Poseidon destroyed his **νηῦς**. He and these men, he says, escaped **αἰπὺς ὄλεθρος**.*

ὣς φάτο πειράζων, ἐμὲ δ' οὐ λάθεν εἰδότα πολλά, 281
ἀλλά μιν ἄψορρον προσέφην δολίοισ' ἐπέεσσι· 282
"νέα μέν μοι κατέαξε Ποσειδάων ἐνοσίχθων, 283
πρὸς πέτρῃσι βαλὼν ὑμῆς ἐπὶ πείρασι γαίης, 284
ἄκρῃ προσπελάσας· ἄνεμος δ' ἐκ πόντου ἔνεικεν· 285
αὐτὰρ ἐγὼ σὺν τοῖσδε ὑπέκφυγον αἰπὺν ὄλεθρον." 286

---

275 **αἰγίοχος,-η,-ον**—aegis-holding, aegis-bearing.
ἀλέγω—care for, be concerned about (+ gen.).

276 ~ **πολύ**—by far, much.
φέρτερος,-η,-ον—stronger, more powerful.
εἰμέν—present, 1st pers. plur. of **εἰμί**.

277 **ἔχθος,-εος, τό**—disfavor, enmity.
ἀλευάμενος—"in order to avoid," "to avoid;" aorist participle of **ἀλέομαι**.
φείδομαι, φείσομαι, πεφιδόμην—spare, refrain from harming, have mercy upon (+ gen.).

278 **σεῦ**—gen. sing. of **σύ**.
εἰ μή—unless.
~ **κελεύω, κελεύσω, ἐκέλευσα**—urge, order, command; **οὐδ'...πεφιδοίμην..., εἰ μὴ θυμός...κελεύοι** – future less vivid condition: "I would not spare…unless my heart should command…." Not exactly a statement to cheer up Odysseus and his men. What adjective was used to describe the **θυμός** of the Cyclops in 9.272?

279 **εἴφ' = εἰπέ**—imperative of **εἶπον**.
ὅπῃ—where.
ἔσχες—"you anchored;" aorist of **ἔχω**:

ἰών—"when you arrived."

~ **εὐεργής,-ές**—well-made.

280 **ἐσχατιή,-ῆς, ἡ**—the most remote part, the farthest part; **ἐπ' ἐσχατιῆς** – on the farthest part [of the island].

ἢ καί—or.

σχεδόν—nearby.

δάω, (aor.) **ἐδάην**—know; **δαείω** – aorist subjunctive.

281 **πειράζω**—test, try; **πειράζων** – "trying [to get information from me]."

λάθεν = ἔλαθεν—aorist of **λανθάνω**; **ἐμὲ δ' οὐ λάθεν** – "but he did not fool me" or "I saw what he was after" (*literally*, but [what he was after] did not escape me).

εἰδότα—"knowing;" perfect active participle, acc. sing. masc. of **οἶδα**; translate as present; modifies **ἐμέ**; **εἰδότα πολλά** – "knowing too much [for him]."

282 **ἄψορρον**—in reply.

δόλιος,-η,-ον—wily, crafty, cunning.

ἐπέεσσι—dat. plur. of **ἔπος**.

283 **νέα**—acc. sing. of **νηῦς**.

μοι—DATIVE OF INTEREST showing possession.

κατάγνυμι, κατάξω, κατέαξα—break in pieces, shatter, wreck.

284 **πέτρῃσι**—dat. plur. of **πέτρη**.

ὑμός,-ή,-όν—your.

πεῖραρ,-ατος, τό—boundary, border; **πείρασι** – dat. plur.

285 **ἄκρη,-ης, ἡ**—cape.

προσπελάζω, προσπελάσω—drive against, dash upon (+ dat.); **προσπελάσας** (aorist active participle) modifies **Ποσειδάων**.

ἔνεικεν = ἤνεικεν—aorist of **φέρω**; understand **νέα** as its object.

286 **τοῖσδε**—"these men here."

ὑπεκφεύγω, (aor.) **ὑπέκφυγον**—escape, avoid.

Scanning Notes

278 The **υ** in **θυμός** is long.

283 **νέα** is scanned as one long syllable (synizesis).

The **α** in **Ποσειδάων** is long.

284 The **υ** in **ὑμῆς** is long.

285 The last **α** in **προσπελάσας** is long.

The Cyclops seizes ***δύω*** *of the* ***ἑταῖροι****, kills them and eats them for his evening meal (****δόρπον****). Seeing his cruel (****σχέτλια****)* ***ἔργα****, the wailing (****κλαίοντες****) men raise their* ***χεῖρες*** *to Zeus. When the Cyclops had eaten his fill of human flesh (****κρέας****), he lay down among his* ***μῆλα****.*

ὣς ἐφάμην, ὁ δέ μ' οὐδὲν ἀμείβετο νηλέϊ θυμῷ,
ἀλλ' ὅ γ' ἀναΐξας ἑτάροισ' ἐπὶ χεῖρας ἴαλλε,
σὺν δὲ δύω μάρψας ὥς τε σκύλακας ποτὶ γαίῃ
κόπτ'· ἐκ δ' ἐγκέφαλος χαμάδις ῥέε, δεῦε δὲ γαῖαν.
τοὺς δὲ διὰ μελεϊστὶ ταμὼν ὁπλίσσατο δόρπον·
ἤσθιε δ' ὥς τε λέων ὀρεσίτροφος, οὐδ' ἀπέλειπεν,
ἔγκατά τε σάρκας τε καὶ ὀστέα μυελόεντα.
ἡμεῖς δὲ κλαίοντες ἀνεσχέθομεν Διὶ χεῖρας,
σχέτλια ἔργ' ὁρόωντες· ἀμηχανίη δ' ἔχε θυμόν.

---

287 Compare this line with 9.272. What differences are there?

288 **ἀναΐσσω, ἀναΐξω, ἀνήιξα**—jump up, rise suddenly.

ἐπιάλλω—put upon; **ἐπὶ...ἴαλλε** – TMESIS; **ἑτάροισ' ἐπὶ χεῖρας ἴαλλε** – "he put his hands upon [my] comrades."

289 **σύν**—"together."

δύω = δύο—two.

μάρπτω, μάρψω, ἔμαρψα—seize, lay hold of, grab.

ὥς τε—like, just like.

σκύλαξ, σκύλακος, ἡ—puppy. (Comparing the men to puppies stresses their helplessness.)

ποτί—upon, against, to (+ dat.).

γαίῃ—"the ground."

290 **κόπτω, κόψω, ἔκοψα**—smash, strike hard; **κόπτ' = κόπτε.**

ἐκ—"out."

ἐγκέφαλος,-ου, ὁ—brains.

χαμάδις—onto the ground.

ῥέω, ῥεύσομαι, ἔρρευσα—flow, run.

δεύω, δεύσω, ἔδευσα—wet, soak.

291 **διατάμνω**, (aor.) **διέταμον**—cut, cut up; **διὰ...ταμών** – TMESIS.

μελεϊστι—limb from limb.

ὁπλίζω, ὁπλίσω, ὥπλισσα—prepare, get ready; *middle*, prepare [something] for oneself; **ὁπλίσσατο = ὡπλίσσατο**.

δόρπον,-ου, τό—evening meal.

292 **ἐσθίω**—eat, devour.

ὀρεσίτροφος,-ον—mountain-bred, reared in the mountains.

ἀπολείπω, ἀπολείψω, ἀπέλιπον—leave [anything] behind, leave [anything uneaten].

293 **ἔγκατα,-ων, τά**—entrails.

σάρξ, σαρκός, ἡ—*singular or plural*, flesh.

ὀστέον,-ου, τό—bone.

μυελόεις,-εσσα,-εν—full of marrow, marrowy.

294 ~ **κλαίω**—weep, wail.

ἀνέχω, ἀνασχήσω, ἀνέσχον or **ἀνέσχεθον**—lift up, hold up.

Διί—dative of **Ζεύς**.

295 **σχέτλιος,-η,-ον**—cruel, hard-hearted.

ἔργον,-ου, τό—deed; **ἔργ' = ἔργα**.

ὁρόωντες—present active participle of **ὁράω**.

ἀμηχανίη,-ης, ἡ—helplessness.

ἔχε = εἶχε—imperfect of **ἔχω**.

Scanning Notes

287 The **υ** in **θυμῷ** is long.

288 The second and third **α** in **ἀναΐξας** are long.

289 The second **α** in **μάρψας** is long.

293 The first **τε** is scanned long. A short final syllable that ends in a vowel and is followed by a word beginning with **σ** can be scanned long.

The **υ** in **μυελόεντα** is long.

295 The **υ** in **θυμόν** is long.

αὐτὰρ ἐπεὶ Κύκλωψ μεγάλην ἐμπλήσατο νηδὺν
ἀνδρόμεα κρέ᾽ ἔδων καὶ ἐπ᾽ ἄκρητον γάλα πίνων,
κεῖτ᾽ ἔντοσθ᾽ ἄντροιο τανυσσάμενος διὰ μήλων.

*Odysseus wants to kill the sleeping Cyclops with his sharp sword (**ξίφος ὀξύ**), but realizes they would then be trapped in the **σπέος** because they cannot move the stone (**λίθος**) blocking the entrance (**θύραι**).*

τὸν μὲν ἐγὼ βούλευσα κατὰ μεγαλήτορα θυμὸν
ἆσσον ἰών, ξίφος ὀξὺ ἐρυσσάμενος παρὰ μηροῦ,
οὐτάμεναι πρὸς στῆθος, ὅθι φρένες ἧπαρ ἔχουσι,
χείρ᾽ ἐπιμασσάμενος· ἕτερος δέ με θυμὸς ἔρυκεν.
αὐτοῦ γάρ κε καὶ ἄμμες ἀπωλόμεθ᾽ αἰπὺν ὄλεθρον·

---

296 **ἐμπίπλημι**—fill; **ἐμπλήσατο** – aorist middle.

νηδύς,-ύος, ἡ—belly.

297 **ἀνδρόμεος,-ον**—human, man's.

κρέας, κρέως, τό—flesh, meat; *plural can have collective meaning*, flesh; **κρέ᾽** = **κρέα** – acc. plur.

~ **ἔδω**—eat (up), devour, consume.

ἐπιπίνω—drink after, drink afterwards; **ἐπ᾽...πίνων** – TMESIS.

ἄκρητος,-ον—unmixed, undiluted (Describing milk this way may be something of a joke. The adjective is normally applied to wine, which was almost always mixed with water before it was drunk. It may foreshadow the **ἄκρητος οἶνος** Odysseus gives the Cyclops later (9.347ff). Or perhaps portraying him as a milk drinker who is unused to wine sets him up to be more susceptible to the effects of that wine.)

γάλα, γάλακτος, τό—milk.

298 **κεῖτ᾽** = **ἐκεῖτο**—imperfect of **κεῖμαι**.

ἔντοσθ᾽ = **ἔντοσθε**—within, inside (+ gen.).

ἄντρον,-ου, τό = **σπέος**.

τανύω, τανύω, ἐτάνυσσα—stretch; **τανυσσάμενος** – aorist middle participle: "stretching himself out."

299 **τόν**—him, *i.e.*, the Cyclops.

βούλευσα = **ἐβούλευσα**—"I considered," "I debated whether to" (+ infinitive).

300 ἆσσον—near.

~ ξίφος,-εος, τό—sword.

~ ὀξύς,-εῖα,-ύ—sharp.

~ ἐρύω, (aor.) εἴρυσ(σ)α—pull; *middle,* draw [a sword].

παρά—"from beside."

μηρός,-οῦ, ὁ—thigh; **παρὰ μηροῦ**, *i.e.*, from the sheath that hung beside his thigh. If he was right-handed, his sword would have been in a sheath on his left side, hanging from a strap that passed over his right shoulder.

301 **οὐτάω,** (aor.) **οὔτησα**—stab, wound; **οὐτάμεναι** – aorist active infinitive with **βούλευσα** in 9.299: "I considered stabbing."

πρὸς στῆθος—"in the chest."

ὅθι—where, in the place where.

φρένες—This word usually refers to the mind, heart, or intelligence, but here has its literal meaning: midriff, diaphragm.

ἧπαρ,-ατος, τό—the liver.

302 **χείρ' = χειρί**—DATIVE OF MEANS.

ἐπιμαίομαι, (aor.) **ἐπεμασσάμην**—feel, touch; **ἐπιμασσάμενος** – "feeling [for the place **ὅθι φρένες ἧπαρ ἔχουσι**]."

ἕτερος...θυμός—"another thought or consideration," "second thoughts."

ἐρύκω—restrain, hold back.

303 **αὐτοῦ**—there.

ἄμμες = ἡμεῖς.

ἀπωλόμεθ' = ἀπωλόμεθα—aorist middle, 1st pers. plur. of **ἀπόλλυμι.**

ὄλεθρον—cognate accusative, *i.e.*, an accusative containing the same idea as the verb.

This line is the apodosis of a past contrary to fact condition with an understood protasis: "[If I had killed the Cyclops,] we also would have died a wretched death there."

Scanning Notes

297 The **ι** in **πίνων** is long.

299 The **υ** in **θυμόν** is long.

302 The last syllable of **ἐπιμασσάμενος** is scanned long. If there is a short vowel in the final syllable of a word and the consonant that follows it is **ν, ρ,** or **ς**, it may be scanned long.

The **υ** in **θυμός** is long.

The **υ** in **ἔρυκεν** is long.

οὐ γάρ κεν δυνάμεσθα θυράων ὑψηλάων
χερσὶν ἀπώσασθαι λίθον ὄβριμον, ὃν προσέθηκεν.
ὣς τότε μὲν στενάχοντες ἐμείναμεν Ἠῶ δῖαν.

---

304 **δυνάμεσθα**—imperfect.

οὐ γάρ κεν δυνάμεσθα—This is the apodosis of a present contrary to fact condition with an understood protasis: [if the Cyclops were dead,] we would not be able.

~ **θύρη,-ης, ἡ**—door (of a room); *plural*, door (of a house), entrance.

ὑψηλός,-ή,-όν—high, tall, lofty.

305 **χερσί(ν)**—dat. plur. of **χείρ**.

ἀπωθέω, ἀπώσω, ἀπέωσα—push [something – acc.] away from [something – gen.]; **ἀπώσασθαι** – aorist middle infinitive, translate as active.

λίθος,-ου, ὁ—a stone.

ὄβριμος,-ον—heavy.

προστίθημι, (aor.) **προσέθηκα**—put [in a certain place], put in position, put in place; the Cyclops is the subject of **προσέθηκεν**.

306 ~ **στενάχω**—groan, moan.

μένω, μενέω, ἔμεινα—await, wait for.

Ἠῶ—acc. of **Ἠώς**.

Scanning Notes

304 The **α** in **θυράων** is long.

The **α** in **ὑψηλάων** is long.

Odyssey Book 9.347-370

The next morning the Cyclops ate two of Odysseus' men for breakfast, then drove his flock out of the cave, covering the entrance with the huge rock as he left. In the evening when he returned, he ate two more of the men for dinner.

Book 9.347-370

Odysseus offers the Cyclops some ***οἶνος****. He drinks it all, then asks Odysseus to give him more and tell him his* ***ὄνομα****, so he might give Odysseus a guest gift (****ξείνιον****).*

“ Κύκλωψ, τῆ, πίε οἶνον, ἐπεὶ φάγες ἀνδρόμεα κρέα,
ὄφρ’ εἰδῇς, οἷόν τι ποτὸν τόδε νηῦς ἐκεκεύθει
ἡμετέρη· σοὶ δ’ αὖ λοιβὴν φέρον, εἴ μ’ ἐλεήσας
οἴκαδε πέμψειας· σὺ δὲ μαίνεαι οὐκέτ’ ἀνεκτῶς.
σχέτλιε, πῶς κέν τίς σε καὶ ὕστερον ἄλλος ἵκοιτο
ἀνθρώπων πολέων; ἐπεὶ οὐ κατὰ μοῖραν ἔρεξας. ”
ὣς ἐφάμην, ὁ δὲ δέκτο καὶ ἔκπιεν· ἥσατο δ’ αἰνῶς
ἡδὺ ποτὸν πίνων καί μ’ ᾔτεε δεύτερον αὖτις·

---

347 **τῆ**—come!, here!

~ **πίνω, πίομαι, ἔπιον**—drink; **πίε** – aorist imperative.

φάγον (aor.)—eat, devour.

348 **εἰδῇς**—aorist subjunctive of **ὁράω**; **ὄφρ’ εἰδῇς** – PURPOSE CLAUSE.

ποτόν,-οῦ, τό—drink; **οἷόν τι ποτὸν τόδε** – “what kind of drink this [was that].”

κεύθω, κεύσω, ἔκευσα, κέκευθα—contain; **ἐκεκεύθει** – pluperfect, 3rd pers. sing.

349 **αὖ**—now.

λοιβή,-ῆς, ἡ—libation (an offering of wine to a god or gods); Odysseus is flattering the Cyclops by claiming he is bringing him a libation as one would to a deity.

φέρον = ἔφερον.

εἰ—in the hope that (+ opt.).

ἐλεέω, (aor.) **ἠλέησα**—pity, take pity on; **ἐλεήσας** – aorist active participle, nom. sing. masc.; agrees with “you,” the subject of **πέμψειας** in the next line.

350 **πέμψειας**—aorist optative, 2nd pers. sing.

μαίνομαι—rage, act like a madman; **μαίνεαι = μαίνῃ** – present, 2nd pers. sing.

ἀνεκτῶς—endurably, bearably; **οὐκέτ’ ἀνεκτῶς** – “unbearably.”

351 σχέτλιος,-η,-ον—cruel, hard-hearted.

τίς—translate with ἄλλος.

καί—"again."

ὕστερον—in the future.

ἵκοιτο—"visit;" aorist optative of ἱκνέομαι; POTENTIAL OPTATIVE.

352 πολέων = πολῶν; ἀνθρώπων πολέων – "of the many men [there are in the world].

κατὰ μοῖραν—properly, rightly.

ἔρεξας—aorist active, 2nd pers. sing. of ῥέζω – do, act.

353 ἐφάμην—imperfect middle with active meaning, 1st pers. sing. of φημί.

δέκτο = ἔδεκτο = ἐδέξατο—aorist of δέχομαι. (Forms lacking thematic vowels [connecting vowels between the verb stem and the endings] are more frequent in Homer than in later Greek.)

~ ἐκπίνω, (aor.) ἔκπιον—drink all.

ἥδομαι, (aor.) ἡσάμην—be pleased.

αἰνῶς—exceedingly.

354 ἡδύς, ἡδεῖα, ἡδύ—sweet, pleasant.

πίνων—modifies "he," the subject of ἥσατο in the preceding line.

αἰτέω, αἰτήσω, ᾔτησα—ask for, request; ᾔτεε – imperfect.

δεύτερον—again, a second time.

~ αὖτις—once more, again.

Scanning Notes

347 κρέα is scanned as one long syllable (synizesis).

354 The ι in πίνων is long.

“ δός μοι ἔτι πρόφρων καί μοι τεὸν οὔνομα εἰπὲ
αὐτίκα νῦν, ἵνα τοι δῶ ξείνιον, ᾧ κε σὺ χαίρῃς.
καὶ γὰρ Κυκλώπεσσι φέρει ζείδωρος ἄρουρα
οἶνον ἐριστάφυλον, καί σφιν Διὸς ὄμβρος ἀέξει·
ἀλλὰ τόδ’ ἀμβροσίης καὶ νέκταρός ἐστιν ἀπορρώξ. ”

*After giving him more **οἶνος**, Odysseus tells the Cyclops that his **ὄνομα** is **Οὖτις**. The Cyclops answers **αὐτίκα** and reveals what Odysseus’ **ξείνιον** will be.*

ὣς ἔφατ’· αὐτάρ οἱ αὖτις ἐγὼ πόρον αἴθοπα οἶνον·
τρὶς μὲν ἔδωκα φέρων, τρὶς δ’ ἔκπιεν ἀφραδίῃσιν.
αὐτὰρ ἐπεὶ Κύκλωπα περὶ φρένας ἤλυθεν οἶνος
καὶ τότε δή μιν ἔπεσσι προσηύδων μειλιχίοισι·
“ Κύκλωψ, εἰρωτᾷς μ’ ὄνομα κλυτόν; αὐτὰρ ἐγώ τοι
ἐξερέω· σὺ δέ μοι δὸς ξείνιον, ὥς περ ὑπέστης.

---

355 **δός**—aorist imperative of **δίδωμι**.
ἔτι—again.
πρόφρων—willingly.
~ **τεός,-ή,-όν**—your.
οὔνομα = ὄνομα

356 **δῶ**—aorist subjunctive of **δίδωμι**, 1st pers. sing.
~ **ξείνιον,-ου, τό**—guest gift, gift given by a host to a guest.
ᾧ—relative pronoun referring to the **ξείνιον**.
χαίρω—take pleasure in (+ dat.); **χαίρῃς**—present subjunctive, 2nd pers. sing.
ᾧ κε σὺ χαίρῃς—relative clause of purpose (a relative clause with **κε(ν)** and a subjunctive verb to express purpose).

357 **ζείδωρος,-ον**—grain-giving, fruitful.
ἄρουρα,-ης, ἡ—earth, soil.

358 **ἐριστάφυλος,-ον**—made from fine grapes.
σφιν—“for them,” *i.e.*, the Cyclopes.
ὄμβρος,-ου, ὁ—rain.
ἀέξω—cause to grow; **ὄμβρος ἀέξει** – “the rain causes [the grapes] to grow.”

359 **τόδ' = τόδε [ποτόν].**

ἀμβροσίη,-ης, ἡ—ambrosia (the food of the gods).

νέκταρ,-αρος, τό—nectar (the drink of the gods).

ἀπορρώξ,-ῶγος, ὁ or **ἡ**—a sample, "as good as," "equal to."

360 **οἱ**—"to him."

πόρον = ἔπορον.

αἶθοψ,-οπος—sparkling, bright.

361 **ἀφραδίη,-ης, ἡ**—*singular or plural*, foolishness, folly; **ἀφραδίῃσιν** – "in his foolishness."

362 **περιέρχομαι**, (aor.) **περιῆλθον** or **περιήλυθον**—go around, come around, encompass; **περὶ...ἤλυθεν** – TMESIS.

φρένας—ACCUSATIVE OF RESPECT.

ἐπεὶ Κύκλωπα περὶ φρένας ἤλυθεν οἶνος—"when the wine had gone to the Cyclops' head."

363 **προσηύδων**—imperfect active, 1st pers. sing. of **προσαυδάω.**

364 **εἰρωτάω**—ask, inquire; *can be followed by double accusatives, the person asked and the thing asked about.*

~ **κλυτός,-όν**—famous, renowned.

365 **ἐξείρω, ἐξερέω**—tell.

ὑφίστημι, (aor.) **ὑπέστην**—promise.

Οὗτις ἐμοί γ' ὄνομα· Οὗτιν δέ με κικλήσκουσι 366
μήτηρ ἠδὲ πατὴρ ἠδ' ἄλλοι πάντες ἑταῖροι." 367
ὣς ἐφάμην, ὁ δέ μ' αὐτίκ' ἀμείβετο νηλέϊ θυμῷ· 368
"Οὗτιν ἐγὼ πύματον ἔδομαι μετὰ οἷσ' ἑτάροισι, 369
τοὺς δ' ἄλλους πρόσθεν· τὸ δέ τοι ξεινήϊον ἔσται." 370

366 **Οὗτις**, (acc.) **Οὗτιν**—Outis (The significance of Odysseus' choice of a false name will be revealed shortly. Odysseus intends **Οὗτις** to be mistaken for **οὔτις** ("nobody," "no man," or "no one"); it is usually translated into English as Nobody or Noman, neither of which sound too much like real English names. Perhaps Outis would not have sounded too convincing in Greek either, but the Cyclops was drunk.)

ἐμοί—DATIVE OF POSSESSION.

Οὗτις ἐμοί γ' ὄνομά [ἐστι].

κικλήσκω—call [by a name].

368 Compare this line with 9.272 and 9.287. What are the similarities and differences?

369 **πύματος,-η,-ον**—last.

ἔδομαι—future of **ἔδω**.

μετά—"among."

370 **τοὺς δ' ἄλλους**—also the object of **ἔδομαι** in 9.369.

πρόσθεν—before, *i.e.*, before Odysseus.

ξεινήϊον = ξείνιον.

ἔσται—future of **εἰμί**.

Scanning Notes

366 The final syllable (**-μα**) in **ὄνομα** is scanned long, even though its vowel is short. Occasionally, a final syllable ending in a short vowel is arbitrarily scanned long simply because it occupies a position in the line that requires a long syllable.

368 The **υ** in **θυμῷ** is long.

369 The last syllable of **πύματον** is scanned long. A final syllable containing a short vowel can be scanned long if it ends with **ν**, **ρ**, or **ς**.

Odyssey Book 9.395-414

After revealing his "gift" to Odysseus, the Cyclops fell over and lay on his back in a drunken sleep. Odysseus and his men got the large wooden stake they had sharpened during the day while he was out of the cave. They put it into the ashes of the fire until it was very hot, then thrust it into the Cyclops' eye.

Book 9.395-414

*The Cyclops screams and pulls the stake (**μοχλός**), stained with blood (**αἷμα**), from his **ὀφθαλμός**. He calls outs loudly (**μεγάλα**) to the Cyclopes who live **ἐν σπήεσσι** nearby.*

σμερδαλέον δὲ μέγ’ ᾤμωξεν, περὶ δ’ ἴαχε πέτρη,
ἡμεῖς δὲ δείσαντες ἀπεσσύμεθ’. αὐτὰρ ὁ μοχλὸν
ἐξέρυσ’ ὀφθαλμοῖο πεφυρμένον αἵματι πολλῷ.
τὸν μὲν ἔπειτ’ ἔρριψεν ἀπὸ ἕο χερσὶν ἀλύων,

---

395 **σμερδαλέον**—terribly.

μέγα—in a loud voice, loudly.

οἰμώζω, οἰμώξομαι, ᾤμωξα—scream, cry out in pain.

περί—around.

ἰάχω—echo, resound.

πέτρη—refers to the rock walls of the cave.

396 **δείσαντες**—from **δείδω**.

ἀποσεύομαι, (aor.) **ἀπεσσύμην**—rush away, dart away.

μοχλός,-οῦ, ὁ—stake.

397 **ἐξερύω**, (aor.) **ἐξέρυσα**—pull [something, acc.] out of [something, gen.]; **ἐξέρυσ’ = ἐξέρυσε**.

φύρω—stain, wet; **πεφυρμένον** – perfect passive participle describing **μοχλόν**.

αἷμα,-ατος, τό—blood.

Odysseus’ plan to blind Polyphemus by driving a stake into his eye would not have worked unless the Cyclops had only one eye. It has been noted that Homer, though describing Cyclopes and their society earlier in Book 9 (9.106-115), never says they are one-eyed; he simply assumes throughout this entire episode that Polyphemus is.

There has been much discussion about Homer’s silence on this point. Some speculate that he did not have to mention it as everyone in his audience knew they only had one eye. Another theory suggests that Cyclopes, traditionally large and powerful, were not traditionally one-eyed. Homer, basing this episode on a folktale about a one-eyed giant, simply made the Cyclops one-eyed for the sake of the story.

An interesting modern theory about the origin of stories about one-eyed cave-dwelling giants concerns fossil bones of Pleistocene dwarf elephants found in Greek and Italian coastal caves. The elephant skulls, much larger than men's, have large central nasal cavities, which could have been mistaken for a single central eye socket. The vertebrae and limb bones would have suggested gigantic size. Someone who found such fossils might easily imagine huge, one-eyed giants.

398 **τόν**—"it;" refers to the **μοχλόν**.

ἔρριψεν—aorist of **ῥίπτω**.

ἕο = αὐτοῦ.

χερσίν—DATIVE OF MEANS.

ἀλύω—be frantic with pain, be beside oneself with pain.

Fig. 4. Henri Matisse. (French, 1869–1954). *The Cyclops* from the series *Ulysses*, 1935. Soft ground etching. 92.79.3. Museum of Art and Archaeology, University of Missouri. Gift of Museum Associates.

Scanning Notes

395 The **ι** in **ἴαχε** is long.

396 **δέ** is scanned long because **δείσαντες** was originally spelled **δϝείσαντες**.

398 The final syllable (**-πο**) in **ἀπό** is scanned long, even though its vowel is short. Occasionally, a final syllable ending in a short vowel is arbitrarily scanned long simply because it occupies a position in the line that requires a long syllable.

The **υ** in **ἀλύων** is long.

αὐτὰρ ὁ Κύκλωπας μεγάλ’ ἤπυεν, οἵ ῥά μιν ἀμφὶς
ᾤκεον ἐν σπήεσσι δι’ ἄκριας ἠνεμοέσσας.

*From outside the **σπέος**, his neighbors ask why he is shouting. When he replies that **Οὖτις** is killing him, they tell him that it must be a sickness (**νοῦσος**) sent by Zeus that afflicts him and recommend that he pray to his **πατήρ**.*

οἱ δὲ βοῆς ἀΐοντες ἐφοίτων ἄλλοθεν ἄλλος,
ἱστάμενοι δ’ εἴροντο περὶ σπέος, ὅττι ἑ κήδοι·
  “τίπτε τόσον, Πολύφημ’, ἀρημένος ὧδ’ ἐβόησας
νύκτα δι’ ἀμβροσίην καὶ ἀΰπνους ἄμμε τίθησθα;
ἦ μή τίς σευ μῆλα βροτῶν ἀέκοντος ἐλαύνει;
ἦ μή τίς σ’ αὐτὸν κτείνει δόλῳ ἠὲ βίηφι;”
  τοὺς δ’ αὖτ’ ἐξ ἄντρου προσέφη κρατερὸς Πολύφημος·
“ὦ φίλοι, Οὖτίς με κτείνει δόλῳ οὐδὲ βίηφιν.”

---

399 **μεγάλ’ = μεγάλα**—loudly.

ἠπύω—call to.

οἵ—relative pronoun referring to **Κύκλωπας**.

ἀμφίς—around, round about (+ acc.).

400 **οἰκέω**—live, dwell.

σπήεσσι—dat. plur. of **σπέος**.

δι’ = διά—“among.”

ἄκρις,-ιος, ἡ—hilltop, peak.

ἠνεμόεις,-εσσα,-εν—wind-blown, windy.

401 **βοή,-ῆς, ἡ**—shouting, crying out.

ἀΐω—hear (+ gen.)

φοιτάω—make one’s way, come; **ἐφοίτων** – imperfect, 3rd pers. plur.

ἄλλοθεν—from another place; **ἄλλοθεν ἄλλος** – some or one from one place, some or one from another place.

402 **ἱστάμενοι**—present middle participle, nom. plur. masc. of **ἵστημι**: “standing.”

εἴρομαι—ask.

περί—round, round about (+ acc.); **περὶ σπέος** goes with **ἱστάμενοι**. Why are the Cyclops’ neighbors standing outside his cave? Why don’t they go in?

ὅττι—what (neuter of **ὅς τις**; introduces the indirect question).

ἑ—"him" (acc. sing. of **εἷο**).

κήδω—trouble, cause pain to.

403 **τίπτε**—why?

Πολύφημος,-ου, ὁ—Polyphemus (this is the first time Homer uses the Cyclops' name); **Πολύφημ' = Πολύφημε**.

ἀρημένος,-η,-ον—hurt, harmed, distressed; **τόσον** with **ἀρημένος**: "distressed so greatly."

~ **βοάω, βοήσομαι, ἐβόησα**—cry aloud, shout, call out.

404 **δι' = διά**.

ἀμβρόσιος,-η,-ον—ambrosial. It is not clear what this word meant when describing night. Several suggestions have been made: "fragrant," "sweet-smelling," "divine," "holy," "immortal."

ἄϋπνος,-ον—sleepless, unable to sleep (**α-** [negative prefix] + **ὕπνος** [sleep]).

ἄμμε = ἡμᾶς.

τίθησθα—present, 2nd pers. sing. of **τίθημι**.

405 **ἦ μή τίς...βροτῶν**—surely no one.

ἀέκων,-ουσα—against one's will, being unwilling; **ἀέκοντος** is used as a participle here; **σευ...ἀέκοντος** – GENITIVE ABSOLUTE: "against your will," "with you unwilling."

ἐλαύνω—drive off.

406 **σ' αὐτόν**—you yourself.

κτείνει—"is trying to kill" (a CONATIVE present).

δόλος,-ου, ὁ—trickery, guile, trick.

βίηφι(ν)—by force.

407 **ἄντρον,-ου, τό = σπέος**.

~ **κρατερός,-ή,-όν**—strong, powerful, mighty.

408 When Polyphemus says **Οὖτις**, which he thinks is Odysseus' name, the other Cyclopes hear **οὔ τις** – "no one."

Scanning Notes

403 The **α** in **ἀρημένος** is long.

οἱ δ' ἀπαμειβόμενοι ἔπεα πτερόεντ' ἀγόρευον·
"εἰ μὲν δὴ μή τίς σε βιάζεται οἶον ἐόντα,
νοῦσόν γ' οὔ πως ἔστι Διὸς μεγάλου ἀλέασθαι,
ἀλλὰ σύ γ' εὔχεο πατρὶ Ποσειδάωνι ἄνακτι."
ὣς ἄρ' ἔφαν ἀπιόντες, ἐμὸν δ' ἐγέλασσε φίλον κῆρ,
ὡς ὄνομ' ἐξαπάτησεν ἐμὸν καὶ μῆτις ἀμύμων.

---

409 **πτερόεντ' = πτερόεντα.**

ἀγόρευον = ἠγόρευον.

410 **βιάζομαι**, (aor.) **ἐβιασάμην**—use violence against, overpower by force.

ἐόντα—present participle, masc. sing of **εἰμί**; **οἶον ἐόντα** describes **σε**.

411 **νοῦσος,-ου, ὁ**—disease, illness; **νοῦσον...Διὸς μεγάλου** – "an illness sent by great Zeus."

οὔ πως ἔστι—it is not possible.

ἀλέομαι, (aor.) **ἠλευάμην**—avoid, escape; **ἀλέασθαι = ἀλεύασθαι**.

The other Cyclopes assume that if no one is hurting him, his suffering must be due to illness.

412 **εὔχομαι**—pray; **εὔχεο** – present imperative.

~ **ἄναξ,-ακτος, ὁ**—lord.

413 **ἔφαν**—imperfect, 3rd pers. plur. of **φημί**.

ἀπιόντες—present active participle, nom. plur. masc. of **ἄπειμι (ἀπό + εἶμι)**.

γελάω, γελάσομαι, ἐγέλασ(σ)α—laugh, smile, rejoice.

414 **ὡς**—[seeing] how.

ὄνομ' = ὄνομα.

ἐξαπατάω, (aor.) **ἐξαπάτησα**—trick, deceive; **ἐξαπάτησεν** is singular to agree with **ὄνομα**, but **μῆτις ἀμύμων** is also the subject of this verb.

μῆτις,-ιος, ἡ—scheme, plan, cunning, shrewdness; **μῆτις** in this line may be a pun on **μή τις** (9. 410).

ἀμύμων,-ον—excellent.

Scanning Notes

412 The **α** in **Ποσειδάωνι** is long.

413 The last syllable of **ἔφαν** is scanned long. A final syllable containing a short vowel can be scanned long if it ends with **ν**, **ρ**, or **ς**.

414 The **υ** in **ἀμύμων** is long.

Odyssey Book 9.502-536

After hiding beneath the Cyclops' sheep to escape from the cave, Odysseus and his men hurried to their ship and set sail. From the ship, Odysseus shouted back to Polyphemus.

Book 9.502-536

Odysseus tells the Cyclops his real ***ὄνομα****.*

" Κύκλωψ, αἴ κέν τίς σε καταθνητῶν ἀνθρώπων 502
ὀφθαλμοῦ εἴρηται ἀεικελίην ἀλαωτύν, 503
φάσθαι Ὀδυσσῆα πτολιπόρθιον ἐξαλαῶσαι, 504
υἱὸν Λαέρτεω, Ἰθάκῃ ἔνι οἰκί' ἔχοντα. " 505

*The Cyclops reveals that a seer (**μάντις**) once told him a **φώς** named Odysseus would rob him of his sight. He urges Odysseus to return so he may give him **ξείνια** and ask Poseidon, his **κλυτὸς πατήρ**, to help Odysseus on his journey.*

ὣς ἐφάμην, ὁ δέ μ' οἰμώξας ἠμείβετο μύθῳ· 506
" ὢ πόποι, ἦ μάλα δή με παλαίφατα θέσφαθ' ἱκάνει. 507
ἔσκε τις ἐνθάδε μάντις ἀνὴρ ἠΰς τε μέγας τε, 508
Τήλεμος Εὐρυμίδης, ὃς μαντοσύνῃ ἐκέκαστο 509
καὶ μαντευόμενος κατεγήρα Κυκλώπεσσιν· 510

---

502 **αἴ**—if.
καταθνητός,-ή,-όν—mortal.

503 **εἴρηται**—present subjunctive; **αἴ κέν...εἴρηται** – protasis of a future more vivid condition: "if anyone…asks about."
ἀεικέλιος,-η,-ον—shameful.
ἀλαωτύς,-ύος, ἡ—blinding (**ἀλαόω** – blind, make blind).

504 **φάσθαι**—infinitive of **φημί**, used as an imperative.
πτολιπόρθιος,-ον—sacker of cities.
ἐξαλαόω, (aor.) **ἐξαλάωσα**—blind; **Ὀδυσσῆα...ἐξαλαῶσαι** – indirect statement.

505 **Λαέρτεω = Λαέρτου.**
Ἰθάκῃ ἔνι = ἐνὶ Ἰθάκῃ.
οἰκία, τά—*plural translated as singular*, home, house, abode; **οἰκί' = οἰκία.**

506 **οἰμώζω, οἰμώξομαι, ᾤμωξα**—cry out in pain or distress.

507 **ὢ πόποι**—oh no!
παλαίφατος,-ον—old, spoken long ago.

θέσφατα,-ων, τό—oracles, prophecy; **θέσφαθ' = θέσφατα**.

με...ἱκάνει—"comes home to me," "comes true."

508 **ἔσκε = ἦν**—"there was."

μάντις,-ιος, ὁ—seer, prophet.

ἠΰς, ἠΰ—good.

μέγας—"tall," "large."

509 **Τήλεμος,-ου, ὁ**—Telemus.

Εὐρυμίδης,-αο, ὁ—son of Eurymus.

μαντοσύνη,-ης, ἡ—art of divination.

καίνυμαι, (perf.) **κέκασμαι**—excel (+ dat. of what one excels in); **ἐκέκαστο** – pluperfect, translate as imperfect.

510 **μαντεύομαι**—be a seer, act as a seer.

καταγηράω, καταγηράσω, κατεγήρασα—grow old; **κατεγήρα** – imperfect.

Κυκλώπεσσιν—may mean "among the Cyclopes" or, taken with **μαντευόμενος**, "for the Cyclopes."

Scanning Notes

505 The **α** in **Λαέρτεω** is long.

-τεω in **Λαέρτεω** is scanned as one long syllable (synizesis).

506 The **α** in **οἰμώξας** is long.

The **υ** in **μύθῳ** is long.

507 The **α** in **ἱκάνει** is long.

510 The second **α** in **κατεγήρα** is long.

ὅς μοι ἔφη τάδε πάντα τελευτήσεσθαι ὀπίσσω,
χειρῶν ἐξ Ὀδυσῆος ἁμαρτήσεσθαι ὀπωπῆς.
ἀλλ' αἰεί τινα φῶτα μέγαν καὶ καλὸν ἐδέγμην
ἐνθάδ' ἐλεύσεσθαι, μεγάλην ἐπιειμένον ἀλκήν·
νῦν δέ μ' ἐὼν ὀλίγος τε καὶ οὐτιδανὸς καὶ ἄκικυς
ὀφθαλμοῦ ἀλάωσεν, ἐπεί μ' ἐδαμάσσατο οἴνῳ.
ἀλλ' ἄγε δεῦρ', Ὀδυσεῦ, ἵνα τοι πὰρ ξείνια θείω,
πομπήν τ' ὀτρύνω δόμεναι κλυτὸν ἐννοσίγαιον·
τοῦ γὰρ ἐγὼ πάϊς εἰμί, πατὴρ δ' ἐμὸς εὔχεται εἶναι.
αὐτὸς δ', αἴ κ' ἐθέλῃσ', ἰήσεται, οὐδέ τις ἄλλος
οὔτε θεῶν μακάρων οὔτε θνητῶν ἀνθρώπων."

---

511 **ἔφη**—imperfect active, 3rd pers. sing. of **φημί**.

τελευτάω, τελευτήσω—carry out, accomplish; *passive*, come to pass; **τελευτήσεσθαι** – future passive infinitive.

ὀπίσσω—in the future.

512 **ἁμαρτάνω, ἁμαρτήσομαι**—lose, be deprived of (+ gen.); **ἁμαρτήσεσθαι** – future infinitive; understand **ἐμέ** as its subject.

ὀπωπή,-ῆς, ἡ—vision, ability to see.

513 **ἐδέγμην**—aorist of **δέχομαι**: "I expected."

514 **ἐπιέννυμι**, (aor.) **ἐπίεσσα**—put on over; **ἐπιειμένος** – perfect passive participle: "clothed in," "wearing."

ἀλκή,-ῆς, ἡ—strength, might.

515 **ἐών**—"one who is."

ὀλίγος—"short."

οὐτιδανός,-ή,-όν—worthless, good for nothing.

ἄκικυς (masc. and fem. adj.)—weak, feeble.

516 **ἀλαόω, ἀλαώσω, ἀλάωσα**—blind, make [acc.] blind in [gen.].

δαμάζω, (aor.) **ἐδάμασσα**—overcome, overpower; **ἐδαμάσσατο** – middle, translate as active.

517 **δεῦρ' = δεῦρο**.

Ὀδυσεῦ—vocative.

παρατίθημι, (aor.) **παρέθηκα**—set, place, or put [acc.] beside [dat.]; **πὰρ...θείω** – TMESIS; aorist subjunctive.

518 **πομπήν**—"safe passage;" object of **δόμεναι**.

ὀτρύνω, ὀτρυνέω, ὤτρυνα—urge, call upon; **ὀτρύνω** – aorist subjunctive.

δόμεναι—aorist infinitive of **δίδωμι**.

ἐννοσίγαιος = ἐνοσίχθων; κλυτὸν ἐννοσίγαιον – "the famous earth-shaker," *i.e.*, Poseidon; object of **ὀτρύνω**.

519 **τοῦ**—"his."

εὔχεται—"he claims."

520 **ἐθέλησ' = ἐθέλησι**—present active subjunctive, 3rd pers. sing.

ἰάομαι, ἰήσομαι, ἰησάμην—heal, cure.

Scanning Notes

513 The **α** in **καλόν** is long.

515 The **ι** in **ἄκικυς** is long.

518 The **υ** in **ὀτρύνω** is long.

520 The first **ι** in **ἰήσεται** is long.

Odysseus replies that he wishes he could send the Cyclops to the ***δόμος*** *of Hades. Polyphemus prays to Poseidon that Odysseus never reach his* ***οἶκος****. If it is fated that he do so, he prays that he arrive after a long time (****ὀψέ****), having lost his* ***ἑταῖροι****, and find* ***πήματα ἐν οἴκῳ****.*

ὣς ἔφατ', αὐτὰρ ἐγώ μιν ἀμειβόμενος προσέειπον·
" αἲ γὰρ δὴ ψυχῆς τε καὶ αἰῶνός σε δυναίμην
εὖνιν ποιήσας πέμψαι δόμον Ἄϊδος εἴσω,
ὡς οὐκ ὀφθαλμόν γ' ἰήσεται οὐδ' ἐνοσίχθων. "
ὣς ἐφάμην, ὁ δ' ἔπειτα Ποσειδάωνι ἄνακτι
εὔχετο, χεῖρ' ὀρέγων εἰς οὐρανὸν ἀστερόεντα·
" κλῦθι, Ποσείδαον γαιήοχε κυανοχαῖτα·
εἰ ἐτεόν γε σός εἰμι, πατὴρ δ' ἐμὸς εὔχεαι εἶναι,
δὸς μὴ Ὀδυσσῆα πτολιπόρθιον οἴκαδ' ἱκέσθαι,
υἱὸν Λαέρτεω, Ἰθάκῃ ἔνι οἰκί' ἔχοντα.

---

523 **αἲ γάρ** + optative—expresses a wish: "would that!"

δυναίμην—present optative.

524 **εὖνις** (masc. and fem. adj.)—deprived of, bereaved of (+ gen.); **εὖνιν** (acc.) agrees with **σε**.

Ἀΐδης,-ος, ὁ—Hades, god of the Underworld where the spirits of the dead go.

εἴσω—into (+ acc.).

"Would that I, having deprived you of soul and life (*literally*, having made you deprived of soul and life) might be able to send you into the house of Hades."

525 **ὡς**—"as surely as."

οὐδ'—not even.

οὐκ...οὐδ'—negatives repeated for emphasis.

Odysseus wishes he were as certain of being able to send Polyphemus to Hades as he is certain that Poseidon will not be able to heal his eye.

527 **εὔχετο**—"he prayed."

χεῖρ' = χεῖρε—acc. dual.

ὀρέγω, ὀρέξω, ὤρεξα—stretch out, hold out.

ἀστερόεις,-εσσα,-εν—starry (**ἀστήρ** – star); this is a standard epithet used with **οὐρανός**; it does not mean it is night time.

528 ~ **κλύω**, (aor.) **ἔκλυον**—hear; **κλῦθι**—imperative.

Ποσείδαον—vocative.

γαιήοχος,-ον—earth-holding (There is dispute about the meaning of this adjective; it may refer to the ocean as surrounding or supporting the earth.)

κυανοχαίτης (masc. adj.)—dark-haired; **κυανοχαῖτα** – vocative.

529 **ἐτεόν**—truly, really, in fact.

εὔχεαι—“you claim;” present tense, 2nd pers. sing.

530 **δός**—“grant that;” aorist imperative of **δίδωμι**; (with accusative and infinitive).

531 Compare 9.530-531 with 9.504-505.

Scanning Notes

523 The **υ** in **ψυχῆς** is long.

524 The **Α** in **Ἄϊδος** is long.

525 The first **ι** in **ἰήσεται** is long.

526 The **α** in **Ποσειδάωνι** is long.

528 The **α** in **Ποσείδαον** is long.

The **υ** in **κυανοχαῖτα** is long.

531 The **α** in **Λαέρτεω** is long.

-τεω in **Λαέρτεω** is scanned as one long syllable (synizesis).

ἀλλ' εἴ οἱ μοῖρ' ἐστὶ φίλους τ' ἰδέειν καὶ ἱκέσθαι 532
οἶκον ἐϋκτίμενον καὶ ἑὴν ἐς πατρίδα γαῖαν, 533
ὀψὲ κακῶς ἔλθοι, ὀλέσας ἄπο πάντας ἑταίρους, 534
νηὸς ἐπ' ἀλλοτρίης, εὕροι δ' ἐν πήματα οἴκῳ." 535
ὣς ἔφατ' εὐχόμενος, τοῦ δ' ἔκλυε κυανοχαίτης. 536

---

532 **οἱ**—DATIVE OF POSSESSION.

μοῖρ' = μοῖρα—fate, destiny.

ἰδέειν = ἰδεῖν.

533 **ἐϋκτίμενος,-η,-ον**—well-built.

ἑός, ἑή, ἑόν—his (own), her (own), its (own).

534 **ὀψέ**—after a long time.

κακῶς—miserably, with suffering.

ἔλθοι—OPTATIVE OF WISH.

ὀλέσας ἄπο = ἀπολέσας—aorist active participle, nom. sing. masc. of **ἀπόλλυμι** – lose.

535 **ἀλλότριος,-η,-ον**—belonging to another, not one's own.

εὕροι—OPTATIVE OF WISH.

οἴκῳ—object of **ἐν**.

536 **τοῦ**—object of **ἔκλυε**. Saying that a god "heard" a prayer is a common Homeric way of indicating that the prayer was granted.

Odysseus' boasting and the revelation of his name to Polyphemus may seem unnecessary, but reputation and heroic pride in one's accomplishments are of great importance in the world of the Homeric hero. Unfortunately, revealing to Polyphemus who has blinded him allows him to curse Odysseus and insure that Poseidon will make the rest of Odysseus' journey as difficult as he can. After this episode, Odysseus will be much more cautious about identifying himself.

Scanning Notes

534 The **α** in **ὀλέσας** is long.

535 The second syllable of **ἀλλοτρίης** is not scanned long even though it is followed by two consonants. If the first consonant is a mute or stop (**π, β, φ, κ, γ, χ, τ, δ,** or **θ**) and the second is either **λ** or **ρ**, the preceding syllable can be scanned short.

536 The **υ** in **κυανοχαίτης** is long.

Odyssey Book 10.28-49

After visiting Aeolus, the keeper of the winds, Odysseus and his men set sail for home. Before they left, Aeolus gave Odysseus a gift – a leather bag containing all the winds that might blow his ships off course as they sailed to Ithaca. Odysseus unfortunately did not tell his companions what the bag contained.

Book 10.28-49

*On the tenth day, they see Ithaca. Sleep (**ὕπνος**) now overcomes Odysseus, since he himself had guided the **νηῦς** the entire time so as to quickly (**θᾶσσον**) reach his **πατρὶς γαῖα**.*

ἐννῆμαρ μὲν ὁμῶς πλέομεν νύκτας τε καὶ ἦμαρ,
τῇ δεκάτῃ δ᾽ ἤδη ἀνεφαίνετο πατρὶς ἄρουρα,
καὶ δὴ πυρπολέοντας ἐλεύσσομεν ἐγγὺς ἐόντες.
ἔνθ᾽ ἐμὲ μὲν γλυκὺς ὕπνος ἐπέλλαβε κεκμηῶτα·
αἰεὶ γὰρ πόδα νηὸς ἐνώμων, οὐδέ τῳ ἄλλῳ
δῶχ᾽ ἑτάρων, ἵνα θᾶσσον ἱκοίμεθα πατρίδα γαῖαν·

*His **ἑταῖροι**, thinking Aeolus has given Odysseus gifts (**δῶρα**) of silver (**ἄργυρος**) and gold (**χρυσός**) that Odysseus is not sharing with them, open the bag. The escaping **ἄνεμοι** blow the **νηῦς** back out to sea, **γαίης ἄπο πατρίδος**.*

οἱ δ᾽ ἕταροι ἐπέεσσι πρὸς ἀλλήλους ἀγόρευον
καί μ᾽ ἔφασαν χρυσόν τε καὶ ἄργυρον οἴκαδ᾽ ἄγεσθαι,
δῶρα παρ᾽ Αἰόλου μεγαλήτορος Ἱπποτάδαο.
ὧδε δέ τις εἴπεσκεν ἰδὼν ἐς πλησίον ἄλλον·
"ὢ πόποι, ὡς ὅδε πᾶσι φίλος καὶ τίμιός ἐστιν
ἀνθρώποισ᾽, ὅτεών κε πόλιν καὶ γαῖαν ἵκηται.

---

28 **ἐννῆμαρ**—for nine days.
ὁμῶς—alike (*with* **νύκτας τε καὶ ἦμαρ** – "by day and night alike").
πλέω, πλεύσομαι, ἔπλευσα—sail; **πλέομεν** – imperfect.

29 **δέκατος,-η,-ον**—tenth; **τῇ δεκάτῃ** [**ἡμέρῃ**] – dative of time when.
ἀναφαίνω, (aor.) **ἀνέφηνα**—reveal; *passive*, be seen, appear.
ἄρουρα,-ης, ἡ—earth, soil; **πατρὶς ἄρουρα** – native land.

30 **πυρπολέω**—tend or keep up a fire; **πυρπολέοντας** – "men tending fires."
λεύσσω—see.
ἐγγύς—near, close; **ἐγγὺς ἐόντες** – describes the subject of **ἐλεύσσομεν**.

31 **ἐπιλαμβάνω, ἐπιλήψομαι, ἐπέλαβον**—lay hold of, seize; **ἐπέλλαβε** = **ἐπέλαβε**.

κάμνω, (aor.) **ἔκαμον**, (perf.) **κέκμηκα**—grow weary, become exhausted; **κεκμηῶτα** – perfect active participle, acc. sing. masc.

32 **πούς, ποδός, ὁ**—foot; **ποὺς νηός** – sheet (a rope or strap fastened to one of the lower corners of a ship's sail, used to control it).

νωμάω, νωμήσω—handle, control; **ἐνώμων** – imperfect, 1st pers. sing.

33 **δῶχ'** = **ἔδωκα**—aorist of **δίδωμι**.

θᾶσσον—"more quickly."

35 **ἔφασαν**—imperfect, 3rd pers. plur. of **φημί**.

οἴκαδ' = **οἴκαδε**.

μ'...ἄγεσθαι—indirect statement after **ἔφασαν**: "that I was bringing for myself..."

36 **δῶρον,-ου, τό**—gift.

Αἴολος,-ου, ὁ—Aeolus, keeper of the winds.

Ἱπποτάδης,-αο, ὁ—son of Hippotas.

37 **εἴπεσκεν**—aorist iterative of **εἶπον**; **τις εἴπεσκεν** – "several kept saying."

ἰδών—"looking."

πλησίον—near by.

38 **ὢ πόποι**—expresses the vexation or displeasure of the **ἑταῖροι**; perhaps translate with a sarcastic "great!" or "look!"

ὅδε—refers to Odysseus.

τίμιος,-α,-ον—honored.

39 **ὅτεων**—gen. plur. masc. of **ὅς τις**.

ὅτεών κε πόλιν καὶ γαῖαν ἵκηται—"whoever's city and land he comes to," "wherever he goes."

Scanning Notes

35 The **υ** in **χρυσόν** is long.

36 The first **ο** in **Αἰόλου** is long.

The second **α** in **Ἱπποτάδαο** is long.

37 **εἴπεσκεν** was originally spelled **ϝείπεσκεν**.

38 The first **ι** in **τίμιος** is long.

πολλὰ μὲν ἐκ Τροίης ἄγεται κειμήλια καλὰ
ληΐδος· ἡμεῖς δ' αὖτε ὁμὴν ὁδὸν ἐκτελέσαντες
οἴκαδε νισόμεθα κενεὰς σὺν χεῖρας ἔχοντες.
καὶ νῦν οἱ τά γε δῶκε χαριζόμενος φιλότητι
Αἴολος. ἀλλ' ἄγε θᾶσσον ἰδώμεθα, ὅττι τάδ' ἐστίν,
ὅσσος τις χρυσός τε καὶ ἄργυρος ἀσκῷ ἔνεστιν."
 ὣς ἔφασαν, βουλὴ δὲ κακὴ νίκησεν ἑταίρων·
ἀσκὸν μὲν λῦσαν, ἄνεμοι δ' ἐκ πάντες ὄρουσαν,
τοὺς δ' αἶψ' ἁρπάξασα φέρεν πόντονδε θύελλα
κλαίοντας, γαίης ἄπο πατρίδος.

---

40 **ἄγεται**—"he is bringing for himself."
κειμήλιον,-ου, τό—treasure.

41 **ληΐς, ληΐδος, ἡ**—booty, spoils of war; **ληΐδος** – "from the spoils of war."
ὁμός,-ή,-όν—the same.
ἐκτελέω, (aor.) **ἐξετέλεσσα**—finish, complete; **ἐκτελέσαντες** – aorist active participle.

42 **νίσομαι**—come back, return.
κενεός,-ά,-όν—empty.
συνέχω, συνέξω, συνέσχον—hold together; **σὺν...ἔχοντες** – TMESIS.

43 **χαρίζομαι**—gratify, show favor, show kindness (+ dat.).
φιλότητι—"for the sake of friendship," "because of friendship."

44 ~ **θᾶσσον**—quickly.
ἰδώμεθα—aorist middle subjunctive; HORTATORY SUBJUNCTIVE.
ὅττι—"what" (neut. acc. sing. of **ὅς τις**).

45 **ὅσσος τις**—"how much."
ἀσκός,-οῦ, ὁ—leather bag; **ἀσκῷ** – dative with **ἔνεστιν**.

46 **νίκησεν = ἐνίκησεν**—"prevailed."
ἑταίρων—*with* **βουλὴ...κακή**.

47 **λῦσαν = ἔλυσαν**—"they untied."
ὀρούω, ὀρούσω, ὤρουσα—rush; **ὄρουσαν = ὤρουσαν**.

48 ~ **αἶψα**—at once.
ἁρπάζω, ἁρπάξω, ἥρπαξα—snatch up, seize.
φέρεν = ἔφερεν.

πόντονδε—toward the open sea, *i.e.*, away from the shore of Ithaca.

θύελλα,-ης, ἡ—violent storm, storm wind, gale.

Scanning Notes

40 The first **α** in **καλά** is long.

42 The **ι** in **νισόμεθα** is long.

The final syllable of **νισόμεθα** is scanned long, even though its vowel is short. Occasionally, a final syllable ending in a short vowel is arbitrarily scanned long simply because it occupies a position in the line that requires a long syllable.

45 The **υ** in **χρυσός** is long.

46 The **ι** in **νίκησεν** is long.

47 The last syllable of **λῦσαν** is scanned long. If there is a short vowel in the final syllable of a word and the consonant that follows it is **ν**, **ρ**, or **ς**, it may be scanned long.

48 The third **α** in **ἁρπάξασα** is long.

Odyssey Book 10.210-347

Having lost all but one ship, Odysseus and his companions reached the island of Aeaea, home of the goddess Circe, the daughter of Helios. When Odysseus saw smoke rising from somewhere in the interior of the island, he sent a group of men led by Eurylochus to investigate.

Book 10.210-347

*Eurylochus' party finds the **δώματα Κίρκης**, which is surrounded by wolves (**λύκοι**) and **λέοντες**, animals she had bewitched with evil drugs (**κακὰ φάρμακα**). They hear the voice (**ὄψ**) of Circe singing from inside the house.*

εὗρον δ' ἐν βήσσῃσι τετυγμένα δώματα Κίρκης 210
ξεστοῖσιν λάεσσι, περισκέπτῳ ἐνὶ χώρῳ. 211
ἀμφὶ δέ μιν λύκοι ἦσαν ὀρέστεροι ἠδὲ λέοντες, 212
τοὺς αὐτὴ κατέθελξεν, ἐπεὶ κακὰ φάρμακ' ἔδωκεν. 213
οὐδ' οἵ γ' ὡρμήθησαν ἐπ' ἀνδράσιν, ἀλλ' ἄρα τοί γε 214
οὐρῇσιν μακρῇσι περισσαίνοντες ἀνέσταν. 215
ὡς δ' ὅτ' ἂν ἀμφὶ ἄνακτα κύνες δαίτηθεν ἰόντα 216
σαίνωσ'· αἰεὶ γάρ τε φέρει μειλίγματα θυμοῦ· 217
ὣς τοὺς ἀμφὶ λύκοι κρατερώνυχες ἠδὲ λέοντες 218
σαῖνον· τοὶ δ' ἔδδεισαν, ἐπεὶ ἴδον αἰνὰ πέλωρα. 219

---

210 **βῆσσα,-ης, ἡ**—small wooded valley, glen, dell.

τεύχω, τεύξω, ἔτευξα, τέτευχα—construct, build; **τετυγμένα** – perfect passive participle: "built," "made."

δώματα—plural used for singular.

Κίρκη,-ης, ἡ—Circe, a goddess who lived on the island Aeaea; daughter of Helios.

211 **ξεστός,-ή,-όν**—polished, smoothed.

λᾶας, λᾶος, ὁ—a stone; **λάεσσι** – dat. plur.; **ξεστοῖσιν λάεσσι** – with **τετυγμένα** in the preceding line.

περίσκεπτος,-ον—elevated.

~ **χῶρος,-ου, ὁ**—place.

212 **μιν**—"it," *i.e.*, the house.

λύκος,-ου, ὁ—wolf.

ὀρέστερος,-α,-ον—mountain-dwelling.

213 **αὐτή**—refers to Circe.

καταθέλγω, καταθέλξω, κατέθελξα—bewitch, enchant.

~ **φάρμακον,-ου, τό**—drug, magical drug, enchanted potion.

214 **ὁρμάω, ὁρμήσω, ὥρμησα**, (aor. pass.) **ὡρμήθην**—move; *middle and passive*, rise, attack, make an attack.

215 **οὐρή,-ῆς, ἡ**—tail.

περισσαίνω—wag; **οὐρῇσιν μακρῇσι περισσαίνοντες** – "wagging their long tails."

~ **ἀνίστημι**, (aor.) **ἀνέστην**—stand up, rise; **ἀνέσταν**—aorist, 3rd pers. plur.

216 **ἄνακτα**—"their master."

κύων, κυνός, ὁ—dog.

δαίτηθεν—from a meal, from a feast.

217 **σαίνω**, (aor.) **ἔσηνα**—fawn, show fondness; **σαίνω' = σαίνωσι** – present subjunctive, 3rd pers. plur.

μειλίγμα, -ατος, τό—something that soothes or makes gentle; **μειλίγματα θυμοῦ** – tidbits or scraps to appease their hunger.

218 **τούς**—them, *i.e.*, Odysseus' men.

κρατερῶνυξ, (gen.) **-υχος**—strong-clawed, with powerful claws.

219 **σαῖνον = ἔσαινον**.

αἰνός,-ή,-όν—terrible.

πέλωρον, τό (only in nom. and acc. forms)—monster.

Scanning Notes

211 The **α** in **λάεσσι** is long.

217 The first **υ** in **θυμοῦ** is long.

ἔσταν δ' ἐν προθύροισι θεᾶς καλλιπλοκάμοιο,
Κίρκης δ' ἔνδον ἄκουον ἀειδούσης ὀπὶ καλῇ
ἱστὸν ἐποιχομένης μέγαν ἄμβροτον, οἷα θεάων
λεπτά τε καὶ χαρίεντα καὶ ἀγλαὰ ἔργα πέλονται.

*Polites urges them to call out (**φθέγγεσθαι**) to the person in the house. When they do, she **αἶψα** comes out, opens the shining doors (**θύραι φαειναί**), and invites them in. Eurylochus remains behind, suspecting a **δόλος**. She serves them **σίτος** in which she mixes evil **φάρμακα**, then strikes them with her magic wand (**ῥάβδος**), turning them into pigs (**σύες**).*

τοῖσι δὲ μύθων ἦρχε Πολίτης, ὄρχαμος ἀνδρῶν,
ὅς μοι κήδιστος ἑτάρων ἦν κεδνότατός τε·
"ὦ φίλοι, ἔνδον γάρ τις ἐποιχομένη μέγαν ἱστὸν
καλὸν ἀοιδιάει, δάπεδον δ' ἅπαν ἀμφιμέμυκεν,
ἢ θεὸς ἠὲ γυνή· ἀλλὰ φθεγγώμεθα θᾶσσον."
ὣς ἄρ' ἐφώνησεν, τοὶ δ' ἐφθέγγοντο καλεῦντες.
ἡ δ' αἶψ' ἐξελθοῦσα θύρας ὤϊξε φαεινὰς
καὶ κάλει· οἱ δ' ἅμα πάντες ἀϊδρείῃσιν ἕποντο·
Εὐρύλοχος δ' ὑπέμεινεν· ὀΐσατο γὰρ δόλον εἶναι.

---

220 **ἔσταν = ἔστησαν**—aorist, 3rd pers. plur. of **ἵστημι**.

πρόθυρον,-ου, τό—doorway (here, the gateway into the courtyard in front of the house); **προθύροισι** – plural used for singular.

καλλιπλόκαμος,-ον—having lovely hair.

221 **ἔνδον**—within, in the house.

ἄκουον = ἤκουον.

ἀείδω—sing; **ἀειδούσης** – present active participle, gen. sing. fem.; modifies **Κίρκης**.

~ **ὄψ, ὀπός, ἡ**—voice.

222 **ἱστὸν ἐποιχομένης**—"walking along the web (the cloth she is weaving)," "going back and forth in front of the web," *i.e.*, following the shuttle as she weaves (see the note on 2.94).

[**τοῖον ἱστὸν**] **οἷα**—such a web as....

223 **λεπτός,-ή,-όν**—fine, delicately woven.

χαρίεις, χαρίεσσα, χαρίεν—pleasing, lovely.

ἀγλαός,-ή,-όν—splendid.

ἔργα—"works," "weaving."

224 **μύθων ἦρχε**—"began to speak," "was the first to speak."

Πολίτης,-ου, ὁ—Polites.

ὄρχαμος,-ου, ὁ—leader.

225 **κήδιστος,-η,-ον**—dearest, closest.

κεδνός,-ή,-όν—devoted, trustworthy.

227 **καλόν**—sweetly.

ἀοιδιάω—sing; **ἀοιδιάει = ἀοιδιᾷ**.

δάπεδον,-ου, τό—floor.

ἀμφιμυκάομαι, (perf.) **ἀμφιμέμυκα**—resound, echo all around.

228 ~ **φθέγγομαι, φθέγξομαι, ἐφθεγξάμην**—call out, shout; **φθεγγώμεθα** – HORTATORY SUBJUNCTIVE.

229 **καλεῦντες**—present active participle, nom. plur. masc. of **καλέω**.

230 ~ **οἴγνυμι**, (aor.) **ὤϊξα**—open.

~ **φαεινός,-ή,-όν**—bright, shining.

231 **κάλει = ἐκάλει**—imperfect: "she invited or summoned [them] in."

~ **ἅμα**—all together.

ἀϊδρείη,-ης, ἡ—ignorance; **ἀϊδρείῃσιν** – plural used for singular; dative of cause – "out of ignorance," "because of their ignorance."

232 **Εὐρύλοχος,-ου, ὁ**—Eurylochus.

ὑπομένω, (aor.) **ὑπέμεινα**—remain or stay behind.

~ **ὀΐομαι, οἰήσομαι, ὠϊσάμην**—think, suspect.

Scanning Notes

221 The **α** in **καλῇ** is long.

222 The **α** in **θεάων** is long.

224 The **υ** in **μύθων** is long.

The **ι** in **Πολίτης** is long.

225 The last syllable of **κήδιστος** is scanned long. If there is a short vowel in the final syllable of a word and the consonant following it is **ν**, **ρ**, or **ς**, it may be scanned long.

227 The **α** in **καλόν** is long.

The **υ** in **ἀμφιμέμυκεν** is long.

230 The **α** in **θύρας** is long.

232 The **ι** in **ὀΐσατο** is long.

εἷσεν δ' εἰσαγαγοῦσα κατὰ κλισμούς τε θρόνους τε, 233
ἐν δέ σφιν τυρόν τε καὶ ἄλφιτα καὶ μέλι χλωρὸν 234
οἴνῳ Πραμνείῳ ἐκύκα· ἀνέμισγε δὲ σίτῳ 235
φάρμακα λύγρ', ἵνα πάγχυ λαθοίατο πατρίδος αἴης. 236
αὐτὰρ ἐπεὶ δῶκέν τε καὶ ἔκπιον, αὐτίκ' ἔπειτα 237
ῥάβδῳ πεπληγυῖα κατὰ συφεοῖσιν ἐέργνυ. 238
οἱ δὲ συῶν μὲν ἔχον κεφαλὰς φωνήν τε τρίχας τε 239
καὶ δέμας, αὐτὰρ νοῦς ἦν ἔμπεδος ὡς τὸ πάρος περ. 240
ὣς οἱ μὲν κλαίοντες ἐέρχατο· τοῖσι δέ Κίρκη 241
πὰρ ἄκυλον βάλανόν τ' ἔβαλεν καρπόν τε κρανείης 242
ἔδμεναι, οἷα σύες χαμαιευνάδες αἰὲν ἔδουσιν. 243

---

233 **εἷσεν**—aorist of **ἕζομαι**: "she seated [them]," "she told [them] to be seated."

εἰσάγω, εἰσάξω, εἰσήγαγον—bring in, lead in.

κλισμός,-οῦ, ὁ—seat.

θρόνος,-ου, ὁ—chair, seat.

234 **σφιν**—"for them."

τυρός,-οῦ, ὁ—cheese.

ἄλφιτον,-ου, τό—barley; *plural*, barley meal.

μέλι, μέλιτος, τό—honey.

χλωρός,-ή,-όν—yellow.

235 **Πράμνειος** (masc. adj.)—Pramnian (It is not clear exactly what "Pramnian" wine meant to Homer's audience. In later times, it referred to a type of wine; at this time, it may refer to a place of origin.)

κυκάω, κυκήσω—stir, mix; **ἐκύκα** – imperfect, 3rd pers. sing.; **ἐν** (line 10.234)... **οἴνῳ Πραμνείῳ ἐκύκα**: "she mixed with Pramnian wine." She is making a **κυκεών**, a thick drink made of wine, grated cheese, barley meal, and honey.

ἀναμίσγω—mix [one thing – acc.] with [another thing – dat.].

236 **λυγρός,-ή,-όν**—harmful, evil.

πάγχυ—wholly, entirely, utterly.

λαθοίατο—aorist middle optative, 3rd pers. plur. of **λανθάνω**.

αἶα,-ης, ἡ—country, land, homeland, native land.

237 **δῶκεν = ἔδωκεν**.

238 **ῥάβδος,-ου, ἡ**—magic wand.

πλήσσω, πλήξω, ἔπληξα, πέπληγα—strike, hit; **πεπληγυῖα** – perfect active participle, nom. sing. fem.

κατέργνυμι—drive into, shut in, confine; **κατὰ...ἐέργνυ** – imperfect, 3rd pers. sing.; TMESIS.

συφεός,-οῦ, ὁ—pigsty; **συφεοῖσιν** – "in the pigsties."

239 ~ **σῦς, συός, ὁ, ἡ**—pig.

ἔχον = εἶχον—imperfect.

φωνή,-ῆς, ἡ—voice.

θρίξ, τριχός, ἡ—*always in plural*, bristles.

240 **δέμας, τό** (only in nom. and acc. forms)—body, figure.

νοῦς = νόος.

ἔμπεδος,-ον—intact, unimpaired.

τὸ πάρος—formerly.

241 **ἐέργω**—confine, shut in; **ἐέρχατο** – pluperfect passive, 3rd pers. plur.

242 **παραβάλλω, παραβαλῶ, παρέβαλον**—throw beside, throw to; **πάρ...ἔβαλεν** – TMESIS.

ἄκυλος,-ου, ὁ—acorn; **ἄκυλον** – singular used for plural.

βάλανος,-ου, ἡ—acorn; **βάλανον** – singular used for plural. (**ἄκυλος** and **βάλανος** refer to acorns from different varieties of oak trees.)

καρπός,-οῦ, ὁ—fruit.

κράνεια,-ης, ἡ—cornel tree.

243 **ἔδμεναι**—present active infinitive of **ἔδω.**

χαμαιευνάς (gen. **-άδος**) (fem. adj.)—ground-sleeping, who sleep on the ground.

Scanning Notes

234 The **υ** in **τυρόν** is long.

235 The **α** in **ἐκύκα** is long.

The **ι** in **σίτῳ** is long.

238 The last syllable of **κατά** is scanned long. A short final syllable that ends in a vowel and is followed by a word beginning with **σ** can be scanned long.

Eurylochus goes ***ἄψ*** *to the* ***νηῦς****. Unable to speak at first, he finally reports that his* ***ἑταῖροι*** *vanished into a* ***δώματα καλά*** *and never came out.*

Εὐρύλοχος δ' ἄψ ἦλθε θοὴν ἐπὶ νῆα μέλαιναν,
ἀγγελίην ἑτάρων ἐρέων καὶ ἀδευκέα πότμον.
οὐδέ τι ἐκφάσθαι δύνατο ἔπος, ἱέμενός περ,
κῆρ ἄχεϊ μεγάλῳ βεβολημένος· ἐν δέ οἱ ὄσσε
δακρυόφιν πίμπλαντο, γόον δ' ὠΐετο θυμός.
ἀλλ' ὅτε δή μιν πάντες ἀγασσάμεθ' ἐξερέοντες,
καὶ τότε τῶν ἄλλων ἑτάρων κατέλεξεν ὄλεθρον·
"ᾔομεν, ὡς ἐκέλευες, ἀνὰ δρυμά, φαίδιμ' Ὀδυσσεῦ·
εὕρομεν ἐν βήσσῃσι τετυγμένα δώματα καλὰ
ξεστοῖσιν λάεσσι, περισκέπτῳ ἐνὶ χώρῳ.
ἔνθα δέ τις μέγαν ἱστὸν ἐποιχομένη λίγ' ἄειδεν
ἢ θεὸς ἠὲ γυνή· τοὶ δ' ἐφθέγγοντο καλεῦντες.

---

244 **θοός,-ή,-όν**—swift.

μέλαιναν—Ship were called "dark" or "black" because their inner and outer surfaces were probably coated with pitch (pine tar), a dark, viscous substance, to make them watertight, and to protect them from the elements and some types of marine life. When hull remains of ancient ships are discovered, pitch is commonly found on them.

245 **ἀγγελίην**—"news."

ἐρέων—future active participle of **εἴρω**; FUTURE PARTICIPLE OF PURPOSE.

ἀδευκής,-ές—harsh, cruel.

πότμος,-ου, ὁ—fate.

246 **ἔκφημι**—utter, speak; **ἐκφάσθαι** – present middle infinitive.

δύνατο = ἐδύνατο.

247 **ἄχος,-εος, τό**—pain, grief, distress.

βολέω—strike; **βεβολημένος** – perfect passive participle with **κῆρ** (ACCUSATIVE OF RESPECT): "stricken in his heart."

ἐν δέ—moreover, besides.

οἱ—"his;" dative of **εἷο**.

248 **δακρυόφιν**—gen. plur. of **δάκρυον**.

πίμπλημι, πλήσω, ἔπλησα—fill (what something is filled with is in the genitive); **πίμπλαντο** – imperfect.

γόος,-ου, ὁ—weeping, lamentation.

ὠΐετο—imperfect of **ὀΐομαι** – "was intent on," "was engrossed with."

249 **ἄγαμαι**, (aor.) **ἠγασσάμην**—wonder, be astonished, be amazed; **ἀγασσάμεθ'** = **ἠγασσάμεθα**.

ἐξερέομαι—ask, question; **μιν πάντες ἀγασσάμεθ' ἐξερέοντες** – "we all questioned him in amazement" (*literally*, questioning him (as we questioned him), we were all amazed).

250 **καταλέγω, καταλέξω, κατέλεξα**—tell, tell about, relate.

ὄλεθρον—Eurylochus does not really know what happened to the men who entered Circe's house but seems to assume they are dead since he never saw them come back out.

251 **ἤομεν**—imperfect of **εἶμι**.

ἀνά—through (+ acc.).

δρυμά,-ῶν, τά—thickets, woods.

~ **φαίδιμος,-ον**—famous, illustrious, renowned; **φαίδιμ'** = **φαίδιμε** – voc.

252 Compare this line with 10.210. How are they different?

253 Compare this line with 10.211.

254 **λίγ'** = **λίγα**—loudly.

ἄειδεν = **ἤειδεν**.

255 **τοί** = **οἱ**.

Compare this line with 10.228. How are they different?

Scanning Notes

246 The last syllable of **δύνατο** is scanned long. **ἔπος** was originally spelled **ϝέπος**. A short final syllable that ends in a vowel followed by a word beginning with **ϝ** can be scanned long.

The **ι** in **ἱέμενος** is long.

248 The **ι** in **ὠΐετο** is long.

The **υ** in **θυμός** is long.

252 The first **α** in **καλά** is long.

253 The **α** in **λάεσσι** is long.

ἡ δ' αἶψ' ἐξελθοῦσα θύρας ὤϊξε φαεινὰς 256
καὶ κάλει· οἱ δ' ἅμα πάντες ἀϊδρείῃσιν ἕποντο· 257
αὐτὰρ ἐγὼν ὑπέμεινα, ὀϊσάμενος δόλον εἶναι. 258
οἱ δ' ἅμ' ἀϊστώθησαν ἀολλέες, οὐδέ τις αὐτῶν 259
ἐξεφάνη· δηρὸν δὲ καθήμενος ἐσκοπίαζον." 260

Odysseus takes up his ***ξίφος*** *and bow. Eurylochus urges him not to go, but Odysseus tells him powerful necessity (**κρατερὴ ἀνάγκη**) compels him.*

ὣς ἔφατ', αὐτὰρ ἐγὼ περὶ μὲν ξίφος ἀργυρόηλον 261
ὤμοιϊν βαλόμην, μέγα χάλκεον, ἀμφὶ δὲ τόξα· 262
τὸν δ' ἂψ ἠνώγεα αὐτὴν ὁδὸν ἡγήσασθαι. 263
αὐτὰρ ὅ γ' ἀμφοτέρῃσι λαβὼν ἐλλίσσετο γούνων 264
καί μ' ὀλοφυρόμενος ἔπεα πτερόεντα προσηύδα· 265
"μή μ' ἄγε κεῖσ' ἀέκοντα, διοτρεφές, ἀλλὰ λίπ' αὐτοῦ. 266

---

257 **ἀϊδρείη,-ης, ἡ**—ignorance.

Lines 10.256-257 are identical to which previous lines?

258 Compare this line with 10.232. How are they different?

259 **ἀϊστόω, ἀϊστώσω, ἠΐστωσα,** (aor. pass.) **ἠϊστώθην**—cause to vanish; *passive*, vanish, disappear; **ἀϊστώθησαν = ἠϊστώθησαν** – aorist passive, 3rd pers. plur.

ἀολλής,-ές—all together, all; **ἀολλέες** – nom. plur. masc.

260 **ἐκφαίνω,** (aor.) **ἐξέφηνα**—bring to light; *passive*, appear, come forth; **ἐξεφάνη** – aorist passive, 3rd pers. sing.

δηρόν—for a long time.

κάθημαι—sit.

σκοπιάζω—watch.

261 **ἀργυρόηλος,-ον**—silver-studded, ornamented with silver nails.

262 **ὦμος,-ου, ὁ**—shoulder; **ὤμοιϊν** – dat. dual; **περὶ...ὤμοιϊν βαλόμην** – "I threw around my shoulders." (He says he threw his sword around his shoulders because the sheath which holds the sword hangs from a strap that passed over his shoulder.)

βαλόμην = ἐβαλόμην – aorist.

χάλκεος,-ον—made of bronze; **μέγα χάλκεον** describes the **ξίφος**.

τόξον,-ου, τό—bow; *plural*, all one's archery equipment, *i.e.*, quiver, bow, and arrows; **ὤμοιϊν βαλόμην** is understood with **ἀμφὶ δὲ τόξα**.

263 **ἠνώγεα**—pluperfect active, 1st pers. sing. of **ἀνώγω**; translate as imperfect.

ἡγέομαι, ἡγήσομαι, ἡγησάμην—lead or show the way; **ἂψ...αὐτὴν ὁδὸν ἡγήσασθαι** – "to lead [me] back the same way."

264 **ἀμφότερος,-η,-ον**—both; **ἀμφοτέρῃσι [χερσί]** – DATIVE OF MEANS.

λίσσομαι—beg; **ἐλλίσσετο** – imperfect.

γούνων—genitive object of **λαβών**.

265 **ὀλοφύρομαι, ὀλοφυροῦμαι, ὠλοφυράμην**—weep.

προσηύδα—imperfect, 3rd pers. sing. of **προσαυδάω**.

266 **κεῖσ' = κεῖσε**—to that place, there.

ἀέκων,-ουσα—against one's will, being unwilling.

διοτρεφής,-ές—cherished by Zeus; **διοτρεφές** – vocative.

λείπω, λείψω, ἔλιπον—leave, leave behind; **λίπ' = λίπε**—aorist imperative.

αὐτοῦ—here.

Scanning Notes

256 The **α** in **θύρας** is long.

258 The **ι** in **ὀϊσάμενος** is long.

263 **-γεα** in **ἠνώγεα** is scanned as one long syllable (synizesis).

265 The **υ** in **ὀλοφυρόμενος** is long.

The last syllable of **ὀλοφυρόμενος** is scanned long because **ἔπεα** was originally spelled **ϝέπεα**.

οἶδα γὰρ ὡς οὔτ' αὐτὸς ἐλεύσεαι οὔτε τιν' ἄλλον
ἄξεις σῶν ἑτάρων. ἀλλὰ ξὺν τοίσδεσι θᾶσσον
φεύγωμεν· ἔτι γάρ κεν ἀλύξαιμεν κακὸν ἦμαρ."
ὣς ἔφατ', αὐτὰρ ἐγώ μιν ἀμειβόμενος προσέειπον·
" Εὐρύλοχ', ἦ τοι μὲν σὺ μέν' αὐτοῦ τῷδ' ἐνὶ χώρῳ
ἔσθων καὶ πίνων κοίλῃ παρὰ νηῒ μελαίνῃ·
αὐτὰρ ἐγὼν εἶμι· κρατερὴ δέ μοι ἔπλετ' ἀνάγκη."
ὣς εἰπὼν παρὰ νηὸς ἀνήϊον ἠδὲ θαλάσσης.

Just before Odysseus gets to Circe's ***δῶμα****, he meets Hermes, who has the appearance of a young man. Hermes gives him an herb which will protect him from Circe's* ***φάρμακα*** *and not allow her to bewitch* ***(θέλγειν)*** *him. He also gives him advice. When Circe tries to strike him with her long* ***(περιμήκης) ῥάβδος****, he should draw his* ***ξίφος*** *and rush at her. When she invites him to her* ***εὐνή****, he must first make her swear a* ***μέγας ὅρκος*** *not to harm him.*

ἀλλ' ὅτε δὴ ἄρ' ἔμελλον ἰὼν ἱερὰς ἀνὰ βήσσας
Κίρκης ἵξεσθαι πολυφαρμάκου ἐς μέγα δῶμα,
ἔνθα μοι Ἑρμείας χρυσόρραπις ἀντεβόλησεν
ἐρχομένῳ πρὸς δῶμα, νεηνίῃ ἀνδρὶ ἐοικώς,
πρῶτον ὑπηνήτῃ, τοῦ περ χαριεστάτη ἥβη·
ἔν τ' ἄρα μοι φῦ χειρὶ ἔπος τ' ἔφατ' ἔκ τ' ὀνόμαζε·

---

267 **οὔτ' = οὔτε.**

αὐτός—"you yourself;" modifies the subject of **ἐλεύσεαι.**

ἐλεύσεαι—future, 2nd pers. sing. of **ἔρχομαι**, here meaning "return," "come back."

268 **ξύν = σύν.**

τοίσδεσι—dat. plur. masc. of **ὅδε** – "these men here."

269 **φεύγωμεν**—HORTATORY SUBJUNCTIVE.

ἔτι—still, yet.

ἀλύσκω, ἀλύξω, ἤλυξα—escape; **ἀλύξαιμεν**—POTENTIAL OPTATIVE.

271 **Εὐρύλοχ' = Εὐρύλοχε.**

μέν' = μένε—imperative.

272 **ἔσθω**—eat.

κοῖλος,-η,-ον—hollow (refers to the fact that there is space inside a ship).

273 **ἔπλετ' = ἔπλετο**—aorist of **πέλομαι**; translate as present.

ἀνάγκη,-ης, ἡ—necessity.

κρατερὴ δέ μοι ἔπλετ' ἀνάγκη—"for I must go" (literally?).

274 **ἀνήϊον**—"I went inland;" imperfect of **ἄνειμι**.

275 **μέλλω**—be about; **ἔμελλον** – with **ἵξεσθαι** in the next line.

276 **πολυφάρμακος,-ον**—knowing many spells or charms, skilled with drugs.

277 **χρυσόρραπις** (masc. and fem. adj.)—with a golden wand (epithet of Hermes).

ἀντιβολέω, ἀντιβολήσω, ἀντεβόλησα—meet, encounter (+ dat.).

278 **ἐρχομένῳ**—modifies **μοι** in the previous line.

νεηνίης,-εω, ὁ—young man, youth; **νεηνίῃ ἀνδρί = νεηνίῃ**.

ἐοικώς—perfect active participle, nom. sing. masc. of **ἔοικα**; translate as present: "resembling," "looking like" (+ dat.).

279 **ὑπηνήτης,-ου, ὁ**—one who is just getting a beard; **πρῶτον ὑπηνήτῃ** – a young man with his first beard.

τοῦ—"whose."

ἥβη,-ης, ἡ—youthful vigor, early manhood, youth; **τοῦ περ χαριεστάτη ἥβη** – "whose youthful vigor [is] indeed most pleasing."

280 **φύω, φύσω, ἔφυσα** or **ἔφυν**—grasp, take hold of; **φῦ = ἔφυ** – aorist, 3rd pers. sing.; **ἐν τ' ἄρα μοι φῦ χειρί** – "he grasped me by the hand."

Scanning Notes

269 The last syllable of **φεύγωμεν** is scanned long. If there is a short vowel in the final syllable of a word and the consonant that follows it is **ν, ρ,** or **ς**, it may be scanned long.

272 The **ι** in **πίνων** is long.

275 The **α** in **ἱεράς** is long.

The **α** in **βήσσας** is long.

277 The **α** in **Ἑρμείας** is long.

The **υ** in **χρυσόρραπις** is long.

“ πῇ δὴ αὖτ’, ὦ δύστηνε, δι’ ἄκριας ἔρχεαι οἶος,
χώρου ἄϊδρις ἐών; ἕταροι δέ τοι οἵδ’ ἐνὶ Κίρκης
ἔρχαται ὥς τε σύες πυκινοὺς κευθμῶνας ἔχοντες.
ἦ τοὺς λυσόμενος δεῦρ’ ἔρχεαι; οὐδέ σέ φημι
αὐτὸν νοστήσειν, μενέεις δὲ σύ γ’ ἔνθα περ ἄλλοι.
ἀλλ’ ἄγε δή σε κακῶν ἐκλύσομαι ἠδὲ σαώσω·
τῆ, τόδε φάρμακον ἐσθλὸν ἔχων ἐς δώματα Κίρκης
ἔρχευ, ὅ κέν τοι κρατὸς ἀλάλκῃσιν κακὸν ἦμαρ.
πάντα δέ τοι ἐρέω ὀλοφώϊα δήνεα Κίρκης.
τεύξει τοι κυκεῶ, βαλέει δ’ ἐν φάρμακα σίτῳ·

---

281 **πῇ**—where?

δύστηνος,-ον—wretched, unfortunate.

ἄκρις,-ιος, ἡ—hill.

ἔρχεαι—present, 2nd person singular of **ἔρχομαι**.

282 **ἄϊδρις,-ι**—ignorant, ignorant of (+ gen.).

ἐών—present participle of **εἰμί**.

ἕταροι...τοι οἵδ’ ἐνὶ Κίρκης—“those companions of yours in [the house] of Circe.”

283 **ἔρχαται**—perfect passive, 3rd pers. plur. of **ἐέργω** – confine.

πυκινούς—“strongly built.”

κευθμών,-ῶνος, ὁ—pen, pigsty.

284 **λυσόμενος**—FUTURE PARTICIPLE OF PURPOSE.

285 **μενέεις**—future tense.

ἔνθα περ—where, there where; **ἔνθα περ ἄλλοι** – there where the others [are *or* remain].

286 **ἐκλύω, ἐκλύσω**—free from, rescue from (what one is rescued from is in the genitive); **ἐκλύσομαι** – future middle, translate as active.

σαόω, σαώσω, ἐσάωσα—save.

287 **τῆ**—here!

φάρμακον ἐσθλόν—refers to an herb that Hermes is going to give Odysseus.

288 **ἔρχευ**—present imperative of **ἔρχομαι**.

ὅ—which (neuter relative pronoun referring to the **φάρμακον**).

κρατός—gen. sing. of **κάρη**; **τοι κρατός** – “from your head.”

ἄλαλκον (aor.)—ward off, keep off; ἀλάλκῃσιν – subjunctive, 3rd pers. sing.; subjunctive used for future.

289 ὀλοφώϊος,-ον—destructive, deadly, malign.

δήνεα,-ων, τά—arts, wiles.

290 τεύχω—make, prepare.

κυκεών,-ῶνος, ὁ—mixed drink or potion made of wine, barley meal, grated cheese, and honey; κυκεῶ – acc. sing.

βαλέει—future tense.

Fig. 5. Fragment from a krater depicting Hermes. Roman, Trajanic period, 98-117 CE. Marble. 88.33. Museum of Art and Archaeology, University of Missouri. Weinberg Fund and Gilbreath-McLorn Museum Fund.

Scanning Notes

281 By synizesis, δή and αὖτ' are run together to form one long syllable. Pronounce as though it were written δ' αὖτ'.

284 The υ in λυσόμενος is long.

286 The υ in ἐκλύσομαι is long.

288 The α in κρατός is long.

290 The ι in σίτῳ is long.

ἀλλ᾽ οὐδ᾽ ὣς θέλξαι σε δυνήσεται· οὐ γὰρ ἐάσει 291
φάρμακον ἐσθλόν, ὅ τοι δώσω, ἐρέω δὲ ἕκαστα. 292
ὁππότε κεν Κίρκη σ᾽ ἐλάσῃ περιμήκεϊ ῥάβδῳ, 293
δὴ τότε σὺ ξίφος ὀξὺ ἐρυσσάμενος παρὰ μηροῦ 294
Κίρκῃ ἐπαΐξαι ὥς τε κτάμεναι μενεαίνων. 295
ἡ δέ σ᾽ ὑποδδείσασα κελήσεται εὐνηθῆναι· 296
ἔνθα σὺ μηκέτ᾽ ἔπειτ᾽ ἀπανήνασθαι θεοῦ εὐνήν, 297
ὄφρα κέ τοι λύσῃ θ᾽ ἑτάρους αὐτόν τε κομίσσῃ· 298
ἀλλὰ κέλεσθαί μιν μακάρων μέγαν ὅρκον ὀμόσσαι 299
μή τί τοι αὐτῷ πῆμα κακὸν βουλευσέμεν ἄλλο, 300
μή σ᾽ ἀπογυμνωθέντα κακὸν καὶ ἀνήνορα θήῃ.” 301

---

291 ~ **θέλγω, θέλξω, ἔθελξα**—bewitch, work spells upon, enchant.

ἐάω, ἐάσω, ἔασα—permit, allow.

292 **ἕκαστα**—“all the things [you need to know].”

293 **ὁππότε κεν** + subjunctive—when.

ἐλάσῃ—aorist subjunctive, 3rd pers. sing. of **ἐλαύνω** – strike.

~ **περιμήκης,-ες**—long.

ῥάβδος,-ου, ἡ—magic wand.

294 **μηρός,-οῦ, ὁ**—thigh.

Compare this line with 9.300.

295 **ἐπαΐσσω,** (aor.) **ἐπήϊξα**—rush at (+ dat.); **ἐπαΐξαι** – infinitive used for imperative.

ὥς τε—like, just like.

κτάμεναι—aorist active infinitive of **κτείνω**.

μενεαίνω—desire, intend, be resolved.

296 **ὑποδείδω, ὑποδείσω, ὑπέδδεισα**—fear, be afraid.

εὐνάω, εὐνήσω, εὔνησα, (aor. pass.) **εὐνήθην**—lull to sleep; *passive*, lie with, have sex.

297 **μηκέτι**—no longer.

ἀπαναίνομαι, (aor.) **ἀπηνηνάμην**—refuse, reject; **ἀπανήνασθαι** – infinitive used for imperative.

~ **εὐνή,-ῆς, ἡ**—bed.

298 **λύσῃ**—aorist subjunctive, 3rd pers. sing.; Circe is the subject.

θ' = τε.

αὐτόν = αὐτόν σε—"you yourself."

κομίζω, κομιῶ, ἐκόμισσα—look after, attend to, care for, provide for; **κομίσσῃ** – aorist subjunctive, 3rd pers. sing.; Circe is the subject; **ὄφρα κε...λύσῃ...κομίσσῃ** – PURPOSE CLAUSE.

299 **κέλεσθαι**—infinitive for imperative.

μιν—"her."

ὀμόσσαι—aorist infinitive of **ὄμνυμι.**

Μακάρων indicates she is to swear the great oath "of the gods," *i.e.*, the unbreakable oath the gods swear by the River Styx.

300 **τοι αὐτῷ**—"for you," "against you."

βουλευσέμεν—future active infinitive; **μή...βουλευσέμεν** spells out the oath Odysseus is to make her swear: "not to be going to devise."

τί, κακόν, and **ἄλλο** modify **πῆμα.**

Compare this line with 5.179. How are they different? To whom was Odysseus speaking in the earlier line?

301 **ἀπογυμνόω, ἀπογυμνώσω**—strip, take the clothes off; **ἀπογυμνωθέντα** – aorist passive participle, acc. sing. masc.

ἀνήνωρ, -ορος (masc. adj.)—deprived of virility, unmanly (**ἀν-** [negative prefix] + **ἀνήρ**).

θήῃ—aorist subjunctive, 3rd pers. sing. of **τίθημι**; **μή...θήῃ** expresses what Hermes fears will happen if Odysseus does not make Circe swear the oath: "lest she make you, when you are stripped of your clothes, cowardly and unmanly."

Scanning Notes

291 The **α** in **ἐάσει** is long.

295 The first **α** in **ἐπαΐξαι** is long.

296 The first **α** in **ὑποδδείσασα** is long.

298 The **υ** in **λύσῃ** is long.

ὣς ἄρα φωνήσας πόρε φάρμακον Ἀργεϊφόντης 302
ἐκ γαίης ἐρύσας καί μοι φύσιν αὐτοῦ ἔδειξε. 303
ῥίζῃ μὲν μέλαν ἔσκε, γάλακτι δὲ εἴκελον ἄνθος· 304
μῶλυ δὲ μιν καλέουσι θεοί, χαλεπὸν δέ τ' ὀρύσσειν 305
ἀνδράσι γε θνητοῖσι· θεοὶ δέ τε πάντα δύνανται. 306

When Odysseus comes ***ἐς δώματα Κίρκης****, she serves him the same drink (****κυκεών****) she gave his* ***ἑταῖροι****, strikes him with her* ***ῥάβδος****, and tells him to go the pigsty (****συφεός****).*

Ἑρμείας μὲν ἔπειτ' ἀπέβη πρὸς μακρὸν Ὄλυμπον 307
νῆσον ἀν' ὑλήεσσαν, ἐγὼ δ' ἐς δώματα Κίρκης 308
ἤϊα· πολλὰ δέ μοι κραδίη πόρφυρε κιόντι. 309
ἔστην δ' εἰνὶ θύρῃσι θεᾶς καλλιπλοκάμοιο· 310
ἔνθα στὰς ἐβόησα, θεὰ δέ μευ ἔκλυεν αὐδῆς. 311
ἡ δ' αἶψ' ἐξελθοῦσα θύρας ὤϊξε φαεινὰς 312
καὶ κάλει· αὐτὰρ ἐγὼν ἑπόμην ἀκαχήμενος ἦτορ. 313

---

302 **πόρε = ἔπορε.**

φάρμακον—"the herb."

303 **ἐρύσας**—aorist active participle, nom. sing. masc. of **ἐρύω**: "pulling."

φύσις,-ιος, ἡ—nature, form, appearance.

αὐτοῦ—"its" (referring to the **φάρμακον**).

304 **ῥίζα,-ης, ἡ**—root [of a tree or plant]; **ῥίζῃ** – "in the root."

ἔσκε = ἦν.

γάλα, γάλακτος, τό—milk.

εἴκελος,-η,-ον—like, resembling (+ dat.).

ἄνθος,-εος, τό—flower, blossom.

305 **μῶλυ, τό**—moly (Probably an imaginary plant. Garlic, which has a white flower and a dark root and was used in antiquity as a protective charm, has been proposed as a possibility. Another suggestion is the snowdrop (*Galanthus nivalis*). It is found in forest glens, grows wild in Greece, has a milk-colored flower, and a dark root. The snowdrop contains galanthamine, which acts as an antidote to stramonium, a possibility for Circe's "evil drug." Stramonium can be derived from a common plant and can produce memory

impairment, delusions, and hallucinations, such as forgetting one's homeland and thinking one is a pig.)

χαλεπός,-ή,-όν—difficult, hard; **χαλεπόν** – "[it is] difficult."

ὀρύσσω, (aor.) **ὄρυξα**—dig up, get out of the ground.

307 **Ὄλυμπος,-ου, ὁ**—Mt. Olympus, the home of the gods.

308 **ὑλήεις,-εσσα,-εν**—wooded.

309 **ἤϊα**—imperfect, 1st pers. sing. of **εἶμι**.

πολλά—greatly.

μοι—DATIVE OF INTEREST showing possession.

κραδίη,-ης, ἡ—heart.

πορφύρω—be troubled; **πόρφυρε** – imperfect.

κίω—go, make one's way, proceed; **κιόντι** – modifies **μοι**.

310 **εἰνί = ἐν**.

καλλιπλόκαμος,-ον—having lovely hair.

Compare this line with 10.220. How are they different?

311 **στάς**—aorist active participle; translate as present.

μευ—gen. sing. of **ἐγώ**.

αὐδή,-ῆς, ἡ—voice.

313 **ἀκαχίζω**—distress, trouble; **ἀκαχήμενος** – perfect passive participle: "distressed," "troubled."

ἦτορ—ACCUSATIVE OF RESPECT.

Compare lines 10.312-313 with 10.230-231 and 10.256-257. What are the differences?

Scanning Notes

308 The **υ** in **ὑλήεσσαν** is long.

309 The **υ** in **πόρφυρε** is long.

311 The **α** in **στάς** is long.

The **α** in **θεά** is long.

312 The **α** in **θύρας** is long.

εἷσε δέ μ' εἰσαγαγοῦσα ἐπὶ θρόνου ἀργυροήλου,
καλοῦ δαιδαλέου· ὑπὸ δὲ θρῆνυς ποσὶν ἦεν·
τεῦχε δέ μοι κυκεῶ χρυσέῳ δέπᾳ, ὄφρα πίοιμι,
ἐν δέ τε φάρμακον ἧκε, κακὰ φρονέουσ' ἐνὶ θυμῷ.
αὐτὰρ ἐπεὶ δῶκέν τε καὶ ἔκπιον οὐδέ μ' ἔθελξε,
ῥάβδῳ πεπληγυῖα ἔπος τ' ἔφατ' ἔκ τ' ὀνόμαζεν·
  "ἔρχεο νῦν συφεόνδε, μετ' ἄλλων λέξο ἑταίρων."

Odysseus draws his ***ξίφος ὀξύ*** *and rushes at Circe* ***ὥς κτάμεναι μενεαίνων****.*

ὣς φάτ', ἐγὼ δ' ἄορ ὀξὺ ἐρυσσάμενος παρὰ μηροῦ
Κίρκῃ ἐπήϊξα ὥς τε κτάμεναι μενεαίνων.
ἡ δὲ μέγα ἰάχουσα ὑπέδραμε καὶ λάβε γούνων
καί μ' ὀλοφυρομένη ἔπεα πτερόεντα προσηύδα·

Circe is amazed that Odysseus can drink her ***φάρμακα*** *and not be bewitched.* ***Οὐδέ τις ἄλλος ἀνήρ*** *has ever done this. She concludes he must be Odysseus, the man Hermes told her would come to her* ***νῆσος*** *on his way home* ***ἐκ Τροίης****.*

  "τίς πόθεν εἰς ἀνδρῶν; πόθι τοι πόλις ἠδὲ τοκῆες;

---

314 **εἷσε**—aorist of **ἕζομαι.**

Compare 10.314 with 10.233. How do they differ? What possession of Odysseus' which he has with him was also described with the adjective **ἀργυρόηλος**?

315 **δαιδάλεος,-η,-ον**—finely-crafted.

θρῆνυς,-υος, ὁ—footstool.

ποσίν—dat. plur. of **πούς**: "for the feet."

ἦεν—imperfect, 3rd pers. sing. of **εἰμί.**

316 **τεῦχε = ἔτευχε.**

χρύσεος,-η,-ον—golden, made of gold.

δέπας,-αος, τό—cup; **δέπᾳ** – dat. sing.

πίοιμι—aorist optative of **πίνω.**

317 **ἧκε**—aorist active, 3rd pers. sing. of **ἵημι**; **ἐν...ἧκε** – "she put in."

φρονέουσ' = φρονέουσα – "intending," "planning."

319 **πεπληγυῖα**—perfect active participle, nom. sing. fem. of **πλήσσω** – strike.

ὀνόμαζεν = ὠνόμαζεν.

ἔπος τ' ἔφατ' ἔκ τ' ὀνόμαζεν—"she addressed [me]" (*literally*, "she spoke a word and called [me] by name aloud;" since at this point Circe does not know Odysseus' name, **ὀνόμαζεν** cannot be taken literally).

320 **ἔρχεο**—imperative.

συφεός,-οῦ, ὁ—pigsty.

λέγω, (aor.) **ἔλεξα**—lay, cause to lie down; *middle,* lay oneself down, lie down; **λέξο** – aorist middle imperative.

321 **ἄορ,-ορος, τό = ξίφος.**

322 Compare 10.321-322 with 10.294-295. How are they different? Who spoke the earlier lines?

323 **μέγα**—loudly.

ἰάχω—shout, shriek.

ὑποτρέχω, (aor.) **ὑπέδραμον**—run in under an enemy's weapon.

324 **ὀλοφύρομαι, ὀλοφυροῦμαι, ὠλοφυράμην**—weep.

Compare 10.324 with 10.265. How are the lines different?

325 **πόθεν**—from what place?

εἶς—2nd pers. sing. of **εἰμί.**

τίς πόθεν εἶς ἀνδρῶν;—"Who are you among men [and] from what place?"

πόθι—where?

τοι—"your."

τοκεύς,-έως, ὁ—parent; **τοκῆες** – nom. plur.

Scanning Notes

315 The **α** in **καλοῦ** is long.

316 The **υ** in **χρυσέῳ** is long.

-εῳ in **χρυσέῳ** is scanned as one long syllable (synizesis).

317 The **υ** in **θυμῷ** is long.

322 The final syllable of **ἐπήϊξα** is scanned long, even though its vowel is short. Occasionally, a final syllable ending in a short vowel is arbitrarily scanned long simply because it occupies a position in the line that requires a long syllable.

323 The last syllable of **μέγα** is scanned long because **ἰάχουσα** originally began with **ϝ**.

324 The **υ** in **ὀλοφυρομένη** is long.

θαῦμά μ’ ἔχει, ὡς οὔ τι πιὼν τάδε φάρμακ’ ἐθέλχθης. 326
οὐδὲ γὰρ οὐδέ τις ἄλλος ἀνὴρ τάδε φάρμακ’ ἀνέτλη, 327
ὅς κε πίῃ καὶ πρῶτον ἀμείψεται ἕρκος ὀδόντων· 328
σοὶ δέ τις ἐν στήθεσσιν ἀκήλητος νόος ἐστίν. 329
ἦ σύ γ’ Ὀδυσσεύς ἐσσι πολύτροπος, ὅν τέ μοι αἰεὶ 330
φάσκεν ἐλεύσεσθαι χρυσόρραπις Ἀργεϊφόντης, 331
ἐκ Τροίης ἀνιόντα θοῇ σὺν νηῒ μελαίνῃ. 332

She invites him into her ***εὐνή****. He refuses until she swears a* ***μέγας ὅρκος*** *not to harm him.*

ἀλλ’ ἄγε δὴ κολεῷ μὲν ἄορ θέο, νῶϊ δ’ ἔπειτα 333
εὐνῆς ἡμετέρης ἐπιβήομεν, ὄφρα μιγέντε 334
εὐνῇ καὶ φιλότητι πεποίθομεν ἀλλήλοισιν.” 335
ὣς ἔφατ’, αὐτὰρ ἐγώ μιν ἀμειβόμενος προσέειπον· 336

---

326 **θαῦμα,-ατος, τό**—wonder, amazement.

πιών—aorist active participle of **πίνω**; describes the subject of **ἐθέλχθης**.

φάρμακ’ = **φάρμακα**.

ἐθέλχθης—aorist passive, 2nd pers. sing. of **θέλγω**.

327 **οὐδὲ...οὐδέ**—repetition of the negative emphasizes the negative idea. One can imagine her stammering in amazement: “Not…not…any other man…”

ἀνατλάω, (aor.) **ἀνέτλην**—withstand.

328 **ὅς**—refers to **οὐδέ τις ἄλλος ἀνήρ**.

πίῃ—aorist subjunctive of **πίνω**.

πρῶτον—“when once,” “once.”

ἀμείψεται—aorist subjunctive (SHORT-VOWEL SUBJUNCTIVE) of **ἀμείβω** – *middle with* ***ἕρκος ὀδόντων***, pass, enter. (**πίῃ** and **ἀμείψεται** are subjunctives in a subordinate clause beginning with **ὅς** which expresses indefiniteness in time.)

ἕρκος,-εος, τό—barrier, fence.

ὀδούς,-όντος, ὁ—tooth; **ἕρκος ὀδόντων** – “the lips” or “the mouth” (*literally*, the barrier of teeth).

καὶ πρῶτον ἀμείψεται ἕρκος ὀδόντων = **καὶ** [**οὗ**] **ἕρκος ὀδόντων** [**φάρμακα**] **πρῶτον ἀμείψεται**—“and whose lips the drug once passed.”

329 **σοί**—DATIVE OF POSSESSION with **στήθεσσιν**.

ἀκήλητος,-ον—impervious to enchantment.

τις...νόος—"the sort of mind," "the kind of mind."

330 **ἐσσι = εἶ.**

πολύτροπος,-ον—resourceful, ingenious.

331 **φάσκω**—say, promise; **φάσκεν = ἔφασκεν**.

332 **ἀνιόντα**—present active participle, acc. sing. masc. of **ἄνειμι** – return; modifies **ὅν** in 10.330.

333 **κολεόν,-οῦ, τό**—sheath or scabbard of a sword; **κολεῷ** – "in its sheath."

ἄορ = ξίφος.

θέο—aorist middle imperative, 2nd pers. sing. of **τίθημι**.

νῶϊ—we two (nom. dual of **ἐγώ**).

334 **ἡμετέρης**—"my."

ἐπιβήομεν—aorist subjunctive of **ἐπιβαίνω** – place oneself upon, "go to" (+ gen.); SHORT-VOWEL SUBJUNCTIVE; HORTATORY SUBJUNCTIVE.

μιγέντε—aorist passive participle, nom. dual of **μίσγω**.

335 **μιγέντε εὐνῇ καὶ φιλότητι**—"having sex" (*literally*, mingling in bed and in love).

πεποίθομεν = πεποίθωμεν—perfect subjunctive of **πείθω** – persuade, believe; *perfect*, trust (+ dat.).

Scanning Notes

331 The **υ** in **χρυσόρραπις** is long.

“ὦ Κίρκη, πῶς γάρ με κέλεαι σοὶ ἤπιον εἶναι, 337
ἥ μοι σῦς μὲν ἔθηκας ἐνὶ μεγάροισιν ἑταίρους, 338
αὐτὸν δ’ ἐνθάδ’ ἔχουσα δολοφρονέουσα κελεύεις 339
ἐς θάλαμόν τ’ ἰέναι καὶ σῆς ἐπιβήμεναι εὐνῆς, 340
ὄφρα με γυμνωθέντα κακὸν καὶ ἀνήνορα θήῃς. 341
οὐδ’ ἂν ἐγώ γ’ ἐθέλοιμι τεῆς ἐπιβήμεναι εὐνῆς, 342
εἰ μή μοι τλαίης γε, θεά, μέγαν ὅρκον ὀμόσσαι, 343
μή τί μοι αὐτῷ πῆμα κακὸν βουλευσέμεν ἄλλο.” 344
ὣς ἐφάμην, ἡ δ’ αὐτίκ’ ἀπώμνυεν, ὡς ἐκέλευον. 345
αὐτὰρ ἐπεί ῥ’ ὄμοσέν τε τελεύτησέν τε τὸν ὅρκον, 346
καὶ τότ’ ἐγὼ Κίρκης ἐπέβην περικαλλέος εὐνῆς. 347

---

337 **κέλεαι**—present, 2nd pers. sing. of **κέλομαι**.

ἤπιος,-η,-ον—well-disposed, gentle.

338 **ἥ**—relative pronoun referring to Circe: “who.”

σῦς—acc. plur.

μοι—“my” (with **ἑταίρους**).

339 **αὐτόν**—[me] myself.

ἐνθάδ’ = ἐνθάδε—here.

δολοφρονέω—plan trickery.

340 **θάλαμος,-ου, ὁ**—bedroom.

ἐπιβήμεναι—aorist active infinitive of **ἐπιβαίνω**.

341 **γυμνόω, γυμνώσω,** (aor. pass.) **ἐγυμνώθην**—make naked; *passive*, become naked; **γυμνωθέντα** – aorist passive participle, acc. sing. masc.

θήῃς—aorist subjunctive of **τίθημι**.

Compare this line with 10.301.

342 **ἐθέλοιμι**—present optative of **ἐθέλω**.

343 **εἰ μή**—unless.

τλαίης—“you bring yourself,” “you make up your mind;” aorist optative of **τλάω**.

ὀμόσσαι—from **ὄμνυμι**.

344 **βουλευσέμεν**—future active infinitive; **μή τί μοι αὐτῷ πῆμα κακὸν βουλευσέμεν ἄλλο** expresses the content of the oath Odysseus wants her to swear.

Compare lines 10.342-344 with 5.177-179. To whom is Odysseus speaking in 5.177-179? How are the passages different?

345 **ἐφάμην**—imperfect middle, 1st pers. sing. of **φημί**; translate as active.

ἀπομνύω, (aor.) **ἀπώμοσα**—swear a negative oath, swear not to do something; **ἀπόμνυεν = ἀπώμνυεν**.

346 **ὄμοσεν = ὤμοσεν** (from **ὄμνυμι**).

τελευτάω, τελευτήσω, τελεύτησα—finish or complete [an oath] in proper form.

ὄμοσέν, τελεύτησέν—translate as pluperfect.

347 **καὶ τότ'**—"then."

περικαλλής,-ές—beautiful; **περικαλλέος** – gen. sing. fem.

Look back at 5.184-187 to read what Calypso said in her oath. On this occasion, we do not hear Circe reciting the oath, only Odysseus reporting that she **αὐτίκ' ἀπώμνυεν**. Perhaps Homer left out the complete oath and included the word **αὐτίκα** to indicate Circe's hurry to get Odysseus into her bed.

Chronologically, the episode with Circe occurred before that with Calypso. It may have been this encounter and Hermes' advice to get the oath that prompted Odysseus to insist on the later oath from Calypso.

Scanning Notes

337 **-λεαι** in **κέλεαι** is scanned as one long syllable (synizesis).

343 The **α** in **θεά** is long.

Odyssey Book 11.100-137

After Circe restored Odysseus' companions to human form, he and his men stayed with her for a year, enjoying her hospitality. When they decided to leave and resume their journey home, Circe told Odysseus he must first make a journey to the Underworld to consult the dead prophet Teiresias.

Book 11.100-137

Teiresias tells Odysseus that he and his ***ἑταῖροι*** *will have their* ***νόστος*** *if they do not harm the* ***βόες*** *and* ***μῆλα*** *of Helios on the* ***νῆσος*** *of Thrinacia.*

“ νόστον δίζηαι μελιηδέα, φαίδιμ’ Ὀδυσσεῦ·
τὸν δέ τοι ἀργαλέον θήσει θεός. οὐ γὰρ ὀΐω
λήσειν ἐννοσίγαιον, ὅ τοι κότον ἔνθετο θυμῷ,
χωόμενος ὅτι οἱ υἱὸν φίλον ἐξαλάωσας.
ἀλλ’ ἔτι μέν κε καὶ ὧς, κακά περ πάσχοντες, ἵκοισθε,
αἴ κ’ ἐθέλῃς σὸν θυμὸν ἐρυκακέειν καὶ ἑταίρων,
ὁππότε κεν πρῶτον πελάσῃς εὐεργέα νῆα
Θρινακίῃ νήσῳ, προφυγὼν ἰοειδέα πόντον,
βοσκομένας δ’ εὕρητε βόας καὶ ἴφια μῆλα
Ἠελίου, ὃς πάντ’ ἐφορᾷ καὶ πάντ’ ἐπακούει.
τὰς εἰ μέν κ’ ἀσινέας ἐάᾳς νόστου τε μέδηαι,
καί κεν ἔτ’ εἰς Ἰθάκην, κακά περ πάσχοντες, ἵκοισθε·

---

100 **δίζημαι**—seek, seek to achieve, strive for; **δίζηαι** – 2nd pers. sing.
μελιηδής,-ές—honey-sweet.
φαίδιμ’ = **φαίδιμε**.

101 **ἀργαλέος,-η,-ον**—difficult.
τοι = **σοι**.
θήσει—future of **τίθημι**.
θεός—*i.e.*, Poseidon.
ὀΐω—think, suppose.

102 **λήσειν**—from **λανθάνω**; understand **σε** as its subject.
ἐννοσίγαιος = **ἐνοσίχθων**.
κότος,-ου, ὁ—anger.
ἔνθετο—store up [acc.] in [dat.]; aorist middle of **ἐντίθημι**.

103 **χώομαι**—be angry.
ὅτι—because.
ἐξαλαόω, (aor.) **ἐξαλάωσα**—blind.

104 **καὶ ὧς**—"even so," *i.e.*, in spite of Poseidon's anger.

ἵκοισθε—POTENTIAL OPTATIVE.

105 **ἐθέλῃς**—"you will be willing;" subjunctive, translate as future.

ἐρυκακέειν—aorist active infinitive of **ἐρύκω**; **σὸν θυμὸν ἐρυκακέειν καὶ ἑταίρων** – "to curb your desire and that of your companions."

106 **ὁππότε κεν πρῶτον**—"when once" (+ subjunctive).

πελάζω, πελάσω, ἐπέλασ(σ)α—bring.

107 **Θρινακίη,-ης, ἡ**—Thrinacia, the island on which Helios kept his cattle.

προφεύγω, προφεύξομαι, προὔφυγον—flee from, escape from.

ἰοειδής,-ές—purple, dark.

108 **βόσκω**—feed; *passive*, graze.

ἴφιος,-α,-ον—fat.

109 **πάντ' = πάντα**.

110 **ἀσινής,-ές**—unharmed.

ἐάω, ἐάσω, ἔασα—let be, do no harm to; **ἐέᾳς = ἐάῃς** – subjunctive; **τὰς εἰ μέν κ' ἀσινέας ἐέᾳς** – "if you will leave them unharmed."

μέδομαι, μεδήσομαι—think about, remember; **μέδηαι = μέδῃ** – present subjunctive, 2nd pers. sing.

Scanning Notes

101 The **ι** in **ὀΐω** is long.

102 The **υ** in **θυμῷ** is long.

103 The last syllable of **χωόμενος** is scanned long. A final syllable containing a short vowel can be scanned long if it ends with **ν, ρ,** or **ς**.

105 The **υ** in **θυμόν** is long.

The **υ** in **ἐρυκακέειν** is long.

108 The first **ι** in **ἴφια** is long.

110 **-εας** in **ἀσινέας** is pronounced as one long syllable (synizesis).

If they harm Helios' livestock, there will be ***ὄλεθρος*** *for the* ***νηῦς*** *and the* ***ἑταῖροι****. Odysseus will return home after a long time (****ὀψέ****) to* ***πήματα*** *in his* ***οἶκος****.*

εἰ δέ κε σίνηαι, τότε τοι τεκμαίρομ' ὄλεθρον 112
νηΐ τε καὶ ἑτάροισ'. αὐτὸς δ' εἴ πέρ κεν ἀλύξῃς, 113
ὀψὲ κακῶς νεῖαι, ὀλέσας ἄπο πάντας ἑταίρους, 114
νηὸς ἐπ' ἀλλοτρίης· δήεις δ' ἐν πήματα οἴκῳ, 115
ἄνδρας ὑπερφιάλους, οἵ τοι βίοτον κατέδουσι 116
μνώμενοι ἀντιθέην ἄλοχον καὶ ἕδνα διδόντες. 117

Teiresias tells Odysseus that after he kills the ***μνηστῆρες****, he must leave his home, taking an oar (****ἐρετμόν****) with him. When he finds people who know nothing about the* ***θάλασσα*** *or* ***νῆες****, he should set the* ***ἐρετμόν*** *in the ground and sacrifice a ram (****ἀρνειός****), a* ***ταῦρος****, and a boar (****κάπρος****) to Poseidon. When he returns home, he should sacrifice to all the* ***θεοί****. Finally, Teiresias makes a prophecy about Odysseus'* ***θάνατος****.*

ἀλλ' ἦ τοι κείνων γε βίας ἀποτείσεαι ἐλθών· 118
αὐτὰρ ἐπὴν μνηστῆρας ἐνὶ μεγάροισι τεοῖσι 119
κτείνῃς ἠὲ δόλῳ ἢ ἀμφαδὸν ὀξέϊ χαλκῷ, 120
ἔρχεσθαι δὴ ἔπειτα, λαβὼν εὐῆρες ἐρετμόν, 121
εἰς ὅ κε τοὺς ἀφίκηαι, οἳ οὐκ ἴσασι θάλασσαν 122
ἀνέρες οὐδέ θ' ἅλεσσι μεμιγμένον εἶδαρ ἔδουσιν· 123

---

112 **σίνομαι**—hurt, harm; **εἰ δέ κε σίνηαι** [**βόας**].

τεκμαίρομαι—foretell, predict; **τεκμαίρομ' = τεκμαίρομαι**.

113 **εἴ περ**—even if.

ἀλύξῃς—from **ἀλύσκω**.

114 **κακῶς**—miserably, with suffering.

νεῖαι—present, 2nd pers. sing. of **νέομαι**; translate as future.

ὀλέσας ἄπο = ἀπολέσας—"having lost," "after losing;" aorist active participle, nom. sing. masc. of **ἀπόλλυμι** – lose.

115 **ἀλλότριος,-η,-ον**—belonging to another.

δήω—find; **δήεις** – present, translate as future.

Compare 11.114-115 with Polyphemus' words in 9.534-535.

116 **ὑπερφίαλος,-ον**—arrogant, insolent, with no concern for the rights of others.

βίοτος,-ου, ὁ—goods, livelihood.

κατέδω—eat up, devour, consume.

117 **μνάομαι**—woo, court.

ἕδνα,-ων, τά— bridal gifts given to the bride's father for the hand of the bride.

διδόντες—"offering."

118 **βίας**—"acts of violence."

ἀποτείσεαι—"you will exact vengeance for;" future middle, 2nd pers. sing. of **ἀποτίνω**.

119 **ἐπήν = ἐπεὶ ἄν**—when, after, as soon as (+ subjunctive).

120 **ἀμφαδόν**—openly.

χαλκός,-οῦ, ὁ = ξίφος.

121 **ἔρχεσθαι**—infinitive used as imperative.

εὐήρης,-ες—well-balanced, easy to handle.

~ **ἐρετμόν,-ου, τό**—oar.

122 **εἰς ὅ κε**—until (+ subjunctive).

ἀφίκηαι—aorist subjunctive, 2nd pers. sing. of **ἀφικνέομαι**.

ἴσασι—3rd pers. plur. of **οἶδα**.

123 **ἀνέρες**—nom. plur. of **ἀνήρ**; **τοὺς...οἳ...ἀνέρες** – "those people who."

ἅλς, ἁλός, ὁ—*sing. and plur.*, salt.

μεμιγμένον—perfect passive participle of **μίσγω** – mix.

εἶδαρ,-ατος, τό—food.

Scanning Notes

112 The first **ι** in **σίνηαι** is long.

114 The **α** in **ὀλέσας** is long.

118 The **α** in **βίας** is long.

122 The first **ι** and the **α** in **ἴσασι** are long.

οὐδ' ἄρα τοὶ ἴσασι νέας φοινικοπαρῄους, 124
οὐδ' εὐήρε' ἐρετμά, τά τε πτερὰ νηυσὶ πέλονται. 125
σῆμα δέ τοι ἐρέω μάλ' ἀριφραδές, οὐδέ σε λήσει· 126
ὁππότε κεν δή τοι συμβλήμενος ἄλλος ὁδίτης 127
φήῃ ἀθηρηλοιγὸν ἔχειν ἀνὰ φαιδίμῳ ὤμῳ, 128
καὶ τότε δὴ γαίῃ πήξας εὐῆρες ἐρετμόν, 129
ῥέξας ἱερὰ καλὰ Ποσειδάωνι ἄνακτι, 130
ἀρνειὸν ταῦρόν τε συῶν τ' ἐπιβήτορα κάπρον, 131
οἴκαδ' ἀποστείχειν ἔρδειν θ' ἱερὰς ἑκατόμβας 132
ἀθανάτοισι θεοῖσι, τοὶ οὐρανὸν εὐρὺν ἔχουσι, 133
πᾶσι μάλ' ἑξείης. θάνατος δέ τοι ἐξ ἁλὸς αὐτῷ 134
ἀβληχρὸς μάλα τοῖος ἐλεύσεται, ὅς κέ σε πέφνῃ 135

---

124 **τοί = οἱ.**

νέας—acc. plur. of **νηῦς**.

φοινικοπάρῃος,-ον—red-cheeked, purple-cheeked (refers to the practice of painting the bow or "cheeks" of a ship bright red or purple).

125 **εὐήρε' = εὐήρεα.**

τά—"which," referring to **ἐρετμά**.

πτερόν,-οῦ, τό—wing.

Although oars are called "wings for ships" (perhaps a metaphor for the rhythmical rise and fall of the oars or for the way they help speed the ship along), they were most important when entering or leaving port or when the sea was calm. The main form of propulsion for Homeric ships was the wind.

126 **σῆμα,-ατος, τό**—sign.

ἀριφραδής,-ές—clear, distinct.

οὐδέ σε λήσει—"you can't miss it."

127 **συμβάλλω, συμβαλῶ, συμέβαλον**—bring together; *middle*, meet, encounter (+ dat.); **συμβλήμενος** – aorist middle participle.

ὁδίτης,-ου, ὁ—traveler.

128 **φήῃ**—subjunctive, 3rd pers. sing. of **φημί**.

ἀθηρηλοιγός,-οῦ, ὁ—winnowing tool (an implement used to separate grain from chaff [husks]).

ἔχειν—**σε** is its understood subject.

ὦμος,-ου, ὁ—shoulder.

129 **πήγνυμι, πήξω, ἔπηξα**—stick, set firmly, plant.

130 **ῥέξας**—"having made," "having performed."

ἱερά,-ῶν, τά—sacrifices, offerings.

131 **ἀρνειός,-οῦ, ὁ**—ram.

ἐπιβήτωρ,-ορος, ὁ—mate.

κάπρος,-ου, ὁ—boar; **συῶν...ἐπιβήτορα** is in apposition to **κάπρον**.

132 **ἀποστείχω**, (aor.) **ἀπέστιχον**—go back, return.

ἔρδω, ἔρξω, ἔρξα—do, perform.

ἀποστείχειν and **ἔρδειν**—infinitives used as imperatives.

ἑκατόμβη,-ης, ἡ—hecatomb, sacrificial offering of a large number of animals (Literally, the word means a sacrifice of one hundred (**ἑκατόν**) oxen (**βοῦς**), but it was used for sacrifices of fewer than one hundred animals and not necessarily oxen.)

134 **ἑξείης**—one after the other, in order; **πᾶσι μάλ' ἑξείης** – to each and every one in order (refers to **ἀθανάτοισι θεοῖσι**).

τοι = σοι.

ἐξ ἁλός—"away from the sea," *i.e.*, on dry land, as opposed to the deaths at sea of his companions.

135 **ἀβληχρός,-ή,-όν**—gentle.

τοῖος,-η,-ον—such; **ἀβληχρὸς μάλα τοῖος** – "such a very gentle."

φένω, (aor.) **ἔπεφνον**—kill; **πέφνῃ** – subjunctive for future.

Scanning Notes

124 The first **ι** and the **α** in **ἴσασι** are long.

The second **ι** in **φοινικοπαρῄους** is long.

127 The **ι** in **ὁδίτης** is long.

129 The **α** in **πῆξας** is long.

130 The **α** in **ῥέξας** is long.

The **ι** in **ἱερά** is long.

The first **α** in **καλά** is long.

The **α** in **Ποσειδάωνι** is long.

132 The **α** in **ἱεράς** is long.

γήρᾳ ὕπο λιπαρῷ ἀρημένον· ἀμφὶ δὲ λαοὶ 136
ὄλβιοι ἔσσονται. τὰ δέ τοι νημερτέα εἴρω." 137

---

136 **γῆρας,-αος, τό**—old age; **γήρᾳ** – dat. sing.
λιπαρός,-ή,-όν—rich, wealthy, comfortable.
ἀρημένος,-η,-ον—worn out, overcome.

137 **ὄλβιος,-ον**—happy, prosperous.
νημερτής,-ές—true.

Scanning Notes

136 The last syllable of **ὕπο** is scanned long. A short final syllable ending in a vowel and followed by a word beginning with **λ** can be scanned long.
The **α** in **ἀρημένον** is long.
The **α** in **λαοί** is long.

Odyssey Book 11.478-491

While in the Underworld, Odysseus saw the ghostly spirit of Achilles, the greatest Greek hero of the Trojan War. Achilles asked Odysseus why he was there.

Book 11.478-491

Odysseus explains he is trying to get home and needed to speak with Teiresias. Achilles, he says, is ***μακάρτατος****, since he was honored like a* ***θεός*** *when he was alive and now has great power among the dead (****νέκυες****). Achilles disagrees, saying he would rather be a poor man living on earth than ruling* ***πάντες νέκυες****.*

" ὦ Ἀχιλεῦ, Πηλῆος υἱέ, μέγα φέρτατ' Ἀχαιῶν, 478
ἦλθον Τειρεσίαο κατὰ χρέος, εἴ τινα βουλὴν 479
εἴποι, ὅπως Ἰθάκην ἐς παιπαλόεσσαν ἱκοίμην· 480
οὐ γάρ πω σχεδὸν ἦλθον Ἀχαιΐδος οὐδέ πω ἁμῆς 481
γῆς ἐπέβην, ἀλλ' αἰὲν ἔχω κακά. σεῖο δ', Ἀχιλλεῦ, 482
οὔ τις ἀνὴρ προπάροιθε μακάρτερος οὔτ' ἄρ' ὀπίσσω· 483
πρὶν μὲν γάρ σε ζωὸν ἐτίομεν ἶσα θεοῖσιν 484
Ἀργεῖοι, νῦν αὖτε μέγα κρατέεις νεκύεσσιν 485
ἐνθάδ' ἐών· τῶ μή τι θανὼν ἀκαχίζευ, Ἀχιλλεῦ." 486
ὣς ἐφάμην, ὁ δέ μ' αὐτίκ' ἀμειβόμενος προσέειπε· 487

---

478 **Ἀχιλ(λ)εύς,-ῆος, ὁ**—Achilles; **Ἀχιλεῦ**—vocative.
Πηλεύς,-ῆος, ὁ—Peleus, father of Achilles.
μέγα—by far.
φέρτατος,-η,-ον—best, bravest.

479 **χρέος,-εος, τό**—need, business; **Τειρεσίαο κατὰ χρέος** – "in need of Teiresias."
εἴ—on the chance that, in the hope that (+ optative).

480 **παιπαλόεις,-εσσα,-εν**—rocky, rugged, craggy.

481 **σχεδόν**—near, close to (+ gen. or dat.).
Ἀχαιΐς,-ίδος (fem. adj.)—Achaean; **Ἀχαιΐδος [γαίης]**.
ἁμός,-ή,-όν—our; *here*, "my."

482 **σεῖο**—GENITIVE OF COMPARISON with **μακάρτερος** in the next line.

483 **προπάροιθε**—before, formerly, in past times.
ὀπίσσω—in the future.
οὔ τις ἀνὴρ προπάροιθε μακάρτερος [ἦν] οὔτ' ἄρ' ὀπίσσω [ἔσσεται].

484 **πρίν**—before, in the past.

ζωός,-ή,-όν—alive, living.

τίω—honor, esteem.

ἶσος,-η,-ον—equal; **ἶσα** – like, equal to (+ dat.) (neut. plur. used as adverb).

485 **Ἀργεῖοι,-ων, οἱ**—Argives (one of the names Homer uses for Greeks).

κρατέω—have power among (+ dat.); **μέγα κρατέεις** – "you have great power among."

~ **νέκυς,-υος, ὁ**—dead body; *plural,* the dead.

486 **ἐών**—present active participle of **εἰμί**.

τῶ—therefore.

θανών—"because you are dead" (*literally,* being dead); aorist active participle of **θνῄσκω**.

ἀκαχίζω—grieve; **ἀκαχίζευ** – present passive imperative, 2nd pers. sing.

Scanning Notes

478 The diphthong **υἱ** in **υἱέ** is scanned short (internal correption).

479 The **α** in **Τειρεσίαο** is long.

481 The **α** in **ἀμῆς** is long.

484 The **ι** in **ἐτίομεν** is long.

“ μὴ δή μοι θάνατόν γε παραύδα, φαίδιμ’ Ὀδυσσεῦ.
βουλοίμην κ’ ἐπάρουρος ἐὼν θητευέμεν ἄλλῳ,
ἀνδρὶ παρ’ ἀκλήρῳ, ᾧ μὴ βίοτος πολὺς εἴη,
ἢ πᾶσιν νεκύεσσι καταφθιμένοισιν ἀνάσσειν.

---

488 **παραυδάω**—speak consolingly of, make light of; **παραύδα** – present imperative.

φαίδιμ’ = **φαίδιμε**.

489 **βουλοίμην**—“I would wish,” “I would choose.”

ἐπάρουρος,-ον—on earth; **ἐπάρουρος ἐών** – “living on earth.”

θητεύω—serve as a hired laborer; **θητευέμεν** – present active infinitive.

490 **παρ’** = **πάρα**—“in the house of” (+ dat.).

ἄκληρος,-ον—landless; **ἀνδρὶ...ἀκλήρῳ**, *i.e.*, a tenant farmer who owns no land. The man who is this person’s hired laborer would be at the very bottom of the social scale.

βίοτος,-ου, ὁ—goods, livelihood, means of living.

εἴη—present optative, 3rd pers. sing. of **εἰμί**. (When there is an optative of wish in a main clause, a verb in a subordinate clause may be optative by assimilation.)

491 **καταφθίω, καταφθίσω, κατέφθισα**, (aor. pass.) **κατεφθίμην**—destroy; *passive*, perish, die.

ἀνάσσω, ἀνάξω, ἄναξα—be a king over, rule over (+ dat.).

Achilles’ stated preferences emphasize the gloomy expectations that were held for life after death. For the most part, the dead are ghostly spirits flitting about with no purpose in the Underworld, unable to utter more than shrill squeaks.

Scanning Notes

488 The last **α** in **παραύδα** is long.

Odyssey Book 12.166-259

Odysseus and his men were sailing home. Circe had warned him about the dangers awaiting them on the voyage – the Sirens, the Planctae, Scylla and Charybdis. She told Odysseus exactly what to do if he wanted to listen to the Sirens' song, but said he must choose whether to face the Planctae or Scylla and Charybdis.

Book 12.166-259

When the ship reaches the ***νῆσος*** *of the Sirens, the* ***ἄνεμος*** *stops. The men begin to use the* ***ἐρετμά****. Odysseus puts wax in his companions' ears (****οὔατα****), then they tie him up securely. As they row quickly past the* ***νῆσος****, the Sirens begin to sing their song (****ἀοιδή****).*

τόφρα δὲ καρπαλίμως ἐξίκετο νηῦς εὐεργὴς
νῆσον Σειρήνοιϊν· ἔπειγε γὰρ οὖρος ἀπήμων.
αὐτίκ' ἔπειτ' ἄνεμος μὲν ἐπαύσατο ἠδὲ γαλήνη
ἔπλετο νηνεμίη, κοίμησε δὲ κύματα δαίμων.
ἀνστάντες δ' ἕταροι νεὸς ἱστία μηρύσαντο,
καὶ τὰ μὲν ἐν νηῒ γλαφυρῇ θέσαν, οἱ δ' ἐπ' ἐρετμὰ
ἑζόμενοι λεύκαινον ὕδωρ ξεστῇσ' ἐλάτῃσιν.
αὐτὰρ ἐγὼ κηροῖο μέγαν τροχὸν ὀξέϊ χαλκῷ
τυτθὰ διατμήξας χερσὶ στιβαρῇσι πίεζον·
αἶψα δ' ἰαίνετο κηρός, ἐπεὶ κέλετο μεγάλη ἲς
Ἠελίου τ' αὐγὴ Ὑπεριονίδαο ἄνακτος·

---

166 **τόφρα**—meanwhile.

καρπαλίμως—swiftly.

ἐξικνέομαι, (aor.) **ἐξικόμην**—arrive at, reach.

167 **Σειρήν,-ῆνος, ἡ**—a Siren, one of two female creatures whose singing lured sailors to their death. (There is dispute over the appearance of the Sirens, for which Homer provides no help as he does not describe them. Most artistic evidence portrays Sirens as part-woman/part-bird creatures, but because Homer does not say they were part bird, many assume they were only women. Whether Homer visualized them as women or as bird-woman hybrids, he seems to have thought they were two in number, as evidenced by **Σειρήνοιϊν** – gen. dual. Later artistic depictions show them singly, in twos, threes, and larger groups.)

ἐπείγω—speed [a ship] on, drive [a ship] before it.

οὖρος,-ου, ὁ—wind, breeze.

ἀπήμων,-ον—favorable.

168 **γαλήνη,-ης, ἡ**—calm, stillness.

169 **ἔπλετο**—"there was"; imperfect of **πέλομαι**.

νηνέμιος,-η,-ον—windless.

κοιμάω, κοιμήσω, ἐκοίμησα—still, calm.

δαίμων,-ονος, ὁ, ἡ—god, goddess, divinity, superhuman power (Odysseus does not know which god was responsible, so he just refers to a **δαίμων**.)

170 **ἀνστάντες**—aorist active participle of **ἀνίστημι**.

νεός—gen. sing. of **νηῦς**.

ἱστίον,-ου, τό—sail; **ἱστία** – plural used for singular.

μηρύομαι, (aor.) **ἐμηρυσάμην**—lower, furl [a sail].

171 **θέσαν**—aorist active, 3rd pers. plur. of **τίθημι**.

172 **λευκαίνω**—make white.

ξεστός,-ή,-όν—polished.

ἐλάτη,-ης, ἡ—pine tree; oar made of pine wood.

173 **κηρός,-οῦ, ὁ**—beeswax.

τροχός,-οῦ, ὁ—round piece, cake.

χαλκός,-οῦ, ὁ = **ξίφος**.

174 **τυτθά**—into small pieces.

διατμήγω, (aor.) **διέτμηξα**—cut.

στιβαρός,-ή,-όν—strong, powerful.

πιέζω, πιέσω, ἐπίεσα—squeeze; **πίεζον** – "I kept squeezing," "I kneaded."

175 **ἰαίνω**, (aor.) **ἴηνα**—warm.

κέλετο—"compelled."

ἶς, ἰνός, ἡ—strength, force; **μεγάλη ἲς** [**στιβαρῶν χειρῶν**].

176 **αὐγή,-ῆς, ἡ**—bright light, "rays."

Ὑπεριονίδης,-αο, ὁ = **Ὑπερίων**.

Scanning Notes

166 The **ι** in **ἐξίκετο** is long.

169 The **υ** in **κύματα** is long.

170 The **υ** in **μηρύσαντο** is long.

176 The first **ι** and the **α** in **Ὑπεριονίδαο** are long.

ἑξείης δ' ἑτάροισιν ἐπ' οὔατα πᾶσιν ἄλειψα.
οἱ δ' ἐν νηΐ μ' ἔδησαν ὁμοῦ χεῖράς τε πόδας τε
ὀρθὸν ἐν ἱστοπέδῃ, ἐκ δ' αὐτοῦ πείρατ' ἀνῆπτον·
αὐτοὶ δ' ἑζόμενοι πολιὴν ἅλα τύπτον ἐρετμοῖς.
ἀλλ' ὅτε τόσσον ἀπῆμεν, ὅσον τε γέγωνε βοήσας,
ῥίμφα διώκοντες, τὰς δ' οὐ λάθεν ὠκύαλος νηῦς
ἐγγύθεν ὀρνυμένη, λιγυρὴν δ' ἔντυνον ἀοιδήν·

---

177 **ἑξείης**—one after the other.

οὖας,-ατος, τό—ear.

ἀλείφω, (aor.) **ἤλειψα**—stop up, plug; **ἐπ' οὔατα...ἄλειψα** – "I stopped up the ears [with wax]."

178 **δέω, δήσω, ἔδησα**—bind, tie.

ὁμοῦ—both at once, at the same time.

179 **ὀρθός,-ή,-όν**—upright.

ἱστοπέδη,-ης, ἡ—an upright beam to which a ship's mast was secured with ropes; it acted as a support post for the mast. It was not as tall as the mast itself but came up only to deck level.

αὐτοῦ—"the mast itself."

πεῖραρ,-ατος, τό—rope, cord; **πείρατ' = πείρατα**.

ἀνάπτω, (aor.) **ἀνῆψα**—fasten, attach.

The best interpretation of this description of the binding of Odysseus seems to be that he was bound hand and foot, then placed standing up on the crossbeam that was located in the middle of the ship. His feet were inside the binding that held the mast to the **ἱστοπέδη** and he was also tied to the mast.

180 **πολιός,-ή,-όν**—gray.

τύπτω, τύψω, ἔτυψα—strike, beat.

181 **ἄπειμι**—be away, be distant (**ἀπό + εἰμί**); **ἀπῆμεν** – imperfect.

γέγωνα (perfect, translate as present)—make oneself heard; **τόσσον ἀπῆμεν, ὅσον τε [τις] γέγωνε βοήσας** – "we were as far away as someone can make himself heard by shouting" (*literally,* as someone shouting makes himself heard).

182 **ῥίμφα**—swiftly.

διώκω—propel; understand **νῆα** as the object of **διώκοντες**.

τὰς δ' οὐ λάθεν—"did not escape their notice." **τάς** refers to the Sirens. **ὠκύαλος νηῦς** is the subject of **λάθεν**.

Fig. 6. Figurine of a Siren. Greek, Hellenistic period, 323-31 BCE. From Mírina, Greece. Terracotta with traces of paint. 64.59. Museum of Art and Archaeology, University of Missouri.

ὠκύαλος,-ον—swift.

183 **ἐγγύθεν**—nearby.

ὄρνυμι—stir up, set in motion; *middle*, rush, move; **ἐγγύθεν ὀρνυμένη** modifies **ὠκύαλος νηῦς** in the previous line.

λιγυρός,-ή,-όν—clear-sounding.

ἐντύνω—begin to sing.

ἀοιδή,-ῆς, ἡ—song.

Scanning Notes

183 The **υ** in **ἔντυνον** is long.

*In their **ἀοιδή**, the Sirens urge Odysseus to stop the **νηῦς** so he may listen to them. Odysseus orders his **ἑταῖροι** to release him, but they just add more ropes. When they row to the point where the Sirens' **ἀοιδή** can no longer be heard, they remove the wax from their **οὔατα** and release Odysseus.*

" δεῦρ' ἄγ' ἰών, πολύαιν' Ὀδυσεῦ, μέγα κῦδος Ἀχαιῶν, 184
νῆα κατάστησον, ἵνα νωϊτέρην ὄπ' ἀκούσῃς. 185
οὐ γάρ πώ τις τῇδε παρήλασε νηῒ μελαίνῃ, 186
πρίν γ' ἡμέων μελίγηρυν ἀπὸ στομάτων ὄπ' ἀκοῦσαι, 187
ἀλλ' ὅ γε τερψάμενος νεῖται καὶ πλείονα εἰδώς. 188
ἴδμεν γάρ τοι πάνθ', ὅσ' ἐνὶ Τροίῃ εὐρείῃ 189
Ἀργεῖοι Τρῶές τε θεῶν ἰότητι μόγησαν, 190
ἴδμεν δ' ὅσσα γένηται ἐπὶ χθονὶ πουλυβοτείρῃ. " 191
ὣς φάσαν ἱεῖσαι ὄπα κάλλιμον· αὐτὰρ ἐμὸν κῆρ 192
ἤθελ' ἀκουέμεναι, λῦσαί τ' ἐκέλευον ἑταίρους 193
ὀφρύσι νευστάζων· οἱ δὲ προπεσόντες ἔρεσσον. 194
αὐτίκα δ' ἀνστάντες Περιμήδης Εὐρύλοχός τε 195
πλείοσί μ' ἐν δεσμοῖσι δέον μᾶλλόν τε πίεζον. 196

---

184 **ἰών**—"as you go by."

πολύαινος,-ον—much-praised, illustrious.

κῦδος,-εος, τό—glory.

185 **καθίστημι**—bring [a ship] to land; **κατάστησον** – aorist imperative.

νωΐτερος,-η,-ον—our (referring to two persons).

ὄπ' = ὄπα—acc. sing. of **ὄψ**.

186 **τῇδε**—here.

παρελαύνω, παρελάσω, παρήλασα—row past.

187 **πρίν**—before; **πρίν** + aorist infinitive – before ___ing.

μελίγηρυς (fem. adj.)—honey-toned, melodious.

στόμα,-ατος, τό—mouth.

188 **ὁ**—*i.e.*, any man who stops to listen.

τέρπω, τέρψω, ἔτερψα—delight, cheer, satisfy; *middle*, take pleasure, be filled with satisfaction.

νεῖται καὶ πλείονα εἰδώς—"departs knowing even more," *i.e.*, "wiser" or "richer in knowledge."

189 **ἴδμεν**—1st pers. plur. of **οἶδα**.

πάνθ' = πάντα.

ὅσ' = ὅσα; πάνθ', ὅσ' – "all things," "all that."

190 **ἰότης,-ητος, ἡ**—will.

μογέω, (aor.) **ἐμόγησα**—suffer.

191 **ὅσσα γένηται**—"all that happens."

χθών, χθονός, ἡ—the earth.

πουλυβότειρα (fem. adj.)—fruitful, all-nourishing.

192 **ἱεῖσαι**—present active participle, nom. plur. fem. of **ἵημι** – "sending forth."

κάλλιμος,-ον—sweet, beautiful.

193 **ἤθελ' = ἤθελε**.

ἀκουέμεναι = ἀκούειν.

194 **ὀφρύς,-ύος, ἡ**—eyebrow.

νευστάζω—nod, motion.

Why did Odysseus not simply speak his orders?

προπίπτω, προπεσοῦμαι, προὔπεσον—bend forward.

ἐρέσσω—row.

195 **Περιμήδης,-εος, ὁ**—Perimedes, one of Odysseus' comrades.

196 **πλείοσι**—dat. plur. masc. of **πλείων**.

δεσμός,-οῦ, ὁ—any means of binding or fastening; *plural*, bonds, ropes.

δέω—bind, tie.

πιέζω, πιέσω, ἐπίεσα—secure tightly, bind tightly.

Scanning Notes

185 The last syllable of **κατάστησον** is scanned long. If there is a short vowel in the final syllable of a word and the consonant that follows it is **ν, ρ,** or **ς**, it may be scanned long.

187 **-εων** in **ἡμέων** is scanned as one long syllable (synizesis).

192 The first **ι** in **ἱεῖσαι** is long.

αὐτὰρ ἐπεὶ δὴ τάς γε παρήλασαν οὐδ᾽ ἔτ᾽ ἔπειτα
φθόγγον Σειρήνων ἠκούομεν οὐδέ τ᾽ ἀοιδήν,
αἶψ᾽ ἀπὸ κηρὸν ἕλοντο ἐμοὶ ἐρίηρες ἑταῖροι,
ὅν σφιν ἐπ᾽ ὠσὶν ἄλειψ᾽, ἐμέ τ᾽ ἐκ δεσμῶν ἀνέλυσαν.

*Now they see smoke (**καπνός**) and **κῦμα** and hear a roaring sound. The **ἑταῖροι** are so frightened they drop their **ἐρετμά**. Odysseus urges them not to lose heart. He tells the steersman (**κυβερνήτης**) to keep the **νηῦς** away from the **καπνός** and the **κῦμα** and to head for the cliff (**σκόπελος**). He does not tell them about Scylla.*

ἀλλ᾽ ὅτε δὴ τὴν νῆσον ἐλείπομεν, αὐτίκ᾽ ἔπειτα
καπνὸν καὶ μέγα κῦμα ἴδον καὶ δοῦπον ἄκουσα.
τῶν δ᾽ ἄρα δεισάντων ἐκ χειρῶν ἔπτατ᾽ ἐρετμά,
βόμβησαν δ᾽ ἄρα πάντα κατὰ ῥόον· ἔσχετο δ᾽ αὐτοῦ
νηῦς, ἐπεὶ οὐκέτ᾽ ἐρετμὰ προήκεα χερσὶν ἔπειγον.
αὐτὰρ ἐγὼ διὰ νηὸς ἰὼν ὤτρυνον ἑταίρους
μειλιχίοισ᾽ ἐπέεσσι παρασταδὸν ἄνδρα ἕκαστον·

---

197 **παρελαύνω, παρελάσω, παρήλασα**—row past.

198 **φθόγγος,-ου, ὁ**—voice.

199 **κηρός,-οῦ, ὁ**—beeswax.

ἐρίηρος,-ον—faithful, trusty; **ἐρίηρες** – nom. plur. masc.

200 **ὅν**—"which;" refers to **κηρόν** in the previous line.

οὖας,-ατος, τό—ear; **ὠσίν** – dat. plur.

ἀλείφω, (aor.) **ἤλειψα**—put in; **ἄλειψ᾽ = ἄλειψα**.

ἀναλύω, ἀναλύσω, ἀνέλυσα—set free, release.

202 **καπνός,-οῦ, ὁ**—smoke.

δοῦπος,-ου, ὁ—loud noise, roaring [of the sea].

At this point, Odysseus must make a choice between two dangerous routes that lie very close together. He knows the risks of each route because Circe described them to him. One choice is to sail by the Planctae, high cliffs constantly struck by great waves which wreck every ship that tries to sail past. Previously, she told him, only Jason's ship, the *Argo*, got safely past them with help from Hera. The smoke (possibly from volcanic activity), the waves, and the noise Odysseus and his crew now see and hear are from the Planctae. (Homer appears to have combined a story of cliffs whose dangerous surf destroyed all who sailed by with the story of the Symplegades, the clashing rocks between which the *Argo* traveled. Another possibility is that there was a version of the story in which the Symplegades no longer moved after Jason's passage and they are now unmoving but still deadly.)

The other route, the one he will choose, is a passage between two cliffs. In one lives Scylla, a monster in a cave high in the cliff. From the cave, she extends six necks, each of which has a head with three rows of teeth, with which she grabs and devours passing sea creatures and sailors. Beside the opposite cliff is the sea goddess, Charybdis, who sucks down sea water in a terrible whirlpool which destroys anything caught in it.

203 **τῶν [ἑταίρων] δεισάντων.**

πέτομαι, πετήσομαι, ἐπτάμην—fly; **ἔπτατ' = ἔπτατο.**

204 **βομβέω, βομβήσω, βόμβησα**—make a clashing noise.

πάντα [ἐρετμά].

ῥόος,-ου, ὁ—current.

When the men dropped their oars in fright, the oars splashed in the water, but were not lost because the oars were held in place by leather straps.

αὐτοῦ—there.

205 **ἔσχετο...νηῦς**—"the ship stopped."

προήκης,-ες—sharp-edged, thin-edged.

ἐπείγω—move, ply.

206 **ὀτρύνω, ὀτρυνέω, ὤτρυνα**—encourage.

207 **παρασταδόν**—standing by, standing beside.

Scanning Notes

200 The **υ** in **ἀνέλυσαν** is long.

204 The last syllable of **κατά** is scanned long. A short final syllable that ends in a vowel and is followed by a word beginning with **ρ** can be scanned long.

206 The **υ** in **ὤτρυνον** is long.

“ ὦ φίλοι, οὐ γάρ πώ τι κακῶν ἀδαήμονές εἰμεν·
οὐ μὲν δὴ τόδε μεῖζον ἔπι κακόν, ἢ ὅτε Κύκλωψ
εἴλει ἐνὶ σπῆϊ γλαφυρῷ κρατερῆφι βίηφιν·
ἀλλὰ καὶ ἔνθεν ἐμῇ ἀρετῇ βουλῇ τε νόῳ τε
ἐκφύγομεν, καί που τῶνδε μνήσεσθαι ὀΐω.
νῦν δ’ ἄγεθ’, ὡς ἂν ἐγὼ εἴπω, πειθώμεθα πάντες.
ὑμεῖς μὲν κώπῃσιν ἁλὸς ῥηγμῖνα βαθεῖαν
τύπτετε κληΐδεσσιν ἐφήμενοι, αἴ κέ ποθι Ζεὺς
δώῃ τόνδε γ’ ὄλεθρον ὑπεκφυγέειν καὶ ἀλύξαι·
σοὶ δέ, κυβερνῆθ’, ὧδ’ ἐπιτέλλομαι· ἀλλ’ ἐνὶ θυμῷ
βάλλευ, ἐπεὶ νηὸς γλαφυρῆς οἰήϊα νωμᾷς·
τούτου μὲν καπνοῦ καὶ κύματος ἐκτὸς ἔεργε
νῆα, σὺ δὲ σκοπέλου ἐπιμαίεο, μή σε λάθῃσι
κεῖσ’ ἐξορμήσασα καὶ ἐς κακὸν ἄμμε βάλῃσθα. ”

---

208 **οὐ...πώ τι**—not at all.

ἀδαήμων,-ον—ignorant of, inexperienced in dealing with (+ gen.).

209 **μείζων,-ον**—comparative of **μέγας**.

ἔπειμι—be upon; **ἔπι = ἔπεστι**; “indeed this [is] not a greater evil [which] is upon [us] than when the Cyclops…”

210 **εἰλέω**, (aor.) **ἔλσα**—pen in, shut in; **εἴλει** [**ἡμᾶς**].

σπῆϊ—dat. sing. of **σπέος**.

βίη,-ης, ἡ—strength, power; **κρατερῆφι βίηφιν** – dat. sing.

211 ~ **ἔνθεν**—from that place.

ἀρετή,-ῆς, ἡ—valor.

βουλή,-ῆς, ἡ—planning, scheming.

212 **ἐκφεύγω**, (aor.) **ἔκφυγον**—escape from.

μνήσεσθαι—future infinitive of **μιμνήσκομαι**; understand **ἡμᾶς** as its subject; “and I think that no doubt [we] will remember these [dangers we are about to face in the same way that we remember escaping from the Cyclops].”

213 **ὡς ἂν ἐγὼ εἴπω**—“as I command.”

πειθώμεθα—HORTATORY SUBJUNCTIVE.

214 **κώπη,-ης, ἡ = ἐρετμόν**.

ῥηγμίς,-ῖνος, ἡ—breaking waves, surf.

215 **τύπτω, τύψω, ἔτυψα**—strike, beat.

κληΐς,-ῗδος, ἡ—rowing bench, *i.e.*, bench where the ship's rowers sit; **κληΐδεσσιν** – "on the rowing benches."

ἕφημαι—be seated, sit on (+ dat.).

αἴ κε—"in the hope that."

ποθί—somehow.

216 **δώῃ**—aorist subjunctive of **δίδωμι**.

217 **κυβερνήτης,-ου, ὁ**—steersman; **κυβερνῆθ' = κυβερνῆτα** – vocative.

ὧδ' = ὧδε—"as follows."

ἐπιτέλλω—*active or middle*, give orders to (+ dat.).

218 **βάλλευ**—middle imperative; **ἐνὶ θυμῷ βάλλευ** – "take it to heart" (literally?).

οἰήϊον,-ου, τό—quarter rudder. Quarter rudders were rudders that looked like large oars, mounted on one or both sides of the stern (rear) section of a ship.

νωμάω, νωμήσω—handle, control.

219 **ἐκτός**—far from (+ gen.).

ἐέργω, ἔρξω, ἔρξα—keep away.

220 ~ **σκόπελος,-ου, ὁ**—cliff, crag. (This refers to the cliff inhabited by Scylla. Odysseus is telling the steersman to stay close to this cliff and away from the smoke and surf of the Planctae, in other words, to take the route that leads between Scylla and Charybdis.)

ἐπιμαίομαι, (aor.) **ἐπεμασσάμην**—steer for, head for (+ gen.); **ἐπιμαίεο** – imperative, 2nd pers. sing.

λάθησι—aorist subjunctive, 3rd pers. sing. of **λανθάνω**.

221 **κεῖσ' = κεῖσε**—to that place, there.

ἐξορμάω, ἐξορμήσω—deviate from a course, swerve; **μή σε λάθησι [νηῦς] κεῖσ' ἐξορμήσασα** – "lest the ship, deviating from its course there, escape your attention," *i.e.*, lest you accidentally let the ship head toward the Planctae.

ἄμμε = ἡμᾶς.

βάλησθα = βάλῃς.

Scanning Notes

209 The **ι** in **ἔπι** is long.

212 The **ι** in **ὀΐω** is long.

215 The first **ι** in **κληΐδεσσιν** is long.

217 The **υ** in **θυμῷ** is long.

219 The **υ** in **κύματος** is long.

221 The first **α** in **ἐξορμήσασα** is long.

ὣς ἐφάμην, οἱ δ' ὦκα ἐμοῖσ' ἐπέεσσι πίθοντο.
Σκύλλην δ' οὐκέτ' ἐμυθεόμην, ἄπρηκτον ἀνίην,
μή πώς μοι δείσαντες ἀπολλήξειαν ἑταῖροι
εἰρεσίης, ἐντὸς δὲ πυκάζοιεν σφέας αὐτούς.

*Although Circe had told him not to try to fight Scylla, Odysseus puts on his armor (**τεύχεα**), takes **δύο** spears, and waits for Scylla on the front deck of the **νηῦς**. But he cannot see her anywhere.*

καὶ τότε δὴ Κίρκης μὲν ἐφημοσύνης ἀλεγεινῆς
λανθανόμην, ἐπεὶ οὔ τί μ' ἀνώγει θωρήσσεσθαι·
αὐτὰρ ἐγὼ καταδὺς κλυτὰ τεύχεα καὶ δύο δοῦρε
μάκρ' ἐν χερσὶν ἑλὼν εἰς ἴκρια νηὸς ἔβαινον
πρῴρης· ἔνθεν γάρ μιν ἐδέγμην πρῶτα φανεῖσθαι
Σκύλλην πετραίην, ἥ μοι φέρε πῆμ' ἑτάροισιν.
οὐδέ πῃ ἀθρῆσαι δυνάμην· ἔκαμον δέ μοι ὄσσε
πάντῃ παπταίνοντι πρὸς ἠεροειδέα πέτρην.

---

222 **ὦκα**—quickly, at once.

πίθοντο = ἐπίθοντο.

223 **Σκύλλη,-ης, ἡ**—Scylla.

οὐκέτ' = οὐκέτι—no more, no further, *i.e.*, no more than mentioning in 12.220 the **σκόπελος** where she lived.

μυθέομαι, μυθήσομαι, μυθησάμην—speak of, mention.

ἄπρηκτος,-ον—against which nothing can be done.

ἀνίη,-ης, ἡ—danger, peril.

224 **μή πως**—"so that...not" (introduces a purpose clause with two optative verbs).

ἀπολλήγω, ἀπολλήξω—stop, cease or desist from (+ gen.); **ἀπολλήξειαν** – aorist optative.

225 **εἰρεσίη,-ης, ἡ**—rowing.

ἐντός—within, inside, *i.e.*, within or in the bottom of the ship.

πυκάζω, (aor.) **πύκασα**—conceal, shut up.

σφέας—them (acc. plur. of **εἷο**).

226 **ἐφημοσύνη,-ης, ἡ**—command.

ἀλεγεινός,-ή,-όν—painful, hard.

227 ἀνώγει—pluperfect, 3rd pers. sing. of ἀνώγω.

θωρήσσομαι—arm oneself.

228 καταδύω, (aor.) κατέδυν—put on; καταδύς – aorist active participle, nom. sing. masc.

κλυτός,-όν—splendid, excellent.

τεύχεα,-ων, τά—armor.

δόρυ, δούρατος or δουρός, τό—spear; δοῦρε – acc. dual.

229 μάκρ' = μακρώ—acc. dual neut. – "long."

ἴκρια,-ων, τά—deck.

230 πρῴρη,-ης, ἡ—ship's bow, prow, forepart of a ship; ἴκρια νηὸς...πρῴρης – the bow deck. (There was a small deck (ἴκρια) on both ends, stern and bow, of Homeric ships.)

ἐδέγμην—"I expected;" aorist of δέχομαι.

φανεῖσθαι—future passive infinitive; μιν...φανεῖσθαι – accusative/infinitive with ἐδέγμην: "that she would be seen."

231 πετραῖος,-η,-ον—rock-dwelling, living among the rocks.

πῆμ' = πῆμα.

232 πῃ—anywhere.

ἀθρέω—see, observe; ἀθρῆσαι – aorist active infinitive.

δυνάμην = ἐδυνάμην.

κάμνω, (aor.) ἔκαμον—grow weary, become exhausted.

233 πάντῃ—in all directions.

παπταίνω—glance, peer; παπταίνοντι – modifies μοι.

ἠεροειδής,-ές—misty.

Scanning Notes

223 The υ in ἐμυθεόμην is long.

The ι in ἀνίην is long.

*The **νηῦς** sails down a narrow passage (**στεινωπός**), trying to avoid the whirlpool of Charybdis. This whirlpool sucks down the **ὕδωρ θαλάσσης**, then throws it up again so high the spray falls on the tops of both **σκόπελοι**. Fear (**δέος**) seizes the men.*

ἡμεῖς μὲν στεινωπὸν ἀνεπλέομεν γοόωντες·
ἔνθεν γὰρ Σκύλλη, ἑτέρωθι δὲ δῖα Χάρυβδις
δεινὸν ἀνερροίβδησε θαλάσσης ἁλμυρὸν ὕδωρ.
ἦ τοι ὅτ' ἐξεμέσειε, λέβης ὣς ἐν πυρὶ πολλῷ
πᾶσ' ἀναμορμύρεσκε κυκωμένη· ὑψόσε δ' ἄχνη
ἄκροισι σκοπέλοισιν ἐπ' ἀμφοτέροισιν ἔπιπτεν.
ἀλλ' ὅτ' ἀναβρόξειε θαλάσσης ἁλμυρὸν ὕδωρ,
πᾶσ' ἔντοσθε φάνεσκε κυκωμένη, ἀμφὶ δὲ πέτρη
δεινὸν βεβρύχει, ὑπένερθε δὲ γαῖα φάνεσκε
ψάμμῳ κυανέη· τοὺς δὲ χλωρὸν δέος ᾕρει.

---

234 **στεινωπός,-οῦ, ἡ**—narrow passage, strait.

ἀναπλέω, ἀναπλεύσομαι—sail through.

γοάω, γοήσομαι, ἐγόησα—weep, wail, groan; **γοόωντες** – present active participle.

235 **ἔνθεν**—"on one side;" **ἔνθεν** [ἦν].

ἑτέρωθι—on the other side, opposite.

Χάρυβδις,-εως, ἡ—Charybdis, the sea goddess who created the deadly whirlpool at the foot of the cliff opposite the cliff in which Scylla lived.

236 **δεινόν**—terribly, dreadfully.

ἀναρροιβδέω, ἀναρροιβδήσω, ἀνερροίβδησα—swallow down, suck down.

~ **ἁλμυρός,-ά,-όν**—salty, briny.

237 **ὅτ'** = **ὅτε**.

ἐξεμέω, ἐξεμέσω—vomit forth, throw up, disgorge; **ἐξεμέσειε** – aorist optative (optative with **ὅτε**).

λέβης,-ητος, ὁ—cauldron, kettle, metal vessel for boiling water; **λέβης ὥς** – "like a cauldron."

πῦρ, πυρός, τό—fire; **ἐν πυρὶ πολλῷ** – "on a large fire."

238 **πᾶσ'** = **πᾶσα**.

ἀναμορμύρω—boil up, foam up; **ἀναμορμύρεσκε** – iterative imperfect.

κυκάω, κυκήσω—foam up, seethe; **πᾶσ'...κυκωμένη** – "all seething."

ὑψόσε—high, up, upwards.

ἄχνη,-ης, ἡ—foam, spray.

239 **ἄκρος,-η,-ον**—topmost part of.

πίπτω, πεσοῦμαι, ἔπεσον—fall.

240 **ἀναβρόχω**, (aor.) **ἀνέβροξα**—swallow down, swallow again, suck down again.

241 **ἔντοσθε**—inside.

φάνεσκε—"she appeared."

ἀμφί—on both sides; **ἀμφὶ δὲ πέτρη** refers to the rock in the two cliffs between which they are sailing.

242 **βέβρυχα** (perfect, translate as present)—roar; **βεβρύχει** – pluperfect, 3rd pers. sing., translate as imperfect.

ὑπένερθε—beneath, below.

γαῖα—refers to the sea floor, visible at the bottom of the whirlpool.

243 **ψάμμος,-ου, ἡ**—sand.

κυάνεος,-η,-ον—dark; **ψάμμῳ κυανέη**: "dark with sand."

τούς—*i.e.*, Odysseus' companions.

χλωρός,-ή,-όν—pale.

ᾕρει—imperfect of **αἱρέω**.

Scanning Notes

236 The **υ** in **ὕδωρ** is long.

238 The **υ** in **ἀναμορμύρεσκε** is long.

240 The **υ** in **ὕδωρ** is long.

242 The **υ** in **βεβρύχει** is long.

243 The **υ** in **κυανέη** is long.

*As the terrified men look toward Charybdis, Scylla seizes and eats **ἕξ** of the **ἑταῖροι**.*

ἡμεῖς μὲν πρὸς τὴν ἴδομεν δείσαντες ὄλεθρον·
τόφρα δέ μοι Σκύλλη γλαφυρῆς ἐκ νηὸς ἑταίρους
ἓξ ἕλεθ', οἳ χερσίν τε βίηφί τε φέρτατοι ἦσαν.
σκεψάμενος δ' ἐς νῆα θοὴν ἅμα καὶ μεθ' ἑταίρους
ἤδη τῶν ἐνόησα πόδας καὶ χεῖρας ὕπερθεν
ὑψόσ' ἀειρομένων· ἐμὲ δὲ φθέγγοντο καλεῦντες
ἐξονομακλήδην, τότε γ' ὕστατον, ἀχνύμενοι κῆρ.

---

244 **τήν** – "her," *i.e.*, Charybdis.

245 **τόφρα**—meanwhile.

Fig. 7. Askos with plastic decoration depicting Scylla (detail). South Italian, late 4th century BCE. Probably from Canosa, Apulia, Italy. Pottery with traces of paint. 2008.172. Museum of Art and Archaeology, University of Missouri. Weinberg Fund and Gilbreath-McLorn Museum Fund.

246 **ἕξ**—six.

ἕλεθ' = ἕλετο—"took as prey;" aorist middle of **αἱρέω**.

χερσίν τε βίηφί τε—"in strength and might."

φέρτατος,-η,-ον—best, most powerful.

247 **σκέπτομαι, σκέψομαι, ἐσκεψάμην**—look, look about, turn one's eyes; **σκεψάμενος** – "when I looked" (he had been looking at Charybdis).

ἅμα—at the same time.

μεθ' = μετά; μεθ' ἑταίρους – "for my companions," "in search of my companions."

248 **ἤδη**—already; modifies **ἀειρομένων** in the next line.

νοέω, νοήσω, ἐνόησα—see, observe, perceive.

ὕπερθεν—above, *i.e.*, the six men are above him as Scylla pulls them off the ship and up to her cave.

249 **ὑψόσ' = ὑψόσε**—upwards.

ἀείρω, (aor.) **ἤειρα**—lift, pick up; *passive*, be taken up and carried off, be lifted, be carried up, rise.

ἐμέ—object of **καλεῦντες** (present active participle, nom. plur. masc. of **καλέω** – call on for help).

φθέγγομαι, φθέγξομαι, ἐφθεγξάμην—call out, shout.

250 **ἐξονομακλήδην**—by name.

ὕστατον—for the last time.

ἄχνυμαι—be distressed, grieve.

κῆρ—ACCUSATIVE OF RESPECT; **ἀχνύμενοι κῆρ** – "in anguish."

ὡς δ' ὅτ' ἐπὶ προβόλῳ ἁλιεὺς περιμήκεϊ ῥάβδῳ
ἰχθύσι τοῖς ὀλίγοισι δόλον κατὰ εἴδατα βάλλων
ἐς πόντον προΐησι βοὸς κέρας ἀγραύλοιο,
ἀσπαίροντα δ' ἔπειτα λαβὼν ἔρριψε θύραζε,
ὣς οἵ γ' ἀσπαίροντες ἀείροντο προτὶ πέτρας.
αὐτοῦ δ' εἰνὶ θύρῃσι κατήσθιε κεκλήγοντας,
χεῖρας ἐμοὶ ὀρέγοντας ἐν αἰνῇ δηϊοτῆτι.
οἴκτιστον δὴ κεῖνο ἐμοῖσ' ἴδον ὀφθαλμοῖσι
πάντων, ὅσσ' ἐμόγησα πόρους ἁλὸς ἐξερεείνων.

---

251 **ὡς δ' ὅτ'**—as when.

πρόβολος,-ου, ὁ—a projecting rock.

ἁλιεῦς,-ῆος, ὁ—fisherman.

ῥάβδος,-ου, ἡ—fishing-rod; **περιμήκεϊ ῥάβδῳ** – DATIVE OF MEANS with **προΐησι** in 12.253.

252 **ἰχθύς,-ύος, ὁ**—fish.

ὀλίγος,-η,-ον—small (a spear would have been used for larger fish rather than rod, line, and bait).

δόλον—"bait."

εἶδαρ,-ατος, τά—food; **εἴδατα** *with* **δόλον** – "food as bait."

253 **προΐησι**—"lets fall," "throws;" present, 3rd person singular of **προΐημι**.

κέρας, κέρατος or **κέραος, τό**—horn [of an animal]. There are many theories about how a horn was used. It was probably a tube of bull's horn around the the fishing line just above the hook to protect the line from being bitten off by a fish.

ἄγραυλος,-ον—dwelling in the fields, field-dwelling.

254 **ἀσπαίρω**—gasp; **ἀσπαίροντα** [**ἰχθύν**].

ἔρριψε—"he throws;" gnomic aorist, an aorist used for a customary action; translated as present.

θύραζε—out [of the sea].

255 **οἵ**—refers to the six men taken by Scylla.

προτί—to, towards (+ acc.).

256 **εἰνί = ἐν**.

θύρῃσι—"the mouth of the cave," "the cave's entrance."

κατεσθίω—devour, eat.

κλάζω, κλάγξω, ἔκλαγξα, κέκλαγγα—scream, shout, shriek; **κεκλήγοντας** – perfect active participle, acc. plur. masc.; translate as present.

257 **ὀρέγω, ὀρέξω, ὤρεξα**—hold out, stretch out.

αἰνός,-ή,-όν—terrible.

δηϊοτής,-ῆτος, ἡ—struggle.

258 **οἴκτιστος,-η,-ον**—most pitiable, most wretched.

259 **πόροι,-ων, οἱ**—pathways.

ἐξερεείνω—traverse, explore.

Odyssey Book 12.429-450

Because Odysseus' companions killed and ate the cattle belonging to Helios, Zeus sent a terrible storm upon them when they sailed from Thrinacia. It destroyed the ship and killed everyone except Odysseus. He lashed the mast and keel of the shattered ship together and, sitting on them, was driven by the winds over the stormy sea.

Book 12.429-450

Odysseus is carried back to the ***σκόπελος*** *of Scylla and* ***δεινή*** *Charybdis. When the whirlpool sucks down the* ***ὕδωρ θαλάσσης****, the mast (****ἱστός****) and keel (****τρόπις****) on which he has been riding go down too. Odysseus catches hold of a large fig tree (****ἐρινεός****), to which he clings until the* ***ἱστός*** *and the* ***τρόπις*** *reappear.*

παννύχιος φερόμην, ἅμα δ' ἠελίῳ ἀνιόντι 429
ἦλθον ἐπὶ Σκύλλης σκόπελον δεινήν τε Χάρυβδιν. 430
ἡ μὲν ἀνερροίβδησε θαλάσσης ἁλμυρὸν ὕδωρ· 431
αὐτὰρ ἐγὼ ποτὶ μακρὸν ἐρινεὸν ὑψόσ' ἀερθείς, 432
τῷ προσφὺς ἐχόμην ὡς νυκτερίς· οὐδέ πῃ εἶχον 433
οὔτε στηρίξαι ποσὶν ἔμπεδον οὔτ' ἐπιβῆναι· 434
ῥίζαι γὰρ ἑκὰς εἶχον, ἀπήωροι δ' ἔσαν ὄζοι 435
μακροί τε μεγάλοι τε, κατεσκίαον δὲ Χάρυβδιν. 436
νωλεμέως δ' ἐχόμην, ὄφρ' ἐξεμέσειεν ὀπίσσω 437
ἱστὸν καὶ τρόπιν αὖτις· ἐελδομένῳ δέ μοι ἦλθον, 438

---

429 **παννύχιος,-ον**—all night long (where English would use an adverb, Greek uses an adjective agreeing with the subject).

ἅμα—with, along with (+ dat.).

431 **ἡ**—"she" (Charybdis).

ἀναρροιβδέω, ἀναρροιβδήσω—swallow down, suck down.

432 **ποτί**—to, towards (+ acc.).

ἐρινεός,-οῦ, ὁ—wild fig tree (Circe had told Odysseus about this tree, which grew on the rock just above the whirlpool.)

ὑψόσε—high, up, upwards.

ἀερθείς—"jumping," "leaping;" aorist passive participle, nom. sing. masc. of **ἀείρω**.

433 **τῷ**—refers to **ἐρινεόν**.

προσφύω, προσφύσω, προσέφυσα—seize, grasp, cling to (+ dat.); **προσφύς** – aorist active participle.

ἐχόμην—"I held on."

νυκτερίς,-ίδος, ἡ—bat.

πῃ—anywhere; **οὐδέ πῃ εἶχον** – "for I had nowhere."

434 **στηρίζω**, (aor.) **ἐστήριξα**—set, find firm footing, plant oneself firmly.

ποσίν—dat. plur. of **πούς**.

ἔμπεδον—firmly; **στηρίξαι ποσὶν ἔμπεδον** – "to plant my feet firmly."

ἐπιβῆναι—"to climb up."

435 **ῥιζα,-ης, ἡ**—root (of a tree or plant).

ἑκάς—far, far away.

εἶχον = ἦσαν.

ἀπήωρος,-ον—high in the air.

ἔσαν = ἦσαν.

ὄζος,-ου, ὁ—branch.

436 **κατασκιάω**—cast a shadow over.

Odysseus must be clinging to the trunk of the fig tree, since he says he could not get a foothold anywhere. The roots are too far below and he is unable to climb up and sit on one of the branches because they are too high in the air.

437 **νωλεμέως**—unceasingly, without rest.

ἐξεμέω, ἐξεμέσω—vomit forth, throw up, disgorge; **ἐξεμέσειεν** – aorist optative (optative with **ὄφρα**); subject is "she" (Charybdis).

ὀπίσσω—back.

438 **ἱστός,-οῦ, ὁ**—mast.

τρόπις, τρόπιος, ἡ—a ship's keel (the beam of wood running down the center of the bottom of a ship). It has also been suggested that **τρόπις**, while usually translated "keel," in this passage actually refers to the mast step. The mast step is the platform resting on the keel that supports the lower end of the mast.

ἐέλδομαι—long for, wish, desire.

Scanning Notes

431 The **υ** in **ὕδωρ** is long.

432 The **ι** in **ἐρινεόν** is long.

433 The **υ** in **προσφύς** is long.

435 **γάρ** is scanned long because **ἑκάς** was originally spelled **ϝεκάς**.

ὄψ'· ἦμος δ' ἐπὶ δόρπον ἀνὴρ ἀγορῆθεν ἀνέστη
κρίνων νείκεα πολλὰ δικαζομένων αἰζηῶν,
τῆμος δὴ τά γε δοῦρα Χαρύβδιος ἐξεφαάνθη.

Odysseus lets himself fall into the ***ὕδωρ***. ***Ἑζόμενος*** *on the pieces of wood, he paddles away, avoiding Scylla and* ***αἰπὺς ὄλεθρος***. *After drifting for nine days (**ἐννῆμαρ**), he reaches Calypso's* ***νῆσος***.

ἧκα δ' ἐγὼ καθύπερθε πόδας καὶ χεῖρε φέρεσθαι,
μέσσῳ δ' ἐνδούπησα παρὲξ περιμήκεα δοῦρα,
ἑζόμενος δ' ἐπὶ τοῖσι διήρεσα χερσὶν ἐμῇσι.
Σκύλλην δ' οὐκέτ' ἔασε πατὴρ ἀνδρῶν τε θεῶν τε
εἰσιδέειν· οὐ γάρ κεν ὑπέκφυγον αἰπὺν ὄλεθρον.
 ἔνθεν δ' ἐννῆμαρ φερόμην, δεκάτῃ δέ με νυκτὶ
νῆσον ἐς Ὠγυγίην πέλασαν θεοί, ἔνθα Καλυψὼ
ναίει ἐϋπλόκαμος, δεινὴ θεὸς αὐδήεσσα,
ἥ μ' ἐφίλει τ' ἐκόμει τε.

---

439 **ὄψ' = ὀψέ**—late, at last, after a long time.

ἦμος—at the time when.

δόρπον,-ου, τό—evening meal; **ἐπὶ δόρπον** – "for the evening meal."

ἀγορῆθεν—from the marketplace.

ἀνέστη—GNOMIC AORIST.

440 **κρίνω**—decide, settle; **κρίνων** describes **ἀνήρ** in the previous line – "the man who decides."

νεῖκος,-εος, τό—quarrel.

δικάζω, δικάσω—pronounce judgment, give a decision; *middle*, seek a judgment or decision.

αἰζηοί,-ῶν, οἱ—young men.

Homer is describing late afternoon or early evening, when the man judging cases would go home for his evening meal. Using this picture from ordinary life to indicate the time draws a sharp contrast between what Odysseus would have been doing if he were leading a normal life at home and the suffering he is currently undergoing.

441 **τῆμος**—then, at that time. (The time is late afternoon/early evening. Since he came to the whirlpool **ἅμα δ' ἠελίῳ ἀνιόντι** (12.429), he has been clinging to the tree all day.)

δόρυ, δουρός, τό—plank; **τά...δοῦρα = ἱστὸν καὶ τρόπιν.**

Χαρύβδιος—"out of Charybdis."

ἐκφαίνω, (aor.) **ἐξέφηνα**—bring to light; *passive*, appear, come forth; **ἐξεφαάνθη** – aorist passive, 3rd pers. sing.

442 **ἧκα**—aorist of **ἵημι**: "I let go," "I unclasped."

καθύπερθε—from above.

χεῖρε—acc. dual.

καθύπερθε...φέρεσθαι—to be carried from above, *i.e.*, to fall.

443 **μέσσῳ**—*i.e.*, in the middle of the water.

ἐνδουπέω, ἐνδουπήσω, ἐνδούπησα—fall in with a splash or thud (+ dat.).

παρέξ—along side of (+ acc.).

περιμήκης,-ες—long.

444 **διερέσσω**, (aor.) **διήρεσα**—row, paddle.

445 **ἐάω, ἐάσω, ἔασα**—allow, permit.

446 **εἰσοράω**, (aor.) **εἰσεῖδον**—see, catch sight of; **Σκύλλην** is the subject of the aorist infinitive **εἰσιδέειν. με** is its understood object.

οὐ γάρ κεν ὑπέκφυγον αἰπὺν ὄλεθρον—the apodosis of a past contrary to fact (had/would have) condition. The understood protasis: "If Zeus had allowed Scylla to catch sight of me."

447 **ἐννῆμαρ**—for nine days.

448 **πελάζω, πελάσω, ἐπέλασ(σ)α**—bring.

449 **ναίω**—live, dwell.

αὐδήεις,-εσσα—speaking with human voice (as opposed to the way the gods speak); **δεινὴ θεὸς αὐδήεσσα** – "the dangerous goddess who can speak the language of men."

450 **κομέω**—look after, care for.

In describing his arrival at Calypso's island (where we first met him in Book 5), Odysseus has now come to the end of the story he has been telling the Phaeacians, the story of what happened to him from the end of the Trojan War until he was shipwrecked upon their coast. The next twelve books of the *Odyssey* describe what happens next – his arrival in Ithaca, the concealment of his identity, his meeting with his son, the return to his palace disguised as a beggar, the destruction of the suitors, and finally, his reunion with Penelope.

Scanning Notes

445 The **α** in **ἔασε** is long.

Appendix 1 – Source Notes

The *Odyssey* has been analyzed, critiqued, and explained for over two thousand years. The interpretations and explanations put forward in this book include ideas and research from many scholars. To give proper credit and to indicate books and articles for further investigation, the sources are listed in this appendix. They are arranged by the line number and the word or idea to which the note refers.

1.1 **no mention of Odysseus' name** Joachim Latacz. *Homer: His Art and His World*, trans. James P. Holoka (Ann Arbor: University of Michigan Press, 1998), 136; Peter Jones, ed. *Homer: Odyssey 1 & 2* (Warminster, England: Aris & Phillips Ltd., 1991), 102.

Μοῦσα Elizabeth Minchin, "The Poet Appeals to His Muse: Homeric Invocations in the Context of Epic Performance," *Classical Journal* 91, no. 1 (Oct.-Nov. 1995): 26-27.

πολύτροπος W. B. Stanford, ed. *The Odyssey of Homer*, Vol. I (Books I-XII), 2nd ed. (London: St. Martins Press, 1959; reprinted 1977), 206; Stephanie West, "Books I-IV," in *A Commentary on Homer's Odyssey, Vol. I: Introduction and Books I-VIII* by Alfred Heubeck, Stephanie West, and J. B. Hainsworth (Oxford: Clarendon Press, 1988), 69.

1.2 **ἱερὸν πτολίεθρον** W. B. Stanford, ed. *The Odyssey of Homer*, Vol. I (Books I-XII), 2nd ed. (London: St. Martins Press, 1959; reprinted 1977), 207; Stephanie West, "Books I-IV," in *A Commentary on Homer's Odyssey, Vol. I: Introduction and Books I-VIII* by Alfred Heubeck, Stephanie West, and J. B. Hainsworth (Oxford: Clarendon Press, 1988), 70.

1.7 **σφετέρῃσιν ἀτασθαλίῃσιν** Stephanie West, "Books I-IV," in *A Commentary on Homer's Odyssey, Vol. I: Introduction and Books I-VIII* by Alfred Heubeck, Stephanie West, and J. B. Hainsworth (Oxford: Clarendon Press, 1988), 71-72; D. M. Jones. *Ethical Themes in the Plot of the Odyssey* (London: University of London, 1954); Howard W. Clarke. *The Art of the Odyssey*, 2nd ed. (Bristol: Bristol Classical Press, 1989), 7. For more discussion of **ἀτασθαλίαι** and whether the fate of Odysseus' men is a good example of this theme, see: Jenny Strauss Clay, "The Beginning of the Odyssey," *American Journal of Philology* 97, no. 4 (Winter 1976): 313-317; Rainer Friedrich, "Thrinakia and Zeus' Ways to Men in the *Odyssey*," *Greek, Roman and Byzantine Studies* 28, no. 4 (Winter 1987): 375-400.

1.10 **εἰπὲ καὶ ἡμῖν** W. B. Stanford, ed. *The Odyssey of Homer*, Vol. I (Books I-XII), 2nd ed. (London: St. Martins Press, 1959; reprinted 1977), 208-9; Stephanie West, "Books I-IV," in *A Commentary on Homer's Odyssey, Vol. I: Introduction and Books I-VIII* by Alfred Heubeck, Stephanie West, and J. B. Hainsworth (Oxford: Clarendon Press, 1988), 73.

1.11 **αἰπύν** Peter Jones, ed. *Homer: Odyssey 1 & 2* (Warminster, England: Aris & Phillips Ltd., 1991), 100; Stephanie West, "Books I-IV," in *A Commentary on Homer's Odyssey, Vol. I: Introduction and Books I-VIII* by Alfred Heubeck, Stephanie West, and J. B. Hainsworth (Oxford: Clarendon Press, 1988), 73; Arie Hoekstra, "Books IX-XII," in *A*

Commentary on Homer's Odyssey, Vol. II: Books IX-XVI by Alfred Heubeck and Arie Hoekstra (Oxford: Clarendon Press, 1990), 282.

1.14 **Καλυψώ** Peter Jones, ed. *Homer: Odyssey 1 & 2* (Warminster, England: Aris & Phillips Ltd., 1991), 100-101; W. J. Woodhouse. *The Composition of the Odyssey* (Oxford: Clarendon Press, 1930), 215-217.

1.22 **Αἰθίοπες** Stephanie West, "Books I-IV," in *A Commentary on Homer's Odyssey, Vol. I: Introduction and Books I-VIII* by Alfred Heubeck, Stephanie West, and J. B. Hainsworth (Oxford: Clarendon Press, 1988), 75; Frank M. Snowden, Jr. *Before Color Prejudice: The Ancient View of Blacks* (Cambridge MA: Harvard University Press, 1983), 56.

1.29 **ἀμύμων** Stephanie West, "Books I-IV," in *A Commentary on Homer's Odyssey, Vol. I: Introduction and Books I-VIII* by Alfred Heubeck, Stephanie West, and J. B. Hainsworth (Oxford: Clarendon Press, 1988), 77; Peter Jones, ed. *Homer: Odyssey 1 & 2* (Warminster, England: Aris & Phillips Ltd., 1991), 103; Matthew Clark, "Formulas, Metre and Type-Scenes," in *The Cambridge Companion to Homer*, ed. Robert Fowler (Cambridge: Cambridge University Press, 2004), 128-130; Steven Lowenstam, "Iros' Mother and the Hand of Penelope: Homeric Diction," in *The Scepter and the Spear: Studies on Forms of Repetition in the Homeric Poems* (Lanham, MD: Rowman & Littlefield, 1993), 46-51; Frederick M. Combellack, "Two Blameless Homeric Characters," *American Journal of Philology* 103, no. 4 (Winter, 1982): 361-368; Anne Amory Parry. *Blameless Aegisthus: A Study in ΑΜΥΜΩΝ and Other Epithets in Homer* (Leiden: E. J. Brill, 1973), 112, 124; Charles Rowan Beye. *The Iliad, The Odyssey, and the Epic Tradition* (Gloucester, MA: Peter Smith, 1972; originally published in 1966, Anchor Books edition, Doubleday), 24-25; *An Intermediate Greek-English Lexicon founded upon the Seventh Edition of Liddell and Scott's Greek-English Lexicon* (Oxford: Clarendon Press, 1972; originally published 1889), s.v. "ἀμύμων."

the Aegisthus story, Homer's version and Aeschylus' version Peter Jones, ed. *Homer: Odyssey 1 & 2* (Warminster, England: Aris & Phillips Ltd., 1991), 104.

1.34 **ὑπὲρ μόρον** Peter Jones, ed. *Homer: Odyssey 1 & 2* (Warminster, England: Aris & Phillips Ltd., 1991), 105; Bernadotte Perrin and Thomas Day Seymour, eds. *Eight Books of Homer's Odyssey with Introduction, Commentary, and Vocabulary* (Boston: Ginn & Co., 1897), Commentary, p. 4.

1.38 **Ἀργεϊφόντης** Stephanie West, "Books I-IV," in *A Commentary on Homer's Odyssey, Vol. I: Introduction and Books I-VIII* by Alfred Heubeck, Stephanie West, and J. B. Hainsworth (Oxford: Clarendon Press, 1988), 79.

1.41 **Agamemnon/Clytemnestra/Orestes story** Irene de Jong. *A Narratological Commentary on the Odyssey* (Cambridge: Cambridge University Press, 2001), 12-14; Edward F. D'Arms and Karl K. Hulley, "The Oresteia-Story in the *Odyssey*," *Transactions of the American Philological Association* 77 (1946): 207-213; Howard W. Clarke. *The Art of the Odyssey*, 2nd ed. (Bristol: Bristol Classical Press, 1989), 10-12; S. Douglas Olson, "The Stories of Agamemnon in Homer's Odyssey," *Transactions of the American Philological Association* 120 (1990): 57-71.

1.47 **Athena's wish as foreshadowing** Stephanie West, "Books I-IV," in *A Commentary on Homer's Odyssey, Vol. I: Introduction and Books I-VIII* by Alfred Heubeck, Stephanie West, and J. B. Hainsworth (Oxford: Clarendon Press, 1988), 80; Irene de Jong. *A Narratological Commentary on the Odyssey* (Cambridge: Cambridge University Press, 2001), 14.

1.54 **Atlas** Stephanie West, "Books I-IV," in *A Commentary on Homer's Odyssey, Vol. I: Introduction and Books I-VIII* by Alfred Heubeck, Stephanie West, and J. B. Hainsworth (Oxford: Clarendon Press, 1988), 81-82.

1.62 **ὠδύσαο** Peter Jones, ed. *Homer: Odyssey 1 & 2* (Warminster, England: Aris & Phillips Ltd., 1991), 108; Irene de Jong. *A Narratological Commentary on the Odyssey* (Cambridge: Cambridge University Press, 2001), 14.

1.72 **ἀτρυγέτοιο** D. M. Jones, "Etymological Notes," *Transactions of the Philological Society* (1953): 51; Simon Pulleyn, ed. *Homer: Iliad, Book One* (Oxford: Oxford University Press, 2000), 207-208.

1.78-79 **ἀντία...ἀέκητι** W. B. Stanford, ed. *The Odyssey of Homer*, Vol. I (Books I-XII), 2nd ed. (London: St. Martins Press, 1959; reprinted 1977), 216.

1.86 **ἐϋπλοκάμῳ** J. B. Hainsworth, "Books V-VIII," in *A Commentary on Homer's Odyssey, Vol. I: Introduction and Books I-VIII* by Alfred Heubeck, Stephanie West, and J. B. Hainsworth (Oxford: Clarendon Press, 1988), 261; Peter Jones, ed. *Homer: Odyssey 1 & 2* (Warminster, England: Aris & Phillips Ltd., 1991), 110.

1.90 **κάρη κομόωντας** Stephanie West, "Books I-IV," in *A Commentary on Homer's Odyssey, Vol. I: Introduction and Books I-VIII* by Alfred Heubeck, Stephanie West, and J. B. Hainsworth (Oxford: Clarendon Press, 1988), 86; Thomas Day Seymour. *Life in the Homeric Age* (1907; reprint, New York: Biblo & Tannen, 1963), 175-176.

Ἀχαιούς Stephanie West, "Books I-IV," in *A Commentary on Homer's Odyssey, Vol. I: Introduction and Books I-VIII* by Alfred Heubeck, Stephanie West, and J. B. Hainsworth (Oxford: Clarendon Press, 1988), 86.

1.91 **suitors mentioned for the first time** Peter Jones, ed. *Homer: Odyssey 1 & 2* (Warminster, England: Aris & Phillips Ltd., 1991), 110.

2.86 **Antinous' attempt to undermine Telemachus' authority** Stephanie West, "Books I-IV," in *A Commentary on Homer's Odyssey, Vol. I: Introduction and Books I-VIII* by Alfred Heubeck, Stephanie West, and J. B. Hainsworth (Oxford: Clarendon Press, 1988), 136; Anne Amory Parry. *Blameless Aegisthus: A Study in AMYMΩN and Other Epithets in Homer* (Leiden: E. J. Brill, 1973): 29-35.

2.94 **ἱστόν** Thomas Day Seymour. *Life in the Homeric Age* (1907; reprint, New York: Biblo & Tannen, 1963), 135; W. W. Merry, ed. *Homer, Odyssey, Books I-XII* (Oxford: Clarendon Press, 1870; reprint, 1932), Notes, p. 31. For more details on looms and weaving, see *The Oxford Classical Dictionary*, 3rd ed., s.v. "textile production," by John Peter Wild.

2.95 **the use of fine threads** Stephanie West, "Books I-IV," in *A Commentary on Homer's Odyssey, Vol. I: Introduction and Books I-VIII* by Alfred Heubeck, Stephanie West, and J. B. Hainsworth (Oxford: Clarendon Press, 1988), 138.

2.96 **Penelope's pretense** Stephanie West, "Books I-IV," in *A Commentary on Homer's Odyssey, Vol. I: Introduction and Books I-VIII* by Alfred

Heubeck, Stephanie West, and J. B. Hainsworth (Oxford: Clarendon Press, 1988), 138.

2.98 **μή...ὄληται** Bernadotte Perrin and Thomas Day Seymour, eds. *Eight Books of Homer's Odyssey with Introduction, Commentary, and Vocabulary* (Boston: Ginn & Co., 1897), Commentary, p. 27.

2.100 **τανηλεγέος** Stephanie West, "Books I-IV," in *A Commentary on Homer's Odyssey, Vol. I: Introduction and Books I-VIII* by Alfred Heubeck, Stephanie West, and J. B. Hainsworth (Oxford: Clarendon Press, 1988), 138.

2.110 **weaving, women, and Penelope** Jane McIntosh Snyder, "The Web of Song: Weaving Imagery in Homer and the Lyric Poets," *Classical Journal* 76, no. 3 (February/March 1981): 193-194; Irene de Jong. *A Narratological Commentary on the Odyssey* (Cambridge: Cambridge University Press, 2001), 50-51.

5.123 **Ὀρτυγίη** J. B. Hainsworth, "Books V-VIII," in *A Commentary on Homer's Odyssey, Vol. I: Introduction and Books I-VIII* by Alfred Heubeck, Stephanie West, and J. B. Hainsworth (Oxford: Clarendon Press, 1988), 266.

5.127 **τριπόλῳ** Edward A. Armstrong, "The Triple-Furrowed Field," *The Classical Review* 57 (1943): 4-5.

5.130 **τρόπις** Samuel Mark. *Homeric Seafaring* (College Station: Texas A&M University Press, 2005), 126-127.

5.140 **ἀτρύγετον** See note on 1.72 above.

5.155 **παρ' οὐκ ἐθέλων ἐθελούσῃ** W. W. Merry, ed. *Homer, Odyssey, Books I-XII* (Oxford: Clarendon Press, 1870; reprint, 1932), Notes, p. 68.

5.163 **σχεδίην** Samuel Mark. *Homeric Seafaring* (College Station: Texas A&M University Press, 2005), 70-96.

5.175 **ἐῖσαι** Samuel Mark. *Homeric Seafaring* (College Station: Texas A&M University Press, 2005), 98-99.

5.179 **Odysseus' speech and what it reveals about him** Charles Rowan Beye. *The Iliad, The Odyssey, and the Epic Tradition* (Gloucester, MA: Peter Smith, 1972; originally published in 1966, Anchor Books edition, Doubleday), 187-188.

5.205 **καὶ ἔμπης** W. B. Stanford, ed. *The Odyssey of Homer*, Vol. I (Books I-XII), 2nd ed. (London: St. Martins Press, 1959; reprinted 1977), 299.

5.217 **μέγεθος** J. B. Hainsworth, "Books V-VIII," in *A Commentary on Homer's Odyssey, Vol. I: Introduction and Books I-VIII* by Alfred Heubeck, Stephanie West, and J. B. Hainsworth (Oxford: Clarendon Press, 1988), 272.

5.227 **Odysseus' sexual relationship with Calypso** M. I. Finley. *The World of Odysseus* (New York: New York Review of Books, 2002; originally published in 1954; revised edition in 1977), 130; James Morrison. *A Companion to Homer's Odyssey* (Westport, CN: Greenwood Press, 2003), 66.

5.337 **αἴθυια** W. Geoffrey Arnott. *Birds in the Ancient World from A to Z* (London and New York: Routledge, 2007), 7-8.

6.119 **αὖτε** Paul Shorey, "The Pathos and Humor of αὖ," *Classical Philology* 23, no. 3 (July 1928): 286.

6.130 **λέων** Thomas Day Seymour. *Life in the Homeric Age* (1907; reprint, New York: Biblo & Tannen, 1963), 372; Stephanie West, "Books I-IV," in *A Commentary on Homer's Odyssey, Vol. I: Introduction and Books I-VIII* by Alfred Heubeck, Stephanie West, and J. B. Hainsworth (Oxford: Clarendon Press, 1988), 213; W. B. Stanford, ed. *The Odyssey of Homer*, Vol. I (Books I-XII), 2nd ed. (London: St. Martins Press, 1959; reprinted 1977), 277.

6.137 **comparison of Odysseus to the lion** Janet Watson, ed. *Homer Odyssey VI & VII* (London: Bristol Classical Press, 2002), 55.

6.142 **supplication** John Gould, "HIKETEIA," *The Journal of Hellenic Studies* 93 (1973): 75-77.

6.186 **λευκώλενος** Allen Rogers Benner. *Selections from Homer's Iliad* (New York: Irvington, 1903), xxv; Simon Pulleyn, ed. *Homer: Iliad, Book One* (Oxford: Oxford University Press, 2000), 140-141.

9. 255 **the Cyclops' questions and Odysseus' actions** Alfred Heubeck, "Books IX-XII," in *A Commentary on Homer's Odyssey, Vol. II: Books IX-XVI* by Alfred Heubeck and Arie Hoekstra (Oxford: Clarendon Press, 1990), 28; W. B. Stanford, ed. *The Odyssey of Homer*, Vol. I (Books I-XII), 2nd ed. (London: St. Martins Press, 1959; reprinted 1977), 357; F. S. Naiden. *Ancient Supplication* (Oxford: Oxford University Press, 2006), 139; Jonathan Shay. *Odysseus in America: Combat Trauma and the Trials of Homecoming* (New York: Scribner, 2002), 45.

piracy Samuel Mark. *Homeric Seafaring* (College Station: Texas A&M University Press, 2005), 18-19; *The Oxford Classical Dictionary*, 3rd ed., s.v. "piracy," by Philip de Souza; Stephanie West, "Books I-IV," in *A Commentary on Homer's Odyssey, Vol. I: Introduction and Books I-VIII* by Alfred Heubeck, Stephanie West, and J. B. Hainsworth (Oxford: Clarendon Press, 1988), 165.

9.267 **gifts for guests** Laura M. Slatkin, "Homer's Odyssey," in *A Companion to Ancient Epic*, ed. John Miles Foley (Malden, MA and Oxford: Blackwell, 2005), 319; Thomas Day Seymour. *Life in the Homeric Age* (1907; reprint, New York: Biblo & Tannen, 1963), 452-453.

9. 289 **σκύλακας** Irene de Jong. *A Narratological Commentary on the Odyssey* (Cambridge: Cambridge University Press, 2001), 241.

9.297 **ἄκρητον** Seth L. Schein, "Odysseus and Polyphemus in the *Odyssey*," *Greek Roman and Byzantine Studies* 11 (1970): 79; W. B. Stanford, ed. *The Odyssey of Homer*, Vol. I (Books I-XII), 2nd ed. (London: St. Martins Press, 1959; reprinted 1977), 358; Alfred Heubeck, "Books IX-XII," in *A Commentary on Homer's Odyssey, Vol. II: Books IX-XVI* by Alfred Heubeck and Arie Hoekstra (Oxford: Clarendon Press, 1990), 30.

9.300 **παρὰ μηροῦ** Thomas Day Seymour. *Life in the Homeric Age* (1907; reprint, New York: Biblo & Tannen, 1963), 666.

9.397 **Cyclopes having only one eye** Robert Mondi, "The Homeric Cyclopes: Folktale, Tradition, and Theme," *Transactions of the American Philological Association* 113 (1983): 17-38; Adrienne Mayor. *The First Fossil Hunters: Paleontology in Greek and Roman Times* (Princeton, NJ: Princeton University Press, 2000), 35-36.

9.536 **τοῦ δ' ἔκλυε** George Eckel Duckworth. *Foreshadowing and Suspense in the Epics of Homer, Apollonius, and Vergil* (New York: Haskell, 1966), 10.

Odysseus telling Polyphemus his name Howard W. Clarke. *The Art of the Odyssey*, 2nd ed. (Bristol: Bristol Classical Press, 1989), 57; Calvin S. Brown, "Odysseus and Polyphemus: The Name and the Curse," *Comparative Literature* 18, no. 3 (September 1966): 193-202; Christopher G. Brown, "In the Cyclops' Cave: Revenge and Justice in *Odyssey* 9," *Mnemosyne* 49, no. 1 (1996): 26-29.

10.32 **πόδα νηός** Samuel Mark. *Homeric Seafaring* (College Station: Texas A&M University Press, 2005), 131.

10.211 **περισκέπτῳ** Alfred Heubeck, "Books IX-XII," in *A Commentary on Homer's Odyssey, Vol. II: Books IX-XVI* by Alfred Heubeck and Arie Hoekstra (Oxford: Clarendon Press, 1990), 55.

10.235 **Πραμνείῳ** Alfred Heubeck, "Books IX-XII," in *A Commentary on Homer's Odyssey, Vol. II: Books IX-XVI* by Alfred Heubeck and Arie Hoekstra (Oxford: Clarendon Press, 1990), 56-57.

10.244 **μέλαιναν** Samuel Mark. *Homeric Seafaring* (College Station: Texas A&M University Press, 2005), 99.

10.272 **κοίλῃ** Samuel Mark. *Homeric Seafaring* (College Station: Texas A&M University Press, 2005), 97.

10.305 **μῶλυ** W. B. Stanford, ed. *The Odyssey of Homer*, Vol. I (Books I-XII), 2nd ed. (London: St. Martins Press, 1959; reprinted 1977), 373-374; Andreas Plaitakis and Roger C. Duvoisin, "Homer's Moly Identified as *Galanthus nivalis*: Physiologic Antidote to Stramonium Poisoning," *Clinical Neuropharmacology* 6, no. 1 (1983): 1-5.

10.347 **oaths of Circe and Calypso** Cathy L. Callaway. "The Oath in Epic Poetry" (Ph.D. diss., University of Washington, 1990), 53, 57.

11.124 **φοινικοπαρῄους** Samuel Mark. *Homeric Seafaring* (College Station: Texas A&M University Press, 2005), 99-100.

11.125 **πτερὰ νηυσί** Samuel Mark. *Homeric Seafaring* (College Station: Texas A&M University Press, 2005), 144-145; W. B. Stanford, ed. *The Odyssey of Homer*, Vol. I (Books I-XII), 2nd ed. (London: St. Martins Press, 1959; reprinted 1977), 386.

11.489 **ἐπάρουρος** Alfred Heubeck, "Books IX-XII," in *A Commentary on Homer's Odyssey, Vol. II: Books IX-XVI* by Alfred Heubeck and Arie Hoekstra (Oxford: Clarendon Press, 1990), 106; W. B. Stanford, ed. *The Odyssey of Homer*, Vol. I (Books I-XII), 2nd ed. (London: St. Martins Press, 1959; reprinted 1977), 398.

11.490 **ἀνδρὶ...ἀκλήρῳ** Alfred Heubeck, "Books IX-XII," in *A Commentary on Homer's Odyssey, Vol. II: Books IX-XVI* by Alfred Heubeck and Arie Hoekstra (Oxford: Clarendon Press, 1990), 106.

11.491 **the afterlife** *The Oxford Classical Dictionary*, 3rd ed., s.v. "death, attitudes to," by Robert S. J. Garland and John Scheid; W. B. Stanford, ed. *The Odyssey of Homer*, Vol. I (Books I-XII), 2nd ed. (London: St. Martins Press, 1959; reprinted 1977), 381.

12.167 **Σειρήνοιϊν** Alfred Heubeck, "Books IX-XII," in *A Commentary on Homer's Odyssey, Vol. II: Books IX-XVI* by Alfred Heubeck and Arie Hoekstra (Oxford: Clarendon Press, 1990), 118-119; Gerald K. Gresseth, "The Homeric Sirens," *Transactions of the American Philological Association* 101 (1970): 211-218.

12.169 **δαίμων** Alfred Heubeck, "Books IX-XII," in *A Commentary on Homer's Odyssey, Vol. II: Books IX-XVI* by Alfred Heubeck and Arie Hoekstra (Oxford: Clarendon Press, 1990), 127.

12.179 **ἱστοπέδη and binding of Odysseus** Samuel Mark. *Homeric Seafaring* (College Station: Texas A&M University Press, 2005), 127-129.

12.202 **the two routes** Alfred Heubeck, "Books IX-XII," in *A Commentary on Homer's Odyssey, Vol. II: Books IX-XVI* by Alfred Heubeck and Arie Hoekstra (Oxford: Clarendon Press, 1990), 121-122, 129.

12.204 **why the oars were not lost** Samuel Mark. *Homeric Seafaring* (College Station: Texas A&M University Press, 2005), 122.

12.218 **οἰήϊα** Samuel Mark. *Homeric Seafaring* (College Station: Texas A&M University Press, 2005), 122-123.

12.229-230 **ἴκρια νηὸς...πρῴρης** Samuel Mark. *Homeric Seafaring* (College Station: Texas A&M University Press, 2005), 115-116.

12.253 **κέρας** Alexander Shewan, "Fishing with a Rod in Homer," in *Homeric Essays* (Oxford: Blackwell, 1935): 427-440; W. B. Stanford, ed. *The Odyssey of Homer*, Vol. I (Books I-XII), 2nd ed. (London: St. Martins Press, 1959; reprinted 1977), 413-414; Alfred Heubeck, "Books IX-XII," in *A Commentary on Homer's Odyssey, Vol. II: Books IX-XVI* by Alfred Heubeck and Arie Hoekstra (Oxford: Clarendon Press, 1990), 132.

12.433-436 **Odysseus and the fig tree** Alfred Heubeck, "Books IX-XII," in *A Commentary on Homer's Odyssey, Vol. II: Books IX-XVI* by Alfred Heubeck and Arie Hoekstra (Oxford: Clarendon Press, 1990), 142.

12.438 **τρόπις** Samuel Mark. *Homeric Seafaring* (College Station: Texas A&M University Press, 2005), 126-127.

12.439-440 **contrast between a normal life for Odysseus and what he is experiencing** W. B. Stanford, ed. *The Odyssey of Homer*, Vol. I (Books I-XII), 2nd ed. (London: St. Martins Press, 1959; reprinted 1977), 418; Alfred Heubeck, "Books IX-XII," in *A Commentary on Homer's Odyssey, Vol. II: Books IX-XVI* by Alfred Heubeck and Arie Hoekstra (Oxford: Clarendon Press, 1990), 142.

Appendix 2 – Some Basic Homeric Forms and Grammar

Homeric Greek contains many forms and usages that differ from Attic Greek, the dialect spoken in Athens in the fifth and fourth centuries B.C.E. and the one taught in most beginning Greek courses. For example, verb augments may be missing. Noun and verb endings as well as word spellings may be quite different.

Homeric Greek is not, however, a dialect that was spoken in one particular place. No group of people spoke it as their everyday language. It is an artificial language, a mixture of words drawn from many dialects and time periods that traveling poets or bards used for the oral composition and performance of their songs. In the generations before Homer (whoever that person or persons may have been), these bards traveled to various gatherings, reciting stories of heroic figures and events. Accompanying themselves with a lyre and composing as they sang, they provided entertainment for aristocratic banquets or at festivals and games.

The language used in these recitations, the language used in the composition of the *Odyssey*, is mainly Ionic (the dialect spoken on the west coast of Asia Minor), but it also has traces of Aeolic (the Greek spoken farther north on the Asia Minor coast) and Arcado-Cypriot (thought to be the language carried to Arcadia and Cyprus by Mycenaeans from the Peloponnese). Many bards over several centuries helped create and pass on this language to succeeding generations of performers. As they moved from place to place, composing and performing their songs, they undoubtedly picked up local words to add to their vocabulary. They modified words to make them fit into the meter; they simply invented others. Over time, the true meaning of some traditional words and expressions was lost, probably not even known by the poets using them, but they remained part of the epic language.

Meter was the primary reason for the use of words from so many different sources. Composing in dactylic hexameter, the poets needed words that would fit into complex metrical patterns. If an Ionic form did not fit the meter and a word from another dialect did, that word would be used instead. If an augmented verb did not work but an unaugmented one did, then the augment was omitted.

The following appendix does not contain every Homeric form or explain every aspect of Homeric grammar. It is just a quick guide to some of the major variations from Attic Greek and the more frequently used forms and constructions that occur in this book.

Nouns

First Declension Feminine

	ἡ ἀοιδή *(song)*	ἡ γαῖα *(land)*	ἡ θεά *(goddess)*
Sing.			
nom.	ἀοιδή	γαῖα	θεά
gen.	ἀοιδῆς	γαίης	θεᾶς
dat.	ἀοιδῇ	γαίῃ	θεᾷ
acc.	ἀοιδήν	γαῖαν	θεάν
voc.	ἀοιδή	γαῖα	θεά
Dual			
nom., acc., voc.	ἀοιδά	γαία	θεά
gen., dat.	ἀοιδῆιν	γαίῃιν	θεῇιν
Plur.			
nom., voc.	ἀοιδαί	γαῖαι	θεαί
gen.	ἀοιδάων (-έων,-ῶν)	γαιάων (-έων,-ῶν)	θεάων (-ῶν)
dat.	ἀοιδῇσι (-ῇς)	γαίῃσι (-ῃς)	θεῇσι (-ῇς,-αῖς)
acc.	ἀοιδάς	γαίας	θεάς

First Declension Masculine

	ὁ Ἀτρεΐδης *(son of Atreus)*	ὁ ἱκέτης *(suppliant)*	ὁ Ἑρμείας *(Hermes)*
Sing.			
nom.	Ἀτρεΐδης	ἱκέτης	Ἑρμείας
gen.	Ἀτρεΐδαο (-εω)	ἱκέταο (-εω)	Ἑρμείαο (-ω)
dat.	Ἀτρεΐδῃ	ἱκέτῃ	Ἑρμείᾳ
acc.	Ἀτρεΐδην	ἱκέτην	Ἑρμείαν
voc.	Ἀτρεΐδη	ἱκέτα	Ἑρμεία
Dual			
nom., acc., voc.	Ἀτρεΐδα	ἱκέτα	
gen., dat.	Ἀτρεΐδῃιν	ἱκέτῃιν	
Plur.			
nom., voc.	Ἀτρεΐδαι	ἱκέται	
gen.	Ἀτρεϊδάων (-έων,-ῶν)	ἱκετάων (-έων,-ῶν)	
dat.	Ἀτρεΐδῃσι (-ῃς)	ἱκέτῃσι (-ῃς)	
acc.	Ἀτρεΐδας	ἱκέτας	

Second Declension

	ὁ θυμός (*heart, mind*)	ἡ νῆσος (*island*)	τὸ μέγαρον (*great hall, palace*)
Sing.			
nom.	θυμός	νῆσος	μέγαρον
gen.	θυμοῦ (-οῖο)	νήσου (-οιο)	μεγάρου (-οιο)
dat.	θυμῷ	νήσῳ	μεγάρῳ
acc.	θυμόν	νῆσον	μέγαρον
voc.	θυμέ	νῆσε	μέγαρον
Dual			
nom., acc., voc.	θυμώ	νήσω	μεγάρω
gen., dat.	θυμοῖιν	νήσοιιν	μεγάροιιν
Plur.			
nom., voc.	θυμοί	νῆσοι	μέγαρα
gen.	θυμῶν	νήσων	μεγάρων
dat.	θυμοῖσι (-οῖς)	νήσοισι (-οις)	μεγάροισι (-οῖς)
acc.	θυμούς	νήσους	μέγαρα

Third Declension

	ὁ ἄναξ (*lord, king*)	ἡ φρήν (*heart, mind*)	τὸ δῶμα (*house*)
Sing.			
nom.	ἄναξ	φρήν	δῶμα
gen.	ἄνακτος	φρενός	δῶματος
dat.	ἄνακτι	φρενί	δώματι
acc.	ἄνακτα	φρένα	δῶμα
voc.	ἄναξ	φρήν	δῶμα
Dual			
nom., acc., voc.	ἄνακτε	φρένε	δώματε
gen., dat.	ἀνάκτοιιν	φρενοῖιν	δωμάτοιιν
Plur.			
nom., voc.	ἄνακτες	φρένες	δώματα
gen.	ἀνάκτων	φρενῶν	δωμάτων
dat.	ἀνάκτεσσι (-εσι)	φρένεσσι (-εσι)	δωμάτεσσι
	ἄναξι	φρεσί	δώμασι
acc.	ἄνακτας	φρένας	δώματα

Common Third Declension Nouns with Irregular Forms

	ἡ νηῦς *(ship)*	τὸ ἔπος *(word)*	ὁ ἀνήρ *(man)*
Sing.			
nom.	νηῦς	ἔπος	ἀνήρ
gen.	νηός, νεός	ἔπεος	ἀνέρος, ἀνδρός
dat.	νηί	ἔπεϊ	ἀνέρι, ἀνδρί
acc.	νῆα, νέα	ἔπος	ἀνέρα, ἄνδρα
voc.	νηῦ	ἔπος	ἆνερ
Dual			
nom., acc., voc.	νῆε	ἔπεε	ἀνέρε, ἄνδρε
gen., dat.	νηοῖιν	ἐπέοιιν	ἀνέροιιν ἀνδροῖιν
Plur.			
nom., voc.	νῆες, νέες	ἔπεα	ἀνέρες, ἄνδρες
gen.	νηῶν, νεῶν	ἐπέων	ἀνέρων, ἀνδρῶν
dat.	νηυσί νήεσσι	ἐπέεσσι ἔπε(σ)σι	ἀνδράσι ἄνδρεσσι
acc.	νῆας, νέας	ἔπεα	ἀνέρας, ἄνδρας

	ὁ, ἡ βοῦς *(bull, cow)*	ἡ πόλις *(city)*	ὁ Ζεύς *(Zeus)*
Sing.			
nom.	βοῦς	πόλις	Ζεύς
gen.	βοός	πόλιος, πόληος	Διός, Ζηνός
dat.	βοΐ	πόλι (-ει,-ιι)	Διί, Ζηνί
acc.	βοῦν, βῶν	πόλιν	Δία, Ζῆνα
voc.	βοῦ	πόλι	Ζεῦ
Dual			
nom., acc., voc.	βόε	πόλιε	
gen., dat.	βοοῖιν	πολίοιιν	
Plur.			
nom., voc.	βόες	πόλιες, πόληες	
gen.	βοῶν	πολίων	
dat.	βόεσσι βουσί	πολίεσσι πόλεσι (-ισι)	
acc.	βόας, βοῦς	πόλιας (-ηας,-ις)	

	ὁ ᾿Οδυσσεύς *(Odysseus)*
Sing.	
nom.	᾿Οδυσσεύς, ᾿Οδυσεύς
gen.	᾿Οδυσσῆος, ᾿Οδυσῆος, ᾿Οδυσσέος, ᾿Οδυσεῦς
dat.	᾿Ουσσῆι, ᾿Οδυσῆι, ᾿Οδυσεῖ
acc.	᾿Οδυσσέα, ᾿Οδυσέα, ᾿Οδυσσῆα, ᾿Οδυσῆα
voc.	᾿Οδυσσεῦ, ᾿Οδυσεῦ

Pronouns

Personal Pronouns

	I	you	he, she, it
Sing.			
nom., voc.	ἐγώ, ἐγών	σύ	—
gen.	ἐμεῖο, ἐμέο, ἐμεῦ, μευ, ἐμέθεν	σεῖο, σέο, σεο, σεῦ, σευ, σέθεν	εἶο, ἕο, ἑο. εὖ, ἕθεν
dat.	ἐμοί, μοι	σοί, τοι, τεΐν	ἑοῖ, οἶ, οἱ
acc.	ἐμέ, με	σέ, σε	μιν, ἕ, ἑ, ἑέ
Dual			
nom., acc., voc.	νῶϊ, νώ	σφῶϊ, σφώ	σφωε
gen., dat.	νῶϊν	σφῶϊν, σφῷν	σφωϊν
Plur.			
nom., voc.	ἡμεῖς, ἄμμες	ὑμεῖς, ὔμμες	—
gen.	ἡμέων, ἡμείων	ὑμείων, ὑμέων	σφείων, σφέων, σφεων, σφῶν
dat.	ἡμῖν, ἄμμι(ν), ἥμιν, ἧμιν	ὑμῖν, ὔμμι(ν), ὕμιν	σφίσι(ν), σφι(ν), σφισι(ν)
acc.	ἡμέας, ἄμμε, ἥμεας, ἧμας	ὑμέας, ὔμμε	σφέας, σφεας, σφε, σφάς

Other Pronouns

The following pronouns have the same forms in the Homeric dialect as in Attic Greek, with ending variations similar to those seen on nouns and adjectives.

relative pronoun:	ὅς, ἥ, ὅ
intensive pronoun:	αὐτός,-ή,-ό
demonstrative pronouns:	(ἐ)κεῖνος,-η,-ο
	ὅδε, ἥδε, τόδε
	οὗτος, αὕτη, τοῦτο

The Definite Article

ὁ, ἡ, τό, the definite article (*the*) in Attic Greek, is more frequently used by Homer as a demonstrative pronoun (*this, that*), a personal pronoun (*he, she, it*), or a relative pronoun (*who, which*) than as an article.

	masc.	fem.	neut.
Sing.			
nom., voc.	**ὁ**	**ἡ**	**τό**
gen.	**τοῦ, τοῖο**	**τῆς**	**τοῦ, τοῖο**
dat.	**τῷ**	**τῇ**	**τῷ**
acc.	**τόν**	**τήν**	**τό**
Dual			
nom., acc., voc.	τώ	τώ	τώ
gen., dat.	**τοῖιν**	**τοῖιν**	**τοῖιν**
Plur.			
nom., voc.	**οἱ, τοί**	**αἱ, ταί**	**τά**
gen.	**τῶν**	**τάων, τῶν**	**τῶν**
dat.	**τοῖσι(ν), τοῖς**	**τῇσι(ν), τῇς**	**τοῖσι(ν), τοῖς**
acc.	**τούς**	**τάς**	**τά**

Case Usages

Genitive

genitive absolute—A participle in agreement with a noun (or a pronoun) in the genitive case that is not connected grammatically to the main construction of the sentence. Expresses time, cause, condition, or circumstances under which an action takes place.

ἦ μή τίς <u>σευ</u> μῆλα βροτῶν <u>ἀέκοντος</u> ἐλαύνει; (*Od.* 9.405)
*Surely no mortal man is driving off your flocks against your will (*literally, *with you being unwilling)?*

genitive of comparison—A genitive used with comparative adjectives or adverbs to indicate the person or thing being compared. Translate with "than."

<u>σεῖο</u> δ', Ἀχιλλεῦ, / οὔ τις ἀνὴρ προπάροιθε μακάρτερος οὔτ' ἄρ' ὀπίσσω· (*Od.* 11.482-483)
No man [was] in the past nor [will be] in the future more blessed than you, Achilles.

Dative

dative of cause—indicates cause or reason.

αὐτῶν γὰρ σφετέρῃσιν ἀτασθαλίῃσιν ὄλοντο (*Od.* 1.7)
For they perished because of their very own criminal folly.

dative of interest—indicates to or for whom something refers or is done. Frequently conveys the idea of possession.

ἀλλά μοι ἀμφ' Ὀδυσῆϊ δαΐφρονι δαίεται ἦτορ (*Od.* 1.48)
But my heart is distressed about wise Odysseus.

dative of means—indicates the instrument or means by which something is done.

αὐτοὶ δ' ἑζόμενοι πολιὴν ἅλα τύπτον ἐρετμοῖς. (*Od.* 12.180)
Sitting, they struck the gray sea with their oars.

dative of place (locative dative)—indicates location or place.

ἤδη γὰρ μάλα πολλὰ πάθον καὶ πολλὰ μόγησα
κύμασι καὶ πολέμῳ· (*Od.* 5.223-224)
For I've already endured very many things and suffered much on the sea and in war.

dative of possession—indicates possession when what is possessed is the subject of the verb εἰμί or a similar verb.

ὅθι τοι μοῖρ' ἐστὶν ἀλύξαι (*Od.* 5.345)
where it is your fate to escape

Accusative

accusative of respect—indicates in what respect the meaning of a verb or adjective is limited or applied.

αὐτὰρ ἐγὼν ἑπόμην ἀκαχήμενος ἦτορ. (*Od.* 10.313)
*But I followed, troubled at heart (*literally, *with respect to my heart).*

Verbs

augments—frequently not used.

ὁ δ' ἀσπερχὲς μενέαινεν / ἀντιθέῳ Ὀδυσῆϊ (*Od.* 1.20-21)
He kept raging unceasingly at godlike Odysseus.

conative present—a present form expressing an attempt or intention.

ἦ μή τίς σ' αὐτὸν κτείνει δόλῳ ἠὲ βίηφι; (*Od.* 9.406)
Surely no one is trying to kill you by trick or by force?

hortatory subjunctive—a present or aorist first-person subjunctive used to express exhortation or warning.

ἀλλὰ φθεγγώμεθα θᾶσσον. (*Od.* 10.228)
But let us call out quickly.

infinitives

infinitive used as imperative—an infinitive can be used to express a command.

ἀλλὰ κέλεσθαί μιν μακάρων μέγαν ὅρκον ὀμόσσαι (*Od.* 10.299)
But command her to swear the great oath of the gods

present active infinitives can have the following endings: –μεν
–μεναι
–έμεναι
–έμεν
–ειν

iteratives indicate repeated past action. Usually unaugmented, iterative imperfects and aorists are formed by adding **–σκ–** and personal endings to stems.

ἔνθα καὶ ἠματίη μὲν ὑφαίνεσκεν μέγαν ἱστόν,
νύκτας δ' ἀλλύεσκεν (*Od.* 2.104-105)
Then during the days she kept weaving on the great piece of cloth, but during the nights she kept unraveling it.

mixed aorist – an aorist with the **σ** of the "first" aorist and the thematic vowel (**ο** or **ε**) of a "second" aorist, for example, **ἐδύσετο** for **ἐδύσατο** (*Od.* 5.352)

optative of wish—The optative without **κε(ν)** or **ἄν** can express a wish referring to the future.

> <u>**εὕροι**</u> **δ' ἐν πήματα οἴκῳ** (*Od.* 9.535)
> *and may he find trouble in his house*

participles

aorist participles can indicate something that happens at the same time as the main verb rather than at a previous time; often translated as present participles.

> **τοῦ ὅ γ' <u>ἐπιμνησθεὶς</u> ἔπε' ἀθανάτοισι μετηύδα·** (*Od.* 1.31)
> *Remembering him, he addressed the gods.*

future participle of purpose—The future participle used to express purpose.

> **ἦ τοὺς <u>λυσόμενος</u> δεῦρ' ἔρχεαι;** (*Od.* 10.284)
> *Are you coming here to release them?*

personal endings that may differ from Attic:

2nd pers. sing. mid./pass.	**–εαι** instead of **–ει**
	–ηαι instead of **–ῃ**
	–σαο instead of **–σω**
3rd pers. plur. mid./pass.	**–αται** instead of **–νται**
	–ατο instead of **–ντο**
3rd pers. plur. aor. pass.	**–εν** instead of **–ησαν**
2nd pers. sing., pres. mid. imperative	**–εο** instead of **–ου**

potential optative—**ἄν** or **κε(ν)** + optative to express a future possibility or likelihood; translated with *may, can, might, could, should.* Sometimes occurs without **ἄν** or **κε(ν)**.

> **ἀλλὰ ξὺν τοίσδεσι θᾶσσον / φεύγωμεν· ἔτι γάρ κεν ἀλύξαιμεν κακὸν ἦμαρ.** (*Od.* 10. 268-269)
> *But let us flee quickly with these men. For we may still escape the evil day.*

purpose clause—a dependent clause expressing purpose can be introduced by **ἵνα, ὅπως, ὄφρα, ὡς**, or **ἕως**. **μή** is used for the negative. The verb is subjunctive after a primary tense (present, future, perfect, or future perfect), optative (sometimes subjunctive) after a secondary tense (imperfect, aorist, or pluperfect). **ἄν** or **κε(ν)** may be used with the subjunctive.

> **αὐτάρ οἱ πρόφρων ὑποθήσομαι οὐδ' ἐπικεύσω,**
> **ὥς κε μάλ' ἀσκηθὴς ἣν πατρίδα γαῖαν ἵκηται.** (*Od.* 5.143-144)
> *But I will willingly give advice to him and not conceal anything, so that he may reach his homeland completely unharmed.*

short-vowel subjunctive—A subjunctive form in which the long thematic vowel before a verb ending, **–η** or **–ω**, is shortened to **–ε** or **–ο**.

> **εὐνῆς ἡμετέρης ἐπιβήομεν** (*Od.* 10.334) *let us get into my bed*

subjunctive for future—A subjunctive may be used to express future time. **κε(ν)** or **ἄν** may be used with it.

> **ὅς κέ σ' ἐέδνοισι βρίσας οἶκόνδ' ἀγάγηται.** (*Od.* 6.159)
> *who, having prevailed with his bridal gifts, will marry you.*

tmesis— In Homeric poetry, some prepositions were used with verbs to convey an idea that in later Greek would be expressed by a compound verb formed from their union. This separation has traditionally been referred to as tmesis (from **τέμνω** – cut). This is actually an incorrect application of the term, since in Homeric Greek the preposition has not been "cut" from the verb. Rather, the two have not yet evolved into a compound verb. (It is correctly applied to instances in Attic Greek where true tmesis occurs and words are actually cut apart, usually for emphasis or parody.)

> **νήπιοι, οἳ κατὰ βοῦς Ὑπερίονος Ἠελίοιο / ἤσθιον·** (*Od.* 1.8-9)
> *the fools, who devoured the cattle of Hyperion Helios*

εἰμί (I am)	Sing.	Dual	Plur.
present indicative	**εἰμί**		**εἰμέν**
	ἐσσί, εἶς	**ἐστόν**	**ἐστέ**
	ἐστί	**ἐστόν**	**εἰσί, ἔασι**
imperfect indicative	**ἦα, ἔα, ἔον**		**ἦμεν**
	ἦσθα, ἔησθα	**ἦστον**	**ἦτε**
	ἦεν, ἔην, ἤην, ἦν	**ἤστην**	**ἦσαν, ἔσαν**
infinitive	**εἶναι, ἔμμεναι, ἔμμεν, ἔμεναι, ἔμεν**		
participle	**ἐών, ἐοῦσα, ἐόν**		

εἶμι (I go)	Sing.	Dual	Plur.
present indicative	**εἶμι**		**ἴμεν**
	εἶσθα	**ἴτον**	**ἴτε**
	εἶσι	**ἴτον**	**ἴασι**
imperfect indicative	**ἤϊα, ἤϊον**		**ἤομεν**
	ἤεισθα	**ἴτον**	**ἦτε**
	ἤϊε, ἦε, ἤει, ἴε	**ἴτην**	**ἤϊσαν, ἦσαν, ἤϊον, ἴσαν**
infinitive	**ἴμεναι, ἴμεν, ἰέναι**		
participle	**ἰών, ἰοῦσα, ἰόν**		

Appendix 3 – Meter and Scansion

Dactylic Hexameter

Meter is the rhythmical pattern of poetry. Unlike English poetry, whose meters involve patterns of stressed and unstressed syllables, Greek meters are patterns of long and short syllables. The meter of Homeric poetry, **dactylic hexameter**, has the following characteristics:

- Each line is divided into **six** sections called **feet** (ἕξ – "six," hence "*hex*ameter").
- The patterns of long and short syllables that can occur within the feet are called **dactyls** and **spondees**.
- A **dactyl** is a pattern of one long, then two short syllables: — ˘ ˘ (The dactyl gets its name from **δάκτυλος** – "finger." Notice the one long and two short sections of your index finger.)
- A **spondee** is a pattern of two long syllables: — —
- Each of the first five feet in a line can be either a dactyl or a spondee. About 95% of the time, the fifth foot is a dactyl. A line with a spondee in the fifth foot is called a **spondaic line**.
- The sixth foot is always a spondee.

Vowels and Diphthongs

short vowels: ᾰ ε ῐ ο ῠ

long vowels: ᾱ η ῑ ῡ ω (Hint: any vowel with a circumflex accent is long.)

diphthongs (a diphthong is a combination of two vowels pronounced together):

αι ει οι ᾳ ῃ ῳ υι αυ ευ ηυ ου

Determining Syllable Length – Basic Rules

SHORT SYLLABLES: A syllable is scanned as a **short** syllable if:

- it contains a single short vowel followed by a single consonant or another vowel with which it does not form a diphthong.

LONG SYLLABLES: A syllable is scanned as a **long** syllable if:

- it contains a long vowel.
- it contains a diphthong.
- it contains a short vowel followed by two or more consonants. (This is very common.)

  Note: Both consonants do not have to be in the same word as the vowel. See the second syllable of **θάλασσαν** (two consonants in the same word) and the last syllables of **ἔσαν** and **πόλεμον** (two consonants in different words) in *Od.* 1.12.

  – ˘ ˘ | – ˘ ˘ | – ˘ ˘ | – ˘ ˘ | – ˘ ˘ | – –

  οἴκοι ἔσαν, πόλεμόν τε πεφευγότες ἠδὲ θάλασσαν·

  Note: A **ρ** at the beginning of a word and **ζ**, **ξ**, and **ψ** in any position are considered double consonants. See the third syllable in **μερμήριξε** in *Od.* 2.93.

  – ˘ ˘ | – – | – ˘ ˘ | – ˘ ˘ | – – | – –

  ἡ δὲ δόλον τόνδ' ἄλλον ἐνὶ φρεσὶ μερμήριξε·

- it is the first or last syllable in the line. Even if these are short syllables, they are scanned as long ones. See the last syllable of **πολλά** in *Od.* 1.1.

– ˘ ˘ | – ˘ ˘ | – ˘ ˘ | – ˘ ˘ | – ˘ ˘ | – –

Ἄνδρα μοι ἔννεπε, Μοῦσα, πολύτροπον, ὃς μάλα πολλὰ

Determining Syllable Length – Exceptions

Sometimes syllables that would be scanned long according to the basic rules can be (although not always are) scanned short and syllables that would be scanned short can be (although not always are) scanned long. If you have a syllable that needs to be the opposite of what it looks like it should be, see if one of these exceptions applies.

Long syllables that can be scanned **SHORT**:

- When a word's final syllable ends with a long vowel or diphthong and the next word begins with a vowel, the syllable can be scanned short. (This very common occurrence is called **correption**.) See **μοι** in *Od.* 1.1.

  – ˘ ˘ | – ˘ ˘ | – ˘ ˘ | – ˘ ˘ | – ˘ ˘ | – –

  Ἄνδρα <u>μοι</u> ἔννεπε, Μοῦσα, πολύτροπον, ὃς μάλα πολλὰ

  Correption within a word (internal correption) can also occur. See the first syllable of **υἱέ** in *Od.* 11.478.

  – ˘ | – – | – ˘ ˘ | – ˘ ˘ | – ˘ ˘ | – –

  ὦ Ἀχιλεῦ, Πηλῆος <u>υἱ</u>έ, μέγα φέρτατ' Ἀχαιῶν,

- If a short vowel is followed by two consonants and the first of the two consonants is a mute or stop (**π**, **β**, **φ**, **κ**, **γ**, **χ**, **τ**, **δ**, or **θ**) and the second is either **λ** or **ρ**, the preceding syllable can be scanned short. See the second syllable of **ἐστί** in *Od.* 1.66.

  – ˘ ˘ | – ˘ ˘ | – ˘ ˘ | – ˘ ˘ | – ˘ ˘ | – –

  ὃς περὶ μὲν νόον ἐ<u>στὶ</u> βροτῶν, περὶ δ' ἱρὰ θεοῖσιν

Short syllables that can be scanned **LONG**:

- When the last syllable of a word ends in a short vowel and the next word begins with a liquid (**λ**, **μ**, **ν**, **ρ**), a digamma (**ϝ**), or a sigma (**σ**), the syllable can be scanned long. See the last syllable of **ἐνί** in *Od.* 1.27.

  – ˘ ˘ | – ˘ ˘ | – ˘ ˘ | – ˘ ˘ | – ˘ ˘ | – –

  Ζηνὸς ἐ<u>νὶ</u> μεγάροισιν Ὀλυμπίου ἁθρόοι ἦσαν.

- When the last syllable of a word ends in a short vowel followed by a single consonant and that consonant is **ν**, **ρ**, or **ς**, the syllable can be scanned long. See the last syllable of **πύματον** in *Od.* 9.369.

  — ˘ ˘ |— ˘ ˘ |— ˘ ˘ |— ˘ ˘ |— ˘ ˘ |— —

  Οὖτιν ἐγὼ πύματον ἔδομαι μετὰ οἷσ' ἑτάροισι,

- When a word's final syllable ends in a short vowel and the syllable occupies a position in the line that requires a long syllable, it can be scanned long. (In other words, it is scanned long because the poet needed a long syllable there.) See the last syllable of **νισόμεθα** in *Od.* 10.42.

  — ˘ ˘ |— ˘ ˘ |— ˘ ˘ |— — |— ˘ ˘ |— —

  οἴκαδε νισόμεθα κενεὰς σὺν χεῖρας ἔχοντες.

Diaeresis, or When is a Diphthong Not a Diphthong?

When a double dot (¨) indicating a **diaeresis** (separation) appears over an **ι** or **υ**, it means that letter does not form a diphthong with the preceding vowel. The two vowels are pronounced as separate syllables. There are two diaereses in *Od.* 1.38.

— —|— —|— ˘ ˘|— ˘ ˘ |— ˘ ˘|— —

Ἑρμείαν πέμψαντες, ἐΰσκοπον Ἀργεϊφόντην,

Digamma

The digamma (**ϝ**), pronounced like the English *w*, was a consonant used in early Greek but no longer in use in Homeric Greek. Sometimes, but not always, a digamma that was once in a word still affects the determination of long and short syllables. In *Od.* 1.92, the last syllable of **εἰλίποδας** is scanned long because **ἕλικας** was originally spelled **ϝέλικας**, putting two consonants after the short **α**.

— ˘ ˘ |— —|— ˘ ˘ |— ˘ ˘ |— ˘ ˘ |— —

μῆλ' ἀδινὰ σφάζουσι καὶ εἰλίποδας ἕλικας βοῦς.

Elision

Elision occurs when a short final vowel (and sometimes a final diphthong) is dropped before a word beginning with a vowel. An apostrophe takes the place of the missing vowel or diphthong. In *Od.* 1.34, **ἄλγε'** equals **ἄλγεα**.

σφῇσιν ἀτασθαλίῃσιν ὑπὲρ μόρον <u>ἄλγε'</u> ἔχουσιν,

Synizesis

Sometimes two vowels or a vowel and a diphthong that are side by side (either in the same word or in separate words) which would normally be pronounced as two syllables are run together, scanned, and pronounced as one long syllable. See **-λεαι** in **κέλεαι** in *Od.* 5.174.

– ˘ ˘ | – ˘ ˘ | – ˘ ˘ |– ˘ ˘ | – ˘ ˘ | – –
ἤ με κέ<u>λεαι</u> σχεδίῃ περάαν μέγα λαῖτμα θαλάσσης,

Appendix 4 - Readings

Readings

The following list will provide a few places to start if you want to find out more about the world of Homer, Homer as an artist, the poems themselves, and some of the issues that arise in the first twelve books of the *Odyssey*. Needless to say, it barely scratches the surface of Homeric scholarship. People have been speculating, researching, and debating about Homer for a very long time and will no doubt continue to do so for a very long time to come.

Introductions to Homer and the *Odyssey*

Beye, Charles Rowan. *The Iliad, the Odyssey, and the Epic Tradition.* New York: Anchor, 1966.

Bowra, C. M. *Homer*. London: Duckworth, 1972.

Camps, W. A. *An Introduction to Homer.* Oxford: Oxford University Press, 1980.

Finley, John H., Jr. *Homer's Odyssey*. Cambridge MA: Harvard University Press, 1978.

Griffin, Jasper. *Homer, The Odyssey*. 2nd ed. Landmarks of World Literature Series. Cambridge: Cambridge University Press, 2004.

Kirk, G. S. *Homer and the Epic*. Cambridge: Cambridge University Press, 1965.

Latacz, Joachim. *Homer: His Art and His World.* Trans. James P. Holoka. Ann Arbor: University of Michigan Press, 1996.

Morrison, James. *A Companion to Homer's Odyssey*. Westport, CT: Greenwood, 2003. (An excellent source for someone coming to Homer for the first time.)

Powell, Barry B. *Homer*. Blackwell Introductions to the Classical World Series. Malden, MA: Blackwell Publishing, 2004.

Rutherford, Richard. *Homer*. Greece and Rome New Surveys in the Classics, no. 26. Oxford: Oxford University Press, 1996.

Slatkin, Laura M. "Homer's *Odyssey*." In *A Companion to Ancient Epic*. Edited by John Miles Foley, pp. 315-329. Malden, MA: Blackwell, 2005.

Taplan, Oliver. "Homer." In *The Oxford History of the Classical World*. Edited by John Boardman, Jasper Griffin, and Oswyn Murray, pp. 50-77. Oxford: Oxford University Press, 1986.

Thalmann, William G. *The Odyssey: An Epic of Return*. New York: Twayne Publishers, 1992.

Specific Issues

Bennet, John. "Homer and the Bronze Age." In *A New Companion to Homer*. Edited by Ian Morris and Barry Powell, pp. 511-533. Leiden and New York: Brill, 1997. Was the world Homer described that of Bronze Age Greece or a later time? This article provides explanations of why there may be Bronze Age elements, but the world was most likely the eighth century B.C.E.

Bittlestone, Robert. *Odysseus Unbound: The Search for Homer's Ithaca*. Cambridge & New York: Cambridge University Press, 2005. Presents the theory that the ancient island of Ithaca is the current Paliki peninsula of the island Kefallinia rather than the island which is today called Ithaki. Separated from Kefallinia by a sea channel in Homer's time, the channel has since been filled in, making the ancient island a peninsula.

Brilliant, Richard. "Kirke's Men: Swine and Sweethearts." In *The Distaff Side: Representing the Female in Homer's Odyssey*. Edited by Beth Cohen, pp. 165-174. New York and Oxford: Oxford University Press, 1995.

Brown, Calvin S. "Odysseus and Polyphemus: The Name and the Curse." *Comparative Literature* 18, no. 3 (Summer, 1966) 193-202.

Brown, Christopher G. "In the Cyclops' Cave: Revenge and Justice in *Odyssey* 9." *Mnemosyne* 49, no. 1 (Feb., 1996): 1-29

Clay, Jenny Strauss. "The Beginning of the Odyssey." *American Journal of Philology* 97, no. 4 (Winter 1976): 313-326. More on **ἀτασθαλίαι**.

D'Arms, Edward F. and Karl K. Hulley. "The Oresteia-Story in the *Odyssey*." *Transactions of the American Philological Association* 77 (1946): 207-213.

Dimock, G. "Crime and Punishment in the *Odyssey*." *Yale Review* 60, no. 2 (Winter, 1971): 199-214.

Finley, M. I. *The World of Odysseus*. Rev. ed. New York: New York Review Books, 2002 (originally published 1954; rev. ed. originally published

1977). A classic work introducing the world of Homeric society and postulating that it reflects the world of Greece in tenth/ninth century B.C.E.

Fowler, Robert. "The Homeric Question." In *The Cambridge Companion to Homer*. Edited by Robert Fowler, pp. 45-55. Cambridge: Cambridge University Press, 2004. Discusses the debate over how and by whom the *Iliad* and the *Odyssey* were composed.

Friedrich, Rainer. "Thrinakia and Zeus' Ways to Men in the *Odyssey*." *Greek Roman, and Byzantine Studies* 28, no. 4 (Winter 1987): 375-400.

Gresseth, Gerald K. "The Homeric Sirens." *Transactions of the American Philological Association* 101 (1970): 203-218.

Halverson, John. "The Succession Issue in the *Odyssey*." *Greece & Rome* 30, no. 2 (Oct., 1986): 119-128. Discusses the nature of Odysseus' position in Ithaca.

Jensen, Minna Skafte. "In What Sense Can the *Iliad* and the *Odyssey* Be Considered Oral Texts?" In *Homer's Odyssey*. Edited by Lillian E. Doherty, pp. 18-28. Oxford: Oxford University Press, 2009. Theorizes that the Homeric works may have been dictated by an oral poet to a scribe.

Jones, D. M. *Ethical Themes in the Plot of the Odyssey*. London; University of London, 1954.

Kearns, Emily. "The Gods in the Homeric Epics." In *The Cambridge Companion to Homer*. Edited by Robert Fowler, pp. 59-73. Cambridge: Cambridge University Press, 2004.

"Lives of Homer." In *Homeric Hymns, Homeric Apocrypha, Lives of Homer*, 295-467, edited and translated by Martin L. West. Loeb Classical Library Vol. 496. Cambridge, MA: Harvard University Press, 2003. Find out what the people in the ancient world believed about the life of their greatest poet.

Luce, J. V. *Celebrating Homer's Landscapes: Troy and Ithaca Revisited*. New Haven: Yale University Press, 1998. Presents the case for identifying ancient Ithaca with modern Ithaki.

Mark, Samuel. *Homeric Seafaring*. College Station: Texas A&M University Press, 2005. Essential source for understanding nautical terminology used in the *Odyssey*.

Mayor, Adrienne. *The First Fossil Hunters: Paleontology in Greek and Roman Times*. Princeton, NJ: Princeton University Press, 2000. Suggests that fossils of prehistoric animals may have inspired mythical creatures in classical mythology.

Minchin, Elizabeth. "The Poet Appeals to His Muse: Homeric Invocations in the Context of Epic Performance." *Classical Journal* 91, no. 1 (Oct.-Nov. 1995): 25-33.

Mondi, Robert. "The Homeric Cyclopes: Folktale, Tradition, and Theme." *Transactions of the American Philological Association* 113 (1983): 17-38.

Morris, Ian and Barry Powell, eds. *A New Companion to Homer*. Leiden and New York: Brill, 1997. Collection of in-depth articles by leading scholars on all aspects of the Homeric works.

Neils, Jenifer. "Les Femmes Fatales: Skylla and the Sirens in Greek Art." In *The Distaff Side: Representing the Female in Homer's Odyssey*. Edited by Beth Cohen, pp. 175-184. New York and Oxford: Oxford University Press, 1995.

Olson, Douglas. "The Stories of Agamemnon in Homer's Odyssey." *Transactions of the American Philological Association* 120 (1990): 57-71.

Olson, S. Douglas. "The Wanderings." In *Blood and Iron: Stories and Storytelling in Homer's Odyssey*, pp. 43-64. Leiden: E. J. Brill, 1995. Discusses Odysseus' relationship with his men during the period covered in Books 9-12.

Plaitakis, Andreas and Roger C. Duvoisin. "Homer's Moly Identified as *Galanthus nivalis*: Physiologic Antidote to Stramonium Poisoning." *Clinical Neuropharmacology* 6, no. 1 (1983): 1-5.

Scodel, Ruth. "The Story-teller and his Audience." In *The Cambridge Companion to Homer*. Edited by Robert Fowler, pp. 45-55. Cambridge: Cambridge University Press, 2004.

Seymour, Thomas Day. *Life in the Homeric Age*. 1907; reprint, New York: Biblo & Tannen, 1963. Information on all aspects of life presented in the Homeric poems.

Shapiro, H. A. "Coming of Age in Phaiakia: The Meeting of Odysseus and Nausikaa." In *The Distaff Side: Representing the Female in Homer's Odyssey*. Edited by Beth Cohen, pp. 155-164. New York and Oxford: Oxford University Press, 1995.

Shay, Jonathan. *Odysseus in America: Combat Trauma and the Trials of Homecoming*. New York: Scribner, 2002. Analyzes the *Odyssey* as an "allegory of many a real veteran's homecoming."

Shein, Seth L. "Odysseus and Polyphemus in the *Odyssey*." *Greek Roman and Byzantine Studies* 11 (1970): 73-83.

Shewan, Alexander. "Fishing with a Rod in Homer." In *Homeric Essays*, 427-440. Oxford: Blackwell, 1935.

Snowden, Frank M., Jr. *Before Color Prejudice: The Ancient View of Blacks*. Cambridge, MA: Harvard University Press, 1983.

Stanford, W. B. "The Homeric Etymology of the Name Odysseus." *Classical Philology* 47, no. 4 (Oct., 1952): 209-213.

The *Odyssey* in Literature, Art, and Media after Homer

Hall, Edith. *The Return of Ulysses: A Cultural History of Homer's Odyssey*. Baltimore: The Johns Hopkins University Press, 2008.

Hardwick, Lorna. "'Shards and Suckers': Contemporary Receptions of Homer." In *The Cambridge Companion to Homer*. Edited by Robert Fowler, pp. 344-362. Cambridge: Cambridge University Press, 2004.

Stanford, W. B. *The Ulysses Theme*. Dallas, TX: Spring Publications, 1992 (originally published Oxford: B. Blackwell, 1954). Analyzes the character of Odysses and his use in literature from ancient times to the twentieth century.

Commentaries

Heubeck, Alfred, Stephanie West, and J.B. Hainsworth. *A Commentary on Homer's Odyssey. Vol. I: Introduction and Books I-VIII*. Oxford: Clarendon Press, 1998.

______ and Arie Hoekstra. *A Commentary on Homer's Odyssey. Vol. II: Books IX-XVI*. Oxford: Clarendon Press, 1990.

Severy, Beth. *Homer: Odyssey I, VI, IX*. Bryn Mawr, PA: Bryn Mawr College, 1991.

Selected Readers with Annotation and Commentary

Beethem, Frank. *Beginning Greek with Homer: An Elementary Course Based on Odyssey V*. London: Bristol Classical Press, 1996; reprinted with corrections 1998.

Garvie, A. F., ed. *Homer, Odyssey, Books VI-VIII* (text with introduction and commentary). Cambridge: Cambridge University Press, 1994; repr. 1999.

Jones, Peter V., ed. *Homer, Odyssey 1 & 2 with an Introduction, Translation and Commentary*. Warminster: Aris & Phillips Ltd., 1991.

Merry, W. W., ed. *Homer, Odyssey, Books I-XII with Introduction, Notes, etc.* Oxford: Clarendon Press, 1932 (originally published 1870).

Muir, J. V., ed. *Homer, Odyssey IX with Introduction and Running Vocabulary*. Bristol: Bristol Classical Press, 2002 (originally published 1980).

Perrin, Bernadotte and Thomas Day Seymour. *Eight Books of Homer's Odyssey with Introduction, Commentary, and Vocabulary*. Boston: Ginn & Company, 1897.

Stanford, W. B., ed. *The Odyssey of Homer with General and Grammatical Introduction, Commentary, and Indexes, Vol. I (Books I-XII)*. 2nd ed. London: St. Martins Press, 1977 (originally published 1959).

Watson, Janet, ed.. *Homer, Odyssey VI & VII with Introduction, Notes & Vocabulary*. Bristol: Bristol Classical Press, 2002.

Greek Text without Notes and Vocabulary

Book 1.1-95

Ἄνδρα μοι ἔννεπε, Μοῦσα, πολύτροπον, ὃς μάλα πολλὰ 1
πλάγχθη, ἐπεὶ Τροίης ἱερὸν πτολίεθρον ἔπερσε· 2
πολλῶν δ’ ἀνθρώπων ἴδεν ἄστεα καὶ νόον ἔγνω, 3
πολλὰ δ’ ὅ γ’ ἐν πόντῳ πάθεν ἄλγεα ὃν κατὰ θυμόν, 4
ἀρνύμενος ἥν τε ψυχὴν καὶ νόστον ἑταίρων. 5
ἀλλ’ οὐδ’ ὧς ἑτάρους ἐρρύσατο, ἱέμενός περ· 6
αὐτῶν γὰρ σφετέρῃσιν ἀτασθαλίῃσιν ὄλοντο, 7
νήπιοι, οἳ κατὰ βοῦς Ὑπερίονος Ἠελίοιο 8
ἤσθιον· αὐτὰρ ὁ τοῖσιν ἀφείλετο νόστιμον ἦμαρ. 9
τῶν ἁμόθεν γε, θεά, θύγατερ Διός, εἰπὲ καὶ ἡμῖν. 10
ἔνθ’ ἄλλοι μὲν πάντες, ὅσοι φύγον αἰπὺν ὄλεθρον, 11
οἴκοι ἔσαν, πόλεμόν τε πεφευγότες ἠδὲ θάλασσαν· 12
τὸν δ’ οἶον, νόστου κεχρημένον ἠδὲ γυναικός, 13
νύμφη πότνι’ ἔρυκε Καλυψώ, δῖα θεάων, 14
ἐν σπέεσι γλαφυροῖσι, λιλαιομένη πόσιν εἶναι. 15
ἀλλ’ ὅτε δὴ ἔτος ἦλθε περιπλομένων ἐνιαυτῶν, 16
τῷ οἱ ἐπεκλώσαντο θεοὶ οἶκόνδε νέεσθαι 17
εἰς Ἰθάκην, οὐδ’ ἔνθα πεφυγμένος ἦεν ἀέθλων 18
καὶ μετὰ οἷσι φίλοισι· θεοὶ δ’ ἐλέαιρον ἅπαντες 19
νόσφι Ποσειδάωνος· ὁ δ’ ἀσπερχὲς μενέαινεν 20
ἀντιθέῳ Ὀδυσῆϊ πάρος ἣν γαῖαν ἱκέσθαι. 21
ἀλλ’ ὁ μὲν Αἰθίοπας μετεκίαθε τηλόθ’ ἐόντας, 22
Αἰθίοπας, τοὶ διχθὰ δεδαίαται, ἔσχατοι ἀνδρῶν, 23
οἱ μὲν δυσομένου Ὑπερίονος, οἱ δ’ ἀνιόντος, 24
ἀντιόων ταύρων τε καὶ ἀρνειῶν ἑκατόμβης. 25
ἔνθ’ ὅ γε τέρπετο δαιτὶ παρήμενος· οἱ δὲ δὴ ἄλλοι 26
Ζηνὸς ἐνὶ μεγάροισιν Ὀλυμπίου ἁθρόοι ἦσαν. 27
τοῖσι δὲ μύθων ἦρχε πατὴρ ἀνδρῶν τε θεῶν τε· 28

Book 1.1-95 (cont.)

μνήσατο γὰρ κατὰ θυμὸν ἀμύμονος Αἰγίσθοιο,
τόν ῥ' Ἀγαμεμνονίδης τηλεκλυτὸς ἔκταν' Ὀρέστης·
τοῦ ὅ γ' ἐπιμνησθεὶς ἔπε' ἀθανάτοισι μετηύδα·
"ὢ πόποι, οἷον δή νυ θεοὺς βροτοὶ αἰτιόωνται.
ἐξ ἡμέων γάρ φασι κάκ' ἔμμεναι· οἱ δὲ καὶ αὐτοὶ
σφῇσιν ἀτασθαλίῃσιν ὑπὲρ μόρον ἄλγε' ἔχουσιν,
ὡς καὶ νῦν Αἴγισθος ὑπὲρ μόρον Ἀτρεΐδαο
γῆμ' ἄλοχον μνηστήν, τὸν δ' ἔκτανε νοστήσαντα,
εἰδὼς αἰπὺν ὄλεθρον, ἐπεὶ πρό οἱ εἴπομεν ἡμεῖς,
Ἑρμείαν πέμψαντες, ἐΰσκοπον Ἀργεϊφόντην,
μήτ' αὐτὸν κτείνειν μήτε μνάασθαι ἄκοιτιν·
ἐκ γὰρ Ὀρέσταο τίσις ἔσσεται Ἀτρεΐδαο,
ὁππότ' ἂν ἡβήσῃ τε καὶ ἧς ἱμείρεται αἴης.
ὣς ἔφαθ' Ἑρμείας, ἀλλ' οὐ φρένας Αἰγίσθοιο
πεῖθ' ἀγαθὰ φρονέων· νῦν δ' ἁθρόα πάντ' ἀπέτεισε."
τὸν δ' ἠμείβετ' ἔπειτα θεὰ γλαυκῶπις Ἀθήνη·
"ὦ πάτερ ἡμέτερε Κρονίδη, ὕπατε κρειόντων,
καὶ λίην κεῖνός γε ἐοικότι κεῖται ὀλέθρῳ,
ὡς ἀπόλοιτο καὶ ἄλλος ὅτις τοιαῦτά γε ῥέζοι.
ἀλλά μοι ἀμφ' Ὀδυσῆϊ δαΐφρονι δαίεται ἦτορ,
δυσμόρῳ, ὃς δὴ δηθὰ φίλων ἄπο πήματα πάσχει
νήσῳ ἐν ἀμφιρύτῃ, ὅθι τ' ὀμφαλός ἐστι θαλάσσης,
νῆσος δενδρήεσσα, θεὰ δ' ἐν δώματα ναίει,
Ἄτλαντος θυγάτηρ ὀλοόφρονος, ὅς τε θαλάσσης
πάσης βένθεα οἶδεν, ἔχει δέ τε κίονας αὐτὸς
μακράς, αἳ γαῖάν τε καὶ οὐρανὸν ἀμφὶς ἔχουσι.
τοῦ θυγάτηρ δύστηνον ὀδυρόμενον κατερύκει,
αἰεὶ δὲ μαλακοῖσι καὶ αἱμυλίοισι λόγοισι
θέλγει, ὅπως Ἰθάκης ἐπιλήσεται· αὐτὰρ Ὀδυσσεύς,

Book 1.1-95 (cont.)

ἱέμενος καὶ καπνὸν ἀποθρῴσκοντα νοῆσαι
ἧς γαίης, θανέειν ἱμείρεται. οὐδέ νυ σοί περ
ἐντρέπεται φίλον ἦτορ, Ὀλύμπιε; οὔ νύ τ' Ὀδυσσεὺς
Ἀργείων παρὰ νηυσὶ χαρίζετο ἱερὰ ῥέζων
Τροίῃ ἐν εὐρείῃ; τί νύ οἱ τόσον ὠδύσαο, Ζεῦ; "
  τὴν δ' ἀπαμειβόμενος προσέφη νεφεληγερέτα Ζεύς·
" τέκνον ἐμόν, ποῖόν σε ἔπος φύγεν ἕρκος ὀδόντων.
πῶς ἂν ἔπειτ' Ὀδυσῆος ἐγὼ θείοιο λαθοίμην,
ὃς περὶ μὲν νόον ἐστὶ βροτῶν, περὶ δ' ἱρὰ θεοῖσιν
ἀθανάτοισιν ἔδωκε, τοὶ οὐρανὸν εὐρὺν ἔχουσιν;
ἀλλὰ Ποσειδάων γαιήοχος ἀσκελὲς αἰὲν
Κύκλωπος κεχόλωται, ὃν ὀφθαλμοῦ ἀλάωσεν,
ἀντίθεον Πολύφημον, ὅου κράτος ἐστὶ μέγιστον
πᾶσιν Κυκλώπεσσι· Θόωσα δέ μιν τέκε νύμφη,
Φόρκυνος θυγάτηρ, ἁλὸς ἀτρυγέτοιο μέδοντος,
ἐν σπέεσι γλαφυροῖσι Ποσειδάωνι μιγεῖσα.
ἐκ τοῦ δὴ Ὀδυσῆα Ποσειδάων ἐνοσίχθων
οὔ τι κατακτείνει, πλάζει δ' ἀπὸ πατρίδος αἴης.
ἀλλ' ἄγεθ' ἡμεῖς οἵδε περιφραζώμεθα πάντες
νόστον, ὅπως ἔλθῃσι· Ποσειδάων δὲ μεθήσει
ὃν χόλον· οὐ μὲν γάρ τι δυνήσεται ἀντία πάντων
ἀθανάτων ἀέκητι θεῶν ἐριδαινέμεν οἶος. "
  τὸν δ' ἠμείβετ' ἔπειτα θεὰ γλαυκῶπις Ἀθήνη·
" ὦ πάτερ ἡμέτερε Κρονίδη, ὕπατε κρειόντων,
εἰ μὲν δὴ νῦν τοῦτο φίλον μακάρεσσι θεοῖσι,
νοστῆσαι Ὀδυσῆα πολύφρονα ὅνδε δόμονδε,
Ἑρμείαν μὲν ἔπειτα, διάκτορον Ἀργεϊφόντην,
νῆσον ἐς Ὠγυγίην ὀτρύνομεν, ὄφρα τάχιστα
νύμφῃ ἐϋπλοκάμῳ εἴπῃ νημερτέα βουλήν,

Book 1.1-95 (cont.)

νόστον Ὀδυσσῆος ταλασίφρονος, ὥς κε νέηται. 87
αὐτὰρ ἐγὼν Ἰθάκηνδε ἐλεύσομαι, ὄφρα οἱ υἱὸν 88
μᾶλλον ἐποτρύνω καί οἱ μένος ἐν φρεσὶ θείω, 89
εἰς ἀγορὴν καλέσαντα κάρη κομόωντας Ἀχαιοὺς 90
πᾶσι μνηστήρεσσιν ἀπειπέμεν, οἵ τέ οἱ αἰεὶ 91
μῆλ' ἁδινὰ σφάζουσι καὶ εἰλίποδας ἕλικας βοῦς. 92
πέμψω δ' ἐς Σπάρτην τε καὶ ἐς Πύλον ἠμαθόεντα 93
νόστον πευσόμενον πατρὸς φίλου, ἤν που ἀκούσῃ, 94
ἠδ' ἵνα μιν κλέος ἐσθλὸν ἐν ἀνθρώποισιν ἔχῃσιν." 95

Book 2.85-110

"Τηλέμαχ' ὑψαγόρη, μένος ἄσχετε, ποῖον ἔειπες 85
ἡμέας αἰσχύνων, ἐθέλοις δέ κε μῶμον ἀνάψαι. 86
σοὶ δ' οὔ τι μνηστῆρες Ἀχαιῶν αἴτιοί εἰσιν, 87
ἀλλὰ φίλη μήτηρ, ἥ τοι περὶ κέρδεα οἶδεν. 88
ἤδη γὰρ τρίτον ἐστὶν ἔτος, τάχα δ' εἶσι τέταρτον, 89
ἐξ οὗ ἀτέμβει θυμὸν ἐνὶ στήθεσσιν Ἀχαιῶν. 90
πάντας μὲν ῥ' ἔλπει, καὶ ὑπίσχεται ἀνδρὶ ἑκάστῳ, 91
ἀγγελίας προϊεῖσα· νόος δέ οἱ ἄλλα μενοινᾷ. 92
ἡ δὲ δόλον τόνδ' ἄλλον ἐνὶ φρεσὶ μερμήριξε· 93
στησαμένη μέγαν ἱστὸν ἐνὶ μεγάροισιν ὕφαινε, 94
λεπτὸν καὶ περίμετρον· ἄφαρ δ' ἡμῖν μετέειπε· 95
κοῦροι, ἐμοὶ μνηστῆρες, ἐπεὶ θάνε δῖος Ὀδυσσεύς, 96
μίμνετ' ἐπειγόμενοι τὸν ἐμὸν γάμον, εἰς ὅ κε φᾶρος 97
ἐκτελέσω, μή μοι μεταμώνια νήματ' ὄληται, 98
Λαέρτῃ ἥρωϊ ταφήϊον, εἰς ὅτε κέν μιν 99
μοῖρ' ὀλοὴ καθέλῃσι τανηλεγέος θανάτοιο, 100
μή τίς μοι κατὰ δῆμον Ἀχαιϊάδων νεμεσήσῃ, 101

Book 2. 85-110 (cont.)

αἴ κεν ἄτερ σπείρου κεῖται πολλὰ κτεατίσσας. 102
ὣς ἔφαθ', ἡμῖν δ' αὖτ' ἐπεπείθετο θυμὸς ἀγήνωρ. 103
ἔνθα καὶ ἠματίη μὲν ὑφαίνεσκεν μέγαν ἱστόν, 104
νύκτας δ' ἀλλύεσκεν, ἐπεὶ δαΐδας παραθεῖτο. 105
ὣς τρίετες μὲν ἔληθε δόλῳ καὶ ἔπειθεν Ἀχαιούς· 106
ἀλλ' ὅτε τέτρατον ἦλθεν ἔτος καὶ ἐπήλυθον ὧραι, 107
καὶ τότε δή τις ἔειπε γυναικῶν, ἣ σάφα ᾔδη, 108
καὶ τήν γ' ἀλλύουσαν ἐφεύρομεν ἀγλαὸν ἱστόν. 109
ὣς τὸ μὲν ἐξετέλεσσε καὶ οὐκ ἐθέλουσ', ὑπ' ἀνάγκης· 110

Book 5.116-191

ὣς φάτο, ῥίγησεν δὲ Καλυψώ, δῖα θεάων, 116
καί μιν φωνήσασ' ἔπεα πτερόεντα προσηύδα· 117
" σχέτλιοί ἐστε, θεοί, ζηλήμονες ἔξοχον ἄλλων, 118
οἵ τε θεαῖς ἀγάασθε παρ' ἀνδράσιν εὐνάζεσθαι 119
ἀμφαδίην, ἤν τίς τε φίλον ποιήσετ' ἀκοίτην. 120
ὣς μὲν ὅτ' Ὠρίων' ἕλετο ῥοδοδάκτυλος Ἠώς, 121
τόφρα οἱ ἠγάασθε θεοὶ ῥεῖα ζώοντες, 122
ἕως μιν ἐν Ὀρτυγίῃ χρυσόθρονος Ἄρτεμις ἁγνὴ 123
οἷσ' ἀγανοῖσι βέλεσσιν ἐποιχομένη κατέπεφνεν. 124
ὣς δ' ὁπότ' Ἰασίωνι ἐϋπλόκαμος Δημήτηρ, 125
ᾧ θυμῷ εἴξασα, μίγη φιλότητι καὶ εὐνῇ 126
νειῷ ἔνι τριπόλῳ· οὐδὲ δὴν ἦεν ἄπυστος 127
Ζεύς, ὅς μιν κατέπεφνε βαλὼν ἀργῆτι κεραυνῷ. 128
ὣς δ' αὖ νῦν μοι ἄγασθε, θεοί, βροτὸν ἄνδρα παρεῖναι. 129
τὸν μὲν ἐγὼν ἐσάωσα περὶ τρόπιος βεβαῶτα 130
οἶον, ἐπεί οἱ νῆα θοὴν ἀργῆτι κεραυνῷ 131
Ζεὺς ἐλάσας ἐκέασσε μέσῳ ἐνὶ οἴνοπι πόντῳ. 132

Book 5.116-191 (cont.)

ἔνθ’ ἄλλοι μὲν πάντες ἀπέφθιθεν ἐσθλοὶ ἑταῖροι,
τὸν δ’ ἄρα δεῦρ’ ἄνεμός τε φέρων καὶ κῦμα πέλασσε.
τὸν μὲν ἐγὼ φίλεόν τε καὶ ἔτρεφον ἠδὲ ἔφασκον
θήσειν ἀθάνατον καὶ ἀγήραον ἤματα πάντα.
ἀλλ’ ἐπεὶ οὔ πως ἔστι Διὸς νόον αἰγιόχοιο
οὔτε παρεξελθεῖν ἄλλον θεὸν οὔθ’ ἁλιῶσαι,
ἐρρέτω, εἴ μιν κεῖνος ἐποτρύνει καὶ ἀνώγει,
πόντον ἐπ’ ἀτρύγετον. πέμψω δέ μιν οὔ πῃ ἐγώ γε·
οὐ γάρ μοι πάρα νῆες ἐπήρετμοι καὶ ἑταῖροι,
οἵ κέν μιν πέμποιεν ἐπ’ εὐρέα νῶτα θαλάσσης.
αὐτάρ οἱ πρόφρων ὑποθήσομαι οὐδ’ ἐπικεύσω,
ὥς κε μάλ’ ἀσκηθὴς ἣν πατρίδα γαῖαν ἵκηται.”
τὴν δ’ αὖτε προσέειπε διάκτορος Ἀργεϊφόντης·
“οὕτω νῦν ἀπόπεμπε, Διὸς δ’ ἐποπίζεο μῆνιν,
μή πώς τοι μετόπισθε κοτεσσάμενος χαλεπήνῃ.”
ὣς ἄρα φωνήσας ἀπέβη κρατὺς Ἀργεϊφόντης·
ἡ δ’ ἐπ’ Ὀδυσσῆα μεγαλήτορα πότνια νύμφη
ἤϊ’, ἐπεὶ δὴ Ζηνὸς ἐπέκλυεν ἀγγελιάων.
τὸν δ’ ἄρ’ ἐπ’ ἀκτῆς εὗρε καθήμενον· οὐδέ ποτ’ ὄσσε
δακρυόφιν τέρσοντο, κατείβετο δὲ γλυκὺς αἰὼν
νόστον ὀδυρομένῳ, ἐπεὶ οὐκέτι ἥνδανε νύμφη.
ἀλλ’ ἦ τοι νύκτας μὲν ἰαύεσκεν καὶ ἀνάγκῃ
ἐν σπέεσι γλαφυροῖσι παρ’ οὐκ ἐθέλων ἐθελούσῃ·
ἤματα δ’ ἂμ πέτρῃσι καὶ ἠϊόνεσσι καθίζων
δάκρυσι καὶ στοναχῇσι καὶ ἄλγεσι θυμὸν ἐρέχθων
πόντον ἐπ’ ἀτρύγετον δερκέσκετο δάκρυα λείβων.
ἀγχοῦ δ’ ἱσταμένη προσεφώνεε δῖα θεάων·
“κάμμορε, μή μοι ἔτ’ ἐνθάδ’ ὀδύρεο, μηδέ τοι αἰὼν

Book 5.116-191 (cont.)

φθινέτω· ἤδη γάρ σε μάλα πρόφρασσ' ἀποπέμψω.
ἀλλ' ἄγε δούρατα μακρὰ ταμὼν ἁρμόζεο χαλκῷ
εὐρεῖαν σχεδίην· ἀτὰρ ἴκρια πῆξαι ἐπ' αὐτῆς
ὑψοῦ, ὥς σε φέρῃσιν ἐπ' ἠεροειδέα πόντον.
αὐτὰρ ἐγὼ σῖτον καὶ ὕδωρ καὶ οἶνον ἐρυθρὸν
ἐνθήσω μενοεικέ', ἅ κέν τοι λιμὸν ἐρύκοι,
εἵματά τ' ἀμφιέσω· πέμψω δέ τοι οὖρον ὄπισθεν,
ὥς κε μάλ' ἀσκηθὴς σὴν πατρίδα γαῖαν ἵκηαι,
αἴ κε θεοί γ' ἐθέλωσι, τοὶ οὐρανὸν εὐρὺν ἔχουσιν,
οἵ μευ φέρτεροί εἰσι νοῆσαί τε κρῆναί τε."
  ὣς φάτο, ῥίγησεν δὲ πολύτλας δῖος Ὀδυσσεύς,
καί μιν φωνήσας ἔπεα πτερόεντα προσηύδα·
  "ἄλλο τι δὴ σύ, θεά, τόδε μήδεαι οὐδέ τι πομπήν,
ἥ με κέλεαι σχεδίῃ περάαν μέγα λαῖτμα θαλάσσης,
δεινόν τ' ἀργαλέον τε· τὸ δ' οὐδ' ἐπὶ νῆες ἐῖσαι
ὠκύποροι περόωσιν, ἀγαλλόμεναι Διὸς οὔρῳ.
οὐδ' ἂν ἐγώ γ' ἀέκητι σέθεν σχεδίης ἐπιβαίην,
εἰ μή μοι τλαίης γε, θεά, μέγαν ὅρκον ὀμόσσαι
μή τί μοι αὐτῷ πῆμα κακὸν βουλευσέμεν ἄλλο."
  ὣς φάτο, μείδησεν δὲ Καλυψώ, δῖα θεάων,
χειρί τέ μιν κατέρεξεν ἔπος τ' ἔφατ' ἔκ τ' ὀνόμαζεν·
  "ἦ δὴ ἀλιτρός γ' ἐσσὶ καὶ οὐκ ἀποφώλια εἰδώς,
οἷον δὴ τὸν μῦθον ἐπεφράσθης ἀγορεῦσαι.
ἴστω νῦν τόδε γαῖα καὶ οὐρανὸς εὐρὺς ὕπερθε
καὶ τὸ κατειβόμενον Στυγὸς ὕδωρ, ὅς τε μέγιστος
ὅρκος δεινότατός τε πέλει μακάρεσσι θεοῖσι,
μή τί τοι αὐτῷ πῆμα κακὸν βουλευσέμεν ἄλλο.
ἀλλὰ τὰ μὲν νοέω καὶ φράσσομαι, ἅσσ' ἂν ἐμοί περ

Book 5.116-191 (cont.)

αὐτῇ μηδοίμην, ὅτε με χρειὼ τόσον ἵκοι· 189
καὶ γὰρ ἐμοὶ νόος ἐστὶν ἐναίσιμος, οὐδέ μοι αὐτῇ 190
θυμὸς ἐνὶ στήθεσσι σιδήρεος, ἀλλ' ἐλεήμων." 191

Book 5.203-227

"διογενὲς Λαερτιάδη, πολυμήχαν' Ὀδυσσεῦ, 203
οὕτω δὴ οἶκόνδε φίλην ἐς πατρίδα γαῖαν 204
αὐτίκα νῦν ἐθέλεις ἰέναι; σὺ δὲ χαῖρε καὶ ἔμπης. 205
εἴ γε μὲν εἰδείης σῇσι φρεσίν, ὅσσα τοι αἶσα 206
κήδε' ἀναπλῆσαι, πρὶν πατρίδα γαῖαν ἱκέσθαι, 207
ἐνθάδε κ' αὖθι μένων σὺν ἐμοὶ τόδε δῶμα φυλάσσοις 208
ἀθάνατός τ' εἴης, ἱμειρόμενός περ ἰδέσθαι 209
σὴν ἄλοχον, τῆς τ' αἰὲν ἐέλδεαι ἤματα πάντα. 210
οὐ μέν θην κείνης γε χερείων εὔχομαι εἶναι, 211
οὐ δέμας οὐδὲ φυήν, ἐπεὶ οὔ πως οὐδὲ ἔοικε 212
θνητὰς ἀθανάτῃσι δέμας καὶ εἶδος ἐρίζειν." 213
τὴν δ' ἀπαμειβόμενος προσέφη πολύμητις Ὀδυσσεύς· 214
"πότνα θεά, μή μοι τόδε χώεο· οἶδα καὶ αὐτὸς 215
πάντα μάλ', οὕνεκα σεῖο περίφρων Πηνελόπεια 216
εἶδος ἀκιδνοτέρη μέγεθός τ' εἰσάντα ἰδέσθαι· 217
ἡ μὲν γὰρ βροτός ἐστι, σὺ δ' ἀθάνατος καὶ ἀγήρως. 218
ἀλλὰ καὶ ὣς ἐθέλω καὶ ἐέλδομαι ἤματα πάντα 219
οἴκαδέ τ' ἐλθέμεναι καὶ νόστιμον ἦμαρ ἰδέσθαι. 220
εἰ δ' αὖ τις ῥαίῃσι θεῶν ἐνὶ οἴνοπι πόντῳ, 221
τλήσομαι ἐν στήθεσσιν ἔχων ταλαπενθέα θυμόν· 222
ἤδη γὰρ μάλα πολλὰ πάθον καὶ πολλὰ μόγησα 223
κύμασι καὶ πολέμῳ· μετὰ καὶ τόδε τοῖσι γενέσθω." 224

Book 5.203-227 (cont.)

ὣς ἔφατ', ἠέλιος δ' ἄρ' ἔδυ καὶ ἐπὶ κνέφας ἦλθεν· 225
ἐλθόντες δ' ἄρα τώ γε μυχῷ σπείους γλαφυροῖο 226
τερπέσθην φιλότητι, παρ' ἀλλήλοισι μένοντες. 227

Book 5.333-353

τὸν δὲ ἴδεν Κάδμου θυγάτηρ, καλλίσφυρος Ἰνώ, 333
Λευκοθέη, ἣ πρὶν μὲν ἔην βροτὸς αὐδήεσσα, 334
νῦν δ' ἁλὸς ἐν πελάγεσσι θεῶν ἐξέμμορε τιμῆς. 335
ἥ ῥ' Ὀδυσῆ' ἐλέησεν ἀλώμενον, ἄλγε' ἔχοντα· 336
αἰθυίῃ δ' εἰκυῖα ποτῇ ἀνεδύσετο λίμνης, 337
ἷζε δ' ἐπὶ σχεδίης καί μιν πρὸς μῦθον ἔειπε· 338
"κάμμορε, τίπτε τοι ὧδε Ποσειδάων ἐνοσίχθων 339
ὠδύσατ' ἐκπάγλως, ὅτι τοι κακὰ πολλὰ φυτεύει; 340
οὐ μὲν δή σε καταφθίσει, μάλα περ μενεαίνων. 341
ἀλλὰ μάλ' ὧδ' ἔρξαι, δοκέεις δέ μοι οὐκ ἀπινύσσειν· 342
εἵματα ταῦτ' ἀποδὺς σχεδίην ἀνέμοισι φέρεσθαι 343
κάλλιπ', ἀτὰρ χείρεσσι νέων ἐπιμαίεο νόστου 344
γαίης Φαιήκων, ὅθι τοι μοῖρ' ἐστὶν ἀλύξαι. 345
τῆ δέ, τόδε κρήδεμνον ὑπὸ στέρνοιο τανύσσαι 346
ἄμβροτον· οὐδέ τί τοι παθέειν δέος οὐδ' ἀπολέσθαι. 347
αὐτὰρ ἐπὴν χείρεσσιν ἐφάψεαι ἠπείροιο, 348
ἂψ ἀπολυσάμενος βαλέειν εἰς οἴνοπα πόντον 349
πολλὸν ἀπ' ἠπείρου, αὐτὸς δ' ἀπονόσφι τραπέσθαι." 350
ὣς ἄρα φωνήσασα θεὰ κρήδεμνον ἔδωκεν, 351
αὐτὴ δ' ἂψ ἐς πόντον ἐδύσετο κυμαίνοντα 352
αἰθυίῃ εἰκυῖα· μέλαν δέ ἑ κῦμ' ἐκάλυψεν. 353

Book 6.115-161

σφαῖραν ἔπειτ᾽ ἔρριψε μετ᾽ ἀμφίπολον βασίλεια· 115
ἀμφιπόλου μὲν ἅμαρτε, βαθείῃ δ᾽ ἔμβαλε δίνῃ. 116
αἱ δ᾽ ἐπὶ μακρὸν ἄϋσαν· ὁ δ᾽ ἔγρετο δῖος Ὀδυσσεύς, 117
ἑζόμενος δ᾽ ὥρμαινε κατὰ φρένα καὶ κατὰ θυμόν· 118
"ὤ μοι ἐγώ, τέων αὖτε βροτῶν ἐς γαῖαν ἱκάνω; 119
ἤ ῥ᾽ οἵ γ᾽ ὑβρισταί τε καὶ ἄγριοι οὐδὲ δίκαιοι, 120
ἦε φιλόξεινοι καί σφιν νόος ἐστὶ θεουδής; 121
ὥς τέ με κουράων ἀμφήλυθε θῆλυς ἀϋτή, 122
Νυμφάων, αἳ ἔχουσ᾽ ὀρέων αἰπεινὰ κάρηνα 123
καὶ πηγὰς ποταμῶν καὶ πίσεα ποιήεντα· 124
ἦ νύ που ἀνθρώπων εἰμὶ σχεδὸν αὐδηέντων. 125
ἀλλ᾽ ἄγ᾽, ἐγὼν αὐτὸς πειρήσομαι ἠδὲ ἴδωμαι." 126
ὣς εἰπὼν θάμνων ὑπεδύσετο δῖος Ὀδυσσεύς, 127
ἐκ πυκινῆς δ᾽ ὕλης πτόρθον κλάσε χειρὶ παχείῃ 128
φύλλων, ὡς ῥύσαιτο περὶ χροῒ μήδεα φωτός. 129
βῆ δ᾽ ἴμεν ὥς τε λέων ὀρεσίτροφος, ἀλκὶ πεποιθώς, 130
ὅς τ᾽ εἶσ᾽ ὑόμενος καὶ ἀήμενος, ἐν δέ οἱ ὄσσε 131
δαίεται· αὐτὰρ ὁ βουσὶ μετέρχεται ἢ ὀΐεσσιν 132
ἠὲ μετ᾽ ἀγροτέρας ἐλάφους· κέλεται δέ ἑ γαστὴρ 133
μήλων πειρήσοντα καὶ ἐς πυκινὸν δόμον ἐλθεῖν· 134
ὣς Ὀδυσεὺς κούρῃσιν ἐϋπλοκάμοισιν ἔμελλε 135
μείξεσθαι, γυμνός περ ἐών· χρειὼ γὰρ ἵκανε. 136
σμερδαλέος δ᾽ αὐτῇσι φάνη κεκακωμένος ἅλμῃ, 137
τρέσσαν δ᾽ ἄλλυδις ἄλλη ἐπ᾽ ἠϊόνας προὐχούσας. 138
οἴη δ᾽ Ἀλκινόου θυγάτηρ μένε· τῇ γὰρ Ἀθήνη 139
θάρσος ἐνὶ φρεσὶ θῆκε καὶ ἐκ δέος εἵλετο γυίων. 140
στῆ δ᾽ ἄντα σχομένη· ὁ δὲ μερμήριξεν Ὀδυσσεύς, 141
ἢ γούνων λίσσοιτο λαβὼν εὐώπιδα κούρην, 142

Book 6.115-161 (cont.)

ἦ αὔτως ἐπέεσσιν ἀποσταδὰ μειλιχίοισι 143
λίσσοιτ', εἰ δείξειε πόλιν καὶ εἵματα δοίη. 144
ὣς ἄρα οἱ φρονέοντι δοάσσατο κέρδιον εἶναι, 145
λίσσεσθαι ἐπέεσσιν ἀποσταδὰ μειλιχίοισι, 146
μή οἱ γοῦνα λαβόντι χολώσαιτο φρένα κούρη. 147
αὐτίκα μειλίχιον καὶ κερδαλέον φάτο μῦθον· 148
"γουνοῦμαί σε, ἄνασσα· θεός νύ τις ἦ βροτός ἐσσι; 149
εἰ μέν τις θεός ἐσσι, τοὶ οὐρανὸν εὐρὺν ἔχουσιν, 150
Ἀρτέμιδί σε ἐγώ γε, Διὸς κούρῃ μεγάλοιο, 151
εἶδός τε μέγεθός τε φυήν τ' ἄγχιστα ἐΐσκω· 152
εἰ δέ τίς ἐσσι βροτῶν, οἳ ἐπὶ χθονὶ ναιετάουσι, 153
τρὶς μάκαρες μὲν σοί γε πατὴρ καὶ πότνια μήτηρ, 154
τρὶς μάκαρες δὲ κασίγνητοι· μάλα πού σφισι θυμὸς 155
αἰὲν ἐϋφροσύνῃσιν ἰαίνεται εἵνεκα σεῖο, 156
λευσσόντων τοιόνδε θάλος χορὸν εἰσοιχνεῦσαν. 157
κεῖνος δ' αὖ περὶ κῆρι μακάρτατος ἔξοχον ἄλλων, 158
ὅς κέ σ' ἐέδνοισι βρίσας οἶκόνδ' ἀγάγηται. 159
οὐ γάρ πω τοιοῦτον ἴδον βροτὸν ὀφθαλμοῖσιν, 160
οὔτ' ἄνδρ' οὔτε γυναῖκα· σέβας μ' ἔχει εἰσορόωντα. 161

Book 6.186-197

τὸν δ' αὖ Ναυσικάα λευκώλενος ἀντίον ηὔδα· 186
"ξεῖν', ἐπεὶ οὔτε κακῷ οὔτ' ἄφρονι φωτὶ ἔοικας, 187
Ζεὺς δ' αὐτὸς νέμει ὄλβον Ὀλύμπιος ἀνθρώποισιν, 188
ἐσθλοῖσ' ἠδὲ κακοῖσιν, ὅπως ἐθέλῃσιν, ἑκάστῳ· 189
καί που σοὶ τά γ' ἔδωκε, σὲ δὲ χρὴ τετλάμεν ἔμπης. 190
νῦν δ', ἐπεὶ ἡμετέρην τε πόλιν καὶ γαῖαν ἱκάνεις, 191

Book 6.186-197 (cont.)

οὔτ' οὖν ἐσθῆτος δευήσεαι οὔτε τευ ἄλλου, 192
ὧν ἐπέοιχ' ἱκέτην ταλαπείριον ἀντιάσαντα. 193
ἄστυ δέ τοι δείξω, ἐρέω δέ τοι οὔνομα λαῶν· 194
Φαίηκες μὲν τήνδε πόλιν καὶ γαῖαν ἔχουσιν, 195
εἰμὶ δ' ἐγὼ θυγάτηρ μεγαλήτορος Ἀλκινόοιο, 196
τοῦ δ' ἐκ Φαιήκων ἔχεται κάρτος τε βίη τε." 197

Book 9.252-306

"ὦ ξεῖνοι, τίνες ἐστέ; πόθεν πλεῖθ' ὑγρὰ κέλευθα; 252
ἤ τι κατὰ πρῆξιν ἦ μαψιδίως ἀλάλησθε 253
οἷά τε ληϊστῆρες ὑπεὶρ ἅλα, τοί τ' ἀλόωνται 254
ψυχὰς παρθέμενοι, κακὸν ἀλλοδαποῖσι φέροντες;" 255
ὣς ἔφαθ', ἡμῖν δ' αὖτε κατεκλάσθη φίλον ἦτορ, 256
δεισάντων φθόγγον τε βαρὺν αὐτόν τε πέλωρον. 257
ἀλλὰ καὶ ὧς μιν ἔπεσσιν ἀμειβόμενος προσέειπον· 258
"ἡμεῖς τοι Τροίηθεν ἀποπλαγχθέντες Ἀχαιοὶ 259
παντοίοισ' ἀνέμοισιν ὑπὲρ μέγα λαῖτμα θαλάσσης, 260
οἴκαδε ἱέμενοι, ἄλλην ὁδὸν ἄλλα κέλευθα 261
ἤλθομεν· οὕτω που Ζεὺς ἤθελε μητίσασθαι. 262
λαοὶ δ' Ἀτρεΐδεω Ἀγαμέμνονος εὐχόμεθ' εἶναι, 263
τοῦ δὴ νῦν γε μέγιστον ὑπουράνιον κλέος ἐστί· 264
τόσσην γὰρ διέπερσε πόλιν καὶ ἀπώλεσε λαοὺς 265
πολλούς· ἡμεῖς δ' αὖτε κιχανόμενοι τὰ σὰ γοῦνα 266
ἱκόμεθ', εἴ τι πόροις ξεινήϊον ἠὲ καὶ ἄλλως 267
δοίης δωτίνην, ἥ τε ξείνων θέμις ἐστίν. 268
ἀλλ' αἰδεῖο, φέριστε, θεούς· ἱκέται δέ τοί εἰμεν. 269
Ζεὺς δ' ἐπιτιμήτωρ ἱκετάων τε ξείνων τε, 270

Book 9.252-306 (cont.)

ξείνιος, ὃς ξείνοισιν ἅμ' αἰδοίοισιν ὀπηδεῖ."
ὣς ἐφάμην, ὁ δέ μ' αὐτίκ' ἀμείβετο νηλέϊ θυμῷ·
"νήπιός εἰς, ὦ ξεῖν', ἢ τηλόθεν εἰλήλουθας,
ὅς με θεοὺς κέλεαι ἢ δειδίμεν ἢ ἀλέασθαι.
οὐ γὰρ Κύκλωπες Διὸς αἰγιόχου ἀλέγουσιν
οὐδὲ θεῶν μακάρων, ἐπεὶ ἦ πολὺ φέρτεροί εἰμεν·
οὐδ' ἂν ἐγὼ Διὸς ἔχθος ἀλευάμενος πεφιδοίμην
οὔτε σεῦ οὔθ' ἑτάρων, εἰ μὴ θυμός με κελεύοι.
ἀλλά μοι εἴφ', ὅπῃ ἔσχες ἰὼν εὐεργέα νῆα,
ἤ που ἐπ' ἐσχατιῆς ἦ καὶ σχεδόν, ὄφρα δαείω."
ὣς φάτο πειράζων, ἐμὲ δ' οὐ λάθεν εἰδότα πολλά,
ἀλλά μιν ἄψορρον προσέφην δολίοισ' ἐπέεσσι·
"νέα μέν μοι κατέαξε Ποσειδάων ἐνοσίχθων,
πρὸς πέτρῃσι βαλὼν ὑμῆς ἐπὶ πείρασι γαίης,
ἄκρῃ προσπελάσας· ἄνεμος δ' ἐκ πόντου ἔνεικεν·
αὐτὰρ ἐγὼ σὺν τοῖσδε ὑπέκφυγον αἰπὺν ὄλεθρον."
ὣς ἐφάμην, ὁ δέ μ' οὐδὲν ἀμείβετο νηλέϊ θυμῷ,
ἀλλ' ὅ γ' ἀναΐξας ἑτάροισ' ἐπὶ χεῖρας ἴαλλε,
σὺν δὲ δύω μάρψας ὥς τε σκύλακας ποτὶ γαίῃ
κόπτ'· ἐκ δ' ἐγκέφαλος χαμάδις ῥέε, δεῦε δὲ γαῖαν.
τοὺς δὲ διὰ μελεϊστὶ ταμὼν ὁπλίσσατο δόρπον·
ἤσθιε δ' ὥς τε λέων ὀρεσίτροφος, οὐδ' ἀπέλειπεν,
ἔγκατά τε σάρκας τε καὶ ὀστέα μυελόεντα.
ἡμεῖς δὲ κλαίοντες ἀνεσχέθομεν Διὶ χεῖρας,
σχέτλια ἔργ' ὁρόωντες· ἀμηχανίη δ' ἔχε θυμόν.
αὐτὰρ ἐπεὶ Κύκλωψ μεγάλην ἐμπλήσατο νηδὺν
ἀνδρόμεα κρέ' ἔδων καὶ ἐπ' ἄκρητον γάλα πίνων,
κεῖτ' ἔντοσθ' ἄντροιο τανυσσάμενος διὰ μήλων.

Book 9.252-306 (cont.)

τὸν μὲν ἐγὼ βούλευσα κατὰ μεγαλήτορα θυμὸν 299
ἆσσον ἰών, ξίφος ὀξὺ ἐρυσσάμενος παρὰ μηροῦ, 300
οὐτάμεναι πρὸς στῆθος, ὅθι φρένες ἧπαρ ἔχουσι, 301
χείρ᾽ ἐπιμασσάμενος· ἕτερος δέ με θυμὸς ἔρυκεν. 302
αὐτοῦ γάρ κε καὶ ἄμμες ἀπωλόμεθ᾽ αἰπὺν ὄλεθρον· 303
οὐ γάρ κεν δυνάμεσθα θυράων ὑψηλάων 304
χερσὶν ἀπώσασθαι λίθον ὄβριμον, ὃν προσέθηκεν. 305
ὣς τότε μὲν στενάχοντες ἐμείναμεν Ἠῶ δῖαν. 306

Book 9.347-370

“Κύκλωψ, τῆ, πίε οἶνον, ἐπεὶ φάγες ἀνδρόμεα κρέα, 347
ὄφρ᾽ εἰδῇς, οἷόν τι ποτὸν τόδε νηῦς ἐκεκεύθει 348
ἡμετέρη· σοὶ δ᾽ αὖ λοιβὴν φέρον, εἴ μ᾽ ἐλεήσας 349
οἴκαδε πέμψειας· σὺ δὲ μαίνεαι οὐκέτ᾽ ἀνεκτῶς. 350
σχέτλιε, πῶς κέν τίς σε καὶ ὕστερον ἄλλος ἵκοιτο 351
ἀνθρώπων πολέων; ἐπεὶ οὐ κατὰ μοῖραν ἔρεξας.” 352
ὣς ἐφάμην, ὁ δὲ δέκτο καὶ ἔκπιεν· ἥσατο δ᾽ αἰνῶς 353
ἡδὺ ποτὸν πίνων καί μ᾽ ᾔτεε δεύτερον αὖτις· 354
“δός μοι ἔτι πρόφρων καί μοι τεὸν οὔνομα εἰπὲ 355
αὐτίκα νῦν, ἵνα τοι δῶ ξείνιον, ᾧ κε σὺ χαίρῃς. 356
καὶ γὰρ Κυκλώπεσσι φέρει ζείδωρος ἄρουρα 357
οἶνον ἐριστάφυλον, καί σφιν Διὸς ὄμβρος ἀέξει· 358
ἀλλὰ τόδ᾽ ἀμβροσίης καὶ νέκταρός ἐστιν ἀπορρώξ.” 359
ὣς ἔφατ᾽· αὐτάρ οἱ αὖτις ἐγὼ πόρον αἴθοπα οἶνον· 360
τρὶς μὲν ἔδωκα φέρων, τρὶς δ᾽ ἔκπιεν ἀφραδίῃσιν. 361
αὐτὰρ ἐπεὶ Κύκλωπα περὶ φρένας ἤλυθεν οἶνος 362
καὶ τότε δή μιν ἔπεσσι προσηύδων μειλιχίοισι· 363

Book 9.347-370 (cont.)

“Κύκλωψ, εἰρωτᾷς μ’ ὄνομα κλυτόν; αὐτὰρ ἐγώ τοι
ἐξερέω· σὺ δέ μοι δὸς ξείνιον, ὥς περ ὑπέστης.
Οὖτις ἐμοί γ’ ὄνομα· Οὖτιν δέ με κικλήσκουσι
μήτηρ ἠδὲ πατὴρ ἠδ’ ἄλλοι πάντες ἑταῖροι.”
ὣς ἐφάμην, ὁ δέ μ’ αὐτίκ’ ἀμείβετο νηλέϊ θυμῷ·
“Οὖτιν ἐγὼ πύματον ἔδομαι μετὰ οἷσ’ ἑτάροισι,
τοὺς δ’ ἄλλους πρόσθεν· τὸ δέ τοι ξεινήϊον ἔσται.”

Book 9.395-414

σμερδαλέον δὲ μέγ’ ᾤμωξεν, περὶ δ’ ἴαχε πέτρη,
ἡμεῖς δὲ δείσαντες ἀπεσσύμεθ’. αὐτὰρ ὁ μοχλὸν
ἐξέρυσ’ ὀφθαλμοῖο πεφυρμένον αἵματι πολλῷ.
τὸν μὲν ἔπειτ’ ἔρριψεν ἀπὸ ἕο χερσὶν ἀλύων,
αὐτὰρ ὁ Κύκλωπας μεγάλ’ ἤπυεν, οἵ ῥά μιν ἀμφὶς
ᾤκεον ἐν σπήεσσι δι’ ἄκριας ἠνεμοέσσας.
οἱ δὲ βοῆς ἀΐοντες ἐφοίτων ἄλλοθεν ἄλλος,
ἱστάμενοι δ’ εἴροντο περὶ σπέος, ὅττι ἑ κήδοι·
“τίπτε τόσον, Πολύφημ’, ἀρημένος ὧδ’ ἐβόησας
νύκτα δι’ ἀμβροσίην καὶ ἀΰπνους ἄμμε τίθησθα;
ἦ μή τίς σευ μῆλα βροτῶν ἀέκοντος ἐλαύνει;
ἦ μή τίς σ’ αὐτὸν κτείνει δόλῳ ἠὲ βίηφι;”
τοὺς δ’ αὖτ’ ἐξ ἄντρου προσέφη κρατερὸς Πολύφημος·
“ὦ φίλοι, Οὖτίς με κτείνει δόλῳ οὐδὲ βίηφιν.”
οἱ δ’ ἀπαμειβόμενοι ἔπεα πτερόεντ’ ἀγόρευον·
“εἰ μὲν δὴ μή τίς σε βιάζεται οἶον ἐόντα,
νοῦσόν γ’ οὔ πως ἔστι Διὸς μεγάλου ἀλέασθαι,
ἀλλὰ σύ γ’ εὔχεο πατρὶ Ποσειδάωνι ἄνακτι.”

Book 9.395-414 (cont.)

ὣς ἄρ' ἔφαν ἀπιόντες, ἐμὸν δ' ἐγέλασσε φίλον κῆρ, 413
ὡς ὄνομ' ἐξαπάτησεν ἐμὸν καὶ μῆτις ἀμύμων. 414

Book 9.502-536

" Κύκλωψ, αἴ κέν τίς σε καταθνητῶν ἀνθρώπων 502
ὀφθαλμοῦ εἴρηται ἀεικελίην ἀλαωτύν, 503
φάσθαι Ὀδυσσῆα πτολιπόρθιον ἐξαλαῶσαι, 504
υἱὸν Λαέρτεω, Ἰθάκῃ ἔνι οἰκί' ἔχοντα. " 505
ὣς ἐφάμην, ὁ δέ μ' οἰμώξας ἠμείβετο μύθῳ· 506
" ὢ πόποι, ἦ μάλα δή με παλαίφατα θέσφαθ' ἱκάνει. 507
ἔσκε τις ἐνθάδε μάντις ἀνὴρ ἠΰς τε μέγας τε, 508
Τήλεμος Εὐρυμίδης, ὃς μαντοσύνῃ ἐκέκαστο 509
καὶ μαντευόμενος κατεγήρα Κυκλώπεσσιν· 510
ὅς μοι ἔφη τάδε πάντα τελευτήσεσθαι ὀπίσσω, 511
χειρῶν ἐξ Ὀδυσῆος ἁμαρτήσεσθαι ὀπωπῆς. 512
ἀλλ' αἰεί τινα φῶτα μέγαν καὶ καλὸν ἐδέγμην 513
ἐνθάδ' ἐλεύσεσθαι, μεγάλην ἐπιειμένον ἀλκήν· 514
νῦν δέ μ' ἐὼν ὀλίγος τε καὶ οὐτιδανὸς καὶ ἄκικυς 515
ὀφθαλμοῦ ἀλάωσεν, ἐπεί μ' ἐδαμάσσατο οἴνῳ. 516
ἀλλ' ἄγε δεῦρ', Ὀδυσεῦ, ἵνα τοι πὰρ ξείνια θείω, 517
πομπήν τ' ὀτρύνω δόμεναι κλυτὸν ἐννοσίγαιον· 518
τοῦ γὰρ ἐγὼ πάϊς εἰμί, πατὴρ δ' ἐμὸς εὔχεται εἶναι. 519
αὐτὸς δ', αἴ κ' ἐθέλῃσ', ἰήσεται, οὐδέ τις ἄλλος 520
οὔτε θεῶν μακάρων οὔτε θνητῶν ἀνθρώπων. " 521
ὣς ἔφατ', αὐτὰρ ἐγώ μιν ἀμειβόμενος προσέειπον· 522
" αἲ γὰρ δὴ ψυχῆς τε καὶ αἰῶνός σε δυναίμην 523
εὖνιν ποιήσας πέμψαι δόμον Ἄϊδος εἴσω, 524
ὡς οὐκ ὀφθαλμόν γ' ἰήσεται οὐδ' ἐνοσίχθων. " 525

Book 9.502-536 (cont.)

ὣς ἐφάμην, ὁ δ’ ἔπειτα Ποσειδάωνι ἄνακτι 526
εὔχετο, χεῖρ’ ὀρέγων εἰς οὐρανὸν ἀστερόεντα· 527
“ κλῦθι, Ποσείδαον γαιήοχε κυανοχαῖτα· 528
εἰ ἐτεόν γε σός εἰμι, πατὴρ δ’ ἐμὸς εὔχεαι εἶναι, 529
δὸς μὴ Ὀδυσσῆα πτολιπόρθιον οἴκαδ’ ἱκέσθαι, 530
υἱὸν Λαέρτεω, Ἰθάκῃ ἔνι οἰκί’ ἔχοντα. 531
ἀλλ’ εἴ οἱ μοῖρ’ ἐστὶ φίλους τ’ ἰδέειν καὶ ἱκέσθαι 532
οἶκον ἐϋκτίμενον καὶ ἑὴν ἐς πατρίδα γαῖαν, 533
ὀψὲ κακῶς ἔλθοι, ὀλέσας ἄπο πάντας ἑταίρους, 534
νηὸς ἐπ’ ἀλλοτρίης, εὕροι δ’ ἐν πήματα οἴκῳ. ” 535
ὣς ἔφατ’ εὐχόμενος, τοῦ δ’ ἔκλυε κυανοχαίτης. 536

Book 10.28-49

ἐννῆμαρ μὲν ὁμῶς πλέομεν νύκτας τε καὶ ἦμαρ, 28
τῇ δεκάτῃ δ’ ἤδη ἀνεφαίνετο πατρὶς ἄρουρα, 29
καὶ δὴ πυρπολέοντας ἐλεύσσομεν ἐγγὺς ἐόντες. 30
ἔνθ’ ἐμὲ μὲν γλυκὺς ὕπνος ἐπέλλαβε κεκμηῶτα· 31
αἰεὶ γὰρ πόδα νηὸς ἐνώμων, οὐδέ τῳ ἄλλῳ 32
δῶχ’ ἑτάρων, ἵνα θᾶσσον ἱκοίμεθα πατρίδα γαῖαν· 33
οἱ δ’ ἕταροι ἐπέεσσι πρὸς ἀλλήλους ἀγόρευον 34
καί μ’ ἔφασαν χρυσόν τε καὶ ἄργυρον οἴκαδ’ ἄγεσθαι, 35
δῶρα παρ’ Αἰόλου μεγαλήτορος Ἱπποτάδαο. 36
ὧδε δέ τις εἴπεσκεν ἰδὼν ἐς πλησίον ἄλλον· 37
“ ὢ πόποι, ὡς ὅδε πᾶσι φίλος καὶ τίμιός ἐστιν 38
ἀνθρώποισ’, ὅτεών κε πόλιν καὶ γαῖαν ἵκηται. 39
πολλὰ μὲν ἐκ Τροίης ἄγεται κειμήλια καλὰ 40
ληΐδος· ἡμεῖς δ’ αὖτε ὁμὴν ὁδὸν ἐκτελέσαντες 41

Book 10.28-49 (cont.)

οἴκαδε νισόμεθα κενεὰς σὺν χεῖρας ἔχοντες. 42
καὶ νῦν οἱ τά γε δῶκε χαριζόμενος φιλότητι 43
Αἴολος. ἀλλ' ἄγε θᾶσσον ἰδώμεθα, ὅττι τάδ' ἐστίν, 44
ὅσσος τις χρυσός τε καὶ ἄργυρος ἀσκῷ ἔνεστιν." 45
ὣς ἔφασαν, βουλὴ δὲ κακὴ νίκησεν ἑταίρων· 46
ἀσκὸν μὲν λῦσαν, ἄνεμοι δ' ἐκ πάντες ὄρουσαν, 47
τοὺς δ' αἶψ' ἁρπάξασα φέρεν πόντονδε θύελλα 48
κλαίοντας, γαίης ἄπο πατρίδος. 49

Book 10.210-347

εὗρον δ' ἐν βήσσῃσι τετυγμένα δώματα Κίρκης 210
ξεστοῖσιν λάεσσι, περισκέπτῳ ἐνὶ χώρῳ. 211
ἀμφὶ δέ μιν λύκοι ἦσαν ὀρέστεροι ἠδὲ λέοντες, 212
τοὺς αὐτὴ κατέθελξεν, ἐπεὶ κακὰ φάρμακ' ἔδωκεν. 213
οὐδ' οἵ γ' ὡρμήθησαν ἐπ' ἀνδράσιν, ἀλλ' ἄρα τοί γε 214
οὐρῇσιν μακρῇσι περισσαίνοντες ἀνέσταν. 215
ὡς δ' ὅτ' ἂν ἀμφὶ ἄνακτα κύνες δαίτηθεν ἰόντα 216
σαίνωσ'· αἰεὶ γάρ τε φέρει μειλίγματα θυμοῦ· 217
ὣς τοὺς ἀμφὶ λύκοι κρατερώνυχες ἠδὲ λέοντες 218
σαῖνον· τοὶ δ' ἔδδεισαν, ἐπεὶ ἴδον αἰνὰ πέλωρα. 219
ἔσταν δ' ἐν προθύροισι θεᾶς καλλιπλοκάμοιο, 220
Κίρκης δ' ἔνδον ἄκουον ἀειδούσης ὀπὶ καλῇ 221
ἱστὸν ἐποιχομένης μέγαν ἄμβροτον, οἷα θεάων 222
λεπτά τε καὶ χαρίεντα καὶ ἀγλαὰ ἔργα πέλονται. 223
τοῖσι δὲ μύθων ἦρχε Πολίτης, ὄρχαμος ἀνδρῶν, 224
ὅς μοι κήδιστος ἑτάρων ἦν κεδνότατός τε· 225
"ὦ φίλοι, ἔνδον γάρ τις ἐποιχομένη μέγαν ἱστὸν 226
καλὸν ἀοιδιάει, δάπεδον δ' ἅπαν ἀμφιμέμυκεν, 227

Book 10.210-347 (cont.)

ἢ θεὸς ἠὲ γυνή· ἀλλὰ φθεγγώμεθα θᾶσσον."
 ὣς ἄρ' ἐφώνησεν, τοὶ δ' ἐφθέγγοντο καλεῦντες.
ἡ δ' αἶψ' ἐξελθοῦσα θύρας ὤϊξε φαεινὰς
καὶ κάλει· οἱ δ' ἅμα πάντες ἀϊδρείῃσιν ἕποντο·
Εὐρύλοχος δ' ὑπέμεινεν· ὀΐσατο γὰρ δόλον εἶναι.
εἷσεν δ' εἰσαγαγοῦσα κατὰ κλισμούς τε θρόνους τε,
ἐν δέ σφιν τυρόν τε καὶ ἄλφιτα καὶ μέλι χλωρὸν
οἴνῳ Πραμνείῳ ἐκύκα· ἀνέμισγε δὲ σίτῳ
φάρμακα λύγρ', ἵνα πάγχυ λαθοίατο πατρίδος αἴης.
αὐτὰρ ἐπεὶ δῶκέν τε καὶ ἔκπιον, αὐτίκ' ἔπειτα
ῥάβδῳ πεπληγυῖα κατὰ συφεοῖσιν ἐέργνυ.
οἱ δὲ συῶν μὲν ἔχον κεφαλὰς φωνήν τε τρίχας τε
καὶ δέμας, αὐτὰρ νοῦς ἦν ἔμπεδος ὡς τὸ πάρος περ.
ὣς οἱ μὲν κλαίοντες ἐέρχατο· τοῖσι δέ Κίρκη
πὰρ ἄκυλον βάλανόν τ' ἔβαλεν καρπόν τε κρανείης
ἔδμεναι, οἷα σύες χαμαιευνάδες αἰὲν ἔδουσιν.
 Εὐρύλοχος δ' ἂψ ἦλθε θοὴν ἐπὶ νῆα μέλαιναν,
ἀγγελίην ἑτάρων ἐρέων καὶ ἀδευκέα πότμον.
οὐδέ τι ἐκφάσθαι δύνατο ἔπος, ἱέμενός περ,
κῆρ ἄχεϊ μεγάλῳ βεβολημένος· ἐν δέ οἱ ὄσσε
δακρυόφιν πίμπλαντο, γόον δ' ὠΐετο θυμός.
ἀλλ' ὅτε δή μιν πάντες ἀγασσάμεθ' ἐξερέοντες,
καὶ τότε τῶν ἄλλων ἑτάρων κατέλεξεν ὄλεθρον·
 "ἤομεν, ὡς ἐκέλευες, ἀνὰ δρυμά, φαίδιμ' Ὀδυσσεῦ·
εὕρομεν ἐν βήσσῃσι τετυγνένα δώματα καλὰ
ξεστοῖσιν λάεσσι, περισκέπτῳ ἐνὶ χώρῳ.
ἔνθα δέ τις μέγαν ἱστὸν ἐποιχομένη λίγ' ἄειδεν
ἢ θεὸς ἠὲ γυνή· τοὶ δ' ἐφθέγγοντο καλεῦντες.

Book 10.210-347 (cont.)

ἡ δ' αἶψ' ἐξελθοῦσα θύρας ὤϊξε φαεινὰς 256
καὶ κάλει· οἱ δ' ἅμα πάντες ἀϊδρείῃσιν ἕποντο· 257
αὐτὰρ ἐγὼν ὑπέμεινα, ὀϊσάμενος δόλον εἶναι. 258
οἱ δ' ἅμ' ἀϊστώθησαν ἀολλέες, οὐδέ τις αὐτῶν 259
ἐξεφάνη· δηρὸν δὲ καθήμενος ἐσκοπίαζον." 260
  ὣς ἔφατ', αὐτὰρ ἐγὼ περὶ μὲν ξίφος ἀργυρόηλον 261
ὤμοιϊν βαλόμην, μέγα χάλκεον, ἀμφὶ δὲ τόξα· 262
τὸν δ' ἂψ ἠνώγεα αὐτὴν ὁδὸν ἡγήσασθαι. 263
αὐτὰρ ὅ γ' ἀμφοτέρῃσι λαβὼν ἐλλίσσετο γούνων 264
καί μ' ὀλοφυρόμενος ἔπεα πτερόεντα προσηύδα· 265
  "μή μ' ἄγε κεῖσ' ἀέκοντα, διοτρεφές, ἀλλὰ λίπ' αὐτοῦ. 266
οἶδα γὰρ ὡς οὔτ' αὐτὸς ἐλεύσεαι οὔτε τιν' ἄλλον 267
ἄξεις σῶν ἑτάρων. ἀλλὰ ξὺν τοίσδεσι θᾶσσον 268
φεύγωμεν· ἔτι γάρ κεν ἀλύξαιμεν κακὸν ἦμαρ." 269
  ὣς ἔφατ', αὐτὰρ ἐγώ μιν ἀμειβόμενος προσέειπον· 270
"Εὐρύλοχ', ἦ τοι μὲν σὺ μέν' αὐτοῦ τῷδ' ἐνὶ χώρῳ 271
ἔσθων καὶ πίνων κοίλῃ παρὰ νηῒ μελαίνῃ· 272
αὐτὰρ ἐγὼν εἶμι· κρατερὴ δέ μοι ἔπλετ' ἀνάγκη." 273
  ὣς εἰπὼν παρὰ νηὸς ἀνήϊον ἠδὲ θαλάσσης. 274
ἀλλ' ὅτε δὴ ἄρ' ἔμελλον ἰὼν ἱερὰς ἀνὰ βήσσας 275
Κίρκης ἵξεσθαι πολυφαρμάκου ἐς μέγα δῶμα, 276
ἔνθα μοι Ἑρμείας χρυσόρραπις ἀντεβόλησεν 277
ἐρχομένῳ πρὸς δῶμα, νεηνίῃ ἀνδρὶ ἐοικώς, 278
πρῶτον ὑπηνήτῃ, τοῦ περ χαριεστάτη ἥβη· 279
ἔν τ' ἄρα μοι φῦ χειρὶ ἔπος τ' ἔφατ' ἔκ τ' ὀνόμαζε· 280
  "πῇ δὴ αὖτ', ὦ δύστηνε, δι' ἄκριας ἔρχεαι οἶος, 281
χώρου ἄϊδρις ἐών; ἕταροι δέ τοι οἵδ' ἐνὶ Κίρκης 282
ἔρχαται ὥς τε σύες πυκινοὺς κευθμῶνας ἔχοντες. 283

Book 10.210-347 (cont.)

ἦ τοὺς λυσόμενος δεῦρ’ ἔρχεαι; οὐδέ σέ φημι
αὐτὸν νοστήσειν, μενέεις δὲ σύ γ’ ἔνθα περ ἄλλοι.
ἀλλ’ ἄγε δή σε κακῶν ἐκλύσομαι ἠδὲ σαώσω·
τῆ, τόδε φάρμακον ἐσθλὸν ἔχων ἐς δώματα Κίρκης
ἔρχευ, ὅ κέν τοι κρατὸς ἀλάλκῃσιν κακὸν ἦμαρ.
πάντα δέ τοι ἐρέω ὀλοφώϊα δήνεα Κίρκης.
τεύξει τοι κυκεῶ, βαλέει δ’ ἐν φάρμακα σίτῳ·
ἀλλ’ οὐδ’ ὧς θέλξαι σε δυνήσεται· οὐ γὰρ ἐάσει
φάρμακον ἐσθλόν, ὅ τοι δώσω, ἐρέω δὲ ἕκαστα.
ὁππότε κεν Κίρκη σ’ ἐλάσῃ περιμήκεϊ ῥάβδῳ,
δὴ τότε σὺ ξίφος ὀξὺ ἐρυσσάμενος παρὰ μηροῦ
Κίρκῃ ἐπαΐξαι ὥς τε κτάμεναι μενεαίνων.
ἡ δέ σ’ ὑποδδείσασα κελήσεται εὐνηθῆναι·
ἔνθα σὺ μηκέτ’ ἔπειτ’ ἀπανήνασθαι θεοῦ εὐνήν,
ὄφρα κέ τοι λύσῃ θ’ ἑτάρους αὐτόν τε κομίσσῃ·
ἀλλὰ κέλεσθαί μιν μακάρων μέγαν ὅρκον ὀμόσσαι
μή τί τοι αὐτῷ πῆμα κακὸν βουλευσέμεν ἄλλο,
μή σ’ ἀπογυμνωθέντα κακὸν καὶ ἀνήνορα θήῃ.”
  ὣς ἄρα φωνήσας πόρε φάρμακον Ἀργεϊφόντης
ἐκ γαίης ἐρύσας καί μοι φύσιν αὐτοῦ ἔδειξε.
ῥίζῃ μὲν μέλαν ἔσκε, γάλακτι δὲ εἴκελον ἄνθος·
μῶλυ δέ μιν καλέουσι θεοί, χαλεπὸν δέ τ’ ὀρύσσειν
ἀνδράσι γε θνητοῖσι· θεοὶ δέ τε πάντα δύνανται.
  Ἑρμείας μὲν ἔπειτ’ ἀπέβη πρὸς μακρὸν Ὄλυμπον
νῆσον ἀν’ ὑλήεσσαν, ἐγὼ δ’ ἐς δώματα Κίρκης
ἤϊα· πολλὰ δέ μοι κραδίη πόρφυρε κιόντι.
ἔστην δ’ εἰνὶ θύρῃσι θεᾶς καλλιπλοκάμοιο·
ἔνθα στὰς ἐβόησα, θεὰ δέ μευ ἔκλυεν αὐδῆς.

Book 10.210-347 (cont.)

ἡ δ' αἶψ' ἐξελθοῦσα θύρας ὤϊξε φαεινὰς
καὶ κάλει· αὐτὰρ ἐγὼν ἑπόμην ἀκαχήμενος ἦτορ.
εἷσε δέ μ' εἰσαγαγοῦσα ἐπὶ θρόνου ἀργυροήλου,
καλοῦ δαιδαλέου· ὑπὸ δὲ θρῆνυς ποσὶν ἦεν·
τεῦχε δέ μοι κυκεῶ χρυσέῳ δέπᾳ, ὄφρα πίοιμι,
ἐν δέ τε φάρμακον ἧκε, κακὰ φρονέουσ' ἐνὶ θυμῷ.
αὐτὰρ ἐπεὶ δῶκέν τε καὶ ἔκπιον οὐδέ μ' ἔθελξε,
ῥάβδῳ πεπληγυῖα ἔπος τ' ἔφατ' ἔκ τ' ὀνόμαζεν·
"ἔρχεο νῦν συφεόνδε, μετ' ἄλλων λέξο ἑταίρων."
ὣς φάτ', ἐγὼ δ' ἄορ ὀξὺ ἐρυσσάμενος παρὰ μηροῦ
Κίρκῃ ἐπήϊξα ὥς τε κτάμεναι μενεαίνων.
ἡ δὲ μέγα ἰάχουσα ὑπέδραμε καὶ λάβε γούνων
καί μ' ὀλοφυρομένη ἔπεα πτερόεντα προσηύδα·
"τίς πόθεν εἰς ἀνδρῶν; πόθι τοι πόλις ἠδὲ τοκῆες;
θαῦμά μ' ἔχει, ὡς οὔ τι πιὼν τάδε φάρμακ' ἐθέλχθης.
οὐδὲ γὰρ οὐδέ τις ἄλλος ἀνὴρ τάδε φάρμακ' ἀνέτλη,
ὅς κε πίῃ καὶ πρῶτον ἀμείψεται ἕρκος ὀδόντων·
σοὶ δέ τις ἐν στήθεσσιν ἀκήλητος νόος ἐστίν.
ἦ σύ γ' Ὀδυσσεύς ἐσσι πολύτροπος, ὅν τέ μοι αἰεὶ
φάσκεν ἐλεύσεσθαι χρυσόρραπις Ἀργεϊφόντης,
ἐκ Τροίης ἀνιόντα θοῇ σὺν νηῒ μελαίνῃ.
ἀλλ' ἄγε δὴ κολεῷ μὲν ἄορ θέο, νῶϊ δ' ἔπειτα
εὐνῆς ἡμετέρης ἐπιβήομεν, ὄφρα μιγέντε
εὐνῇ καὶ φιλότητι πεποίθομεν ἀλλήλοισιν."
ὣς ἔφατ', αὐτὰρ ἐγώ μιν ἀμειβόμενος προσέειπον·
"ὦ Κίρκη, πῶς γάρ με κέλεαι σοὶ ἤπιον εἶναι,
ἥ μοι σῦς μὲν ἔθηκας ἐνὶ μεγάροισιν ἑταίρους,
αὐτὸν δ' ἐνθάδ' ἔχουσα δολοφρονέουσα κελεύεις

Book 10.210-347 (cont.)

ἐς θάλαμόν τ' ἰέναι καὶ σῆς ἐπιβήμεναι εὐνῆς,
ὄφρα με γυμνωθέντα κακὸν καὶ ἀνήνορα θήῃς.
οὐδ' ἂν ἐγώ γ' ἐθέλοιμι τεῆς ἐπιβήμεναι εὐνῆς,
εἰ μή μοι τλαίης γε, θεά, μέγαν ὅρκον ὀμόσσαι,
μή τί μοι αὐτῷ πῆμα κακὸν βουλευσέμεν ἄλλο."
  ὣς ἐφάμην, ἡ δ' αὐτίκ' ἀπώμνυεν, ὡς ἐκέλευον.
αὐτὰρ ἐπεί ῥ' ὄμοσέν τε τελεύτησέν τε τὸν ὅρκον,
καὶ τότ' ἐγὼ Κίρκης ἐπέβην περικαλλέος εὐνῆς.

Book 11.100-137

  "νόστον δίζηαι μελιηδέα, φαίδιμ' Ὀδυσσεῦ·
τὸν δέ τοι ἀργαλέον θήσει θεός. οὐ γὰρ ὀΐω
λήσειν ἐννοσίγαιον, ὅ τοι κότον ἔνθετο θυμῷ,
χωόμενος ὅτι οἱ υἱὸν φίλον ἐξαλάωσας.
ἀλλ' ἔτι μέν κε καὶ ὧς, κακά περ πάσχοντες, ἵκοισθε,
αἴ κ' ἐθέλῃς σὸν θυμὸν ἐρυκακέειν καὶ ἑταίρων,
ὁππότε κεν πρῶτον πελάσῃς εὐεργέα νῆα
Θρινακίῃ νήσῳ, προφυγὼν ἰοειδέα πόντον,
βοσκομένας δ' εὕρητε βόας καὶ ἴφια μῆλα
Ἠελίου, ὃς πάντ' ἐφορᾷ καὶ πάντ' ἐπακούει.
τὰς εἰ μέν κ' ἀσινέας ἐάᾳς νόστου τε μέδηαι,
καί κεν ἔτ' εἰς Ἰθάκην, κακά περ πάσχοντες, ἵκοισθε·
εἰ δέ κε σίνηαι, τότε τοι τεκμαίρομ' ὄλεθρον
νηΐ τε καὶ ἑτάροισ'. αὐτὸς δ' εἴ πέρ κεν ἀλύξῃς,
ὀψὲ κακῶς νεῖαι, ὀλέσας ἄπο πάντας ἑταίρους,
νηὸς ἐπ' ἀλλοτρίης· δήεις δ' ἐν πήματα οἴκῳ,
ἄνδρας ὑπερφιάλους, οἵ τοι βίοτον κατέδουσι
μνώμενοι ἀντιθέην ἄλοχον καὶ ἕδνα διδόντες.

Book 11.100-137 (cont.)

ἀλλ' ἦ τοι κείνων γε βίας ἀποτείσεαι ἐλθών· 118
αὐτὰρ ἐπὴν μνηστῆρας ἐνὶ μεγάροισι τεοῖσι 119
κτείνῃς ἠὲ δόλῳ ἢ ἀμφαδὸν ὀξέϊ χαλκῷ, 120
ἔρχεσθαι δὴ ἔπειτα, λαβὼν εὐῆρες ἐρετμόν, 121
εἰς ὅ κε τοὺς ἀφίκηαι, οἳ οὐκ ἴσασι θάλασσαν 122
ἀνέρες οὐδέ θ' ἅλεσσι μεμιγμένον εἶδαρ ἔδουσιν· 123
οὐδ' ἄρα τοὶ ἴσασι νέας φοινικοπαρῄους, 124
οὐδ' εὐήρε' ἐρετμά, τά τε πτερὰ νηυσὶ πέλονται. 125
σῆμα δέ τοι ἐρέω μάλ' ἀριφραδές, οὐδέ σε λήσει· 126
ὁππότε κεν δή τοι συμβλήμενος ἄλλος ὁδίτης 127
φήῃ ἀθηρηλοιγὸν ἔχειν ἀνὰ φαιδίμῳ ὤμῳ, 128
καὶ τότε δὴ γαίῃ πήξας εὐῆρες ἐρετμόν, 129
ῥέξας ἱερὰ καλὰ Ποσειδάωνι ἄνακτι, 130
ἀρνειὸν ταῦρόν τε συῶν τ' ἐπιβήτορα κάπρον, 131
οἴκαδ' ἀποστείχειν ἔρδειν θ' ἱερὰς ἑκατόμβας 132
ἀθανάτοισι θεοῖσι, τοὶ οὐρανὸν εὐρὺν ἔχουσι, 133
πᾶσι μάλ' ἑξείης. θάνατος δέ τοι ἐξ ἁλὸς αὐτῷ 134
ἀβληχρὸς μάλα τοῖος ἐλεύσεται, ὅς κέ σε πέφνῃ 135
γήρᾳ ὕπο λιπαρῷ ἀρημένον· ἀμφὶ δὲ λαοὶ 136
ὄλβιοι ἔσσονται. τὰ δέ τοι νημερτέα εἴρω." 137

Book 11.478-491

"ὦ Ἀχιλεῦ, Πηλῆος υἱέ, μέγα φέρτατ' Ἀχαιῶν, 478
ἦλθον Τειρεσίαο κατὰ χρέος, εἴ τινα βουλὴν 479
εἴποι, ὅπως Ἰθάκην ἐς παιπαλόεσσαν ἱκοίμην· 480
οὐ γάρ πω σχεδὸν ἦλθον Ἀχαιΐδος οὐδέ πω ἁμῆς 481
γῆς ἐπέβην, ἀλλ' αἰὲν ἔχω κακά. σεῖο δ', Ἀχιλλεῦ, 482
οὔ τις ἀνὴρ προπάροιθε μακάρτερος οὔτ' ἄρ' ὀπίσσω· 483

Book 11.478-491 (cont.)

πρὶν μὲν γάρ σε ζωὸν ἐτίομεν ἶσα θεοῖσιν 484
Ἀργεῖοι, νῦν αὖτε μέγα κρατέεις νεκύεσσιν 485
ἐνθάδ' ἐών· τῶ μή τι θανὼν ἀκαχίζευ, Ἀχιλλεῦ." 486
ὣς ἐφάμην, ὁ δέ μ' αὐτίκ' ἀμειβόμενος προσέειπε· 487
"μὴ δή μοι θάνατόν γε παραύδα, φαίδιμ' Ὀδυσσεῦ. 488
βουλοίμην κ' ἐπάρουρος ἐὼν θητευέμεν ἄλλῳ, 489
ἀνδρὶ παρ' ἀκλήρῳ, ᾧ μὴ βίοτος πολὺς εἴη, 490
ἢ πᾶσιν νεκύεσσι καταφθιμένοισιν ἀνάσσειν. 491

Book 12.166-259

τόφρα δὲ καρπαλίμως ἐξίκετο νηῦς εὐεργὴς 166
νῆσον Σειρήνοιϊν· ἔπειγε γὰρ οὖρος ἀπήμων. 167
αὐτίκ' ἔπειτ' ἄνεμος μὲν ἐπαύσατο ἠδὲ γαλήνη 168
ἔπλετο νηνεμίη, κοίμησε δὲ κύματα δαίμων. 169
ἀνστάντες δ' ἕταροι νεὸς ἱστία μηρύσαντο, 170
καὶ τὰ μὲν ἐν νηῒ γλαφυρῇ θέσαν, οἱ δ' ἐπ' ἐρετμὰ 171
ἑζόμενοι λεύκαινον ὕδωρ ξεστῇσ' ἐλάτῃσιν. 172
αὐτὰρ ἐγὼ κηροῖο μέγαν τροχὸν ὀξέϊ χαλκῷ 173
τυτθὰ διατμήξας χερσὶ στιβαρῇσι πίεζον· 174
αἶψα δ' ἰαίνετο κηρός, ἐπεὶ κέλετο μεγάλη ἲς 175
Ἠελίου τ' αὐγὴ Ὑπεριονίδαο ἄνακτος· 176
ἑξείης δ' ἑτάροισιν ἐπ' οὔατα πᾶσιν ἄλειψα. 177
οἱ δ' ἐν νηΐ μ' ἔδησαν ὁμοῦ χεῖράς τε πόδας τε 178
ὀρθὸν ἐν ἱστοπέδῃ, ἐκ δ' αὐτοῦ πείρατ' ἀνῆπτον· 179
αὐτοὶ δ' ἑζόμενοι πολιὴν ἅλα τύπτον ἐρετμοῖς. 180
ἀλλ' ὅτε τόσσον ἀπῆμεν, ὅσον τε γέγωνε βοήσας, 181
ῥίμφα διώκοντες, τὰς δ' οὐ λάθεν ὠκύαλος νηῦς 182
ἐγγύθεν ὀρνυμένη, λιγυρὴν δ' ἔντυνον ἀοιδήν· 183

Book 12.166-259 (cont.)

“ δεῦρ’ ἄγ’ ἰών, πολύαιν’ Ὀδυσεῦ, μέγα κῦδος Ἀχαιῶν,
νῆα κατάστησον, ἵνα νωϊτέρην ὄπ’ ἀκούσῃς.
οὐ γάρ πώ τις τῇδε παρήλασε νηῒ μελαίνῃ,
πρίν γ’ ἡμέων μελίγηρυν ἀπὸ στομάτων ὄπ’ ἀκοῦσαι,
ἀλλ’ ὅ γε τερψάμενος νεῖται καὶ πλείονα εἰδώς.
ἴδμεν γάρ τοι πάνθ’, ὅσ’ ἐνὶ Τροίῃ εὐρείῃ
Ἀργεῖοι Τρῶές τε θεῶν ἰότητι μόγησαν,
ἴδμεν δ’ ὅσσα γένηται ἐπὶ χθονὶ πουλυβοτείρῃ. ”
ὣς φάσαν ἱεῖσαι ὄπα κάλλιμον· αὐτὰρ ἐμὸν κῆρ
ἤθελ’ ἀκουέμεναι, λῦσαί τ’ ἐκέλευον ἑταίρους
ὀφρύσι νευστάζων· οἱ δὲ προπεσόντες ἔρεσσον.
αὐτίκα δ’ ἀνστάντες Περιμήδης Εὐρύλοχός τε
πλείοσί μ’ ἐν δεσμοῖσι δέον μᾶλλόν τε πίεζον.
αὐτὰρ ἐπεὶ δὴ τάς γε παρήλασαν οὐδ’ ἔτ’ ἔπειτα
φθόγγον Σειρήνων ἠκούομεν οὐδέ τ’ ἀοιδήν,
αἶψ’ ἀπὸ κηρὸν ἕλοντο ἐμοὶ ἐρίηρες ἑταῖροι,
ὅν σφιν ἐπ’ ὠσὶν ἄλειψ’, ἐμέ τ’ ἐκ δεσμῶν ἀνέλυσαν.
ἀλλ’ ὅτε δὴ τὴν νῆσον ἐλείπομεν, αὐτίκ’ ἔπειτα
καπνὸν καὶ μέγα κῦμα ἴδον καὶ δοῦπον ἄκουσα.
τῶν δ’ ἄρα δεισάντων ἐκ χειρῶν ἔπτατ’ ἐρετμά,
βόμβησαν δ’ ἄρα πάντα κατὰ ῥόον· ἔσχετο δ’ αὐτοῦ
νηῦς, ἐπεὶ οὐκέτ’ ἐρετμὰ προήκεα χερσὶν ἔπειγον.
αὐτὰρ ἐγὼ διὰ νηὸς ἰὼν ὤτρυνον ἑταίρους
μειλιχίοισ’ ἐπέεσσι παρασταδὸν ἄνδρα ἕκαστον·
“ ὦ φίλοι, οὐ γάρ πώ τι κακῶν ἀδαήμονές εἰμεν·
οὐ μὲν δὴ τόδε μεῖζον ἔπι κακόν, ἢ ὅτε Κύκλωψ
εἶλει ἐνὶ σπῆϊ γλαφυρῷ κρατερῆφι βίηφιν·
ἀλλὰ καὶ ἔνθεν ἐμῇ ἀρετῇ βουλῇ τε νόῳ τε

Book 12.166-259 (cont.)

ἐκφύγομεν, καί που τῶνδε μνήσεσθαι ὀΐω.
νῦν δ' ἄγεθ', ὡς ἂν ἐγὼ εἴπω, πειθώμεθα πάντες.
ὑμεῖς μὲν κώπῃσιν ἁλὸς ῥηγμῖνα βαθεῖαν
τύπτετε κληΐδεσσιν ἐφήμενοι, αἴ κέ ποθι Ζεὺς
δώῃ τόνδε γ' ὄλεθρον ὑπεκφυγέειν καὶ ἀλύξαι·
σοὶ δέ, κυβερνῆθ', ὧδ' ἐπιτέλλομαι· ἀλλ' ἐνὶ θυμῷ
βάλλευ, ἐπεὶ νηὸς γλαφυρῆς οἰήϊα νωμᾷς·
τούτου μὲν καπνοῦ καὶ κύματος ἐκτὸς ἔεργε
νῆα, σὺ δὲ σκοπέλου ἐπιμαίεο, μή σε λάθῃσι
κεῖσ' ἐξορμήσασα καὶ ἐς κακὸν ἄμμε βάλῃσθα."
  ὣς ἐφάμην, οἱ δ' ὦκα ἐμοῖσ' ἐπέεσσι πίθοντο.
Σκύλλην δ' οὐκέτ' ἐμυθεόμην, ἄπρηκτον ἀνίην,
μή πώς μοι δείσαντες ἀπολλήξειαν ἑταῖροι
εἰρεσίης, ἐντὸς δὲ πυκάζοιεν σφέας αὐτούς.
καὶ τότε δὴ Κίρκης μὲν ἐφημοσύνης ἀλεγεινῆς
λανθανόμην, ἐπεὶ οὔ τί μ' ἀνώγει θωρήσσεσθαι·
αὐτὰρ ἐγὼ καταδὺς κλυτὰ τεύχεα καὶ δύο δοῦρε
μάκρ' ἐν χερσὶν ἑλὼν εἰς ἴκρια νηὸς ἔβαινον
πρῴρης· ἔνθεν γάρ μιν ἐδέγμην πρῶτα φανεῖσθαι
Σκύλλην πετραίην, ἥ μοι φέρε πῆμ' ἑτάροισιν.
οὐδέ πῃ ἀθρῆσαι δυνάμην· ἔκαμον δέ μοι ὄσσε
πάντῃ παπταίνοντι πρὸς ἠεροειδέα πέτρην.
  ἡμεῖς μὲν στεινωπὸν ἀνεπλέομεν γοόωντες·
ἔνθεν γὰρ Σκύλλη, ἑτέρωθι δὲ δῖα Χάρυβδις
δεινὸν ἀνερροίβδησε θαλάσσης ἁλμυρὸν ὕδωρ.
ἦ τοι ὅτ' ἐξεμέσειε, λέβης ὣς ἐν πυρὶ πολλῷ
πᾶσ' ἀναμορμύρεσκε κυκωμένη· ὑψόσε δ' ἄχνη
ἄκροισι σκοπέλοισιν ἐπ' ἀμφοτέροισιν ἔπιπτεν.

Book 12.166-259 (cont.)

ἀλλ’ ὅτ’ ἀναβρόξειε θαλάσσης ἁλμυρὸν ὕδωρ, 240
πᾶσ’ ἔντοσθε φάνεσκε κυκωμένη, ἀμφὶ δὲ πέτρη 241
δεινὸν βεβρύχει, ὑπένερθε δὲ γαῖα φάνεσκε 242
ψάμμῳ κυανέη· τοὺς δὲ χλωρὸν δέος ᾕρει. 243
ἡμεῖς μὲν πρὸς τὴν ἴδομεν δείσαντες ὄλεθρον· 244
τόφρα δέ μοι Σκύλλη γλαφυρῆς ἐκ νηὸς ἑταίρους 245
ἓξ ἕλεθ’, οἳ χερσίν τε βίηφί τε φέρτατοι ἦσαν. 246
σκεψάμενος δ’ ἐς νῆα θοὴν ἅμα καὶ μεθ’ ἑταίρους 247
ἤδη τῶν ἐνόησα πόδας καὶ χεῖρας ὕπερθεν 248
ὑψόσ’ ἀειρομένων· ἐμὲ δὲ φθέγγοντο καλεῦντες 249
ἐξονομακλήδην, τότε γ’ ὕστατον, ἀχνύμενοι κῆρ. 250
ὡς δ’ ὅτ’ ἐπὶ προβόλῳ ἁλιεὺς περιμήκεϊ ῥάβδῳ 251
ἰχθύσι τοῖς ὀλίγοισι δόλον κατὰ εἴδατα βάλλων 252
ἐς πόντον προΐησι βοὸς κέρας ἀγραύλοιο, 253
ἀσπαίροντα δ’ ἔπειτα λαβὼν ἔρριψε θύραζε, 254
ὣς οἵ γ’ ἀσπαίροντες ἀείροντο προτὶ πέτρας. 255
αὐτοῦ δ’ εἰνὶ θύρῃσι κατήσθιε κεκλήγοντας, 256
χεῖρας ἐμοὶ ὀρέγοντας ἐν αἰνῇ δηϊοτῆτι. 257
οἴκτιστον δὴ κεῖνο ἐμοῖσ’ ἴδον ὀφθαλμοῖσι 258
πάντων, ὅσσ’ ἐμόγησα πόρους ἁλὸς ἐξερεείνων. 259

Book 12.429-450

παννύχιος φερόμην, ἅμα δ’ ἠελίῳ ἀνιόντι 429
ἦλθον ἐπὶ Σκύλλης σκόπελον δεινήν τε Χάρυβδιν. 430
ἡ μὲν ἀνερροίβδησε θαλάσσης ἁλμυρὸν ὕδωρ· 431
αὐτὰρ ἐγὼ ποτὶ μακρὸν ἐρινεὸν ὑψόσ’ ἀερθείς, 432
τῷ προσφὺς ἐχόμην ὡς νυκτερίς· οὐδέ πῃ εἶχον 433
οὔτε στηρίξαι ποσὶν ἔμπεδον οὔτ’ ἐπιβῆναι· 434

Book 12.429-450 (cont.)

ῥίζαι γὰρ ἑκὰς εἶχον, ἀπήωροι δ’ ἔσαν ὄζοι
μακροί τε μεγάλοι τε, κατεσκίαον δὲ Χάρυβδιν.
νωλεμέως δ’ ἐχόμην, ὄφρ’ ἐξεμέσειεν ὀπίσσω
ἱστὸν καὶ τρόπιν αὖτις· ἐελδομένῳ δέ μοι ἦλθον,
ὄψ’· ἦμος δ’ ἐπὶ δόρπον ἀνὴρ ἀγορῆθεν ἀνέστη
κρίνων νείκεα πολλὰ δικαζομένων αἰζηῶν,
τῆμος δὴ τά γε δοῦρα Χαρύβδιος ἐξεφαάνθη.
ἧκα δ’ ἐγὼ καθύπερθε πόδας καὶ χεῖρε φέρεσθαι,
μέσσῳ δ’ ἐνδούπησα παρὲξ περιμήκεα δοῦρα,
ἑζόμενος δ’ ἐπὶ τοῖσι διήρεσα χερσὶν ἐμῇσι.
Σκύλλην δ’ οὐκέτ’ ἔασε πατὴρ ἀνδρῶν τε θεῶν τε
εἰσιδέειν· οὐ γάρ κεν ὑπέκφυγον αἰπὺν ὄλεθρον.
  ἔνθεν δ’ ἐννῆμαρ φερόμην, δεκάτῃ δέ με νυκτὶ
νῆσον ἐς Ὠγυγίην πέλασαν θεοί, ἔνθα Καλυψὼ
ναίει ἐϋπλόκαμος, δεινὴ θεὸς αὐδήεσσα,
ἥ μ’ ἐφίλει τ’ ἐκόμει τε.

Glossary

Α, α

ἀβληχρός,-ή,-όν—gentle

ἀγαθός,-ή,-όν—good

ἀγάλλομαι—exult in, delight in (+ dat.)

ἄγαμαι, ἀγάσσομαι, ἠγασ(σ)άμην—grudge, be jealous of, begrudge, bear a grudge against (+ dat.); wonder, be astonished, be amazed

Ἀγαμεμνονίδης,-ου, ὁ—son of Agamemnon (Orestes)

Ἀγαμέμνων,-ονος, ὁ—Agamemnon, king of Mycenae; leader of the Greek forces in the Trojan War

ἀγανός,-ή,-όν—gentle

ἀγγελίη,-ης, ἡ—message, news

ἄγε, ἄγετε—come! *(imperative of* ***ἄγω*** *used as an interjection)*; **εἰ δ' ἄγε** – come!, come on!, come now!

ἀγήνωρ,-ορος (masc. and fem. adj.)—manly, bold, proud

ἀγήραος,-ον—ageless, not subject to old age

ἀγήρως = ἀγήραος

ἀγλαός,-ή,-όν—splendid, bright, fine

ἁγνός,-ή,-όν—holy, pure

ἀγορεύω, ἀγορεύσω, ἠγόρευσα—speak, say, utter

ἀγορή,-ῆς, ἡ—assembly; marketplace, place of assembly

ἄγραυλος,-ον—dwelling in the fields, field-dwelling

ἄγριος,-η,-ον—fierce, savage, barbarous, uncivilized

ἀγρότερος,-η,-ον—wild

ἄγχιστα—most closely, very closely

ἀγχοῦ—near, close by

ἄγω, ἄξω, ἤγαγον—lead, bring; *middle with* ***οἰκόνδε*** – marry, take as a wife

ἀδαήμων,-ον—ignorant of, inexperienced in dealing with (+ gen.)

ἀδευκής,-ές—harsh, cruel

ἀδινός,-ή,-όν—thick-thronging

ἄεθλος,-ου, ὁ—contest; *plural*, struggles, hardships, trials, troubles

ἀείδω, ἀείσομαι, ἤεισα—sing

ἀεικέλιος,-η,-ον—shameful, wretched

ἀείρω, (aor.) **ἤειρα**—lift, pick up; *passive*, be taken up and carried off, be lifted, be carried up, rise

ἀέκητι—against the will of, without the good will of (+ gen.)

ἀέκων,-ουσα—against one's will, being unwilling

ἀέξω—cause to grow

ἄημι—blow

ἀθάνατος,-η,-ον—immortal; *plural as a noun*, immortals, gods

Ἀθήνη,-ης, ἡ—Athena, goddess of the arts, intelligence, and war

ἀθηρηλοιγός,-οῦ, ὁ—winnowing tool, an implement used to separate grain from chaff (husks)

ἀθρέω—see, observe, perceive

ἀθρόοι,-αι,-α—all together

αἰ, αἴ—if, if only; *with* ***κε(ν)*** *and subjunctive*, in the hope that, provided that; ***αἴ γάρ*** *with optative expresses a wish*
αἶα,-ης, ἡ—country, land, homeland, native land; **πατρὶς αἶα** – native land
αἰγίοχος,-η,-ον—aegis-holding, aegis-bearing (see note on 5.137)
Αἴγισθος,-ου, ὁ—Aegisthus (see note on 1.29)
αἰδέομαι—honor, respect
Ἀΐδης,-ος, ὁ—Hades, god of the Underworld where the spirits of the dead go
αἰδοῖος,-η,-ον—worthy of respect
ἀϊδρείη,-ης, ἡ—ignorance
ἄϊδρις,-ι—ignorant, ignorant of (+ gen.)
αἰεί—always, continually, constantly
αἰέν—always, continually, constantly
αἰζηοί,-ῶν, οἱ—young men
Αἰθίοπες,-ων, οἱ—Ethiopians (see note on 1.22)
αἶθοψ,-οπος—sparkling, bright
αἴθυια,-ης, ἡ—some type of diving sea bird, possibly a cormorant
αἷμα,-ατος, τό—blood
αἱμύλιος,-ον—wheedling, flattering
αἰνός,-ή,-όν—terrible
αἰνῶς—exceedingly, strongly
Αἴολος,-ου, ὁ—Aeolus, keeper of the winds
αἰπεινός,-ή,-όν—steep, towering
αἰπύς,-εῖα,-ύ—utter, sheer
αἱρέω, αἱρήσω, εἷλον or **ἕλον**—take, choose; seize, take hold of; *middle*, take, take as prey
αἶσα,-ης, ἡ—fate, destiny
ἀϊστόω, ἀϊστώσω, ἠΐστωσα, (aor. pass.) **ἠϊστώθην**—cause to vanish; *passive*, vanish, disappear
αἰσχύνω—blame, put to shame, dishonor
αἰτέω, αἰτήσω, ᾔτησα—ask for, request
αἰτιάομαι—blame
αἴτιος,-η,-ον—guilty, at fault, to blame
αἶψα—at once, quickly
ἀΐω—hear (+ gen.)
αἰών,-ῶνος, ὁ—life
ἀκαχίζω—distress, grieve, trouble
ἀκήλητος,-ον—impervious to enchantment
ἀκιδνότερος,-η,-ον—less admirable
ἄκικυς (masc. and fem. adj.)—weak, feeble
ἄκληρος,-ον—landless
ἀκοίτης,-ου, ὁ—husband
ἄκοιτις,-ιος, ἡ—wife
ἀκούω, ἀκούσομαι, ἤκουσα—hear, hear about, listen *(can take accusative or genitive object; also genitive of person from whom something is heard)*

ἄκρη,-ης, ἡ—cape, headland, promontory
ἄκρητος,-ον—unmixed, undiluted
ἄκρις,-ιος, ἡ—hilltop, peak, hill
ἄκρος,-η,-ον—topmost, topmost part of
ἀκτή,-ῆς, ἡ—beach, shore
ἄκυλος,-ου, ὁ—acorn
ἄλαλκον (aor.)—ward off, keep off
ἀλάομαι, ἀλήσομαι, ἀλήθην, ἀλάλημαι—wander, rove
ἀλαόω, ἀλαώσω, ἀλάωσα—blind, take the sight from, make [acc.] blind in [gen.]
ἀλαωτύς,-ύος, ἡ—blinding
ἄλγος,-εος, τό—pain, suffering; *plural*, hardships, misfortunes
ἀλεγεινός,-ή,-όν—painful, hard
ἀλέγω—care for, be concerned about (+ gen.)
ἀλείφω, (aor.) **ἤλειψα**—stop up, plug, put in
ἀλέομαι, (aor.) **ἠλευάμην**—avoid, escape
ἁλιεῦς,-ῆος, ὁ—fisherman
ἁλιόω, (aor.) **ἡλίωσα**—frustrate
ἀλιτρός,-οῦ, ὁ—rogue, rascal
ἀλκή,-ῆς, ἡ—strength, might
Ἀλκίνοος,-ου, ὁ—Alcinous, king of the Phaeacians
ἀλλ' = ἀλλά
ἀλλά—but
ἀλλήλων (gen. plur.)—one another, each other
ἀλλοδαπός,-ή,-όν—foreign, belonging to another land
ἄλλοθεν—from another place; **ἄλλοθεν ἄλλος** – some or one from one place, some or one from another place
ἄλλος,-η,-ο—other, another, besides, in addition; **ἄλλοθεν ἄλλος** – some or one from one place, some or one from another place; **ἄλλυδις ἄλλος** – some in one direction, some in another
ἀλλότριος,-η,-ον—belonging to another, not one's own
ἄλλυδις—to another place, in another direction; **ἄλλυδις ἄλλος** – some in one direction, some in another
ἀλλύω—undo, unravel
ἄλλως—otherwise, differently, in some other form, in another way
ἄλμη,-ης, ἡ—seawater, brine, dried sea-spray
ἁλμυρός,-ά,-όν—salty, briny
ἄλοχος,-ου, ἡ—wife
ἅλς, ἁλός, ἡ—the sea
ἅλς, ἁλός, ὁ—*sing. and plur.*, salt
ἀλύσκω, ἀλύξω, ἤλυξα—escape
ἀλύω—be frantic with pain, be beside oneself with pain
ἄλφιτον,-ου, τό—barley; *plural*, barley meal
ἄμ = ἀνά

ἅμα—*prep.*, with, along with, together with (+ dat.); *adv.*, all together, at the same time

ἁμαρτάνω, ἁμαρτήσομαι, ἥμαρτον—miss, fail to hit (+ gen.); lose, be deprived of (+ gen.)

ἀμβροσίη,-ης, ἡ—ambrosia (the food of the gods)

ἀμβρόσιος,-η,-ον—ambrosial

ἄμβροτος,-ον—immortal, divine

ἀμείβω, ἀμείψω, ἤμειψα—exchange; *middle*, answer, reply; *with* ***ἕρκος ὀδόντων***, enter, pass

ἀμηχανίη,-ης, ἡ—helplessness

ἄμμε = ἡμᾶς—acc. of **ἡμεῖς**

ἄμμες = ἡμεῖς

ἀμόθεν—from any point, from somewhere

ἀμός,-ή,-όν—our

ἀμύμων,-ον—blameless (see note on 1.29)

ἀμφαδίην—openly, publicly

ἀμφαδόν—openly

ἀμφέρχομαι, (aor.) **ἀμφήλυθον**—surround

ἀμφί—*prep.*, about, concerning (+ gen.); around, about, concerning (+ dat.); round about, around (+ acc.); *adv.*, round, round about, on both sides

ἀμφιέννυμι, ἀμφιέσω—put [clothing] on

ἀμφιμυκάομαι, (perf.) **ἀμφιμέμυκα**—resound, echo all around

ἀμφίπολος,-ου, ἡ—female servant, maid

ἀμφίρυτος,-η,-ον—encircled by the sea, sea-girt

ἀμφίς—*prep.*, around, round about (+ acc.); *adv.*, apart

ἀμφότερος,-η,-ον—both

ἄν—*may add an idea of indefiniteness or indicate a condition; where Attic used* ***ἄν****, Homer much more often used* ***κε(ν)***

ἀν' = ἀνά

ἀνά—on, upon (+ dat.); through, throughout, in (+ acc.)

ἀναβρόχω, (aor.) **ἀνέβροξα**—swallow down, swallow again, suck down again

ἀνάγκη,-ης, ἡ—necessity, compulsion, constraint; **ὑπ' ἀνάγκης** – under compulsion; **ἀνάγκῃ** – under compulsion, against one's will, of necessity

ἀναδύομαι, ἀναδύσομαι, ἀνεδυσάμην—rise up from out of, emerge from (+ gen.)

ἀναΐσσω, ἀναΐξω, ἀνήϊξα—jump up, rise suddenly

ἀναλύω, ἀναλύσω, ἀνέλυσα—set free, release

ἀναμίσγω—mix [one thing – acc.] with [another thing – dat.]

ἀναμορμύρω—boil up, foam up, seethe

ἄναξ, ἄνακτος, ὁ—lord, king, master

ἀναπίμπλημι, (aor.) **ἀνέπλησα**—endure

ἀναπλέω, ἀναπλεύσομαι—sail through

ἀνάπτω, (aor.) **ἀνῆψα**—attach, fasten upon

ἀναρροιβδέω, ἀναρροιβδήσω, ἀνερροίβδησα—swallow down, suck down

ἄνασσα,-ης, ἡ—queen, lady

ἀνάσσω, ἀνάξω, ἄναξα—be king over, be ruler over (+ dat.)
ἀνατλάω, (aor.) **ἀνέτλην**—withstand
ἀναφαίνω, (aor.) **ἀνέφηνα**—reveal; *passive*, appear, be seen
ἀνδάνω, ἁδήσω, ἕαδον—please, delight, be pleasing
ἀνδρόμεος,-ον—human, man's
ἄνειμι—come back, go back, return, go inland, go up; *with reference to the sun*, rise
ἀνεκτῶς—endurably, bearably
ἄνεμος,-ου, ὁ—wind
ἀνέχω, ἀνέξω or **ἀνασχήσω, ἀνέσχον** or **ἀνέσχεθον**—lift up, hold up
ἀνήνωρ,-ορος (masc. adj.)—deprived of virility, unmanly (**ἀν** [negative prefix] + **ἀνήρ**)
ἀνήρ, ἀνδρός or **ἀνέρος, ὁ**—man, husband
ἄνθος,-εος, τό—flower, blossom
ἄνθρωπος,-ου, ὁ—man, human being
ἀνίη,-ης, ἡ—danger, peril
ἀνίστημι, (aor.) **ἀνέστην**—stand up, rise
ἀνστάς,-άντος—aorist active participle, masc. of **ἀνίστημι**
ἄντα—*prep.*, in front of, before (+ gen.); *adv.*, facing someone, in front of someone
ἀντία—against (+ gen.)
ἀντιάω, ἀντιόω, ἠντίασα—meet, encounter; receive, accept
ἀντιβολέω, ἀντιβολήσω, ἀντεβόλησα—meet, encounter (+ dat.)
ἀντίθεος,-η,-ον—godlike, *i.e.*, strong, good-looking
ἀντίον—in reply; ***ἀντίον αὐδάω*** – address
ἄντρον,-ου, τό—cave
ἀνώγω, (perf.) **ἄνωγα**—urge, advise, order, command; *perfect may be translated as present, pluperfect as imperfect*
ἀοιδή,-ῆς, ἡ—song
ἀοιδιάω—sing
ἀολλής,-ές—all together, all
ἄορ,-ορος, τό—sword
ἀπ' = ἀπό
ἀπαμείβομαι—answer, reply
ἀπαναίνομαι, (aor.) **ἀπηνηνάμην**—refuse, reject
ἅπας, ἅπασα, ἅπαν—all, the whole
ἄπειμι—go away, depart
ἄπειμι—be away, be distant
ἀπεῖπον (aor.)—speak one's mind freely
ἀπεπλάγχθην (aor. pass.)—be driven off course
ἀπήμων,-ον—favorable
ἀπήωρος,-ον—high in the air
ἀπινύσσω—lack understanding, lack sense, lack judgment
ἀπό—*prep.*, from, away from, far from (+ gen.); *adv.*, from, away from, away
ἀποβαίνω, ἀποβήσομαι, ἀπέβην—depart, go away
ἀπογυμνόω, ἀπογυμνώσω—strip, take the clothes off
ἀποδύω, ἀποδύσω, ἀπέδυν—take off

ἀποθρῴσκω—rise up from (+ gen.)

ἀπολείπω, ἀπολείψω, ἀπέλιπον—leave behind, leave

ἀπολλήγω, ἀπολλήξω—stop, cease or desist from (+ gen.)

ἀπόλλυμι, ἀπολέσσω, ἀπώλεσα, ἀπόλωλα—destroy, kill, lose; *middle, passive, and perfect active*, perish, die

ἀπολύω, ἀπολύσω, ἀπέλυσα—loosen; *middle*, undo, loosen from

ἀπομνύω, (aor.) **ἀπώμοσα**—swear a negative oath, swear not to do something

ἀπονόσφι—away

ἀποπέμπω—send on one's way, arrange for one's departure

ἀπορρώξ,-ῶγος, ὁ or **ἡ**—a sample

ἀποσεύομαι, (aor.) **ἀπεσσύμην**—rush away, dart away

ἀποσταδά—standing at a distance

ἀποστείχω, (aor.) **ἀπέστιχον**—go back, return

ἀποτίνω, ἀποτείσω, ἀπέτεισα—pay the penalty for, pay for; *middle*, exact a penalty for, take vengeance for

ἀποφθίνω, (aor. pass.) **ἀπεφθίθην**—destroy; *middle and passive*, die, perish

ἀποφώλιος,-ον—empty, useless

ἄπρηκτος,-ον—against which nothing can be done

ἄπυστος,-ον—unaware, without knowledge

ἀπωθέω, ἀπώσω, ἀπέωσα—push [something – acc.] away from [something – gen.]

ἄρ' = ἄρα

ἄρα or **ἄρ** or **ῥα** or **ῥ'**—then, in fact; *often difficult to translate; may simply add emphasis*

ἀργαλέος,-η,-ον—difficult

Ἀργεῖοι,-ων, οἱ—Argives (one of the names Homer used for Greeks)

Ἀργεϊφόντης,-ου, ὁ—Argeiphontes, epithet of Hermes (see note on 1.38)

ἀργής,-ῆτος (masc. and fem. adj.)—bright, flashing

ἀργυρόηλος,-ον—silver-studded, ornamented with silver nails

ἄργυρος,-ου, ὁ—silver

ἀρετή,-ῆς, ἡ—valor

ἀρημένος,-η,-ον—hurt, harmed, distressed; worn out, overcome

ἀριφραδής,-ές—clear, distinct

ἁρμόζω—put together, construct

ἀρνειός,-οῦ, ὁ—ram

ἄρνυμαι—achieve, gain

ἄρουρα,-ης, ἡ—earth, soil; **πατρὶς ἄρουρα** – native land

ἁρπάζω, ἁρπάξω, ἥρπαξα—snatch up, seize

Ἄρτεμις,-ιδος, ἡ—Artemis, goddess of the hunt, sister of Apollo, daughter of Zeus and Leto

ἄρχω, ἄρξω, ἦρξα—begin

ἀσινής,-ές—unharmed

ἀσκελές—unrelentingly

ἀσκηθής,-ές—unhurt, unharmed

ἀσκός,-οῦ, ὁ—leather bag

ἀσπαίρω—gasp

ἀσπερχές—vehemently

ἅσσα = ἅ τινα, neut. acc. plur. of **ὅς τις**

ἆσσον—near

ἀστερόεις,-εσσα,-εν—starry

ἄστυ,-εος, τό—city, town

ἄσχετος,-ον—unrestrained, ungovernable

ἀτάρ = αὐτάρ

ἀτασθαλίαι,-ῶν, αἱ—recklessness, criminal folly, wickedness

ἀτέμβω—mistreat, toy with

ἄτερ—without (+ gen.)

Ἄτλας, Ἄτλαντος, ὁ—Atlas

Ἀτρεΐδης,-αο or **-εω, ὁ**—son of Atreus (can refer to either of the two sons of Atreus, Agamemnon, the king of Mycenae and the commander-in-chief of the Greek forces at Troy, and Menelaus, the king of Sparta and the husband of Helen, whose abduction by Paris, a prince of Troy, led to the Trojan War)

ἀτρύγετος,-ον—barren, unfruitful (see note on 1.72)

αὖ—again, now, in reply; *with **δέ**,* on the other hand

αὐγή,-ῆς, ἡ—bright light

αὐδάω, αὐδήσω, ηὔδησα—say, speak; *with **ἀντίον***, address

αὐδή,-ῆς, ἡ—voice

αὐδήεις,-εσσα—speaking with human voice (as opposed to the way the gods speak)

αὖθι—here, right here, on this spot

ἄϋπνος,-ον—sleepless, unable to sleep

αὐτάρ—but, however, indeed, and, and then; *may mark a contrast with a preceding phrase containing **μέν***

αὖτ' = αὖτε

αὖτε—furthermore, in turn, but, on the contrary, on the other hand; *may simply mark a transition or continuation; can indicate impatience –* ***now, this*** *time*

ἀϋτή,-ῆς, ἡ—shout, cry

αὐτίκα—at once

αὖτις—again, once more

αὐτός,-ή,-ό—self, same; him, her, it (3rd person pronoun in cases other than nominative)

αὐτοῦ—there, here

αὔτως—merely, only, just

αὔω, ἀΰσω, ἤϋσα—shout, cry out

ἀφαιρέομαι, (aor.) **ἀφειλόμην**—take away

ἄφαρ—at once, immediately, without delay

ἀφικνέομαι, (aor.) **ἀφικόμην**—reach, come to, come into the presence of

ἀφραδίη,-ης, ἡ—*singular or plural*, foolishness, folly

ἄφρων,-ον—foolish

Ἀχαιϊάς,-άδος, ἡ—Achaean woman

Ἀχαιΐς,-ίδος (fem. adj.)—Achaean

Ἀχαιοί,-ῶν, οἱ—Achaeans (the name Homer most commonly uses for Greeks. In the *Odyssey*, it is frequently used to refer to the people of Ithaca and the surrounding islands.)

Ἀχιλ(λ)εύς,-ῆος, ὁ—Achilles, greatest Greek warrior in the Trojan War; son of Peleus and Thetis

ἄχνη,-ης, ἡ—foam, spray

ἄχνυμαι—be distressed, grieve

ἄχος,-εος, τό—distress, pain, grief, sorrow

ἄψ—back, back again, again, once more

ἄψορρον—in reply, back

Β, β

βαθύς,-εῖα,-ύ—deep

βαίνω, βήσομαι, ἔβην or **ἔβησα, βέβηκα**—come, go, walk, start, set out

βάλανος,-ου, ἡ—acorn

βάλλω, βαλέω, ἔβαλον—throw, toss, strike; put on [clothes, armor, or weapons]

βαρύς,-εῖα,-ύ—heavy, grievous; *referring to a voice*, deep

βασίλεια,-ης, ἡ—princess

βεβολημένος—perfect passive participle of **βολέω**

βέβρυχα (perf., translate as pres.)—roar

βέλος,-εος, τό—arrow

βένθος,-εος, τό—depth (of the sea); *plural*, the depths, the deepest recesses (of the sea)

βῆ = **ἔβη**—aorist of **βαίνω**

βῆσσα,-ης, ἡ—glen, dell, small wooded valley

βιάζομαι, (aor.) **ἐβιασάμην**—use violence against, overpower by force

βίη,-ης, ἡ—strength, power; *plural*, acts of violence, wrongful acts

βίηφι(ν) = **βίη**—by force, in strength

βίοτος,-ου, ὁ—goods, livelihood, means of living

βοάω, βοήσομαι, ἐβόησα—cry aloud, call out, shout

βοή,-ῆς, ἡ—shouting, crying out

βολέω—strike; **βεβολημένος** – perfect passive participle

βομβέω, βομβήσω, βόμβησα—make a clashing noise

βόσκω—feed; *passive*, graze

βουλεύω, βουλεύσω, ἐβούλευσα—ponder, think about, deliberate, consider, plan, contrive, devise

βουλή,-ῆς, ἡ—counsel, advice, plan, resolve, planning, scheming; decree

βούλομαι, βουλήσομαι—want, wish

βοῦς, βοός, ὁ or **ἡ**—bull, cow; *plural*, cattle

βρίθω, βρίσω, ἔβρισα—prevail

βροτός,-οῦ, ὁ or **ἡ**—mortal, mortal man, man; *as masc. and fem. adj.*, **βροτός** – mortal

Γ, γ

γ' = **γε**

γαῖα,-ης, ἡ—earth, land, country, native land, the ground; **πατρὶς γαῖα** – one's fatherland, home, native land
γαιήοχος,-ον—earth-holding (epithet of Poseidon, possibly referring to the ocean surrounding or supporting the earth)
γάλα, γάλακτος, τό—milk
γαλήνη,-ης, ἡ—calm, stillness
γαμέω, γαμέω, ἔγημα—*with a man as a subject*, marry; *middle, with a woman as a subject*, give herself in marriage, get married
γάμος,-ου, ὁ—marriage, wedding
γάρ—for, since, seeing that
γαστήρ,-έρος, ἡ—belly
γε—indeed, to be sure, at least; *often simply adds emphasis*
γέγωνα (perf.)—make oneself heard; *perfect translated as present, pluperfect as imperfect*
γελάω, γελάσομαι, ἐγέλασσα—laugh, smile, rejoice
γῆ, γῆς, ἡ—earth, land, country, native land
γῆρας,-αος, τό—old age
γίγνομαι, γενήσομαι, ἐγενόμην—become, be, be born, happen; come upon, befall, be the lot of (+ dat.)
γιγνώσκω, γνώσομαι, ἔγνων—get to know, gain knowledge of, learn
γλαυκῶπις,-ιδος (fem. adj.)—gleaming-eyed, bright-eyed, flashing-eyed (epithet of Athena)
γλαφυρός,-ή,-όν—hollow
γλυκύς,-εῖα,-ύ—sweet
γοάω, γοήσομαι, ἐγόησα—weep, wail, groan
γόνυ, γουνός or **γούνατος, τό**—knee
γόος,-ου, ὁ—weeping, lamentation
γοῦνα—acc. plur. of **γόνυ**
γουνοῦμαι—entreat, beseech, humbly beg
γυῖα,-ων, τά—limbs
γυμνός,-ή,-όν—naked
γυμνόω, γυμνώσω, (aor. pass.) **ἐγυμνώθην**—make naked; *passive*, become naked
γυνή, γυναικός, ἡ—wife, woman, female servant; **γύναι** (voc.) – ma'am, my lady (a respectful or courteous way to address a woman)

Δ, δ

δ' = δέ
δαιδάλεος,-η,-ον—finely-crafted
δαίμων,-ονος, ὁ or **ἡ**—god, goddess, divinity, superhuman power
δαίς, δαιτός, ἡ—meal, feast, banquet
δαΐς, δαΐδος, ἡ—torch
δαίτηθεν—from a meal, from a feast
δαΐφρων,-ονος—wise, skillful
δαίω—divide; *passive*, be divided, be troubled, be distressed

δαίω—set on fire; *passive*, blaze, burn

δάκρυον,-ου, τό or **δάκρυ,-υος, τό**—tear; *singular can be used for plural*

δαμάζω, (aor.) **ἐδάμασσα**—overcome, overpower

δάπεδον,-ου, τό—floor

δάω, (aor.) **ἐδάην**—know

δέ—and, but, for, then; **ἐν δέ** – besides, moreover

-δε—*suffix indicating motion towards*

δείδω, δείσομαι, ἔδ(δ)εισα, δείδοικα or **δείδια**—fear, be afraid; *perfect translated as present*

δείκνυμι, δείξω, ἔδειξα—show, point out

δεινόν—terribly, dreadfully, fearfully

δεινός,-ή,-όν—terrible, fearful

δέκατος,-η,-ον—tenth

δέμας, τό (only in nom. and acc. forms)—body, figure

δενδρήεις,-εσσα,-εν—woody, wooded, full of trees

δέος, δέους, τό—fear, reason for fear

δέπας,-αος, τό—cup, drinking cup

δέρκομαι, (aor.) **ἔδρακον**—look

δεσμός,-οῦ, ὁ—any means of binding or fastening; *plural*, bonds, ropes

δεύομαι, δευήσομαι—lack, be without, not have (+ gen.)

δεῦρο—to this place, hither

δεύτερον—again, a second time

δεύω, δεύσω, ἔδευσα—wet, soak

δέχομαι, δέξομαι, ἐδεξάμην or **ἐδέγμην**—accept, receive, expect

δέω, δήσω, ἔδησα—bind, tie

δή—indeed, now, really; *often simply adds emphasis*

δηθά—for a long time, long

δηϊοτής-ῆτος, ἡ—struggle

Δημήτηρ,-τερος or **-τρος, ἡ**—Demeter, sister of Zeus, goddess of grain, the harvest and agriculture

δῆμος,-ου, ὁ—community, country, land, realm

δήν—for a long time, for long

δήνεα,-ων, τά—arts, wiles

δηρόν—for a long time

δήω—find

δι' = διά

διά—through, among (+ gen.); through, among, by means of (+ acc.)

διάκτορος,-ου, ὁ—guide (epithet of Hermes; refers to the fact that he serves as a guide for travelers and for the dead as they go to the Underworld)

διαπέρθω, (aor.) **διέπερσα**—sack, lay waste, destroy utterly

διατάμνω, (aor.) **διέταμον**—cut, cut up

διατμήγω, (aor.) **διέτμηξα**—cut

δίδωμι, (δι)δώσω, ἔδωκα—give, send, afflict with

διερέσσω, (aor.) **διήρεσα**—row, paddle

δίζημαι—strife for, seek, seek to achieve

Διί—dat. of **Ζεύς**

δικάζω, δικάσω—pronounce judgment, give a decision; *middle*, seek a judgment or decision

δίκαιος,-α,-ον—civilized

δίνη,-ης, ἡ—whirlpool or eddy [in a river]

διογενής,-ές—descended from Zeus (epithet of heroes)

δῖος,-α,-ον—divine, glorious, bright, famous, noble, shining; **δῖα θεάων** – glorious among goddesses

Διός—gen. of **Ζεύς**

διοτρεφής,-ές—cherished by Zeus

διχθά—in two

διώκω—propel

δοάσσατο (impersonal aorist)—it seemed (= Attic **ἔδοξε**)

δοκέω—seem, appear

δόλιος,-η,-ον—wily, crafty, cunning

δόλος,-ου, ὁ—trickery, guile, cunning, trick, treachery, trap, bait

δολοφρονέω—plan trickery

δόμος,-ου, ὁ—house, home

δόρπον,-ου, τό—evening meal

δόρυ, δούρατος or **δουρός, τό**—tree, spear, plank

δοῦπος,-ου, ὁ—loud noise, roaring [of the sea]

δρυμά,-ῶν, τά—thickets, woods

δύναμαι, δυνήσομαι, ἐδυνησάμην or **ἐδυνάσθην**—be able, have the power or ability or strength to; be powerful

δύο or **δύω** (indeclinable)—two

δύσμορος,-ον—ill-fated, unlucky

δύστηνος,-ον—wretched, unhappy, miserable, unfortunate

δύω or **δύο** (indeclinable)—two

δύω, δύσω, ἔδυν or **ἔδυσα**—*active or middle*, go, enter, make one's way, plunge; *with reference to the sun or a constellation*, go into [the Ocean], set

δῶμα,-ατος, τό—house; *plural sometimes used for singular*

δῶρον,-ου, τό—gift, present

δωτίνη,-ης, ἡ—gift, present

Ε, ε

ἑ—him, her, it (acc. sing. of **εἷο**)

ἐάω, ἐάσω, ἔασα—permit, allow; let be, do no harm

ἐγγύθεν—nearby

ἐγγύς—near, close

ἐγείρω, ἐγερῶ, ἤγειρα—awaken [someone], wake [someone] up; *middle*, wake up

ἔγκατα,-ων, τά—entrails

ἐγκέφαλος,-ου, ὁ—brains

ἔγνων—aorist of **γιγνώσκω**

ἐγώ, ἐμεῖο—I, me
ἐγών = **ἐγώ**
ἐδητύς,-ύος, ἡ—food
ἔδνα,-ων, τά—bridal gifts given to the bride's father for the hand of the bride
ἔδω, ἔδομαι—eat, eat up, devour, consume
ἔεδνα,-ων, τά—bridal gifts given to the bride's father for the hand of the bride
ἔειπον = **εἶπον**
ἐέλδομαι—long for (+ gen.); wish, desire (+ infinitive)
ἐέργω—confine, shut in; keep away
ἕζομαι, (aor.) **εἷσα**—sit, sit up, sit down; *aorist*, place, seat, tell to be seated
ἔθελξα—aorist of **θέλγω**
ἐθέλχθην—aorist passive of **θέλγω**
ἐθέλω, ἐθελήσω, ἠθέλησα—wish, want, be willing
ἔθηκα—aorist of **τίθημι**
εἰ—if; **εἴ περ** – even if; **εἴ τε...εἴ τε** – whether…or; **εἰ** + optative – to see if, in the hope that, on the chance that; **εἰ δ' ἄγε** – come!, come on!, come now!
εἶδαρ,-ατος, τό—food
εἶδος,-εος, τό—appearance, form, looks
εἰδώς—knowing; *perfect active participle of* **οἶδα**; *translate as present*
εἴκελος,-η,-ον—like, resembling (+ dat.)
εἴκω, (aor.) **εἶξα**—yield to (+ dat.)
εἰλίπους,-πουν (gen. **-ποδος**)—with rolling gait, lumbering
εἷλον—aorist of **αἱρέω**
εἰλέω, (aor.) **ἔλσα**—pen in, shut in
εἷμα,-ατος, τό—garment; *plural*, clothes, clothing
εἶμι—go; *referring to time*, pass
εἰμί, ἔσ(σ)ομαι—be, exist, live
εἰν = **ἐν**
εἵνεκα—because of, on account of, for (+ gen.)
εἰνί = **ἐν**
εἷο (gen.)—him, her, it; himself, herself, itself
εἶπον or **ἔειπον** (aor.)—say, tell, speak; order, command
εἰρεσίη,-ης, ἡ—rowing
εἴρομαι—ask, ask about
εἴρω, ἐρέω—tell
εἰρωτάω—ask, inquire; *can be followed by a double accusative, the person asked and what is being asked about*
εἰς—to, into (+ acc.); **εἰς ὅ κε** (+ subjunctive) – until; **εἰς ὅτε κε** (+ subjunctive) – for the time when
εἶς—present, 2nd pers. sing. of **εἰμί**
εἶσα—aorist of **ἕζομαι**
εἰσάγω, εἰσάξω, εἰσήγαγον—bring or lead in
εἰσάντα—in the face, face to face
ἐΐσκω—consider [someone/thing – acc.] like [someone/thing – dat.], compare to, liken

εἰσοιχνέω—enter
εἰσοράω, (aor.) **εἰσεῖδον**—look at, see, catch sight of
ἔϊσος,-η,-ον—equal; *of ships*, well-balanced (and therefore able to turn quickly)
εἴσω—into (+ acc.)
ἐκ, ἐξ—*prep.*, out of, from, away from (+ gen.); *adv.*, out, away, from; *with* ***ὀνομάζω***, aloud
ἑκάς—far away, far
ἕκαστος,-η,-ον—each; *plural*, all
ἑκατόμβη,-ης, ἡ—hecatomb, sacrificial offering of a large number of animals (see note on 1.25)
ἐκλύω, ἐκλύσω—free from, rescue from (what one is rescued from is in the genitive)
ἐκμείρομαι—have, have one's share of (+ gen.)
ἐκπάγλως—vehemently, strongly, deeply
ἐκπίνω, (aor.) **ἔκπιον**—drink all
ἐκτελέω, (aor.) **ἐξετέλεσσα**—finish, complete
ἐκτός—far from (+ gen.)
ἐκφαίνω, (aor.) **ἐξέφηνα**—bring to light; *passive*, appear, come forth
ἐκφεύγω, (aor.) **ἔκφυγον**—escape from
ἔκφημι—utter, speak
ἐλάτη,-ης, ἡ—pine tree; oar
ἐλαύνω, (aor.) **ἤλασα**—drive, drive off, strike
ἔλαφος,-ου, ἡ—deer
ἐλεαίρω—pity, feel pity (for)
ἐλεέω, (aor.) **ἠλέησα**—pity, take pity on, feel pity for
ἐλεήμων,-ον—compassionate, merciful
ἐλεύσομαι—future of **ἔρχομαι**
ἕλιξ (gen. **-ικος**) (masc. and fem. adj.)—with twisted horns
ἕλον—aorist of **αἱρέω**
ἔλπω—cause to hope, give hope to, make hopeful
ἐμβάλλω, (aor.) **ἐνέβαλον**—put or place or throw [something (acc.)] in or into [something (dat.)]
ἐμέ = με
ἔμεινα—aorist of **μένω**
ἐμός,-ή,-όν—my, mine
ἔμπεδον—firmly
ἔμπεδος,-ον—intact, unimpaired
ἔμπης—in any case, nevertheless, all the same
ἐμπίπλημι—fill
ἐν, ἐνί, εἰν, εἰνί—*prep.*, in, on, among (+ dat.); *adv.*, in, there, therein; **ἐν δέ** – besides, moreover
ἐναίσιμος,-ον—intent on what is right
ἔνδον—within, in the house
ἐνδουπέω, ἐνδουπήσω, ἐνδούπησα—fall in with a splash or thud (+ dat.)
ἔνεικα = ἤνεικα—aorist of **φέρω**

ἔνειμι—be in (+ dat.)

ἔνθ' = ἔνθα

ἔνθα—then, there, where

ἐνθάδε—here

ἔνθεν—from which, from that place; **ἔνθεν...ἑτέρωθι** – on one side…on the other side

ἐνί = ἐν

ἐνιαυτός,-οῦ, ὁ—year, a cycle of seasons

ἐννέπω—tell of, tell about, tell the tale of

ἐννῆμαρ—for nine days

ἐννοσίγαιος,-ου, ὁ—earth-shaker (epithet of Poseidon, who was believed to cause earthquakes)

ἐνοσίχθων,-ονος, ὁ—earth-shaker (epithet of Poseidon, who was believed to cause earthquakes)

ἐντίθημι, ἐνθήσω—put upon, put on board; *middle*, store up [acc.] in [dat.]

ἐντός—within, inside

ἔντοσθε(ν)—*prep.*, within, inside (+ gen.); *adv.*, inside

ἐντρέπομαι—care, be moved

ἐντύνω—begin to sing

ἐξ = ἐκ; **ἐξ οὗ** – since

ἕξ (indeclinable)—six

ἐξαιρέω, (aor.) **ἐξεῖλον**—take out; *middle*, take [something – acc.] away from [someone or something – gen.]

ἐξαλαόω, (aor.) **ἐξαλάωσα**—blind

ἐξαπατάω, (aor.) **ἐξαπάτησα**—trick, deceive

ἑξείης—in a row, one after the other, in order

ἐξείρω, ἐξερέω—tell

ἐξεμέω, ἐξεμέσω—vomit forth, throw up, disgorge

ἐξερεείνω—traverse, explore

ἐξερέομαι—ask, question

ἐξερύω, (aor.) **ἐξέρυσα**—pull out of (+ gen.)

ἐξέρχομαι, ἐξελεύσομαι, ἐξῆλθον—go out, come out

ἐξετέλεσσα—aorist of **ἐκτελέω**

ἐξικνέομαι, (aor.) **ἐξικόμην**—arrive at, reach

ἐξονομακλήδην—by name

ἐξορμάω, ἐξορήσω—deviate from a course, swerve

ἔξοχον—beyond (+ gen.)

ἔοικα (perfect, translate as present)—be fitting, be suitable; be like, resemble (+ dat.); be reasonable, be likely; seem to be

ἑός, ἑή, ἑόν—his (own), her (own), its (own)

ἐπ' = ἐπί

ἐπαΐσσω, (aor.) **ἐπήϊξα**—rush at (+ dat.)

ἐπακούω—hear

ἐπάρουρος,-ον—on earth

ἔπεα—nom. or acc. plur. of **ἔπος**

ἐπέεσσι(ν)—dat. plur. of **ἔπος**

ἐπεί—when, after, since; *with subjunctive*, whenever

ἐπείγω—press hard, urge; be eager for; *of wind*, speed [a ship] on, drive [a ship] before it; *of oars*, ply, move

ἔπειμι—be upon

ἔπειτ' = **ἔπειτα**

ἔπειτα—then

ἐπέοικε (impersonal)—it is fitting (+ acc. and infinitive)

ἐπέρχομαι, (aor.) **ἐπῆλθον** or **ἐπήλυθον**—come on, come upon, come round, return

ἐπήϊξα—aorist of **ἐπαΐσσω**

ἐπήν = **ἐπεὶ ἄν**—when, after, as soon as (+ subjunctive)

ἐπήρετμος,-ον—fitted with oars

ἐπί—*prep.*, on, upon (+ gen.); by, beside, upon (+ dat.); to, towards, among, throughout, over, on, during (+ acc.); *adv.*, thereon, thereupon

ἐπιάλλω—lay upon, put upon

ἐπιβαίνω, (aor.) **ἐπέβην**—set foot upon, board [a ship]; climb up, get up on, place oneself upon; make one's way to, reach (+ gen.)

ἐπιβήτωρ,-ορος, ὁ—mate

ἐπιέννυμι, (aor.) **ἐπίεσσα**—put on over; **ἐπιειμένος** – perfect passive participle: wearing, clothed in

ἐπικεύθω, ἐπικεύσω—conceal, hide

ἐπέκλυον (aor.)—hear, listen to (+ gen.)

ἐπικλώθω, (aor.) **ἐπέκλωσα**—*active and middle*, grant, assign as one's destiny

ἐπιλαμβάνω, ἐπιλήψομαι, ἐπέλαβον—lay hold of, seize

ἐπιλανθάνομαι, ἐπιλήσομαι—forget (+ gen.)

ἐπιμαίομαι, (aor.) **ἐπεμασσάμην**—strive for, struggle for (+ gen.); feel, touch; steer for, head for (+ gen.)

ἐπιμιμνήσκομαι, (aor.) **ἐπεμνήσθην**—remember, think of (+ gen.)

ἐπιπείθομαι—be persuaded

ἐπιπίνω—drink after, drink afterwards

ἐπιτέλλω—*active or middle*, give orders to (+ dat.)

ἐπιτιμήτωρ,-ορος, ὁ—protector, avenger

ἐπιφράζω, (aor. pass.) **ἐπεφράσθην**—*middle and passive*, think of [doing – expressed with an infinitive]

ἐποίχομαι, ἐποιχήσομαι—attack; *with* ***ἱστόν***, walk along, go back and forth in front of

ἕπομαι, ἕψομαι, ἑσπόμην—follow, go with, accompany (+ dat.)

ἐποπίζομαι—respect, have regard for

ἔπος,-εος, τό—word; **ἔπεα πτερόεντα** – winged words (see note on 5.117)

ἐποτρύνω—urge, urge on, rouse to action

ἔργον,-ου, τό—deed, work

ἔρδω, ἔρξω, ἔρξα—do, perform

ἔρεξα—aorist of **ῥέζω**

ἐρέσσω—row

ἐρετμόν,-ου, τό—oar
ἐρέχθω—break, rend
ἐρέω—future of **εἴρω**
ἐριδαίνω, (aor.) **ἐρίδηνα**—contend
ἐρίζω—compete with, rival (+ dat.)
ἐρίηρος,-ον—faithful, trusty; *plural*, **ἐρίηρες**
ἐρινεός,-οῦ, ὁ—wild fig tree
ἐριστάφυλος,-ον—made from fine grapes
ἕρκος,-εος, τό—barrier, fence; *with* ***ὀδόντων***, the lips, the mouth ("the barrier of teeth")
Ἑρμείας, **Ἑρμείω, ὁ**—Hermes, the messenger of the gods
ἔρριψα—aorist of **ῥίπτω**
ἔρρω—go (with an implication of pain, difficulty, or misfortune)
ἐρυθρός,-ά,-όν—red
ἐρύκω, ἐρύξω, ἤρυξα or **ἠρύκακον**—detain, restrain; ward off, keep from; hold back
ἐρύω, (aor.) **εἴρυσ(σ)α**—pull; *middle*, draw [a sword]
ἔρχομαι, ἐλεύσομαι, ἦλθον or **ἤλυθον, εἰλήλουθα** or **ἐλήλυθα**—come, go; return, come back, come home
ἐς—into, to (+ acc.)
ἐσθής,-ῆτος, ἡ—clothing
ἐσθίω—eat, devour
ἐσθλός,-ή,-όν—good, excellent
ἔσθω—eat
ἐσσί—present, 2nd pers. sing. of **εἰμί**
ἔστην—aorist of **ἵστημι**
ἐσχατιή,-ῆς, ἡ—the most remote part, the farthest part
ἔσχατος,-ον—most remote
ἔτ' = ἔτι
ἑταῖρος,-ου, ὁ—companion, comrade
ἕταρος,-ου, ὁ—companion, comrade
ἐτεόν—truly, really, in fact
ἕτερος,-η,-ον—another, other
ἑτέρωθι—on the other side, opposite; **ἔνθεν...ἑτέρωθι** – on one side…on the other side
ἔτι—still, yet, again; *with negative*, no more, no longer
ἔτος,-εος, τό—year
ἐΰ, εὖ—well
εὐεργής,-ές—well-made
εὐήρης,-ες—well-balanced, easy to handle
ἐϋκτίμενος,-η,-ον—well-built
εὐνάω, εὐνήσω, εὔνησα, (aor. pass.) **εὐνήθην**—lull to sleep; *passive*, go to bed, lie with, have sex, make love
εὐνή,-ῆς, ἡ—bed
εὖνις (masc. and fem. adj.)—deprived of, bereaved of (+ gen.); **εὖνιν** – acc. sing.
ἐϋπλόκαμος,-ον—with beautiful braids, having well-braided hair

εὑρίσκω, (aor.) **εὗρον**—find, come upon, discover
Εὐρύλοχος,-ου, ὁ—Eurylochus, one of Odysseus' companions
Εὐρυμίδης,-αο, ὁ—son of Eurymus (patronymic of Telemus)
εὐρύς,-εῖα,-ύ—broad, wide
ἐΰσκοπος,-ον—sharp-sighted
ἐϋφροσύνη,-ης, ἡ—gladness, happiness, joy; *plural can be used for singular*
εὔχομαι, εὔξομαι, ηὐξάμην—claim, declare; pray
εὐῶπις,-ιδος (fem. adj.)—attractive, fair-faced
ἔφαθ' = ἔφατο—imperfect middle with active meaning, 3rd pers. sing. of **φημί**
ἐφάμην—imperfect middle with active meaning of **φημί**
ἐφάπτομαι—touch (+ gen.)
ἔφασαν—imperfect active, 3rd pers. plur. of **φημί**
ἔφατ' = ἔφατο—imperfect middle with active meaning, 3rd pers. sing. of **φημί**
ἐφευρίσκω, (aor.) **ἐφεῦρον**—discover, find, surprise
ἔφη—imperfect active, 3rd pers. sing. of **φημί**
ἔφημαι—be seated, sit on (+ dat.)
ἐφημοσύνη,-ης, ἡ—command
ἐφοράω—see, look upon
ἔχθος,-εος, τό—disfavor, enmity
ἔχω, ἕξω, ἔσχον or **ἐσχεθον**—have, hold; hold back, restrain; inhabit, occupy; *middle*, hold onto, cling, stick (can take a gen. object); depend
ἐών, ἐοῦσα, ἐόν—present participle of **εἰμί**
ἕως—while, so long as, until

Ζ, ζ

ζείδωρος,-ον—grain-giving, fruitful
Ζεύς, Διός or **Ζηνός**—Zeus, king of the gods; **Ζεῦ** – voc.
ζηλήμων,-ον (gen. **-ονος**)—jealous, envious
Ζηνός = Διός—gen. sing. of **Ζεύς**
ζωός,-ή,-όν—alive, living
ζώω—live

Η, η

ἦ—in truth, truly, indeed; *can introduce a question*
ἤ, ἠέ, ἦ, ἦε—or, than, whether; **ἤ** or **ἠέ...ἤ** or **ἦ** or **ἦε** or **ἠέ** – whether...or, either...or
ἡβάω, ἡβήσω, ἥβησα—be in the prime of youth, be young; *aorist*, come to manhood
ἥβη,-ης, ἡ—youthful vigor, early manhood, youth
ἡγέομαι, ἡγήσομαι, ἡγησάμην—lead or show the way
ἠδ' = ἠδέ
ἠδέ—and; **τε...ἠδέ** – both...and
ἤδη—now, already
ἥδομαι, (aor.) **ἡσάμην**—be pleased
ἡδύς, ἡδεῖα, ἡδύ—sweet, pleasant
ἠέ = ἤ

ἦε = **ἤ**

ἠέλιος,-ου, ὁ—the sun (= Attic **ἥλιος**)

Ἠέλιος,-ου, ὁ—Helios, the sun god (= Attic **Ἥλιος**)

ἠεροειδής,-ές—misty

ἠϊών,-όνος, ἡ—beach, shore

ἧκα—aorist of **ἵημι**

ἦλθον—aorist of **ἔρχομαι**

ἠμαθόεις,-εσσα,-εν—sandy

ἦμαρ,-ατος, τό—day

ἠμάτιος,-η,-ον—by day, during the daytime

ἡμεῖς, ἡμέων—we, us

ἡμέρη,-ης, ἡ—day

ἡμέτερος,-η,-ον—our

ἦμος—when, at the time when

ἤν = **εἰ ἄν**—if, if by chance, in the hope that

ἤνεικα—aorist of **φέρω**

ἠνεμόεις,-εσσα,-εν—wind-blown, windy

ἧπαρ,-ατος, τό—the liver

ἤπειρος,-ου, ἡ—the land *(as opposed to the sea)*

ἤπιος,-η,-ον—well-disposed, kind, gentle

ἠπύω—call to

ᾕρει—imperfect, 3rd pers. sing. of **αἱρέω**

ἥρως, ἥρωος, ὁ—warrior, hero, man

ἦ τοι—indeed, in truth, truly, to be sure

ἦτορ, τό (only in nom. and acc. sing. forms)—heart, spirit

ηὔδα—imperfect of **αὐδάω**

ἠΰς, ἠΰ—good

Ἠώς, Ἠοῦς, ἡ—Eos, goddess of dawn

Θ, θ

θ' = **τε**

θάλαμος,-ου, ὁ—bedroom

θάλασσα,-ης, ἡ—the sea

θάλος,-εος, τό—young shoot or branch, young person

θάμνος,-ου, ὁ—bush, shrub; *plural*, thicket

θάνατος,-ου, ὁ—death

θάρσος,-εος, τό—courage, boldness

θᾶσσον—quickly; the sooner, more quickly

θαῦμα,-ατος, τό—wonder, amazement

θεά,-ᾶς, ἡ—goddess; **δῖα θεάων** – glorious among goddesses

θεῖος,-η,-ον—godlike, excellent

θέλγω, θέλξω, ἔθελξα, (aor. pass.) **ἐθέλχθην**—bewitch, beguile; work spells upon, enchant

θέμις,-ιστος, ἡ—customary right, what is due according to custom

-θεν—*suffix indicating place from, e.g.,* ***Τροίηθεν*** *– from Troy*
θεός,-οῦ, ὁ or **ἡ**—god, goddess
θεουδής,-ές—god-fearing
θέσφατα,-ων, τά—oracles, prophecy
θῆλυς,-υ—female, feminine
θην—in truth, surely
θητεύω—serve as a hired laborer
θνήσκω, (aor.) **ἔθανον**—die, be killed, be dead
θνητός,-ή,-όν—mortal
θοός,-ή,-όν—swift
Θόωσα,-ης, ἡ—Thoosa, a nymph, the mother of the Cyclops Polyphemus
θρῆνυς,-υος, ὁ—footstool
Θρινακίη,-ης, ἡ—Thrinacia, the island where Helios kept his cattle
θρίξ, τριχός, ἡ—*always in plural,* hair; bristles [of pigs]
θρόνος,-ου, ὁ—chair, seat
θυγάτηρ,-τρός or **-τέρος, ἡ**—daughter
θύελλα,-ης, ἡ—violent storm, storm wind, gale
θυμός,-οῦ, ὁ—heart, soul, life, mind, feelings, desire, spirit
θύραζε—out
θύρη,-ης, ἡ—door (of a room); *plural,* door (of a house), entrance
θωρήσσομαι—arm oneself

Ι, ι
ἰαίνω, (aor.) **ἴηνα**—warm, cheer, gladden
ἰάομαι, ἰήσομαι, ἰησάμην—heal, cure
Ἰασίων,-ωνος, ὁ—Iasion, a mortal from Crete, lover of Demeter; their son was Plutus, the god of wealth
ἰαύω—sleep, pass the night
ἰάχω—shout, shriek; echo, resound
ἴδον—aorist of **ὁράω**
ἱέμενος,-η,-ον—present middle participle of **ἵημι**
ἱερά,-ῶν, τά—sacrifices, offerings
ἱερός,-ή,-όν—holy, sacred, divine
ἵζω—sit down, seat oneself
ἵημι, ἥσω, ἧκα—send, send forth, throw, hurl, put, place; *middle,* long for, desire, be eager to go in a specific direction, hasten
Ἰθάκη,-ης, ἡ—Ithaca, an island off the west coast of Greece; Odysseus' home
ἱκάνω—come to, reach, be (at), find oneself (at); come upon, affect; *present can have a perfect sense, imperfect can have a pluperfect sense*
ἱκέτης,-ου, ὁ—suppliant
ἱκνέομαι, ἵξομαι, ἱκόμην—arrive at, reach, come to
ἴκρια,-ων, τά—deck (of a ship), planks of the deck
ἵκω, ἱξῶ, ἶξον—come to, come upon, be upon
ἱμείρομαι, (aor.) **ἱμειράμην**—long, long for, wish, desire; *can take gen. object*

ἵνα—so that, in order that
Ἰνώ,-όος, ἡ—Ino (see note on 5.333)
ἰοειδής,-ές—purple, dark
ἰότης,-ητος, ἡ—will, desire
Ἱπποτάδης,-αο, ὁ—son of Hippotas (Aeolus)
ἴς, ἰνός, ἡ—strength, force
ἶσος,-η,-ον—equal; *neut. plur. as an adverb*, **ἶσα** – like, equal to (+ dat.)
ἵστημι, στήσω, ἔστησα or **ἔστην, ἔστηκα**—stand, set up, place, put, cause to be in a specific place
ἱστίον,-ου, τό—sail; *plural used for singular*
ἱστοπέδη,-ης, ἡ—upright beam to which a ship's mast was secured (see note on 12.179)
ἱστός,-οῦ, ὁ—loom; warp (the vertical threads on a loom); web (the cloth being woven on a loom); a ship's mast
ἴφιος,-α,-ον—fat
ἰχθύς,-ύος, ὁ—fish
ἰών—present participle of **εἶμι**

Κ, κ
κ' = κε
κάδ = κατά
Κάδμος,-ου, ὁ—Cadmus, founder of Thebes, the leading city of Boeotia
καθαιρέω, (aor.) **καθεῖλον**—seize, take
κάθημαι—sit
καθίζω—sit
καθίστημι—bring [a ship] to land
καθύπερθε—down from above, from above
καί—and, also, even, too; *can add emphasis*; **καὶ...καί** – both...and; **τε...καί** – both…and; **καὶ ὣς** – even so, nevertheless
καίνυμαι, (perf.) **κέκασμαι**—excel (+ dat. of what one excels in)
κακόν,-οῦ, τό—evil, misfortune, trouble
κακός,-ή,-όν—evil, bad, destructive, disastrous, cowardly
κακόω—befoul, make dirty
κακῶς—miserably, with suffering
καλέω, (aor.) **ἐκάλεσ(σ)α**—call, summon; name; call on for help
κάλλιμος,-ον—sweet, beautiful
καλλιπλόκαμος,-ον—having lovely hair
καλλίσφυρος,-ον—with beautiful ankles
καλόν—sweetly
καλός,-ή,-όν—handsome, beautiful, lovely, fine, well-made, well-constructed
καλύπτω, καλύψω, ἐκάλυψα—cover, hide
Καλυψώ,-όος or **-οῦς, ἡ**—Calypso, a nymph, daughter of Atlas; she lived on the island Ogygia, where she detained Odysseus for seven years
κάμμορος,-ον—ill-fated, wretched

κάμνω, (aor.) **ἔκαμον**, (perf.) **κέκμηκα**—grow weary, become exhausted

καπνός,-οῦ, ὁ—smoke

κάπρος,-ου, ὁ—boar

κάρη, κρατός, τό—head; *can have a masc. acc. sing* – ***κρᾶτα***

κάρηνον,-ου, τό—top, summit

καρπαλίμως—swiftly, quickly

καρπός,-οῦ, ὁ—fruit

κάρτος,-εος, τό—strength, power

κασίγνητος,-ου, ὁ—brother

κατά—*prep.*, down from (+ gen.); down through, down by, down along, along, within, on, upon, throughout (+ acc.); *adv.*, down

καταγηράω, καταγηράσω, κατεγήρασα—grow old

κατάγνυμι, κατάξω, κατέαξα—break in pieces, shatter, wreck

καταδύω, (aor.) **κατέδυν**—put on

καταθέλγω, καταθέλξω, κατέθελξα—bewitch, enchant

καταθνητός,-ή,-όν—mortal

κατακλάω, (aor.) **κατέκλασα**, (aor. pass.) **κατεκλάσθην**—break

κατακτείνω, κατακτενῶ, κατέκτεινα—kill

καταλέγω, καταλέξω, κατέλεξα—tell, tell about, recount, relate

καταλείπω, καλλείψω, κάλλιπον—leave, abandon, leave behind

καταρρέζω, (aor.) **κατέρεξα**—stroke, caress, pat

κατασκιάω—cast a shadow over

καταφένω, (aor.) **κατέπεφνον**—kill, slay

καταφθίω, καταφθίσω, κατέφθισα, (aor. pass.) **κατεφθίμην**—destroy; *passive*, perish, die

κατέδω—eat up, devour, consume

κατείβω—let flow, shed; *middle*, flow, flow down; pass away, ebb away

κατέργνυμι—drive into, shut in, confine

κατερύκω, κατερύξω—restrain, hold back, keep back, stop, detain, keep from leaving

κατεσθίω—devour, eat

κε(ν)—*may add an idea of indefiniteness or indicate a condition; where Attic used* ***ἄν****, Homer much more often used* ***κε(ν)****;* **αἴ κε(ν)** – in the hope that, provided that (+ subjunctive); **εἰς ὅ κε** – until (+ subjunctive)

κεάζω, (aor.) **ἐκέασ(σ)α**—split, shatter, break in pieces

κεδνός,-ή,-όν—devoted, trustworthy

κεῖμαι—lie, lie dead

κειμήλιον,-ου, τό—treasure

κεῖνος,-η,-ο—that, that one; *plural*, those (= **ἐκεῖνος,-η,-ο**)

κεῖσε—to that place, there

κέλευθα,-ων, τά—ways, paths; **ὑγρὰ κέλευθα** – watery ways, *i.e.*, the sea

κελεύω, κελεύσω, ἐκέλευσα—urge, order, command

κέλομαι, κελήσομαι—order, command, urge

κεν = κε

κενεός,-ά,-όν—empty

κέρας, κέρατος or **κέραος, τό**—horn [of an animal]
κεραυνός,-οῦ, ὁ—thunderbolt
κερδαλέος,-η,-ον—cunning, wily, clever, shrewd
κερδίων,-ον—better, best
κέρδος,-εος, τό—profit, device, plan; *plural*, cunning arts, craft, guile
κευθμών,-ῶνος, ὁ—pen, pigsty
κεύθω, κεύσω, ἔκευσα, κέκευθα—contain; have in it, hold
κεφαλή,-ῆς, ἡ—the head
κήδιστος,-η,-ον—dearest, closest
κῆδος,-εος, τό—trouble, pain; *plural*, sorrows, troubles, sufferings, cares
κήδω—trouble, cause pain to
κῆρ, κῆρος, τό—heart, soul, *i.e.*, the seat of emotion and feelings
κηρός,-οῦ, ὁ—beeswax
κικλήσκω—call [by a name]
Κίρκη,-ης, ἡ—Circe, a nymph, daughter of Helios
κιχάνομαι—arrive at, come to, find oneself at
κίω—go, make one's way, proceed
κίων,-ονος, ὁ or **ἡ**—pillar, column
κλάζω, κλάγξω, ἔκλαγξα, κέκλαγγα—scream, shout, shriek
κλαίω—weep, wail
κλάω, κλάσω, ἔκλασα—break, break off
κλέος, τό (only in nom. and acc. forms)—report; fame, glory, reputation, honor
κληῖς,-ῖδος, ἡ—rowing bench, *i.e.*, bench where a ship's rowers sit
κλισμός,-οῦ, ὁ—seat
κλυτός,-όν—famous, renowned; splendid, excellent, fine
κλύω, (aor.) **ἔκλυον**—hear (can have a gen. object)
κνέφας,-αος, τό—darkness, night
κοῖλος,-η,-ον—hollow
κοιμάω, κοιμήσω, ἐκοίμησα—still, calm
κολεόν,-οῦ, τό—sheath or scabbard of a sword
κομάω—have long or abundant hair, wear long hair; **κάρη κομόωντες** – long-haired
κομέω—look after, care for
κομίζω, κομιῶ, ἐκόμισσα—look after, care for, provide for, attend to
κόπτω, κόψω, ἔκοψα—smash, strike hard
κοτέομαι, κοτέσσομαι—be angry with; *aorist*, grow angry with (+ dat.)
κότος,-ου, ὁ—anger
κούρη,-ης, ἡ—daughter, girl, young woman
κοῦρος,-ου, ὁ—young man
κραδίη,-ης, ἡ—heart
κραίνω, (aor.) **ἔκρηνα**—accomplish, bring to pass, carry out
κράνεια,-ης, ἡ—cornel tree
κρᾶτα—acc. sing. of **κάρη**
κρατερός,-ή,-όν—strong, powerful, mighty
κρατερῶνυξ,-υχος—strong-clawed, with powerful claws

κρατέω—have power among (+ dat.)
κράτος,-εος, τό—strength, power
κρατύς (masc. adj.)—strong, mighty
κρέας, κρέως, τό—flesh, meat; *nom. and acc. plur.* – **κρέα**
κρείων,-οντος, ὁ—ruler, lord, king
κρήδεμνον,-ου, τό—woman's head covering, veil
κρίνω—decide, settle
Κρονίδης,-ου, ὁ—son of Cronus (Zeus)
κτάμεναι—aorist active infinitive of **κτείνω**
κτεατίζω, (aor.) **κτεάτισσα**—gain, acquire, win
κτείνω, κτενέω, ἔκτεινα or **ἔκτανον** or **ἔκταν**—kill
κυάνεος,-η,-ον—dark
κυανοχαίτης (masc. adj.)—dark-haired
κυβερνήτης,-ου, ὁ—steersman of a ship
κῦδος,-εος, τό—glory
κυκάω, κυκήσω—stir, mix; foam up, seethe
κυκεών,-ῶνος, ὁ—mixed drink or potion made of wine, barley meal, grated cheese, and honey; **κυκεῶ** – acc. sing.
Κύκλωψ,-ωπος, ὁ—Cyclops
κῦμα,-ατος, τό—wave, waves (of the sea)
κυμαίνω—surge
κύων, κυνός, ὁ—dog
κώπη,-ης, ἡ—oar

Λ, λ

λᾶας, λᾶος, ὁ—a stone
λαβών—aorist active participle of **λαμβάνω**
Λαέρτης,-ου, ὁ—Laertes, father of Odysseus (see note on 2.99)
Λαερτιάδης,-εω, ὁ—son of Laertes (Odysseus)
λαῖτμα,-ατος, τό—gulf, abyss
λαμβάνω, λήψομαι, ἔλαβον—take, grab, seize, take hold of; (can take object in gen.)
λανθάνω, λήσω, ἔλαθον—escape the notice of, elude, not attract the attention of; *middle*, forget, cease to remember (+ gen.)
λαός,-οῦ, ὁ—*singular and plural*, people, army, men
λέβης,-ητος, ὁ—cauldron, kettle, metal vessel for boiling water
λέγω, (aor.) **ἔλεξα**—lay, cause to lie down; *middle*, lay oneself down, lie down
λείβω—shed, pour out
λείπω, λείψω, ἔλιπον—leave, leave behind
λεπτός,-ή,-όν—of fine threads, fine, delicately woven
λευκαίνω—make white
Λευκοθέη,-ης, ἡ—Leucothea, the name by which Ino was known after she became a sea goddess (see note on 5.333)
λευκώλενος,-ον—white-armed (see note on 6.186)
λεύσσω—see

λέων,-οντος, ὁ—lion
λήθω—escape the notice of
ληΐς,-ΐδος, ἡ—booty, spoils of war
ληϊστήρ,-ῆρος, ὁ—pirate
λήσω—future of **λανθάνω**
λίγα—loudly, in clear tones
λιγυρός,-ή,-όν—clear-sounding
λίην—very much; **καὶ λίην**—truly, surely
λίθος,-ου, ὁ—a stone
λιλαίομαι—desire
λίμνη,-ης, ἡ—the sea
λιμός,-οῦ, ὁ—hunger
λιπαρός,-ή,-όν—rich, wealthy, comfortable
λίσσομαι, (aor.) **ἐλ(λ)ισάμην**—beg, beseech, entreat, supplicate
λόγος,-ου, ὁ—word, story, tale
λοιβή,-ῆς, ἡ—libation, drink-offering
λυγρός,-ή,-όν—evil, harmful
λύκος,-ου, ὁ—wolf
λύω, λύσω, ἔλυσα—loosen, free, release

Μ, μ
μ' = με
μαίνομαι—rage, act like a madman
μάκαρ (masc. and fem. adj.)—happy, blessed
μακρόν—loudly
μακρός,-ή,-όν—tall, lofty, great, long
μάλ' = μάλα
μάλα—very, quite; *adds emphasis*
μαλακός,-ή,-όν—soft, gentle
μᾶλλον—more, much, the more
μαντεύομαι—be a seer, act as a seer
μάντις,-ιος, ὁ—seer, prophet
μαντοσύνη,-ης, ἡ—art of divination
μάρπτω, μάρψω, ἔμαρψα—seize, lay hold of, grab
μαψιδίως—at random, without a determined course
μέγα—very, greatly; loudly, with a loud voice; by far
μεγάλα—loudly
μεγαλήτωρ,-ορος (masc. and fem. adj.)—great-hearted, great, daring, heroic
μέγαρον,-ου, τό—great hall, main room, dining hall; house, palace; *plural often used for singular*
μέγας, μεγάλη, μέγα—great, large, tall
μέγεθος,-εος, τό—height, stature
μέγιστος,-η,-ον—superlative of **μέγας**
μέδομαι, μεδήσομαι—think about, remember

μέδων,-οντος, ὁ—ruler, lord

μεθ' = μετά

μεθίημι, μεθήσω, μεθῆκα—let go, give up

μείζων,-ον—comparative of **μέγας**

μειδάω, (aor.) **μείδησα**—smile

μειλίγμα,-ατος, τό—something that soothes; tidbits, scraps

μειλίχιος,-η,-ον—pleasing, winning, gentle, mild

μέλας, μέλαινα, μέλαν—dark, black

μελεϊστί—limb from limb

μέλι,-ιτος, τό—honey

μελίγηρυς (fem. adj.)—honey-toned, melodious

μελιηδής,-ές—honey-sweet

μέλλω—be going or be about [to do something]

μέν—in truth, indeed; *may call attention to or mark a contrast with a following statement which contains* **δέ**.

μενεαίνω—rage, be enraged, be angry at; desire, intend, be inclined or resolved [to do something], be set on [doing something]

μενοεικής,-ές—abundant, plentiful

μενοινάω—plan, turn over [in one's mind]

μένος,-εος, τό—courage, passion, vehement emotion, spirit, determination, anger, rage

μένω, μενέω, ἔμεινα—remain, stay, await, wait for

μερμηρίζω, (aor.) **ἐμερμήριξα**—turn over in one's mind, ponder, consider, devise, contrive

μέσ(σ)ος,-η,-ον—the middle of

μετ' = μετά

μετά—among, along with (+ gen.); among, with (+ dat.); to, towards, to join, after, going behind, next to, for, in search of (+ acc.)

μετακιάθω—visit

μεταμώνιος,-ον—coming to nothing, vain, useless

μεταυδάω—speak, utter

μετέειπον (aor.)—address, speak to (+ dat.)

μετέρχομαι, μετελεύσομαι, μετῆλθον—go among (+ dat.); go after, pursue (+ acc.)

μετόπισθε(ν)—*prep.*, behind (+ gen.); *adv.*, later, afterwards, in the future

μευ—gen. sing. of **ἐγώ**

μή—not, lest; *after a verb of fearing, introduces a clause expressing what is feared*

μηδ' = μηδέ

μηδέ—and not, but not; **μηδέ...μηδέ** – not even…nor

μήδεα,-ων, τά—genitals

μήδομαι, μήσομαι—plan, contrive, intend, devise, plot

μηκέτι—no longer

μῆλον,-ου, τό—sheep; *plural*, sheep, flock of sheep

μῆνις,-ιος, ἡ—anger, wrath

μηρός,-οῦ, ὁ—thigh

μηρύομαι, (aor.) **ἐμηρυσάμην**—lower, furl [a sail]
μήτε—and not; **μήτε...μήτε** – neither…nor
μήτηρ, μητέρος or **μητρός, ἡ**—mother
μητίομαι, μητίσομαι, ἐμητισάμην—devise, plan, bring about
μῆτις,-ιος, ἡ—scheme, plan, cunning, shrewdness
μιμνήσκομαι, μνήσομαι, ἐμνησάμην—remember, recall, call to mind (+ gen. or acc.)
μίμνω—wait
μιν—him, her, it (acc. sing. of **εἶο**)
μίσγω, μίξω, ἔμιξα or **ἔμειξα**, (perf. mid.) **μέμιγμαι**, (aor. pass.) **ἐμίγην**—mix, mingle; *middle and passive*, mingle with, join, set oneself among (+ dat.); have sex with (+ dat.)
μνάομαι—woo, court
μνηστήρ,-ῆρος, ὁ—suitor
μνηστός,-ή,-όν—lawfully married, wedded
μογέω, (aor.) **ἐμόγησα**—suffer
μοῖρα,-ης, ἡ—fate, destiny, doom; **κατὰ μοῖραν** – properly, rightly
μόρος,-ου, ὁ—fate, destiny, what is allotted by fate, one's lot
Μοῦσα,-ης, ἡ—a Muse, one of the goddesses of music, poetry, and song
μοχλός,-οῦ, ὁ—stake
μυελόεις,-εσσα,-εν—full of marrow, marrowy
μυθέομαι, μυθήσομαι, μυθησάμην—speak of, mention
μῦθος,-ου, ὁ—something spoken, word, speech, story, tale, request; *plural*, words, a speech
μυχός,-οῦ, ὁ—the innermost part
μῶλυ, τό—moly, the herb given to Odysseus by Hermes to protect him against Circe's magic (see note on 10.305)
μῶμος,-ου, ὁ—fault, disapproval

Ν, ν
ναιετάω—live, dwell, have one's home
ναίω—live, dwell
Ναυσικάα,-ας, ἡ—Nausicaa, Phaeacian princess, daughter of Alcinous and Arete
νεηνίης,-εω, ὁ—young man, youth
νεῖκος,-εος, τό—quarrel
νειός,-οῦ, ἡ—fallow field (one that has been plowed but left unplanted)
νέκταρ,-αρος, τό—nectar (the drink of the gods)
νέκυς,-υος, ὁ—dead body; *plural*, the dead
νεμεσάω, (aor.) **ἐνεμέσησα**—blame, reproach (+ dat.)
νέμω—allot, assign, distribute
νέομαι—go or come back, return; proceed, go, depart
νευστάζω—nod, motion
νεφεληγερέτης,-αο, ὁ—the cloud-gatherer (epithet of Zeus)
νέω—swim
νηδύς,-ύος, ἡ—belly

νηλεής,-ές—pitiless, ruthless
νῆμα,-ατος, τό—yarn, thread; *plural*, weaving, woven work
νημερτής,-ές—unerring, infallible, certain, true
νηνέμιος,-η,-ον—windless
νήπιος,-η,-ον—foolish, thoughtless, senseless; **νήπιος** – a fool
νῆσος,-ου, ἡ—island
νηῦς, νηός or **νεός, ἡ**—ship
νικάω, νικήσω, ἐνίκησα—conquer, overcome, be victorious, prevail
νίσομαι—come back, return
νοέω, νοήσω, ἐνόησα—observe, perceive, notice, see; think, plan, devise
νόος or **νοῦς,-ου, ὁ**—mind, nature, way of thinking, intention, intelligence, attitude, outlook, will, intent, purpose, disposition
νοστέω, νοστήσω, νόστησα—return
νόστιμος,-ον—belonging or pertaining to a return or homecoming
νόστος,-ου, ὁ—return, homecoming; arrival, coming to, reaching (a specific place)
νόσφι(ν)—*prep.*, except (+ gen.); *adv.*, away, far away
νοῦς = νόος
νοῦσος,-ου, ἡ—disease, illness
νυ—now, indeed, then, therefore; *may be used to add emphasis*
νυκτερίς,-ίδος, ἡ—bat
νύμφη,-ης, ἡ—nymph, a minor female divinity usually associated with an aspect of nature (trees, mountains, springs, rivers, the sea) or places (caves, islands)
νῦν—now; **νῦν δέ** – but as it is
νύξ, νυκτός, ἡ—night
νῶϊ—nom., acc., or voc. dual of **ἐγώ**
νωΐτερος,-η,-ον—our (referring to two persons)
νωλεμέως—unceasingly, continually, without rest
νωμάω, νωμήσω—handle, control
νῶτον,-ου, τό—back; *plural may be used for singular*; **νῶτα θαλάσσης** – the surface of the sea

Ξ, ξ

ξεινήϊον,-ου, τό—guest gift, *i.e.,* a gift given by a host to a guest
ξείνιον,-ου, τό—guest gift, *i.e.,* a gift given by a host to a guest
ξείνιος,-α,-ον—protective of guests and strangers; **Ζεὺς ξείνιος** – Zeus, protector of guests and strangers
ξεῖνος,-ου, ὁ—stranger, guest
ξεστός,-ή,-όν—polished, smoothed
ξίφος,-εος, τό—sword
ξύν = σύν

Ο, ο

ὁ, ἡ, τό—the; he, she, it; this, that; who, which
ὄβριμος,-ον—heavy

ὅδε, ἥδε, τόδε—this, this one here
ὁδίτης,-ου, ὁ—traveler
ὁδός,-οῦ, ἡ—journey, way, path
ὀδούς, ὀδόντος, ὁ—tooth; ***ἕρκος ὀδόντων*** – the lips, the mouth ("the barrier of teeth")
ὀδύρομαι—long for, weep for; grieve, weep, sorrow, lament
Ὀδυσ(σ)εύς,-ῆος, ὁ—Odysseus
ὀδύσσομαι, (aor.) **ὠδυσάμην**—be angry with, hate (+ dat.)
ὄζος,-ου, ὁ—branch
ὅθι—in the place where, at the place where, where
οἱ, οἷ—dat. of **εἷο**: him, her, it
οἷα—like, as
οἴγνυμι, (aor.) **ὤϊξα**—open
οἶδα (perfect, translate as present)—know
οἰήϊον,-ου, τό—quarter rudder (Quarter rudders were rudders that looked like large oars, mounted on one or both sides of the stern (rear) section of a ship.)
οἴκαδε—to one's home, homewards, home
οἰκέω—live, dwell
οἰκία, τά—*plural translated as singular*, house, abode, home
οἴκοι—at home
οἶκόνδε—to one's home, homewards
οἶκος,-ου, ὁ—home, house
οἴκτιστος,-η,-ον—most pitiable, most wretched
οἰμώζω, οἰμώξομαι, ᾤμωξα—scream, cry out in pain or distress
οἶνος,-ου, ὁ—wine
οἶνοψ,-οπος (masc. adj.)—dark like wine, wine-dark, purple
ὀΐομαι or **ὀΐω, οἰήσομαι, ὠϊσάμην**—think, suppose, suspect
οἶος,-η,-ον—alone
οἷος,-η,-ον—what kind of, what, what sort of; such as
ὄϊς, ὄϊος, ὁ or **ἡ**—sheep
ὀΐω = ὀΐομαι
ὄλβιος,-ον—happy, prosperous, fortunate
ὄλβος,-ου, ὁ—happiness, good fortune, prosperity
ὄλεθρος,-ου, ὁ—destruction, death
ὀλίγος,-η,-ον—little, short, small
ὄλλυμι, ὀλέσω, ὤλεσα, ὄλωλα—destroy, kill; *middle and passive (and perfect active)*, be destroyed, perish, die, come to nothing
ὀλοός,-ή,-όν—destructive, deadly
ὀλοόφρων,-ονος—malicious, destructive, malevolent
ὀλοφύρομαι, ὀλοφυροῦμαι, ὠλοφυράμην—weep
ὀλοφώϊος,-ον—destructive, deadly, malign
Ὀλύμπιος,-ον—Olympian; *as a name*, the Olympian (Zeus)
Ὄλυμπος,-ου, ὁ—Mt. Olympus, the home of the gods
ὄμβρος,-ου, ὁ—rain
ὄμνυμι, ὀμοῦμαι, ὤμοσ(σ)α—swear

ὁμός,-ή,-όν—the same

ὁμοῦ—together, at the same time, both at once

ὀμφαλός,-οῦ, ὁ—the center, the navel

ὁμῶς—alike

ὄνομα,-ατος, τό—name

ὀνομάζω, ὀνομάσω, ὠνόμασα—call by name (**ὄνομα**), speak to, address

ὀξύς,-εῖα,-ύ—sharp

ὅπῃ—where

ὀπηδέω—follow, accompany, act as a protector (+ dat.)

ὄπισθεν—behind

ὀπίσσω, ὀπίσω—in the future; back, backwards

ὁπλίζω, ὁπλίσω, ὥπλισσα—prepare, get ready; *middle*, prepare [something] for oneself

ὁπότε, ὁππότε—when, whenever; *with* ***κε(ν)*** *or* ***ἄν*** + *subjunctive – indicates something that will happen in the future*; *with optative when referring to an event which often occurred in the past*

ὅππῃ—where

ὁππότε = ὁπότε

ὅππως = ὅπως

ὄπωπα—perfect of **ὁράω**

ὀπωπή,-ῆς, ἡ—vision, ability to see

ὅπως, ὅππως—so that, in order that, that; in what way, how, as

ὁράω, ὄψομαι, εἶδον or **ἴδον, ὄπωπα**—see, look at

ὀρέγω, ὀρέξω, ὤρεξα—hold out, stretch out

ὀρεσίτροφος,-ον—mountain-bred, reared in the mountains

ὀρέστερος,-α,-ον—mountain-dwelling, from the mountains

Ὀρέστης,-αο, ὁ—Orestes, son of Agamemnon

ὀρθός,-ή,-όν—upright, straight

ὅρκος,-ου, ὁ—oath

ὁρμαίνω, (aor.) **ὥρμηνα**—ponder, consider

ὁρμάω, ὁρμήσω, ὥρμησα, (aor. pass.) **ὡρμήθην**—move; *middle and passive*, rise, attack, make an attack

ὄρνυμι—stir up, set in motion; *middle*, rush, move

ὄρος,-εος, τό—mountain

ὀρούω, ὀρούσω, ὤρουσα—rush

Ὀρτυγίη,-ης, ἡ—Ortygia (see note on 5.123)

ὀρύσσω, (aor.) **ὄρυξα**—dig up, get out of the ground

ὄρχαμος,-ου, ὁ—leader

ὅς, ἥ, ὅ—who, which, that; *can also be used as a demonstrative pronoun*

ὅς, ἥ, ὅν—his own, her own, its own

ὅσ(σ)ος,-η,-ον—as many as, all that, how many, how much, such as; **τόσσος...ὅσος** – such…as

ὄσσε (only in nom. and acc. dual neut. forms)—eyes

ὀστέον,-ου, τό—bone

ὅς τις or **ὅτις, ἥ τις, ὅ τι** or **ὅττι**—whoever, whatever, whichever, who, what
ὅτε—when (+ indicative); when, whenever (+ optative or subjunctive); **εἰς ὅτε κέ(ν)** (+ subjunctive) – for the time when
ὅτι, ὅττι—that; because, since, in that, seeing that
ὅτις = ὅς τις
ὀτρύνω, ὀτρυνέω, ὤτρυνα—send; urge, encourage, call upon
ὅττι = ὅτι
ὅττι—neuter of **ὅς τις**
οὐ, οὐκ, οὐκί, οὐχ—not, no; **οὔ τι** – not at all
οὖας,-ατος, τό—ear
οὐδ' = οὐδέ
οὐδέ—but not, and not, not even, nor; **οὐδέ τι** – not at all, in no way
οὐδέν—not at all, in no way, by no means
οὔθ' = οὔτε
οὐκ = οὐ
οὐκέτι—no longer, no more, no further
οὐκί = οὐ
οὖν—now, therefore, then, to be sure; *may add stress to an affirmative idea*
οὕνεκα—because, seeing that, that
οὔνομα,-ατος, τό—name (= **ὄνομα**)
οὐρανός,-οῦ, ὁ—the heavens, the sky; **οὐρανόθεν** – from the sky, from the heavens
οὐρή,-ῆς, ἡ—tail
οὖρος,-ου, ὁ—wind, breeze, fair wind
οὔτ' = οὔτε
οὐτάω (aor.) **οὔτησα**—stab, wound
οὔτε—and not, nor; **οὔτε...οὔτε** – neither…nor
οὐτιδανός,-ή,-όν—worthless, good for nothing
Οὖτις, (acc.) **Οὖτιν**—Outis (When trapped in the Cyclops' cave, Odysseus tells the Cyclops this is his name; its meaning would be "no one," "nobody," "no man.")
οὗτος, αὕτη, τοῦτο—this
οὕτω—in this way, thus, so
ὀφθαλμός,-οῦ, ὁ—eye
ὄφρα—until, so that, in order that (with indicative, subjunctive, or optative); **τόφρα...ὄφρα** – so long…until
ὀφρύς,-ύος, ἡ—eyebrow
οὐχ = οὐ
ὄψ, ὀπός, ἡ—voice
ὀψέ—late, at last, after a long time

Π, π

πάγχυ—wholly, entirely, utterly
παιπαλόεις,-εσσα,-εν—rocky, rugged, craggy
πάϊς or **παῖς, παιδός, ὁ, ἡ**—child, son, daughter
παλαίφατος,-ον—old, spoken long ago

παννύχιος,-ον—all night long
πάντῃ—in all directions
παντοῖος,-η,-ον—of all sorts, of every kind; *with reference to winds*, all, blowing from all directions
παπταίνω—glance, peer
παρ' or **πάρ** = **παρά**
παρά—*prep.*, from (+ gen.); beside, by, near (+ dat.); to, to the side of, beside, by, near (+ acc.); *adv.*, beside, near
παραβάλλω, παραβαλῶ, παρέβαλον—throw beside, throw to
παρασταδόν—standing by, standing beside
παρατίθημι, (aor.) **παρέθηκα**—set or place beside; *middle*, risk
παραυδάω—speak consolingly of, make light of
πάρειμι—be here with; be with; be available, be at one's disposal (+ dat.)
παρελαύνω, παρελάσω, παρήλασα—row past
παρέξ—along side of (+ acc.)
παρεξέρχομαι, (aor.) **παρεξῆλθον**—slip past, get past, defeat, frustrate
παρευνάζομαι—lie beside, go to bed with, sleep with (implies a sexual relationship) (+ dat.)
πάρημαι—sit at, sit in enjoyment of (+ dat.)
πάρος—before, in the past; *with aorist infinitive*, before ___ing; **τὸ πάρος** – formerly
πᾶς, πᾶσα, πᾶν—all, every, all kinds of
πάσχω, πείσομαι, ἔπαθον—suffer, endure, undergo
πατήρ, πατρός or **πατέρος, ὁ**—father
πατρίς,-ίδος (fem. adj.)—of one's fathers; *with **γαῖα** or **ἄρουρα** or **αἶα***, one's fatherland, home, native land
παύω, παύσω, ἔπαυσα—bring to an end, cause to stop; *middle and passive*, stop, cease
παχύς,-εῖα, ύ—strong
πείθω, πείσω, ἔπεισα or **ἔπιθον, πέποιθα**—persuade, convince, induce to believe; *middle*, obey (+ dat.); *perfect*, trust, rely on (+ dat.)
πειράζω—test, try
πειράομαι, πειρήσομαι, ἐπειρησάμην—try, try to find out, try to discover, test; make an attempt on, attack (can take gen. object)
πεῖραρ,-ατος, τό—end, boundary, border; rope, cord
πέλαγος,-εος, τό—the deep sea
πελάζω, πελάσω, ἐπέλασ(σ)α—bring, carry
πέλω or **πέλομαι**—be
πέλωρον, τό (only in nom. and acc. forms)—monster
πέμπω, πέμψω, ἔπεμψα—send, convey
πέπληγα—perfect of **πλήσσω**
περ—even though, although, though; very, even, indeed, at all; **εἴ περ** – even if
περάω—cross, traverse, make one's way across
πέρθω, (aor.) **ἔπερσα**—sack, lay waste, destroy

περί—*prep.*, about, concerning (+ gen.); around, standing over (+ dat.); round, round about (+ acc.); *adv.*, beyond all others, to an extraordinary degree, beyond measure, exceedingly; around, round and round

περιβαίνω, περιβήσομαι, περιέβην, περιβέβηκα—be astride, straddle, have a leg on each side of (+ gen.)

περίειμι—be superior, excel, surpass, exceed (+ gen.)

περιέρχομαι, (aor.) **περιῆλθον** or **περιήλυθον**—go around, come around, encompass

περικαλλής,-ές—well-constructed, fine, beautiful

περίμετρος,-ον—very large, very long; *with ἱστός* – consisting of long threads

Περιμήδης,-εος, ὁ—Perimedes, one of Odysseus' comrades

περιμήκης,-ες—long

περιπέλομαι—go around, revolve

περίσκεπτος,-ον—elevated

περισσαίνω—wag [a tail]

περιφράζομαι—consider, think about

περίφρων (masc. and fem. adj.)—prudent, wise, sensible

πέτομαι, πετήσομαι, ἐπτάμην—fly

πετραῖος,-η,-ον—rock-dwelling, living among the rocks

πέτρη,-ης, ἡ—rock, cliff

πεύθομαι, πεύσομαι—hear of, learn of, find out about (can take acc. or gen. object)

πη—anywhere

πῇ—where?

πηγή,-ῆς, ἡ—spring, source [of a river]

πήγνυμι, πήξω, ἔπηξα—construct, build; stick, set firmly, plant

Πηλεύς,-ῆος, ὁ—Peleus, father of Achilles

πῆμα,-ατος, τό—misery, woe, suffering, evil

Πηνελόπεια,-ης, ἡ—Penelope, wife of Odysseus

πιέζω, πιέσω, ἐπίεσα—squeeze, bind tightly, secure tightly

πίμπλημι, πλήσω, ἔπλησα—fill

πίνω, πίομαι, ἔπιον—drink

πίπτω, πεσοῦμαι, ἔπεσον—fall

πῖσος,-εος, τό—meadow

πιών—aorist active participle of **πίνω**

πλάζω, (aor.) **ἔπλαγξα**, (aor. pass.) **ἐπλάγχθην**—drive, drive from one's course; *middle and passive*, be driven, be tossed about, be forced to wander, wander, roam

πλείων,-ον—more

πλέω, πλεύσομαι, ἔπλευσα—sail, sail over

πλησίον—near by

πλήσσω, πλήξω, ἔπληξα, πέπληγα—strike, hit

πόθεν—from what place?

ποθί—somehow

πόθι—where?

ποιέω, ποιήσω, ἐποίησα—make

ποιήεις,-εσσα,-εν—grassy

ποῖος,-η,-ον—what kind!, what sort!, what!

πόλεμος,-ου, ὁ—war, battle

πολιός,-ή,-όν—gray

πόλις,-ιος, ἡ—city

Πολίτης,-ου, ὁ—Polites, one of Odysseus' comrades

πολλά—much, greatly

πολλόν—far, greatly, much

πολλός,-ή,-όν—much, many; *neut. plur. as an adverb*, **πολλά** – greatly, much; *neut. sing. as an adverb*, **πολλόν** – greatly, much, far

πολύ—much, far, by far, greatly

πολύαινος,-ον—much-praised, illustrious

πολύμητις,-ιος (masc. and fem. adj.)—crafty, shrewd, of many devices

πολυμήχανος,-ον—resourceful, ever-ready

πολύς, πολλή, πολύ—much, many; in great quantity, in abundance; numerous, great, vast

πολύτλας (masc. adj.)—much-enduring

πολύτροπος,-ον—ingenious, of many devices, resourceful; much-traveled, much-wandering

πολυφάρμακος,-ον—knowing many charms or spells, skilled with drugs

Πολύφημος,-ου, ὁ—Polyphemus, a Cyclops, son of Poseidon

πολύφρων,-ονος (masc. and fem. adj.)—much-thinking, intelligent, sensible, ingenious, skillful

πομπή,-ῆς, ἡ—a sending away, a sending home

πόντος,-ου, ὁ—sea, the open sea

πόποι—*used with* **ὤ** *to express surprise, anger, disappointment, grief, sorrow, vexation, rebuke, disgust, displeasure, or a desire to draw attention to something*

πόροι,-ων, οἱ—pathways

πορφύρω—be troubled

πόρω, (aor.) **ἔπορον**—give, inflict

Ποσειδάων,-ωνος, ὁ—Poseidon, god of the sea

πόσις,-ιος, ὁ—husband

ποτ' = ποτέ

ποταμός,-οῦ, ὁ—river

ποτέ—once; at any time, ever; some day, at some time

ποτή,-ῆς, ἡ—flight

ποτί—upon, against, on, at, to (+ dat.); to, towards (+ acc.)

πότμος,-ου, ὁ—fate

πότνα (fem. adj.)—revered, honored (a title of honor given to goddesses and women)

πότνια (fem. adj.)—revered, honored (a title of honor given to goddesses and women)

ποτόν,-οῦ, τό—drink

που—somewhere; perhaps; no doubt, I suppose

πουλυβότειρα,-ης (fem. adj.)—fruitful, all-nourishing

πούς, ποδός, ὁ—foot; **ποὺς νηός** – sheet (a rope or strap fastened to one of the lower corners of a ship's sail, used to control it)

Πράμνειος (masc. adj.)—Pramnian
πρῆξις,-ιος, ἡ—business
πρίν—*conj.*, before, until (+ infinitive); *adv.*, before, formerly, in the past, once; **πρίν** + aorist infinitive – before ___ing
πρό—*prep.*, in front, before (+ gen. or loc.); *adv.*, beforehand, in advance
πρόβολος, -ου, ὁ—a projecting rock
προέχω or **προὔχω**—jut out, project
προήκης,-ες—sharp-edged, thin-edged
πρόθυρον,-ου, τό—doorway; *plural may be used for singular*
προΐημι, προήσω, προέηκα—send, let go
προπάροιθε(ν)—in past times, formerly, before
προπίπτω, προπεσοῦμαι, προὔπεσον—bend forward
πρός—upon, against, in contact with (+ dat.); to, against (+ acc.)
προσαυδάω—speak to, address; *can take two accusative objects*
προσέειπον (aor.)—speak to, address
προσέφη—imperfect active, 3rd pers. sing. of **πρόσφημι**
προσέφην—imperfect active, 1st pers. sing. of **πρόσφημι**
πρόσθε(ν)—before
προσπελάζω, προσπελάσω—drive against, dash upon (+ dat.)
προστίθημι, (aor.) **προσέθηκα**—put in position, put in place, put [in a certain place]
πρόσφημι—speak to, address
προσφύω, προσφύσω, προσέφυσα—seize, grasp, cling to (+ dat.)
προσφωνέω, προσφωνήσω—speak
προτί—to, towards (+ acc.)
προὔχω or **προέχω**—jut out, project
προφεύγω, προφεύξομαι, προὔφυγον—flee from, escape from
πρόφρων,-ονος (masc. and fem. adj. often used as an adverb)—cheerful(ly), gracious(ly), kind(ly), willing(ly); **πρόφρασσα** – alternate nom. sing. fem. form
πρῴρη,-ης, ἡ—ship's bow, prow, forepart of a ship
πρῶτα or **τὰ πρῶτα**—first
πρῶτον—first, for the first time
πτερόεις,-εσσα,-εν—winged; **ἔπεα πτερόεντα** – winged words (see note on 5.117)
πτερόν,-οῦ, τό—wing
πτολίεθρον,-ου, τό—city
πτολιπόρθιος,-ον—sacker of cities
πτόρθος,-ου, ὁ—branch [of a tree]
πυκάζω, (aor.) **πύκασα**—conceal, shut up
πυκινός,-ή,-όν—thick, dense; strongly built; tightly-thronged; shrewd
Πύλος,-ου, ἡ—Pylos, a kingdom on the southwestern coast of the Peloponnese; ruled by Nestor
πύματος,-η,-ον—last
πῦρ, πυρός, τό—fire
πυρπολέω—tend or keep up a fire
πω—yet, ever; **οὔ πω** – never yet, never, not at all

πως—in any way; **οὔ πως** – in no way, not at all, not yet
πῶς—how?

Ρ, ρ
ῥ' = ἄρα
ῥα = ἄρα
ῥάβδος,-ου, ἡ—magic wand; fishing rod
ῥαίω, ῥαίσω, ἔρραισα—shatter, wreck
ῥέζω, ῥέξω, ἔρεξα—do, act, perform, accomplish
ῥεῖα—easily, with ease, lightly
ῥέω, ῥεύσομαι, ἔρρευσα—flow, run, gush forth
ῥηγμίς,-ῖνος, ἡ—breaking waves, surf
ῥιγέω, ῥιγήσω, ἐρρίγησα—shudder, shudder with fear
ῥιζα,-ης, ἡ—root [of a tree or plant]
ῥίμφα—swiftly
ῥίπτω, ῥίψω, ἔρριψα—throw
ῥοδοδάκτυλος,-ον—rosy-fingered (see note on 5.121)
ῥόος,-ου, ὁ—current [of the sea]
ῥύομαι, (aor.) **ἐρρυσάμην**—rescue, save, protect, cover

Σ, σ
σ' = σέ—acc. sing. of **σύ**
σαίνω, (aor.) **ἔσηνα**—fawn, show fondness
σαόω, σαώσω, ἐσάωσα—save, protect
σάρξ, σαρκός, ἡ—*singular or plural*, flesh
σάφα—clearly, well, exactly
σέβας, τό (only in nom., acc., and voc. forms)—a feeling of awe, wonder
σέθεν—gen. sing of **σύ**
σεῖο—gen. sing. of **σύ**
Σειρήν,-ῆνος, ἡ—a Siren, one of two female creatures whose singing lured sailors to their death (see note on 12.167)
σεῦ or **σευ**—gen. sing. of **σύ**
σῆμα,-ατος, τό—sign, indication
σιδήρεος,-η,-ον—made of iron, hard as iron
σίνομαι—hurt, harm
σῖτος,-ου, ὁ—bread, food
σκέπτομαι, σκέψομαι, ἐσκεψάμην—look, look about, turn one's eyes
σκόπελος,-ου, ὁ—rock, crag, cliff
σκοπιάζω—watch
σκύλαξ, σκύλακος, ἡ—puppy
Σκύλλη,-ης, ἡ—Scylla, a monster with six heads who lived in a cave on a cliff opposite Charybdis. Her heads, each equipped with three rows of teeth, darted out of the cave to seize and devour passing sea creatures or sailors.
σμερδαλέον—loudly, vehemently, terribly

σμερδαλέος,-η,-ον—terrible
σός, σή, σόν—your, yours
Σπάρτη,-ης, ἡ—Sparta, the chief city of Laconia, home of King Menelaus and his wife, Helen
σπεῖος = σπέος
σπεῖρον,-ου, τό—shroud; *plural*, clothes, garments, clothing
σπέος or **σπεῖος, σπείους, τό**—cave, cavern
σπέσσι—dat. plur. of **σπέος**
στεινωπός,-οῦ, ἡ—narrow passage, strait
στενάχω—groan, moan
στέρνον,-ου, τό—chest
στῆθος,-εος, τό—breast, chest; chest, breast, or heart as the seat of emotion and feeling; *always plural, translate as singular when it refers to one person*
στηρίζω, (aor.) **ἐστήριξα**—set, find firm footing, plant oneself firmly
στιβαρός,-ή,-όν—strong, powerful
στόμα,-ατος, τό—mouth
στοναχή,-ῆς, ἡ—groan, sigh
Στύξ, Στυγός, ἡ—the Styx, the underworld river by which the gods swore their most solemn oaths (see note on 5.185)
σύ, σεῖο—you; **τοι** – dat. sing.
συμβάλλω, συμβαλῶ, συμέβαλον—bring together; *middle*, meet, encounter
σύν or **ξύν**—*prep.*, with (+ dat.); *adv.*, together
συνέχω, συνέξω, συνέσχον—hold together
σῦς, συός, ὁ or **ἡ**—pig
συφεός,-οῦ, ὁ—pigsty
σφάζω—slaughter
σφαῖρα,-ης, ἡ—ball
σφε—them (acc. plur. of **εἶο**)
σφέας—them (acc. plur. of **εἶο**)
σφέτερος,-η,-ον—their
σφι(ν)—them (dat. plur. of **εἶο**)
σφισι—them (dat. plur. of **εἶο**)
σφός, σφή, σφόν—their, their own
σχεδίη,-ης, ἡ—vessel, craft (see note on 5. 163)
σχεδόν—*prep.*, near, close to (+ gen. or dat.); *adv.*, close, nearby
σχέτλιος,-η,-ον—cruel, hard-hearted

Τ, τ
τ' = τε
ταλαπείριος,-ον—much-suffering
ταλαπενθής,-ές—patient in suffering, bearing up against trouble
ταλασίφρων,-ονος (masc. and fem. adj.)—steadfast, stout-hearted
τάμνω, (aor.) **ἔταμον**—cut
τανηλεγής,-ές—pitiless, remorseless

τανύω, τανύω, ἐτάνυσσα—stretch, put, place

ταῦρος,-ου, ὁ—bull

ταφήϊος,-η,-ον—of or for burial; *as a noun*, **ταφήϊον** – shroud, burial robe

τάχα—soon, quickly

τάχιστα—most quickly, at once, with great speed

τε—and; *can mark a statement as general or proverbial;* **τε...καί** or **τε...τε** or **τε...ἠδέ** – both…and

Τειρεσίης,-αο, ὁ—Teiresias, a blind seer from Thebes, whom Odysseus consulted in the Underworld

τεκμαίρομαι—foretell, predict

τέκνον,-ου, τό—child

τελευτάω, τελευτήσω, τελεύτησα—carry out, accomplish, perform; finish or complete [an oath] in proper form

τεός,-ή,-όν—your

τέρπω, τέρψω, ἔτερψα—delight, cheer, satisfy; *middle and passive*, enjoy oneself, take pleasure, give oneself up to pleasure or enjoyment, be filled with satisfaction

τέρσομαι—be dry, become dry

τέταρτος,-η,-ον—fourth

τέτρατος,-η,-ον—fourth

τευ—gen. sing. of **τις**

τεύχεα,-ων, τά—armor

τεύχω, τεύξω, ἔτευξα, τέτευχα—make, prepare; build, construct

τῇ—here!, come!; *followed by an imperative*

τῇδε—here

τηλεκλυτός,-όν—famous, well-known, far-famed

Τηλέμαχος,-ου, ὁ—Telemachus, son of Odysseus and Penelope

Τήλεμος,-ου, ὁ—Telemus, a seer

τηλόθεν—from far away

τηλόθι—far away

τῆμος—then, at that time

τι—in any way, at all

τί—why?, for what reason?

τίθημι, θήσω, ἔθηκα—put, place, set, make, cause to be

τίκτω, τέξω, ἔτεκον—give birth to, bear

τιμή,-ῆς, ἡ—honor, respect

τίμιος,-α,-ον—honored

τίπτε—why?

τις, τι—some(one), some(thing), any(one), any(thing), a certain, many a one; **οὔ τι** or **οὐδέ τι**– not at all

τίς, τί—who?, what?, which?

τίσις,-εως, ἡ—vengeance, retribution, revenge

τίω—honor, esteem

τλάω, τλήσομαι, ἔτλην—bear, endure, hold out, be patient, suffer; dare, bring oneself [to do something]; make up one's mind [to do something]

τοι—dat. sing. of **σύ**

τοι—in truth, certainly, surely, indeed, I tell you, let me tell you, you (must) know; *may mark a statement as a general truth or a personal conviction*

τοί = οἱ—nom. plur. masc. of **ὁ**

τοῖος,-η,-ον—such

τοιόσδε,-ήδε,-όνδε—such, of such nature

τοιοῦτος,-αύτη,-οῦτον—such, of such a kind

τοκεύς,-έως, ὁ—parent; **τοκῆες** – nom. plur.

τόξον,-ου, τό—bow; *plural*, all one's archery equipment (quiver, bow, and arrows)

τόσον—so much, so greatly, to so great an extent

τόσσος,-η,-ον—so many, so much, of such magnitude, so great; **τόσσος...ὅσος** – such…as

τότ' = τότε

τότε—then

τόφρα—while, meanwhile, for an indicated amount of time, for so long; **τόφρα...ὄφρα** – so long…until; **τόφρα...ἦος** – so long…until

τρέπω, τρέψω, ἔτρεψα or **ἔτραπον**—turn

τρέφω—tend, look after

τρέω, (aor.) **ἔτρεσα**—flee, run away frightened

τρίετες—for three years

τρίπολος,-ον—triple-furrowed (see note on 5.127)

τρίς—three times, thrice

τρίτος,-η,-ον—the third

Τροίη,-ης, ἡ—Troy (the city); the Troad (the area in the northwest corner of Asia Minor controlled by the city of Troy)

Τροίηθεν—from Troy

τρόπις, τρόπιος, ἡ—a ship's keel (the beam of wood running down the center of the bottom of a ship) (see note on 5.130)

τροχός,-οῦ, ὁ—round piece, cake

Τρῶες,-ων, οἱ—Trojans

τύπτω, τύψω, ἔτυψα—strike, beat

τυρός,-οῦ, ὁ—cheese

τυτθά—into small pieces

τῶ or **τῷ**—therefore, in those circumstances

Υ, υ

ὑβριστής,-οῦ, ὁ—violent person

ὑγρός,-ή,-όν—liquid, fluid, watery; **ὑγρὰ κέλευθα**—watery ways, *i.e.,* the sea

ὕδωρ,-ατος, τό—water

υἱός,-οῦ, ὁ—son

ὕλη,-ης, ἡ—forest, woods

ὑλήεις,-εσσα,-εν—woody, wooded

ὑμεῖς or **ὔμμες, ὑμέων**—you (plur.)

ὑμός,-ή,-όν—your

ὑπ' = **ὑπό**

ὕπατος,-η,-ον—highest, supreme

ὑπείρ = **ὑπέρ**

ὑπεκφεύγω (aor.) **ὑπέκφυγον**—escape, avoid

ὑπένερθε—beneath, below

ὑπέρ—above, over (+ gen.); over, beyond (+ acc.)

ὕπερθε(ν)—above

Ὑπεριονίδης,-αο, ὁ = **Ὑπερίων**

Ὑπερίων,-ονος, ὁ—Hyperion, a name or title for Helios, the sun god

ὑπερφίαλος,-ον—arrogant, insolent, with no concern for the rights of others

ὑπηνήτης,-ου, ὁ—one who is just getting a beard

ὑπίσχομαι—promise, give a promise, make promises

ὕπνος,-ου, ὁ—sleep

ὑπό—*prep.,* under, from under, by reason of (+ gen.); under, beneath (+ dat.); under, underneath (+ acc.); *adv.*, underneath, beneath, under

ὑποδείδω, ὑποδείσω, ὑπέδδεισα—fear, be afraid

ὑποδύομαι, ὑποδύσομαι, ὑπεδυσάμην—emerge from under, come out from under (+ gen.)

ὑπομένω, (aor.) **ὑπέμεινα**—remain or stay behind

ὑποτίθημι, ὑποθήσω—place under; *middle*, give advice

ὑποτρέχω, (aor.) **ὑπέδραμον**—run in under an enemy's weapon

ὑπουράνιος,-ον—under heaven (**ὑπό** + **οὐρανός**)

ὕστατον—for the last time

ὕστερον—afterwards, in the future

ὑφαίνω, (aor.) **ὕφηνα**—weave, devise, contrive

ὑφίστημι, (aor.) **ὑπέστην**—promise

ὑψαγόρης,-ου, ὁ—boaster, bold talker

ὑψηλός,-ή,-όν—high, tall, lofty

ὑψόσε—high, up, upwards

ὑψοῦ—aloft, high

ὕω—rain; *passive*, be rained on

Φ, φ

φάγον (aor.)—eat, devour

φαεινός,-ή,-όν—bright, shining

φαίδιμος,-ον—famous, illustrious, renowned

Φαίηκες,-ων, οἱ—the Phaeacians

φαίνω, φανέω, ἔφηνα, (aor. pass.) **ἐφάνην**—show, reveal; *middle and passive*, appear, be seen

φάρμακον,-ου, τό—drug, magical drug, enchanted potion

φᾶρος,-εος, τό—robe

φασι—present active, 3rd pers. plur. of **φημί**

φάσκω—say, promise

φάτ' = **φάτο**

φάτο = ἔφατο—imperfect middle with active meaning, 3rd pers. sing. of **φημί**
φείδομαι, φείσομαι, πεφιδόμην—spare, refrain from harming, have mercy upon (+ gen.)
φένω, (aor.) **ἔπεφνον**—kill
φέριστος,-η,-ον—best, noblest; *used in vocative as a form of address*, noblest sir
φέρτατος,-η,-ον—best, bravest, most powerful
φέρτερος,-η,-ον—stronger, more powerful
φέρω, οἴσω, ἤνεικα—bring, carry, bear
φεύγω, φεύξομαι, ἔφυγον, πέφευγα—flee, escape, escape from
φημί, φήσω, ἔφησα—say, speak, declare, assert; *translate middle as active*
φθέγγομαι, φθέγξομαι, ἐφθεγξάμην—speak, call out, speak loud and clear, shout
φθίνω—waste away
φθόγγος,-ου, ὁ—voice
φιλέω—love, welcome
φιλόξεινος,-ον—hospitable, friendly to strangers
φίλος,-η,-ον—dear, beloved, pleasing, friendly, kindly; one's own
φίλος,-ου, ὁ—friend
φιλότης, φιλότητος, ἡ—love, affection; sex, making love, sexual intercourse
φοινικοπάρῃος,-ον—red-cheeked, purple-cheeked
φοιτάω—make one's way, come
Φόρκυς,-υνος, ὁ—Phorcys, a sea god
φράζω, φράσω, ἔφρασα—point out, show; *middle*, consider, plan, devise, think of
φρεσί(ν)—dat. plur. of **φρήν**
φρνήν, φρενός, ἡ—mind, heart, intelligence; midriff, diaphragm; *plural forms often used for singular* (see note on 1.42)
φρονέω—consider, debate, ponder; plan, intend, desire
φύγον—aorist of **φεύγω**
φυή,-ῆς, ἡ—stature
φυλάσσω, φυλάξω—guard, watch over, look after
φύλλον,-ου, τό—leaf
φύρω—stain, wet
φύσις,-ιος, ἡ—nature, form, appearance
φυτεύω—cause, bring about
φύω, φύσω, ἔφυσα or **ἔφυν**—take hold of, grasp
φωνέω, φωνήσω, ἐφώνησα—speak
φωνή,-ῆς, ἡ—voice
φώς, φωτός, ὁ—person, man

Χ, χ

χαίρω—rejoice at, take pleasure in (+ dat.); *imperative*, hello, good-bye, farewell, good luck to you
χαλεπαίνω, (aor.) **ἐχαλέπηνα**—do violence to, be hard upon (+ dat.)
χαλεπός,-ή,-όν—difficult, hard
χάλκεος,-ον—made of bronze

χαλκός,-οῦ, ὁ—bronze; sword, ax
χαμάδις—onto the ground
χαμαιευνάς,-άδος (fem. adj.)—ground-sleeping, who sleep on the ground
χαρίεις, χαρίεσσα, χαρίεν—pleasing, lovely
χαριέστατος,-ον—superlative of **χαρίεις**
χαρίζομαι—gratify, show favor, show kindness; honor, seek favor (+ dat.)
Χάρυβδις,-εως or **-ιος, ἡ**—Charybdis, a sea goddess who created a deadly whirlpool at the foot of the cliff opposite the cliff where Scylla lived
χείρ, χειρός, ἡ—hand, arm; *plural*, strength, might
χερείων,-ον—inferior, less worthy, worse
χερσί(ν)—dat. plur. of **χείρ**
χθών, χθονός, ἡ—the earth
χλωρός,-ή,-όν—yellow, pale
χόλος,-ου, ὁ—anger, wrath
χολόω, χολώσω, ἐχόλωσα, (perf. mid.) **κεχόλωμαι**—enrage, make angry; *middle and passive*, be angry, be angry at, be provoked to anger at (+ dat. of the person with whom one is angry or genitive of cause of the anger)
χορός,-οῦ, ὁ—dancing, the dance
χράομαι, χρήσομαι, ἐχρησάμην, κέχρημαι—yearn for, desire, long for (+ gen.)
χρείω,-οῦς, ἡ—need, necessity
χρέος,-εος, τό—need, business
χρή (impersonal)—there is need, it is necessary
χρύσεος,-η,-ον—golden, made of gold
χρυσόθρονος,-ον—with a golden throne, golden-throned
χρυσόρραπις (masc. and fem. adj.)—with a golden wand (epithet of Hermes)
χρυσός,-οῦ, ὁ—gold
χρώς, χρωτός, ὁ—body
χώομαι—be angry
χῶρος,-ου, ὁ—place

Ψ, ψ
ψάμμος,-ου, ἡ—sand
ψυχή,-ῆς, ἡ—life, soul

Ω, ω
ὦ or **ὤ**—o, oh; **ὤ μοι** – oh!, alas!
Ὠγυγίη,-ης, ἡ—Ogygia, the island on which Calypso lived
ὧδε—thus, in this way
ᾤϊξα—aorist of **οἴγνυμι**
ὦκα—quickly, at once
ὠκύαλος,-ον—swift
ὠκύπορος,-ον—swift-sailing
ὦμος,-ου, ὁ—shoulder
ὤμοσ(σ)α—aorist of **ὄμνυμι**

ὥρη,-ης, ἡ—season

Ὠρίων,-ωνος, ὁ—Orion, a great hunter

ὡς—how, in what way, in the same way, as, so that, that, when, as soon as; **καὶ ὡς** – even so, nevertheless

ὥς or **ὣς**—so, thus, in this way, in this manner

Printed and bound by CPI Group (UK) Ltd, Croydon, CR0 4YY

13/04/2025

14656530-0004